P9-AOK-150

...etings

Princeton. 1933.

"Moo"

PLAY PARADE

Play Parade

DESIGN FOR LIVING

CAVALCADE

PRIVATE LIVES

BITTER SWEET

POST-MORTEM

THE VORTEX

HAY FEVER

PLAY PARADE

by Noel Coward

GARDEN CITY, NEW YORK
DOUBLEDAY, DORAN & COMPANY, INC.
MCMXXXIII

PRINTED AT THE *Country Life Press*, GARDEN CITY, N. Y., U. S. A.

EDITION DESIGNED BY ROBERT JOSEPHY

DECORATIONS BY RICHARD KELLY

COPYRIGHT, 1924, 1925, 1929, 1930, 1931, 1932, 1933
BY NOEL COWARD
ALL RIGHTS RESERVED

FIRST EDITION

CONTENTS

INTRODUCTION

WHEN Nelson Doubleday suggested to me that he would like to publish an omnibus volume containing seven of the most representative of my works, I stepped, for an instant, into eminent old age, and, smiling quaveringly across the years at irresponsible youngsters ploughing through my musty old plays, I thanked God that the hurly-burly was over. I could now retire in peace to my dim library and mellowing Kentish garden, and there, with my memories as sole companions, dream away the end of my days.

A little of my old fire returned to me in course of the ensuing argument as to which *were* the most representative of my works, and with senile obstinacy, I insisted upon the following. *The Vortex, Hay Fever, Bitter Sweet, Private Lives, Post Mortem, Cavalcade,* and *Design for Living*. These seem to me to be the most successfully experimental among my output of the last ten years.

I find it very interesting nowadays, now that I have fortunately achieved a definite publicity value, to read criticisms and analyses of my plays written by people of whom I have never heard and whom I have certainly never seen, and who appear to have an insatiable passion for labelling everything with a motive. They search busily behind the simplest of my phrases, like old ladies peering under the bed for burglars, and are not content until they have unearthed some definite, and usually quite inaccurate, reason for my saying this or that. This strange mania I can only suppose is the distinctive feature of a critical mind as opposed to a creative one. It seems to me that a professional writer should be animated by no other motive than the desire to write, and, by doing so, to earn his living.

The original motive for *Cavalcade*, for instance, was a long-cherished ambition to write a big play on a big scale, and to produce it at the London Coliseum. I toyed for a while with the thought of a French Revolution epic, a pageant of the Second Empire, and various other ideas which might give me enough scope for intimate chacterizations against a background of crowd scenes. One day I happened to see in a back number of the *Illustrated London News* a photograph of a troopship leaving for the Boer War. Very soon after this the whole scheme of the play fell into my mind, and, after relating it to C. B. Cochran, and asking him to get me the Coliseum at all costs, I left for New York to play *Private Lives*. A few months later I received a cable from him saying that the Coliseum was unobtainable, but that I could have Drury Lane provided that I would guarantee an approximate opening date. This was slightly agitating, but I cabled back that the play would be ready for production by the end of September.

When I returned to London in May, I carefully examined the facilities of the Drury Lane stage in company with G. E. Calthrop, who constructed the whole show with me in addition to designing all the scenery and dresses, and we retired to the country, after a series of conferences, to build the play according to blueprints, time changes, electrical installations, and hydraulic lifts. I had not one moment to waste on patriotic fervour.

After a slight delay, owing to two extra hydraulic lifts which we had to install, *Cavalcade* was finally launched in October, and with it came the Deluge. A very gratifying Deluge. Letters of congratulation. Crowds in the streets. Superlatives in the press. I was told, on all sides, that I had done "a big thing" and that a peerage was the least I could expect from a grateful monarch. I was also congratulated upon my uncanny shrewdness in slapping on a strong patriotic play two weeks before a general election which was bound to result in a sweeping Conservative majority. (Here I must regretfully admit that during rehearsals I was so very much occupied in the theatre and, as usual, so bleakly uninterested in politics that I had not the remotest idea, until a few days before production, that there was going to be an election at all! However, there was, and its effect on the box office was considerable.)

The excitement continued for the two weeks that I remained in London after the play had opened, and I left for South America, flushed with heroism and extremely tired. I could relax on the boat and reflect that although it was undoubtedly very pleasant to read in the press that my country was proud of me, I had escaped the grave danger of taking the idea seriously. True there had been a few uneasy highbrows who had deplored my fall from sophisticated wit into the bathos of jingoism, and had even gone so far as to suggest that the whole thing was a wily commercial trick, conceived, written, and produced in a spirit of cynical mockery, with my tongue fairly wedged in my cheek, but these shrill small voices were drowned out by the general trumpetings of praise.

The only thing that escaped notice in the uproar was the fact that *Cavalcade*, apart from its appeal as a spectacle, actually possessed two or three really well-written scenes, notably the funeral of Queen Victoria, and the outbreak of the war in 1914. These two scenes had both dignity and brevity.

Now that the whole thing is done, and has become an "epic," and "The Play of the Century," and "The Picture of the Generation," I can meditate blissfully upon the good fortune that prompted me to pick up just that particular number of the *Illustrated London News*, instead of one of a later date depicting the storming of the Winter Palace at St. Petersburg.

The Vortex was written in 1923 and produced on November 25th at the Everyman Theatre, Hampstead. It was an immediate success and established me both as a playwright and as an actor, which was very fortunate, because up until then I had not proved myself to be so hot in either capacity. With this success came many pleasurable trappings. A car. New suits. Silk shirts. An extravagant amount of pyjamas and dressing gowns, and a still more extravagant amount of publicity. I was photographed, and interviewed, and photographed again. In the street. In the park. In my dressing room. At my piano. With my dear old mother, without my dear old mother—and, on one occasion, sitting up in an overelaborate bed looking like a heavily doped Chinese Illusionist. This last photograph, I believe, did me a good deal of harm. People glancing at it concluded at once, and with a certain justification, that I was undoubtedly a weedy sensualist in the last stages of physical and moral degeneration, and that they had better hurry off to see me in my play before my inevitable demise placed that faintly macabre pleasure beyond their reach. This attitude, while temporarily very good for business, became irritating after a time, and for many years I was seldom mentioned in the press without allusions to "cocktails," "post-war hysteria," and "decadence."

My original motive in *The Vortex* was to write a good play with a whacking good part in it for myself, and I am thankful to say, with a few modest reservations, that I succeeded. It is a good play, and although I am fully aware that it could be a good deal better, I am quite reasonably satisfied with it. At the time, I need hardly add, I considered it a masterpiece. At all events, the first night of its production at the Henry Miller Theatre, New York, was a very great moment in my life, and for this I shall never cease to be grateful.

Hay Fever is considered by many to be my best comedy. Whether or not this assertion is true, posterity, if it gives it a glance, will be able to judge with more detachment than I. At any rate it has certainly proved to be a great joy to amateurs, owing, I suppose, to the smallness of its cast, and the fact that it has only one set, which must lead them, poor dears, to imagine that it is easy to act. This species of delusion being common to amateurs all over the world, no word of mine shall be spoken, no warning finger of experience raised, to discourage them, beyond the timorous suggestion that from the professional stand-point, *Hay Fever* is far and away one of the most difficult plays to perform that I have ever encountered.

To begin with, it has no plot at all, and remarkably little action. Its general effectiveness therefore depends upon expert technique from each and every member of the cast. The level of acting in the original London production, led brilliantly by Miss Marie Tempest, was extremely high, consequently the play was a tremendous success. The press naturally and inevitably described it as "thin," "tenuous," and "trivial," because those are their stock phrases for anything later in date and lighter in texture than *The Way of the World*, and it ran, tenuously and triumphantly, for a year.

In America it fared less well. Miss Laura Hope Crews was enthusiastically torn to shreds by the critics for overacting, which indeed she did, but with the very extenuating circumstance that her supporting cast was so uniformly dreary that if she hadn't, I gravely doubt if any of the audience would have stayed in the theatre at all. I am very much attached to *Hay Fever*. I enjoyed writing it and producing it, and I have frequently enjoyed watching it.

Bitter Sweet has given me more complete satisfaction than anything else I have ever written up till now. Not especially on account of its dialogue, or its lyrics, or its music, or its production, but as a whole. In the first place, it achieved and sustained the original mood of its conception more satisfactorily than a great deal of my other work. And in the second place, that particular mood of seminostalgic sentiment, when well done, invariably affects me very pleasantly. In *Bitter Sweet* it did seem to me to be well done, and I felt accordingly very happy about it.

The late William Bolitho, in an article on *Bitter Sweet* published in the New York *World* (one of the very few journalistic excursions relating to myself that I have ever wished, proudly, to keep), finished his essay with a discussion of the quality of the play. He said of this: ". . . You find it faintly when you look over old letters the rats have nibbled at, one evening you don't go out; there is a little of it, impure and odorous, in the very sound of barrel organs, in quiet squares in the evenings, puffing out in gusts that intoxicate your heart. It is all right for beasts to have no memories; but we poor humans have to be compensated."

Private Lives was conceived in Tokyo, written in Shanghai, and produced in London in September, 1930, after a preliminary try-out in the provinces. It was described in the papers variously, as being, "tenuous," "thin," "brittle," "gosasmer," "iridescent," and "delightfully daring." All of which connoted, to the public mind, "cocktails," "evening dress," "repartee," and irreverent allusions to copulation, thereby causing a gratifying number of respectable people to queue up at the box office.

There is actually more to the play than this, however, but on the whole not very much. It is a reasonably well-constructed duologue for two experienced performers, with a couple of extra puppets thrown in to assist the plot and to provide contrast. There is a well-written love scene in Act One, and a certain amount of sound sex psychology underlying the quarrel scenes in Act Two.

As a complete play, it leaves a lot to be desired, principally owing to my dastardly and conscienceless behaviour towards Sibyl and Victor, the secondary characters. These, poor things, are little better than ninepins, lightly wooden, and only there at all in order to be repeatedly knocked down and stood up again. Apart from this, *Private Lives*, from the playwright's point of view, may or may not be considered interesting, but at any rate, from the point of view of technical acting, it is very interesting indeed.

To begin with, there is no further plot and no further action after Act One, with the exception of the rough-and-tumble fight at the curtain of Act Two. Before this, there is exactly forty minutes of dialogue between the leading protagonists, Amanda and Elyot, which naturally demands from them the maximum of resource and comedy experience, as every night, according to the degree of responsiveness from the audience, the attack and tempo of the performance must inevitably vary. This means a constant ear cocked in the direction of the stalls, listening for that first sinister cough of boredom, and, when it comes, a swiftly exchanged glance of warning and an immediate and, it is to be hoped, imperceptible speeding up of the scene until the next sure-fire laugh breaks and it is permissible to relax and breathe more easily for a moment.

This strenuous watchfulness is of course necessary in the playing of any high comedy scene, but as a general rule the considerate author provides lifelines for his actors, in the shape of sharply etched cameos for the subsidiary members of the cast, who can make bustling little entrances and exits in order to break the monotony. He may even, on occasion, actually provide a sustained plot for them to hang on to when all else fails.

In the second act of *Private Lives*, however, there was no help from the author over and above a few carefully placed laugh lines, and, taken all in all, it was more tricky and full of pitfalls than anything I have ever attempted as an actor. But fortunately, for me, I had the inestimable advantage of playing it with Gertrude Lawrence, and so three quarters of the battle was won before the curtain went up.

Post-Mortem was written primarily as a gesture to myself. And now that the hysteria of its mood has evaporated from my mind, I perceive that it is a slightly more "jejeune" gesture than I altogether bargained for.

There are certain moments of genuine passion in it which redeem it from bathos, but on the whole I fear that it is sadly confused and unbalanced. All the same, it was an experiment, and, far from regretting it, I am exceedingly glad I made it, because, as a writer, it undoubtedly did me a power of good. It opened a lot of windows in my brain and allowed me to let off a great deal of steam which might have remained sizzling inside me and combusted later on, to the considerable detriment of *Calvacade* and *Design for Living*.

My emotions while writing it were violent. Much more violent than in any of my previous labours. And I can only say that it was fortunate for my immediate friends that this particular confinement took place on a P. and O. boat returning from the East, where my alternate moans of despair and screams of ecstasy could only disturb two acidulated planters' wives in the adjoining cabin.

Post Mortem was not actually written for the theatre. But, as I felt at the time, perhaps erroneously, that I had a lot to say, I put it into play form, for the simple reason that I felt more at home in that than in any other.

It has not yet been produced, although one day perhaps it will be. I think it might probably be quite effective, provided that it is expertly directed and acted.

Design for Living as a project rather than as a play sat patiently at the back of my mind for eleven years. It had to wait until Lynn Fontanne, Alfred Lunt, and I had arrived, by different roads, at the exact moment in our careers when we felt that we could all three play together with a more or less equal degree of success.

We had met, discussed, argued, and parted again many times, knowing that it was something that we wanted to do very much indeed, and searching wildly through our minds for suitable characters. At one moment we were to be three foreigners. Lynn, Eurasian; Alfred, German; and I, Chinese. At another we were to be three acrobats, rapping out "Allez Oops" and flipping handkerchiefs at one another. A further plan was that the entire play should be played in a gigantic bed, dealing with life and love in the Schnitzler manner. This, however, was hilariously discarded, after Alfred had suggested a few stage directions which, if followed faithfully, would undoubtedly have landed all three of us in gaol.

Finally, when the whole idea seemed to have sunk out of sight for ever, I got a cable from them in the Argentine, where I happened to be at the moment, saying, "Contract with the Guild up in June—we shall be free—what about it?"

From that moment onwards my travelling lacked that sense of detachment which up to then had been its principal charm. Patagonia, Chile, Peru, and Colombia presented themselves in turn, less as strange thrilling countries brimming with historical interest than as painted theatrical backgrounds, against which three attractive, witty characters changed their minds and their colours with the rapidity of chameleons, but failed, unlike chameleons, to achieve even the meagre satisfaction of being alive.

It was not until several months later, when I was on a small Norwegian freight boat travelling from Panama to Los Angeles, that the play suddenly emerged, and, with a superb disregard for the mountains and jungles and plains I had traversed in search of it and, without even a salute to the flamboyant Mexican coastline on the starboard horizon, placed its own *mise en scène* firmly in Paris, London, and New York.

Since then *Design for Living* has been produced, published, and reviewed. It has been liked and disliked, and hated and admired, but never, I think, sufficiently loved by any but its three leading actors. This, perhaps, was only to be expected, as its central theme, from the point of view of the average, must appear to be definitely antisocial. People were certainly interested and entertained and occasionally even moved by it, but it seemed, to many of them, "unpleasant." This sense of "unpleasantness" might have been mitigated for them a little if they had realized that the title was ironic rather than dogmatic. I never intended for a moment that the design for living suggested in the play should apply to anyone outside its three principal characters, Gilda, Otto, and Leo. These glib, overarticulate, and amoral creatures force their lives into fantastic shapes and problems because they cannot help themselves. Impelled chiefly by the impact of their personalities each upon the other, they are like

moths in a pool of light, unable to tolerate the lonely outer darkness, and equally unable to share the light without colliding constantly and bruising one another's wings.

The end of the play is equivocal. The three of them, after
various partings and reunions and partings again, after torturing
and loving and hating one another, are left together as the curtain falls, laughing. Different minds found different meanings in
this laughter. Some considered it to be directed against Ernest,
Gilda's husband, and the time-honoured friend of all three. If
so, it was certainly cruel, and in the worst possible taste. Some
saw in it a lascivious anticipation of a sort of triangular carnal
frolic. Others, with less ribald imaginations, regarded it as a
meaningless and slightly inept excuse to bring the curtain down.
I as author, however, prefer to think that Gilda and Otto and
Leo were laughing at themselves.

Noel Coward.

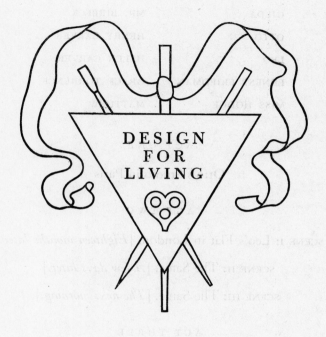

DESIGN
FOR
LIVING

CHARACTERS

GILDA   MR. BIRBECK

OTTO   HENRY CARVER

LEO   HELEN CARVER

ERNEST FRIEDMAN   GRACE TORRENCE

MISS HODGE   MATTHEW

ACT ONE

Otto's Studio in Paris

ACT TWO

SCENE I: Leo's Flat in London. [*Eighteen months later.*]

SCENE II: The Same. [*A few days later.*]

SCENE III: The Same. [*The next morning.*]

ACT THREE

SCENE I: Ernest's Apartment in New York. [*Two years later.*]

SCENE II: The Same. [*The next morning.*]

Time: THE PRESENT

ACT ONE: SCENE I

THE SCENE *is rather a shabby studio in Paris. There is a large window at the back looking out onto roof tops. Down stage, on the Left, there is a door leading onto the stairs, which in turn lead to the street. Up stage, on the Right, there is a door leading into a small kitchen.*

When the curtain rises, it is about ten o'clock on a spring morning, and the studio is empty. Gilda comes in from the kitchen carrying a coffee pot and a milk jug. She places them on a table just under the window, which is already laid with cups and plates, etc. Gilda is a good-looking woman of about thirty.

Suddenly there is a knock on the door Left. She gives a quick glance towards it, and then goes swiftly and silently into the bedroom. In a moment she returns, closing the bedroom door carefully behind her. There is another knock on the door. She opens it, admitting Ernest Friedman. He is any age between forty and fifty, rather precise in manner. He carries a large package, obviously a picture, done up in brown paper.

GILDA: Ernest!

ERNEST: May I come in?

GILDA: I'd no idea you were back.

ERNEST: I arrived last night. [*He comes in and puts down the package.*]

GILDA: What's that?

3

ERNEST: Something exquisite, superb.

GILDA: The Matisse?

ERNEST: Yes.

GILDA: You got it, after all.

ERNEST: It's unbelievable.

GILDA: Undo it quickly!

ERNEST: Otto must see it, too.

GILDA: He's asleep.

ERNEST: Wake him up, then.

GILDA: Not now, Ernest; he's had the most awful neuralgia all night.

ERNEST: Neuralgia?

GILDA: Yes; all up one side of his face and down the other side.

ERNEST [*undoing the package*]: Wake him up. One look at this will take away his neuralgia immediately.

GILDA: No, really. He's only just dropped off. He's been in agony. I've dosed him with aspirin and given him a hot-water bottle here, and another one just there——

ERNEST [*petulantly*]: I didn't know anyone had so many hot-water bottles.

GILDA: I still have one more, in case it spreads.

ERNEST: It really is very irritating. I take the trouble to drag this large picture all the way round here and Otto chooses to have neuralgia.

GILDA: He didn't choose to have it. He hated having it. His little face is all pinched and strained.

ERNEST: Otto's face is enormous.

GILDA: Show me the picture, Ernest, and try not to be disagreeable.

ERNEST [*grumbling*]: It's an anticlimax.

GILDA: Thank you, dear.

ERNEST: It's no use pretending to be hurt. You know you don't really care for anybody's pictures except Otto's.

GILDA: Do you want some coffee?

ERNEST: Why are there two cups, if Otto has neuralgia?

GILDA: Habit. There are always two cups.

ERNEST [*propping up the picture, facing up stage*]: There!

GILDA [*scrutinizing it*]: Yes, it's good.

ERNEST: Stand further back.

GILDA [*obliging*]: Very good indeed. How much?

ERNEST: Eight hundred pounds.

GILDA: Did you bargain?

ERNEST: No, that was their price.

GILDA: I think you were right. Dealers or private owners?

ERNEST: Dealers.

GILDA: Here's your coffee.

ERNEST [*taking the cup and still looking at the picture*]: It's strangely unlike all the other work, isn't it?

GILDA: What are you going to do with it?

ERNEST: Wait a little.

GILDA: And then resell?

ERNEST: I expect so.

GILDA: It will need a room to itself.

ERNEST: None of your decorating schemes. Hands off!

GILDA: Don't you think I'm a good decorator?

ERNEST: Not particularly.

GILDA: Darling Ernest!

ERNEST [*back at the picture*]: Otto will go mad when he sees it.

GILDA: You think Otto's good, don't you? You think he's all right?

ERNEST: Coming along. Coming along very nicely.

GILDA: Better than that. Much better!

ERNEST: Lady Jaguar, defending her young!

GILDA: Otto isn't my young.

ERNEST: Oh, yes, he is. Otto's everybody's young.

GILDA: You think he's weak, don't you?

ERNEST: Certainly, I do.

GILDA: And that I'm strong?

ERNEST: Strong as an ox!

GILDA: You've called me a jaguar and an ox within the last two minutes. I wish you wouldn't be quite so zoological.

ERNEST: A temperamental ox, Gilda. Sometimes a hysterical ox; and, at the moment, an over-vehement ox! What's the matter with you this morning?

GILDA: The matter with me?

ERNEST: There's a wild gleam in your eye.

GILDA: There always is. It's one of my greatest charms! I'm surprised that you never noticed it before.

ERNEST: The years are creeping on me, Gilda. Perhaps my perceptions are getting dulled.

GILDA [absently]: Perhaps they are.

ERNEST: If, in my dotage, I become a bore to you, you won't scruple to let me know, will you?

GILDA: Don't be an idiot!

ERNEST [ruminatively]: Perhaps it was wrong of me to arrive unexpectedly; I should have written you a little note making an appointment.

GILDA: Be a nice bluebottle and stop buzzing at me, will you?

ERNEST: You're a striking-looking woman—particularly when a little distrait. It's a pity Otto's paintings of you have always been so tranquil. He's missed something.

GILDA: The next time he paints me, you must be here to lash me with gay witticisms.

ERNEST: Surely, in my rôle of bitter old family friend, I can demand a little confidence! You could tell me quite safely, you know, if anything's wrong. I might even be able to help, with a senile word or two.

GILDA: Nothing is wrong, I tell you.

ERNEST: Nothing at all?

GILDA: Shall I make you some toast?

ERNEST: No, thank you.

GILDA: It's very hot today, isn't it?

ERNEST: Why not open the window?

GILDA: I never thought of it. [*She opens the window almost violently.*] There!—I'm sick of this studio; it's squalid! I wish I were somewhere quite different. I wish I were somebody quite different. I wish I were a nice-minded British matron, with a husband, a cook, and a baby. I wish I believed in God and the *Daily Mail* and "Mother India"!

ERNEST: I wish you'd tell me what's upsetting you.

GILDA: Glands, I expect. Everything's glandular. I read a book about it the other day. Ernest, if you only realized what was going on inside you, you'd be bitterly offended!

ERNEST: I'm much more interested in what's going on inside you.

GILDA: I'll tell you. All the hormones in my blood are working overtime. They're rushing madly in and out of my organs like messenger boys.

ERNEST: Why?

GILDA: Perhaps it's a sort of presentiment.

ERNEST: Psychic. I see. Well, well, well!

GILDA: Yes, I hear voices. I hear my own voice louder than any of the others, and it's beginning to bore me. Would you describe me as a super-egoist, Ernest?

ERNEST: Yes, dear.

GILDA: Thinking of myself too much, and not enough of other people?

ERNEST: No. Thinking of other people too much through yourself.

GILDA: How can anyone do otherwise?

ERNEST: Detachment of mind.

GILDA: I haven't got that sort of mind.

ERNEST: It's an acquired attitude and difficult to achieve, but, believe me, well worth trying for.

GILDA: Are you presenting yourself as a shining example?

ERNEST: Not shining, my dear, just dully effulgent.

GILDA: How should I start? Go away alone with my thoughts?

ERNEST: With all my detachment I find it very difficult to regard your painful twistings and turnings with composure.

GILDA: Why?

ERNEST [*blandly*]: Because I'm very fond of you.

GILDA: Why?

ERNEST: I don't know. A tedious habit, I suppose. After all, I was very attached to your mother.

GILDA: Yes, I know. Personally, I never cared for her very much. A bossy woman.

ERNEST: I don't think you should allude to the dead as "bossy."

GILDA: No reverence. That's my trouble. No reverence.

ERNEST: I feel vaguely paternal towards you.

GILDA: Yes, Ernest.

ERNEST: And your behaviour confuses me.

GILDA: My painful twistings and turnings.

ERNEST: Exactly.

GILDA: What did you mean by that?

ERNEST: Will you explain one thing to me really satisfactorily?

GILDA: What?

ERNEST: Why don't you marry Otto?

GILDA: It's very funny that underneath all your worldly

wisdom you're nothing but a respectable little old woman in a jet bonnet.

ERNEST: You don't like being disapproved of, do you?

GILDA: Does anybody?

ERNEST: Anyhow, I don't disapprove of you, yourself—of course, you're as obstinate as a mule——

GILDA: There you go again! "Strong as an ox!" "Obstinate as a mule!" Just a pack of Animal Grab—that's what I am! Bring out all the other cards. "Gentle as a dove!" "Playful as a kitten!" "Black as a crow!"——

ERNEST: "Brave as a lion!"——

GILDA: Oh, no, Ernest! You couldn't think that, disapproving of me as you do.

ERNEST: I was about to explain, when you so rudely interrupted, that it isn't you, yourself, I disapprove of. It's your mode of life.

GILDA [*laughing slightly*]: Oh, I see!

ERNEST: Your life is so dreadfully untidy, Gilda.

GILDA: I'm not a tidy person.

ERNEST: You haven't yet answered my original question.

GILDA: Why I don't marry Otto?

ERNEST: Yes. Is there a real reason, or just a lot of faintly affected theories?

GILDA: There's a very real reason.

ERNEST: Well?

GILDA: I love him. [*She glances towards the bedroom door and says louder*]: I love him.

ERNEST: All right! All right, there's no need to shout.

GILDA: Yes, there is, every need. I should like to scream.

ERNEST: That would surely be very bad for Otto's neuralgia.

GILDA [*calming down*]: The only reasons for me to marry

would be these: To have children; to have a home; to have a background for social activities, and to be provided for. Well, I don't like children; I don't wish for a home; I can't bear social activities, and I have a small but adequate income of my own. I love Otto deeply, and I respect him as a person and as an artist. To be tied legally to him would be repellent to me and to him, too. It's not a dashing bohemian gesture to Free Love: we just feel like that, both of us. Now, are you satisfied?

ERNEST: If you are.

GILDA: You're impossible, Ernest. You sit there looking quizzical, and it maddens me!

ERNEST: I am quizzical.

GILDA: Well, be something else, for God's sake!

ERNEST: I suppose you know Leo is back?

GILDA [*jumping slightly*]: What?

ERNEST: I said, "I suppose you know Leo is back?"

GILDA [*tremendously astonished*]: It's not true!

ERNEST: Didn't he let you know?

GILDA [*eagerly*]: When did he arrive? Where's he staying?

ERNEST: He arrived yesterday on the *Mauretania*. I had a note from him last night.

GILDA: Where's he staying?

ERNEST: You'll be shocked when I tell you.

GILDA: Quickly!—Quickly!

ERNEST: The George V.

GILDA [*going off into peals of laughter*]: He must be raving! The George V! Oh, dear, oh, dear! Leo, at the George V! It's a glorious picture. Marble bathrooms and private balconies! Leo in all that grandeur! It isn't possible.

ERNEST: I gather he's made a good deal of money.

GILDA: That's not enough excuse. He ought to be ashamed of himself!

ERNEST: I can't understand him, not letting you know he was back. I fully expected to find him here.

GILDA: He'll appear sooner or later.

ERNEST: Are you glad he's made money?

GILDA: Why do you ask that?

ERNEST: Curiosity.

GILDA: Of course I'm glad. I adore Leo!

ERNEST: And Otto? What about Otto?

GILDA [*irritably*]: What do you mean, "What about Otto?"

ERNEST: Will he be glad, too?

GILDA: You're too ridiculous sometimes, Ernest. What are you suspecting? What are you trying to find out?

ERNEST: Nothing. I was only wondering.

GILDA: It's all right. I know what you're getting at; but you're wrong as usual. Everybody's always wrong about Leo and Otto and me. I'm not jealous of Leo's money and success, and Otto won't be either when he knows. That's what you were suspecting, wasn't it?

ERNEST: Perhaps.

GILDA [*turning away*]: I think you should grasp the situation a little better, having known us all for so long.

ERNEST: Otto and Leo knew each other first.

GILDA: Yes, yes, yes, yes—I know all about that! I came along and spoilt everything! Go on, dear——

ERNEST: I didn't say that.

GILDA [*sharply*]: It's what you meant.

ERNEST: I think, perhaps, you may have spoilt yourself a little.

GILDA: Distrust of women frequently sets in at your age, Ernest.

ERNEST: I cannot, for the life of me, imagine why I'm so fond of you. You have such abominable manners.

GILDA: It's probably the scarlet life I live, causing me to degenerate into a shrew.

ERNEST: Very likely.

GILDA [*suddenly, leaning over the back of his chair, with her arms around him*]: I'm sorry—about my bad manners, I mean. Please forgive me. You're a darling, and you love us a lot, don't you? All three of us? Me a little less than Otto and Leo because I'm a woman and, therefore, unreliable. Isn't that true?

ERNEST [*patting her hand*]: Quite.

GILDA [*leaving him*]: Your affection is a scared thing, though. Too frightened; too apprehensive of consequences. Leave us to grapple with the consequences, my dear. We're bound to have a bad time every now and then, but, at least, we know it. We're aware of a whole lot of things. Look at us clearly as human beings, rather peculiar human beings, I grant you, and don't be prejudiced by our lack of social grace. I laughed too loudly just now at the thought of Leo being rich and rare. Too loudly because I was uneasy, not jealous. I don't want him to be any different, that's all.

ERNEST: I see.

GILDA: Do you? Do you really? I doubt it. I don't see how anyone outside could. But I would like you to understand one thing absolutely and completely. I love Otto—whatever happens, I love Otto.

ERNEST: I never suggested for a moment that you didn't.

GILDA: Wait. Wait and see. The immediate horizon is grey and forbidding and dangerous. You don't know what I'm talking about and you probably think I've gone mad, and I can't explain —not now. But, darling Ernest, there's a crisis on. A full-blooded, emotional crisis; and when I need you, which I expect will be very soon, I shall yell! I shall yell like mad!

ERNEST: I knew you were in a state about something.

GILDA: Nasty shrewd little instincts shooting out and discovering things lurking in the atmosphere. It's funny about atmosphere, isn't it? Strong inside thoughts make outside impressions. Imprints on the ether. A horrid sort of spiritual television.

ERNEST: Quite.

GILDA: Well, are you satisfied now? You felt something was the matter, and you were right. It's always pleasant to be right, isn't it?

ERNEST: Not by any means.

GILDA: You're right about something else, too.

ERNEST: What?

GILDA: Women being unreliable. There are moments in life when I look upon my own damned femininity with complete nausea. There!

ERNEST [smiling]: Good!

GILDA: I don't like women at all, Ernest; and I like myself least of any of them.

ERNEST: Never mind.

GILDA: I do mind. I mind bitterly. It humiliates me to the dust to think that I can go so far, clearly and intelligently, keeping faith with my own standards—which are not female standards at all—preserving a certain decent integrity, not using any tricks; then suddenly, something happens, a spark is struck and down I go into the mud! Squirming with archness, being aloof and desirable, consciously alluring, snatching and grabbing, evading and surrendering, dressed and painted for victory. An object of strange contempt!

ERNEST: A lurid picture, perhaps a trifle exaggerated.

GILDA: I wish it were. I wish it were.

ERNEST: Drink a little coffee.

GILDA: Perhaps you're right. [She sits down suddenly.]

ERNEST [pouring it out]: There!

GILDA: Thank you, Ernest. You're a great comfort. [*She sips a little.*] It's not very nice, is it?

ERNEST: Disgusting!

GILDA: I must have burnt it.

ERNEST: You did, dear.

GILDA: How lovely to be you!

ERNEST: In heaven's name, why?

GILDA: You're a permanent spectator. You deal in pictures. You look at pictures all day long, good pictures and bad pictures; gay pictures and gloomy pictures, and you know why they're this or why they're that, because you're critical and knowledgeable and wise. You're a clever little dear, that's what you are—a clever little dear! [*She begins to laugh again.*]

ERNEST: Gilda, stop it!

GILDA: Take a look at this, my darling. Measure it with your eyes. Portrait of a woman in three cardinal colours. Portrait of a too loving spirit tied down to a predatory feminine carcass.

ERNEST: This is definitely macabre.

GILDA: Right, again!

ERNEST: I think I'd better go. You ought to lie down or something.

GILDA [*hysterically*]: Stay a little longer, you'll find out so much.

ERNEST: I don't want to find out anything. You're scaring me to death.

GILDA: Courage, Ernest. Be brave. Look at the whole thing as a side show. People pay to see freaks. Walk up! Walk up and see the Fat Lady and the Monkey Man and the Living Skeleton and the Three Famous Hermaphrodites!——

[*There is a noise outside in the passage. The door bursts open, and Otto fairly bounds into the room. He is tall and good-looking, wearing a travelling coat and hat, and carrying a suitcase and a large package of painting materials.*]

GILDA: Otto!

OTTO [*striking an attitude*]: I've come home!

GILDA: You see what happens when I crack the whip!

OTTO: Little Ernest! How very sweet to see you! [*He kisses him.*]

GILDA: When did you leave Bordeaux?

OTTO: Night train, dear heart.

GILDA: Why didn't you telegraph?

OTTO: I don't hold with these modern innovations.

ERNEST: This is very interesting.

OTTO: What's very interesting?

ERNEST: Life, Otto. I was just meditating upon Life.

OTTO [*to Gilda*]: I've finished the picture.

GILDA: Really? Completely finished it?

OTTO: Yes, it's fine. I brought it away with me. I made the old fool sit for hours and wouldn't let her see, and afterwards when she did she made the most awful scene. She said it was out of drawing and made her look podgy; then I lost my temper and said it was overeating and lack of exercise that made her look podgy, and that it was not only an exquisite painting but unfalteringly true to life. Then she practically ordered me out of the house! I don't suppose she'll ever pay me the rest of the money, but to hell with her! If she doesn't, I shall have the picture.

ERNEST: Unwise, but, I am sure, enjoyable.

[*There is silence.*]

OTTO: Well?

GILDA: Well what?

OTTO: What on earth's the matter?

GILDA: Why should you think anything's the matter?

OTTO [*looking from one to the other*]: Have your faces lit up? No. Have you rushed at me with outstretched arms? No. Are you, either of you, even remotely pleased to see me? Obviously NO!

Something dreadful has happened and you're trying to decide how to break the news to me. What is it? Tell me at once! What's the matter?

ERNEST [*with slight malice*]: Gilda has neuralgia.

OTTO: Nonsense! She's as strong as a horse.

GILDA [*laughing wildly*]: Oh, my God!

OTTO [*to Ernest*]: What's she "Oh, my God-ing" about?

ERNEST: It's glandular. Everything's glandular.

OTTO: Have you both gone mad?

GILDA: Don't take off your coat and hat.

OTTO: What?

GILDA [*very slowly and distinctly*]: I said, "Don't take off your coat and hat."

OTTO [*humouring her*]: Very well, darling, I won't, I promise you. As a matter of fact, I said to myself only this morning, "Otto," I said, "Otto, you must never, never be parted from your coat and hat! Never, never, never!"

GILDA: There's a surprise for you, darling. A beautiful surprise!

OTTO: What?

GILDA: You must go to the George V at once.

OTTO: The George V?

GILDA: Yes. That's the surprise.

OTTO: Who is it? Who's at the George V?

GILDA: Leo.

OTTO: You're not serious? He couldn't be.

GILDA: He is. He came back on the *Mauretania*. His play is still running in Chicago, and he's sold the movie rights and he's made thousands!

OTTO: Have you seen him?

GILDA: Of course! Last night.

ERNEST: Well, I'm damned!

GILDA: I told you you didn't understand, Ernest. [*To Otto*]: If you'd only let me know you were coming, we could have both met you at the station. It would have been so lovely! Leo will be furious. You must go to him at once and bring him back here and we'll make some sort of a plan for the day.

OTTO: This is good, good, better thank good! An excellent, super homecoming! I was thinking of him last night, bumping along in that awful train. I thought of him for hours, I swear I did. Cross my hand with silver, lady, I'm so definitely the Gipsy Queen! Oh, God, how marvellous! He'll be able to go to Annecy with us.

GILDA: He's got to go back to New York, and then to London.

OTTO: Splendid! We'll go with him. He's been away far too long. Come on—— [*He seizes Gilda's hand.*]

GILDA: No.

ERNEST: What are you going to do?

GILDA: Stay here and tidy up. You go with Otto to fetch Leo. You said my life was untidy, didn't you? Well, I'm taking it to heart!

OTTO: Come on, Gilda; it doesn't matter about tidying up.

GILDA: Yes, it does. It does! It's the most important thing in the world—an orderly mind; that's the thing to have.

OTTO: He's probably brought us presents, and if he's rich they'll be expensive presents. Very nice! Very nice, indeed. Come along, Ernest, my little honey—we'll take a taxi.

ERNEST: I don't think I'll go.

OTTO: You must. He likes seeing you almost as much as us. Come on! [*He grabs Ernest by the shoulders and shoves him towards the door.*]

GILDA: Of course, go, Ernest, and come back too and we'll all celebrate. I'm yelling! Can't you hear me yelling like mad?

OTTO: What on earth are you talking about?

GILDA: A bad joke, and very difficult to explain.

OTTO: Good-morning, darling! I never kissed you good-morning.

GILDA: Never mind about that now. Go on, both of you, or he'll have gone out. You don't want to miss him.

OTTO [*firmly kissing her*]: Good-morning, darling.

GILDA [*suddenly stiffening in his arms*]: Dearest——

[*Otto and Ernest go to the door.*]

GILDA [*suddenly*]: Otto——

OTTO [*turning*]: Yes?

GILDA [*smiling gaily, but with a slight strain in her voice*]: I love you very much, so be careful crossing roads, won't you? Look to the right and the left and all around everything, and don't do anything foolish and impulsive. Please remember, there's a dear——

OTTO: Be quiet, don't pester me with your attentions! [*To Ernest as they go out*]: She's crazy about me, poor little thing; just crazy about me.

[*They go out. Gilda stands quite still for a moment or two staring after them; then she sits down at a table. Leo comes out of the bedroom. He is thin and nervous and obviously making a tremendous effort to control himself. He walks about aimlessly for a little and finishes up looking out of the window, with his back to Gilda.*]

LEO: What now?

GILDA: I don't know.

LEO: Not much time to think.

GILDA: A few minutes.

LEO: Are there any cigarettes?

GILDA: Yes, in that box.

LEO: Want one?

GILDA: No.

LEO [*lighting one*]: It's nice being human beings, isn't it? I'm sure God's angels must envy us.

GILDA: Whom do you love best? Otto or me?

LEO: Silly question.

GILDA: Answer me, anyhow.

LEO: How can I? Be sensible! In any case, what does it matter?

GILDA: It's important to me.

LEO: No, it isn't—not really. That's not what's important. What we did was inevitable. It's been inevitable for years. It doesn't matter who loves who the most; you can't line up things like that mathematically. We all love each other a lot, far too much, and we've made a bloody mess of it! That was inevitable, too.

GILDA: We must get it straight, somehow.

LEO: Yes, we must get it straight and tie it up with ribbons with a bow on the top. Pity it isn't Valentine's Day!

GILDA: Can't we laugh a little? Isn't it a joke? Can't we make it a joke?

LEO: Yes, it's a joke. It's a joke, all right. We can laugh until our sides ache. Let's start, shall we?

GILDA: What's the truth of it? The absolute, deep-down truth? Until we really know that, we can't grapple with it. We can't do a thing. We can only sit here flicking words about.

LEO: It should be easy, you know. The actual facts are so simple. I love you. You love me. You love Otto. I love Otto. Otto loves you. Otto loves me. There now! Start to unravel from there.

GILDA: We've always been honest, though, all of us. Honest with each other, I mean. That's something to go on, isn't it?

LEO: In this particular instance, it makes the whole thing far more complicated. If we were ordinary moral, high-thinking citizens we could carry on a backstairs affair for weeks without saying a word about it. We could lunch and dine together, all three, and not give anything away by so much as a look.

GILDA: If we were ordinary moral, high-thinking citizens we shouldn't have had an affair at all.

LEO: Perhaps not. We should have crushed it down. And the more we crushed it down the more we should have resented Otto, until we hated him. Just think of hating Otto——

GILDA: Just think of him hating us.

LEO: Do you think he will?

GILDA [*inexorably*]: Yes.

LEO [*walking about the room*]: Oh, no, no—he mustn't! It's too silly. He must see how unimportant it is, really.

GILDA: There's no question of not telling him, is there?

LEO: Of course not.

GILDA: We could pretend that you just arrived here and missed them on the way.

LEO: So we could, dear—so we could.

GILDA: Do you think we're working each other up? Do you think we're imagining it to be more serious than it really is?

LEO: Perhaps.

GILDA: Do you think, after all, he may not mind quite so dreadfully?

LEO: He'll mind just as much as you or I would under similar circumstances. Probably a little bit more. Imagine that for a moment, will you? Put yourself in his place.

GILDA [*hopelessly*]: Oh, don't!

LEO: Tell me one thing. How sorry were you last night, when once you realized we were in for it?

GILDA: I wasn't sorry at all. I gave way utterly.

LEO: So did I.

GILDA: Very deep inside, I had a qualm or two. Just once or twice.

LEO: So did I.

GILDA: But I stamped on them, like killing beetles.

LEO: A nice way to describe the pangs of a noble conscience!

GILDA: I enjoyed it all, see! I enjoyed it thoroughly from the very first moment. So there!

LEO: All right! All right! So did I.

GILDA [*defiantly*]: It was romantic. Suddenly, violently romantic! The whole evening was "Gala." You looked lovely, darling —very smooth and velvety—and your manner was a dream! I'd forgotten about your French accent and the way you move your hands, and the way you dance. A sleek little gigolo!

LEO: You must try not to be bitter, dear.

GILDA: There seemed to be something new about you: something I'd never realized before. Perhaps it's having money. Perhaps your success has given you a little extra glamour.

LEO: Look at me now, sweet! It's quite chilly, this morning light. How do I appear to you now?

GILDA [*gently*]: The same.

LEO: So do you, but that's because my eyes are slow at changing visions. I still see you too clearly last night to be able to realize how you look this morning. You were very got up—very got up, indeed, in your green dress and your earrings. It was "Gala," all right—strong magic!

GILDA: Coloured lights, sly music, overhanging trees, paper streamers—all the trappings.

LEO: Champagne, too, just to celebrate, both of us hating it.

GILDA: We drank to Otto. Perhaps you remember that as well?

LEO: Perfectly.

GILDA: How could we? Oh, how could we?

LEO: It seemed quite natural.

GILDA: Yes, but we knew in our hearts what we were up to. It was vile of us.

LEO: I'll drink Otto's health until the day I die! Nothing could change that ever.

GILDA: Sentimentalist!

LEO: Deeper than sentiment: far, far deeper. Beyond the reach of small enchantments.

GILDA: Was that all it was to you? A small enchantment?

LEO: That's all it ever is to anybody, if only they knew.

GILDA: Easy wisdom. Is it a comfort to you?

LEO: Not particularly.

GILDA [*viciously*]: Let's have some more! "Passion's only transitory," isn't it? "Love is ever fleeting!" "Time is a great healer." Trot them all out, dear.

LEO: Don't try to quarrel with me.

GILDA: Don't be so wise and assured and knowing, then. It's infuriating.

LEO: I believe I was more to blame than you, really.

GILDA: Why?

LEO: I made the running.

GILDA: *You* made the running! [*She laughs.*]

LEO: A silly pride made me show off to you, parade my attraction for you, like a mannequin. New spring model, with a few extra flounces!

GILDA: That's my story, Leo; you can't steal it from me. I've been wallowing in self-abasement, dragging out my last night's femininity and spitting on it. I've taken the blame onto myself for the whole thing. Ernest was quite shocked; you should have been listening at the door.

LEO: I was.

GILDA: Good! Then you know how I feel.

LEO: Lot of damned hysteria.

GILDA: Possibly, but heartfelt at the moment.

LEO: Can't we put an end to this flagellation party now?

GILDA: We might just as well go on with it, it passes the time.

LEO: Until Otto comes back.

GILDA: Yes. Until Otto comes back.

LEO [*walking up and down*]: I expect jealousy had something to do with it, too.

GILDA: Jealousy?

LEO: Yes. Subconscious and buried deep, but there all the same; there for ages, ever since our first meeting when you chose Otto so firmly.

GILDA: Another of those pleasant little galas! The awakening of spring! Romance in a café! Yes, sir! "Yes, sir, three bags full!"

LEO: A strange evening. Very gay, if I remember rightly.

GILDA: Oh, it was gay, deliriously gay, thick with omens!

LEO: Perhaps we laughed at them too hard.

GILDA: You and Otto had a row afterwards, didn't you?

LEO: Yes, a beauty.

GILDA: Blows?

LEO: Ineffectual blows. Otto fell into the bath!

GILDA: Was there any water in it?

LEO: Not at first.

GILDA [*beginning to laugh*]: Leo, you didn't——?

LEO [*also beginning to laugh*]: Of course I did; it was the obvious thing to do.

GILDA: Couldn't he get out?

LEO: Every time he tried, I pushed him back.

GILDA [*now laughing helplessly*]: Oh, the poor darling!——

LEO [*giving way*]: Finally—he—he got wedged——

GILDA: This is hysteria! Stop it, stop it——

LEO [*sinking down at the table with his head in his hands, roaring with laughter*]: It—it was a very narrow bath, far—far—too narrow——

GILDA [*collapsing at the other side of the table*]: Shut up, for heaven's sake! Shut up——

[*They are sitting there, groaning with laughter, when Otto comes into the room.*]

OTTO: Leo!

[*They both look up, and the laughter dies away from their faces. Leo rises and comes slowly over to Otto. He takes both his hands and stands looking at him.*]

LEO: Hello, Otto.

OTTO: Why did you stop laughing so suddenly?

LEO: It's funny how lovely it is to see you.

OTTO: Why funny?

GILDA: Where's Ernest?

OTTO: He wouldn't come back with me. He darted off in a taxi very abruptly when we found Leo wasn't at the hotel. He seemed to be in a fluster.

LEO: Ernest's often in a fluster. It's part of his personality, I think.

OTTO: Ernest hasn't got a personality.

GILDA: Yes, he has; but it's only a very little one, gentle and prim.

OTTO: You've changed, Leo. Your face looks different.

LEO: In what way different?

OTTO: I don't know, sort of odd.

LEO: I was very seasick on the *Mauretania*. Perhaps that changed it.

GILDA: They call the *Mauretania* "The Greyhound of the Ocean." I wonder why?

LEO: Because it's too long and too thin and leaps up and down.

GILDA: Personally, I prefer the *Olympic*. It's a good-natured boat and cozy, also it has a Turkish bath.

LEO: I dearly love a Turkish bath.

OTTO: Have you both gone crazy?

LEO: Yes. Just for a little.

OTTO: What does that mean?

GILDA: Lots of things, Otto. Everything's quite horrid.

OTTO: I'm awfully puzzled. I wish you'd both stop hinting and tell me what's happened.

LEO: It's serious, Otto. Please try to be wise about it.

OTTO [*with slight irritation*]: How the hell can I be wise about it if I don't know what it is?

LEO [*turning away*]: Oh, God! This is unbearable!

OTTO [*fighting against the truth that's dawning on him*]: It wouldn't be what I think it is, would it? I mean, what's just dropped into my mind. It isn't that, is it?

GILDA: Yes.

LEO: Yes.

OTTO [*very quietly*]: Oh, I see.

GILDA [*miserably*]: If only you wouldn't look like that.

OTTO: I can't see that it matters very much how I look.

LEO: We're—we're both equally to blame.

OTTO: When did you arrive? When—when did—don't you think you'd better tell me a little more?

LEO [*swiftly*]: I arrived yesterday afternoon, and the moment I'd left my bags at the hotel I came straight here, naturally. Gilda and I dined together, and I spent the night here.

OTTO: Oh—oh, did you?

LEO [*after a long pause*]: Yes, I did.

OTTO: This is the second bad entrance I've made this morning. I don't think I'd better make any more.

GILDA: Otto—darling—please, listen a minute!

OTTO: What is there to listen to? What is there for you to say?

GILDA: Nothing. You're quite right. Nothing at all.

OTTO: Have you planned it? Before, I mean?

LEO: Of course not.

OTTO: Was it in your minds?

LEO: Yes. It's been in all our minds, for ages. You know that.

OTTO: You couldn't have controlled yourself? Not for my sake, alone, but for all that lies between us?

LEO: We could have, I suppose. But we didn't.

OTTO [*still quiet, but trembling*]: Instead of meanly taking advantage of my being away, couldn't you have waited until I came back, and told me how you felt?

LEO: Would that have made things any better?

OTTO: It would have been honest, at least.

LEO [*with sudden violence*]: Bunk! We're being as honest as we know how! Chance caught us, as it was bound to catch us eventually. We were doomed to it from the very first moment. You don't suppose we enjoy telling you, do you? You don't suppose I like watching the pleasure at seeing me fade out of your eyes? If it wasn't that we loved you deeply, both of us, we'd lie to you and deceive you indefinitely, rather than inflict this horror on ourselves.

OTTO [*his voice rising slightly*]: And what about the horror you're inflicting on me?

GILDA: Don't argue, Leo. What's the use of arguing?

OTTO: So, you love me, do you? Both of you love me deeply! I don't want a love that can shut me out and make me feel more utterly alone than I've ever felt in my life before.

GILDA: Don't say that—it's not true! You couldn't be shut out —ever! Not possibly. Hold on to reason for a moment, for the sake of all of us—hold on to reason! It's our only chance. We've known this might happen any day; we've actually discussed it, quite calmly and rationally, but then there wasn't any emotion mixed up with it. Now there is, and we've got to fight it. It's distorting and overbalancing everything—don't you see? Oh, please, please try to see——

OTTO: I see all right. Believe me, I see perfectly!

GILDA: You don't, really—it's hopeless.

OTTO: Quite hopeless.

GILDA: It needn't be, if only we can tide over this moment.

OTTO: Why should we tide over this moment? It's a big moment! Let's make the most of it. [*He gives a little laugh.*]

LEO: I suppose that way of taking it is as good as any.

GILDA: No, it isn't—it isn't.

OTTO: I still find the whole thing a little difficult to realize completely. You must forgive me for being so stupid. I see quite clearly; I hear quite clearly; I know what's happened quite clearly, but I still don't quite understand.

LEO: What more do you want to understand?

OTTO: Were you both drunk?

GILDA: Of course we weren't.

OTTO: Then that's ruled out. One thing is still bewildering me very much. Quite a small trivial thing. You are both obviously strained and upset and unhappy at having to tell me. Isn't that so?

GILDA: Yes.

OTTO: Then why were you laughing when I came in?

LEO: Oh, what on earth does that matter?

OTTO: It matters a lot. It's very interesting.

LEO: It was completely irrelevant. Hysteria. It had nothing to do with anything.

OTTO: Why were you both laughing when I came in?

LEO: It was hysteria, I tell you.

OTTO: Were you laughing at me?

LEO [*wildly*]: Yes, we were! We were! We were laughing at you being wedged in the bath. That's what we were laughing at.

GILDA: Shut up, Leo! Stop it.

LEO [*giving way*]: And I shall laugh at that until the end of my days—I shall roll about on my 'eath bed thinking about it—and there are other things I shall ,augh at, too. I shall laugh at you now, in this situation, being hurt and grieved and immeasurably calm. What right have you to be hurt and grieved, any more than Gilda and me? We're having just as bad a time as you are, probably worse. I didn't stamp about with a martyr's crown on when you rushed off with her, in the first place; I didn't look wistful and say I was shut out. And I don't intend to stand any of that nonsense from you! What happened between Gilda and me last night is actually completely unimportant—a sudden flare-up—and although we've been mutually attracted to each other for years, it wasn't even based on deep sexual love! It was just an unpremeditated roll in the hay and we enjoyed it very much, so there!

OTTO [*furiously*]: Well, one thing that magnificent outburst has done for me is this: I don't feel shut out any more. Do you hear? Not any more! And I'm extremely grateful to you. You were right about me being hurt and grieved. I was. But that's over, too. I've seen something in you that I've never seen before; in all these years I've never noticed it—I never realized that, deep down underneath your superficial charm and wit, you're nothing but a cheap, second-rate little opportunist, ready to sacrifice anything, however sacred, to the excitement of the moment——

GILDA: Otto! Otto—listen a minute; please listen——

OTTO [*turning to her*]: Listen to what? A few garbled explanations and excuses, fully charged with a hundred-per-cent feminine emotionalism, appealing to me to hold on to reason and intelligence as it's "our only chance." I don't want an "only chance"—I don't want a chance to do anything but say what I have to say and leave you both to your own god-damned devices! Where was this much vaunted reason and intelligence last night? Working overtime, I'm sure. Working in a hundred small female ways. I expect your reason and intelligence prompted you to wear your green dress, didn't it? With the emerald earrings? And your green shoes, too, although they hurt you when you dance. Reason must have whispered kindly in your ear on your way back here in the taxi. It must have said, "Otto's in Bordeaux, and Bordeaux is a long way away, so everything will be quite safe!" That's reason, all right—pure reason——

GILDA [*collapsing at the table*]: Stop it! Stop it! How can you be so cruel! How can you say such vile things?

OTTO [*without a break*]: I hope "intelligence" gave you a little extra jab and suggested that you lock the door? In furtive, under-hand affairs doors are always locked——

LEO: Shut up, Otto. What's the use of going on like that?

OTTO: Don't speak to me—old, old Loyal Friend that you are! Don't speak to me, even if you have the courage, and keep out of my sight from now onwards——

LEO: Bravo, Deathless Drama!

OTTO: Wrong again. Lifeless Comedy. You've set me free from a stale affection that must have died ages ago without my realizing it. Go ahead, my boy, and do great things! You've already achieved a Hotel de Luxe, a few smart suits, and the woman I loved. Go ahead, maybe there are still higher peaks for you to climb. Good luck, both of you! Wonderful luck! I wish you were dead and in hell! [*He slams out of the room as the curtain falls.*]

ACT TWO: SCENE I

THE SCENE *is Leo's flat in London. It is only a rented flat but very comfortably furnished. Two French windows at the back open onto a small balcony, which, in turn, overlooks a square. It is several floors up, so only the tops of trees can be seen; these are brown and losing their leaves, as it is autumn. Down stage, on the Right, are double doors leading to the hall. Above these, a small door leads to the kitchen. On the Left, up stage, another door leads to the bedroom and bathroom. There is a large picture of Gilda, painted by Otto, hanging on the wall. The furniture may be left to the producer's discrimination.*

DISCOVERED: *When the curtain rises, it is about ten-thirty in the morning. Eighteen months have passed since Act One. The room is strewn with newspapers. Gilda is lying on the sofa, reading one; Leo is lying face downwards on the floor, reading another one.*

LEO [*rolling over on his back and flinging the paper in the air*]: It's a knockout! It's magnificent! It'll run a year.

GILDA: Two years.

LEO: Three years.

GILDA: Four years, five years, six years! It'll run for ever. Old ladies will be trampled to death struggling to get into the pit. Women will have babies regularly in the upper circle bar during the big scene at the end of the second act——

LEO [*complacently*]: Regularly as clockwork.

GILDA: The *Daily Mail* says it's daring and dramatic and witty.

LEO: The *Daily Express* says it's disgusting.

GILDA: I should be cut to the quick if it said anything else.

LEO: The *Daily Mirror*, I regret to say, is a trifle carping.

GILDA: Getting uppish, I see. Naughty little thing!

LEO [*reading the* Daily Mirror]: "*Change and Decay* is gripping throughout. The characterization falters here and there, but the dialogue is polished and sustains a high level from first to last and is frequently witty, nay, even brilliant——"

GILDA: I love "Nay."

LEO [*still reading*]: "But"—here we go, dear!—"But the play, on the whole, is decidedly thin."

GILDA: My God! They've noticed it.

LEO [*jumping up*]: Thin—thin! What do they mean "thin"?

GILDA: Just thin, darling. Thin's thin all the world over and you can't get away from it.

LEO: Would you call it thin?

GILDA: Emaciated.

LEO: I shall write fat plays from now onwards. Fat plays filled with very fat people!

GILDA: You mustn't let your vibrations be upset by the *Daily Mirror*. It means to be kind. That's why one only looks at the pictures.

LEO: The *Daily Sketch* is just as bad.

GILDA [*gently*]: Just as good, dear—just as good.

LEO: Let's have another look at Old Father *Times*.

GILDA: It's there, behind the *Telegraph*.

LEO [*glancing through it*]: Noncommittal, but amiable. A minute, if slightly inaccurate, description of the plot.

GILDA [*rising and looking over his shoulder*]: Only a few of the names wrong.

LEO: They seem to have missed the main idea of the play.

GILDA: You mustn't grumble; they say the lines are provocative.

LEO: What *could* they mean by that?

GILDA: Anyhow, you can't expect a paper like the *Times* to be really interested in your petty little excursions in the theatre. After all, it is the organ of the nation.

LEO: That sounds vaguely pornographic to me.

[*The telephone rings.*]

LEO [*answering it*]: Hallow! Hallow—'oo is it speaking?— H'if—if you will kaindly 'old the line for a moment, h'I will ascertain. [*He places his hand over the receiver.*] Lady Brevell!

GILDA: Tell her to go to hell.

LEO: It's the third time she's rung up this morning.

GILDA: No restraint. That's what's wrong with Society nowadays.

LEO [*at telephone again*]: Hallow, hallow!—I am seu very sorry but Mr. Mercuré is not awake yet. 'E 'ad a very tiring night what with one thing and another. H'is there any message?— Lunch on the third—or dinner on the seventh.—Yes, I'll write it daown—not at all!—Thenk you.

GILDA [*seriously*]: How do you feel about all that?

LEO: Amused.

GILDA: I'm not sure that I do.

LEO: It's only funny, really.

GILDA: Yes, but dangerous.

LEO: Are you frightened that my silly fluffy little head will be turned?

GILDA: No, not exactly, but it makes me uncomfortable, this snatching that goes on. Success is far more perilous than failure, isn't it? You've got to be doubly strong and watchful and wary.

LEO: Perhaps I shall survive.

GILDA: You'll survive all right, in the long run—I don't doubt that for a moment. It's me I was worrying about.

LEO: Why?

GILDA: Not me, alone. Us.

LEO: Oh, I see.

GILDA: Maybe I'm jealous of you. I never thought of that.

LEO: Darling, don't be silly!

GILDA: Last year was bad enough. This is going to be far worse.

LEO: Why be scared?

GILDA: Where do we go from here? That's what I want to know.

LEO: How would you feel about getting married?

GILDA [*laughing*]: It's not that, dear!

LEO: I know it isn't, but——

GILDA: But what?

LEO: It might be rather fun. We'd get a lot more presents now than if we'd done it before.

GILDA: A very grand marriage. St. Margaret's, Westminster?

LEO: Yes, with a tremendous "do" at Claridge's afterwards.

GILDA: The honeymoon would be thrilling, wouldn't it? Just you and me, alone, finding out about each other.

LEO: I'd be very gentle with you, very tender.

GILDA: You'd get a sock in the jaw, if you were!

LEO [*shocked*]: Oh, how volgar! How inexpressibly volgar!

GILDA: It's an enjoyable idea to play with, isn't it?

LEO: Let's do it.

GILDA: Stop! Stop, stop—you're rushing me off my feet!

LEO: No, but seriously, it's a much better plan than you think. It would ease small social situations enormously. The more successful I become, the more complicated everything's going to get. Let's do it, Gilda.

GILDA: No.

LEO: Why not?

GILDA: It wouldn't do. Really, it wouldn't.

LEO: I think you're wrong.

GILDA: It doesn't matter enough about the small social situations, those don't concern me much, anyway. They never have and they never will. I shouldn't feel cozy, married! It would upset my moral principles.

LEO: Doesn't the Eye of Heaven mean anything to you?

GILDA: Only when it winks!

LEO: God knows, it ought to wink enough at our marriage.

GILDA: Also, there's another thing.

LEO: What?

GILDA: Otto.

LEO: Otto!

GILDA: Yes. I think he'd hate it.

LEO: I wonder if he would.

GILDA: I believe so. There'd be no reason for him to, really; but I believe he would.

LEO: If only he'd appear again we could ask him.

GILDA: He will, sooner or later; he can't go on being cross for ever.

LEO: Funny, about Otto.

GILDA: Screamingly funny.

LEO: Do you love him still?

GILDA: Of course. Don't you?

LEO [*sighing*]; Yes.

GILDA: We couldn't *not* love Otto, really.

LEO: Could you live with him again?

GILDA: No, I don't think so; that part of it's dead.

LEO: We were right, weren't we? Unconditionally right.

GILDA: Yes. I wish it hadn't been so drastic, though, and violent and horrid. I hated him being made so unhappy.

LEO: We weren't any too joyful ourselves, at first.

GILDA: Conscience gnawing at our vitals.

LEO: Do you think—do you think he'll ever get over it, enough for us all to be together again?

GILDA [*with sudden vehemence*]: I don't want all to be together again.

[*The telephone rings.*]

LEO: Damn!

GILDA [*humming*]: Oh, Death, where is thy sting-a-ling-a-ling——

LEO [*at telephone*]: Hallow! Hallow—Neo, I'm afraid he's eout. [*He hangs up.*]

GILDA: Why don't you let Miss Hodge answer the telephone? It would save you an awful lot of trouble.

LEO: Do you think she could?

GILDA: I don't see why not; she seems in full possession of most of her faculties.

LEO: Where is she?

GILDA: She's what's known as "doing the bedroom."

LEO [*calling*]: Miss Hodge—Miss Hodge——

GILDA: We ought to have a valet in a white coat, really. Think if television came in suddenly, and everyone who rang up was faced with Miss Hodge!

[*Miss Hodge enters. She is dusty and extremely untidy.*]

MISS HODGE: Did you call?

LEO: Yes, Miss Hodge.

MISS HODGE: I was doing the bedroom.

LEO: Yes, I know you were and I'm sorry to disturb you, but I have a favour to ask you.

MISS HODGE [*suspiciously*]: Favour?

LEO: Yes. Every time the telephone rings, will you answer it for me?

MISS HODGE [*with dignity*]: If I 'appen to be where I can 'ear it, I will with pleasure.

LEO: Thank you very much. Just ask who it is speaking and tell them to hold the line.

MISS HODGE: 'Ow long for?

LEO: Until you've told me.

MISS HODGE: All right. [*She goes back into the bedroom.*]

LEO: I fear no good will come of that.

GILDA: Do you think while I am here alone in the evenings, when you are rushing madly from party to party, I might find out about Miss Hodge's inner life?

[*The telephone rings.*]

LEO: There now!

[*They both wait while the telephone continues to ring.*]

GILDA [*sadly*]: Two valets in two white coats, that's what we need, and a secretary and an upper housemaid!

[*The telephone continues to ring.*]

LEO: Perhaps I'd better answer it, after all.

GILDA: No, let it ring. I love the tone.

[*Miss Hodge comes flying in breathlessly, and rushes to the telephone.*]

MISS HODGE [*at telephone*]: 'Allo! 'Allo! 'Allo-'allo-'allo-'allo!——

GILDA: This is getting monotonous.

MISS HODGE [*continuing*]: 'Allo, 'allo—'allo! 'Allo——

GILDA [*conversationally*]: Tell me, Mr. Mercuré, what do you think of the modern girl?

LEO [*politely*]: A silly bitch.

GILDA: How cynical!

MISS HODGE: . . . 'allo, 'allo, 'allo, 'allo—'Allo! 'Allo—— [*She turns to them despondently.*] There don't seem to be anyone there.

LEO: Never mind, Miss Hodge. We mustn't hope for too much, at first. Thank you very much.

MISS HODGE: Not at all, sir. [*She goes out again.*]

GILDA: I feel suddenly irritated.

LEO: Why?

GILDA: I don't know. Reaction, I expect, after the anxiety of the last few days. Now it's all over and everything seems rather blank. How happy are you, really?

LEO: Very, I think.

GILDA: I don't work hard enough, not nearly hard enough; I've only done four houses for four silly women since we've been in England.

LEO: Monica Jevon wants you to do hers the moment she comes back.

GILDA: That'll make the fifth silly woman.

LEO: She's not so particularly silly.

GILDA: She's nice, really, nicer than most of them, I suppose. Oh, dear!

LEO: Cigarette? [*He throws her one.*]

GILDA: Ernest was right.

LEO: How do you mean? When?

GILDA: Ages ago. He said my life was untidy. And it is untidy. At this moment it's untidier than ever. Perhaps you're wise about our marrying; perhaps it would be a good thing. I'm developing into one of those tedious unoccupied women, who batten on men and spoil everything for them. I'm spoiling the excitement of your success for you now by being tiresome and gloomy.

LEO: Do you think marriage would automatically transform you into a busy, high-spirited Peg-o'-My-Heart?

GILDA: Something's missing, and I don't know what it is.

LEO: Don't you?

GILDA: No. Do you?

LEO: Yes, I do. I know perfectly well what's missing——
[*The telephone rings again.*]

GILDA: I'll do it this time. [*She goes to the telephone.*] Hallo!
Yes.—Oh, yes, of course! How do you do?—Yes, he's here, I'll
call him.—What?—I'm sure he'd love to.—That's terribly sweet
of you, but I'm afraid I can't. —No, I've got to go to Paris —
No, only for a few days.

LEO: Who is it?

GILDA [*with her hand over the receiver*]: Mrs. Borrowdale. She
wants you for the week-end.—[*Into telephone again*]: Here he is.

LEO [*taking telephone*]: Hallo, Marion.—Yes, wasn't it marvellous?—Terrified out of my seven senses.—What?—Well, I'm
not sure——

GILDA [*hissing at him*]: Yes, you are—quite sure!

LEO: Just hold on one minute while I look at my book.—
[*He puts his hand over the receiver.*] What will you do if I go?

GILDA: Commit suicide immediately, don't be so silly——

LEO: Why didn't you accept, too? She asked you.

GILDA: Because I don't want to go.

LEO [*at telephone*]: No, there isn't a thing down for Saturday.
I'd love to come.—Yes, that'll be grand.—Good-bye. [*He comes
over to Gilda.*] Why don't you want to come? She's awfully amusing, and the house is lovely.

GILDA: It's much better for you to go alone.

LEO: All right. Have it your own way.

GILDA: Don't think I'm being tiresome again, there's a darling!
I just couldn't make the effort—that's the honest-to-God reason.
I'm no good at house parties; I never was.

LEO: Marion's house parties are different. You can do what
you like and nobody worries you.

GILDA: I can never find what I like in other people's houses,
and everybody worries me.

LEO: I suppose I must be more gregarious than you. I enjoy meeting new people.

GILDA: I enjoy meeting new people, too, but not second-hand ones.

LEO: As I said before, Marion's house parties are extremely amusing. She doesn't like "second-hand" people, as you call them, any more than you do. Incidentally, she's a very intelligent woman herself and exceedingly good company.

GILDA: I never said she wasn't intelligent, and I'm sure she's excellent company. She has to be. It's her job.

LEO: That was a cheap gibe—thoroughly cheap——

[*The telephone rings again. Miss Hodge surprisingly appears almost at once. They sit silent while she answers it.*]

MISS HODGE [*at telephone*]: 'Allo! 'Allo—yes——[*She holds out the telephone to Leo.*] 'Ere, it's for you.

LEO [*hopelessly*]: Dear God! [*He takes it and Miss Hodge goes out.*] Hallo!—Yes, speaking.—*Evening Standard?*—Oh, all right, send him up.

GILDA: This is a horrible morning.

LEO: I'm sorry.

GILDA: You needn't be. It isn't your fault.

LEO: Yes, it is, I'm afraid. I happen to have written a successful play.

GILDA [*exasperated*]: Oh, really—— [*She turns away.*]

LEO: Well, it's true, isn't it? That's what's upsetting you?

GILDA: Do you honestly think that?

LEO: I don't know. I don't know what to think. This looks like a row but it hasn't even the virtue of being a new row. We've had it before several times, and just lately more than ever. It's inevitable that the more successful I become, the more people will run after me. I don't believe in their friendship, and I don't take them seriously, but I enjoy them. Probably a damn sight more than they enjoy me! I enjoy the whole thing. I've worked hard for it all my life. Let them all come! They'll drop me, all right, when they're tired of me; but maybe I shall get tired first.

GILDA: I hope you will.

LEO: What does it matter, anyhow?

GILDA: It matters a lot.

LEO: I don't see why.

GILDA: They waste your time, these ridiculous celebrity hunters, and they sap your vitality.

LEC: Let them! I've got lots of time and lots of vitality.

GILDA: That's bravado. You're far too much of an artist to mean that, really.

LEO: I'm far too much of an artist to be taken in by the old cliché of shutting out the world and living for my art alone. There's just as much bunk in that as there is in a cocktail party at the Ritz.

GILDA: Something's gone. Don't you see?

LEO: Of course something's gone. Something always goes. The whole business of living is a process of readjustments. What are you mourning for? The dear old careless days of the Quartier Latin, when Laife was Laife!

GILDA: Don't be such a fool!

LEO: Let's dress up poor, and go back and pretend, shall we?

GILDA: Why not? That, at least, would be a definite disillusionment.

LEO: Certainly, it would. Standing over the skeletons of our past delights and trying to kick them to life again. That wouldn't be wasting time, would it?

GILDA: We needn't go back, or dress up poor, in order to pretend. We can pretend here. Among all this——[*She kicks the newspapers.*] With the trumpets blowing and the flags flying and the telephone ringing, we can still pretend. We can pretend that we're happy.

[*She goes out of the room as the telephone rings. Leo stands looking after her for a moment, and then goes to the desk.*]

LEO [*at telephone*]: Hallo!—What?—Yes, speaking.—Very well, I'll hold the line——

[*Miss Hodge comes in from the hall.*]

MISS HODGE: There's a gentleman to see you. He says he's from the *Evening Standard*.

LEO: Show him in.

[*Miss Hodge goes out.*]

LEO [*at telephone*]: Hallo—yes! Hallo there, how are you? Of course, for hours, reading the papers.—Yes, all of them marvellous——

[*Mr. Birbeck enters. Leo motions him to sit down.*] I'm so glad—it was thrilling, wasn't it?—Did he really? That's grand!—Nonsense, it's always nice to hear things like that—of course, I'd love to.—Black tie or white tie—no tie at all! That'll be much more comfortable.—Good-bye.—What?—No, really? So soon? You'll know it by heart.—Yes, rather.—Good-bye! [*He hangs up the telephone.*] I'm so sorry.

MR. BIRBECK [*shaking hands*]: I'm from the *Standard*.

LEO: Yes, I know.

MR. BIRBECK: I've brought a photographer. I hope you don't mind? We thought a little study of you in your own home would be novel and interesting.

LEO [*bitterly*]: I'm sure it would.

MR. BIRBECK: First of all, may I ask you a few questions?

LEO: Certainly, go ahead. Cigarette?

MR. BIRBECK: No, thank you. I'm not a smoker myself.

LEO [*taking one and lighting it*]: I am.

MR. BIRBECK [*producing notebook*]: This is not your first play, is it?

LEO: No, my seventh. Two of them have been produced in London within the last three years.

MR. BIRBECK: What were their names?

LEO: *The Swift River* and *Mrs. Draper.*

MR. BIRBECK: How do you spell "Mrs. Draper"?

LEO: The usual way—m r s   d r a p e r.

MR. BIRBECK: Do you care for sport?

LEO: Yes, madly.

MR. BIRBECK: Which particular sport do you like best?

LEO: No particular one. I'm crazy about them all.

MR. BIRBECK: I see. [*He writes.*] Do you believe the talkies will kill the theatre?

LEO: No. I think they'll kill the talkies.

MR. BIRBECK [*laughing*]: That's very good, that is! It really is.

LEO: Not as good as all that.

MR. BIRBECK: There's a question that interests our lady readers very much——

LEO: What's that?

MR. BIRBECK: What is your opinion of the modern girl?

LEO [*without flinching*]: Downright; straightforward; upright.

MR. BIRBECK: You approve of the modern girl, then?

LEO: I didn't say so.

MR. BIRBECK: What are your ideas on marriage?

LEO: Garbled.

MR. BIRBECK: That's good, that is. Very good!

LEO [*rising*]: Don't put it, though—don't write down any of this interview; come and see me again.

MR. BIRBECK: Why, what's wrong?

LEO: The whole thing's wrong, Mr.——

MR. BIRBECK: Birbeck.

LEO: Mr. Birbeck. The whole business is grotesque. Don't you see now grotesque it is?

MR. BIRBECK: I'm afraid I don't understand.

LEO: Don't you ever feel sick inside when you have to ask those questions?

MR. BIRBECK: No, why should I?

LEO: Will you do me a very great favour?

MR. BIRBECK: What is it?

LEO: Call in your photographer. Photograph me—and leave me alone.

MR. BIRBECK [*offended*]: Certainly.

LEO: Don't think me rude. I'm just rather tired, that's all.

MR. BIRBECK: I quite understand. [*He goes out into the hall and returns in a moment with the photographer.*] Where do you think would be best?

LEO: Wherever you say.

MR. BIRBECK: Just here?

LEO [*taking his stand just in front of the desk*]: All right.

MR. BIRBECK: Perhaps I could come and see you again sometime when you're not so tired?

LEO: Yes, of course. Telephone me.

MR. BIRBECK: Tomorrow?

LEO: Yes, tomorrow.

MR. BIRBECK: About eleven?

LEO: Yes. About eleven.

MR. BIRBECK: Now, then—are you ready?

[*Gilda comes out of the bedroom, dressed for the street. She goes over to Leo and puts her arms round his neck.*]

GILDA: I'm going to do a little shopping—— [*Then softly*]: Sorry, darling——

LEO: All right, sweet.

[*Gilda goes out.*]

MR. BIRBECK: Just a little smile!

[*Leo smiles as the curtain falls.*]

ACT TWO: SCENE II

THE SCENE *is the same, a few days later.*

It is evening, and Miss Hodge has just finished laying a cold supper on a bridge table in front of the sofa. She regards it thoughtfully for a moment, and then goes to the bedroom door.

MISS HODGE: Your supper's all ready, ma'am.

GILDA [*in bedroom*]: Thank you, Miss Hodge. I shan't want you any more tonight, then.

[*Miss Hodge goes off into the kitchen. Gilda comes out of the bedroom. She is wearing pyjamas and a dressing gown. She goes over to the desk, on which there is a parcel of books. She undoes the parcel and scrutinizes the books, humming happily to herself as she does so. Miss Hodge reënters from the kitchen, this time in her coat and hat.*]

GILDA: Hello, Miss Hodge! I thought you'd gone.

MISS HODGE: I was just putting on me 'at. I think you'll find everything you want there.

GILDA: I'm sure I shall. Thank you.

MISS HODGE: Not at all; it's a pleasure, I'm sure.

GILDA: Oh, Miss Hodge, do you think it would be a good idea if Mr. Mercuré and I got married?

MISS HODGE: I thought you was married.

GILDA: Oh, I'd forgotten. We never told you, did we?

MISS HODGE: You certainly didn't.

GILDA: Well, we're not.

MISS HODGE [*thoughtfully*]: Oh, I see.

GILDA: Are you shocked?

MISS HODGE: It's no affair of mine, ma'am—miss.

GILDA: What do you think about marriage?

MISS HODGE: Not very much, miss, having had a basinful me-self, in a manner of speaking.

GILDA [*surprised*]: What!

MISS HODGE: Hodge is my maiden name. I took it back in—in disgust, if you know what I mean.

GILDA: Have you been married much, then?

MISS HODGE: Twice, all told.

GILDA: Where are your husbands now?

MISS HODGE: One's dead, and the other's in Newcastle.

GILDA [*smiling*]: Oh.

MISS HODGE: Well, I'll be getting 'ome now, if there's nothing else you require?

GILDA: No, there's nothing else, thank you. Good-night.

MISS HODGE: Good-night, miss.

[*Miss Hodge goes out. Gilda laughs to herself; pours herself out a glass of Sherry from the bottle on the table, and settles onto the sofa with the books. Otto comes in from the hall and stands in the doorway, looking at her.*]

OTTO: Hallo, Gilda!

GILDA [*turning sharply and staring at him*]: It's not true!

OTTO [*coming into the room*]: Here we are again!

GILDA: Oh, Otto!

OTTO: Are you pleased?

GILDA: I don't quite know yet.

OTTO: Make up your mind, there's a dear.

GILDA: I'll try.

OTTO: Where's Leo?

GILDA: Away. He went away this afternoon.

OTTO: This seems a very nice flat.

GILDA: It is. You can see right across to the other side of the square on a clear day.

OTTO: I've only just arrived.

GILDA: Where from?

OTTO: New York. I had an exhibition there.

GILDA: Was it successful?

OTTO: Very, thank you.

GILDA: I've decided quite definitely now: I'm ecstatically pleased to see you.

OTTO: That's lovely.

GILDA: How did you get in?

OTTO: I met an odd-looking woman going out. She opened the door for me.

GILDA: That was Miss Hodge. She's had two husbands.

OTTO: I once met a woman who'd had four husbands.

GILDA: Aren't you going to take off your hat and coat?

OTTO: Don't you like them?

GILDA: Enormously. It was foolish of me to ask whether your exhibition was successful. I can see it was! Your whole personality reeks of it.

OTTO [*taking off his hat and coat*]: I'm disappointed that Leo isn't here.

GILDA: He'll be back on Monday.

OTTO: How is he, please?

GILDA: Awfully well.

OTTO: Oh, dear! Oh, dear, oh, dear—I feel very funny! I feel as if I were going to cry, and I don't want to cry a bit.

GILDA: Let's both cry, just a little!

OTTO: Darling, darling Gilda!

[*They rush into each other's arms and hug each other.*]

OTTO: It's all, all right now, isn't it?

GILDA: More than all right.

OTTO: I was silly to stay away so long, wasn't I?

GILDA: That was what Leo meant the other morning when he said he knew what was missing.

OTTO: Me?

GILDA: Of course.

OTTO: I'm terribly glad he said that.

GILDA: We were having a row, trying to find out why we weren't quite as happy as we should be.

OTTO: Do you have many rows?

GILDA: Quite a lot, every now and then.

OTTO: As many as we used to?

GILDA: About the same. There's a bit of trouble on at the moment, really. He's getting too successful and sought after. I'm worried about him.

OTTO: You needn't be. It won't touch him—inside.

GILDA: I'm afraid, all the same; they're all so shrill and foolish, clacking at him.

OTTO: I read about the play in the train. It's a riot, isn't it?

GILDA: Capacity—every performance.

OTTO: Is it good?

GILDA: Yes, I think so.

OTTO: Only think so?

GILDA: Three scenes are first rate, especially the last act. The beginning of the second act drags a bit, and most of the first act's too facile—you know what I mean—he flips along with easy swift dialogue, but doesn't go deep enough. It's all very well played.

OTTO: We'll go on Monday night.

GILDA: Will you stay, now that you've come back?

OTTO: I expect so. It depends on Leo.

GILDA: Oh!

OTTO: He may not want me to.

GILDA: I think he'll want you to, even more than I do!

OTTO: Why do you say that?

GILDA: I don't know. It came up suddenly, like a hiccup.

OTTO: I feel perfectly cozy about the whole business now, you know—no trailing ends of resentment—I'm clear and clean, a newly washed lamb, bleating for company!

GILDA: Would you like some Sherry?

OTTO: Very much indeed.

GILDA: Here, have my glass. I'll get another. We'll need another plate as well and a knife and fork.

OTTO [*looking over the table*]: Cold ham, salad: what's that blob in the pie dish?

GILDA: Cold rice pudding. Delicious! You can have jam with it and cream.

OTTO [*without enthusiasm*]: How glorious.

[*Gilda runs into the kitchen and returns in a moment with plate and knife and fork, etc.*]

GILDA: Here we are!

OTTO: I expected more grandeur.

GILDA: Butlers and footmen?

OTTO: Yes, just a few. Concealed lighting, too. There's something a thought sordid about that lamp over there. Did you decorate this room?

GILDA: You know perfectly well I didn't.

OTTO: Well, you should.

GILDA: Do you want anything stronger to drink than Sherry?

OTTO: No, Sherry's all right. It's gentle and refined, and imparts a discreet glow. Of course, I'm used to having biscuits with it.

GILDA: There aren't any biscuits.

OTTO [*magnificently*]: It doesn't matter.

GILDA: Do sit down, darling.

OTTO [*drawing up a chair*]: What delicious-looking ham! Where *did* you get it?

GILDA: I have it specially sent from Scotland.

OTTO: Why Scotland?

GILDA: It lives there when it's alive.

OTTO: A bonny country, Scotland, if all I've heard is correct, what with the banshees wailing and the four-leaved shamrock.

GILDA: That's Ireland, dear.

OTTO: Never mind. The same wistful dampness distinguishes them both.

GILDA [*helping him to ham*]: I knew you'd arrive soon.

OTTO [*helping her to salad*]: Where's Leo gone, exactly?

GILDA: Smart house party in Hampshire. Bridge, backgammon, several novelists, and a squash court that nobody uses.

OTTO: The Decoration of Life—that's what that is.

GILDA: Slightly out of drawing, but terribly amusing.

OTTO: It won't last long. Don't worry.

GILDA: Tell me where you've been, please, and what you've seen and what you've done. Is your painting still good, or has it deteriorated just a little? I'm suspicious, you see! Dreadfully suspicious of people liking things too much—things that matter, I mean. There's too much enthusiasm for Art going on nowadays. It smears out the highlights.

OTTO: You're certainly in a state, aren't you?

GILDA: Yes, I am. And it's getting worse.

OTTO: Turbulent! Downright turbulent.

GILDA: There isn't any mustard.

OTTO: Never mind: I don't want any, do you?

GILDA: I don't know, really. I'm always a little undecided about mustard.

OTTO: It might pep up the rice pudding!

GILDA: Strange, isn't it? This going on where we left off?

OTTO: Not quite where we left off, thank God.

GILDA: Wasn't it horrible?

OTTO: I was tortured with regrets for a long while. I felt I ought to have knocked Leo down.

GILDA: I'm awfully glad you didn't. He hates being knocked down.

OTTO: Then, of course, he might have retaliated and knocked me down!

GILDA: You're bigger than he is.

OTTO: He's more wiry. He once held me in the bath for twenty minutes while he poured cold water over me.

GILDA [*laughing*]: Yes, I know!

OTTO [*laughing too*]: Oh, of course—that's what you were both laughing at when I came in that day, wasn't it?

GILDA [*weakly*]: Yes, it was very, very unfortunate.

OTTO: An unkind trick of Fate's, to have dropped it into your minds just then.

GILDA: It made a picture, you see—an unbearably comic picture—we were both terribly strained and unhappy; our nerves were stretched like elastic, and that snapped it.

OTTO: I think that upset me more than anything.

GILDA: You might have known it wasn't you we were laughing at. Not you, yourself.

OTTO: It's exactly a hundred and twenty-seven years ago to-day.

GILDA: A hundred and twenty-eight.

OTTO: We've grown up since then.

GILDA: I do hope so, just a little.

OTTO: I went away on a freight boat, you know. I went for thousands of miles and I was very unhappy indeed.

GILDA: And very seasick, I should think.

OTTO: Only the first few days.

GILDA: Not steadily?

OTTO: As steadily as one can be seasick.

GILDA: Do you know a lot about ships now?

OTTO: Not a thing. The whole business still puzzles me dreadfully. I know about starboard and port, of course, and all the different bells; but no one has yet been able to explain to me satisfactorily why, the first moment a rough sea occurs, the whole thing doesn't turn upside down!

GILDA: Were you frightened?

OTTO: Petrified, but I got used to it.

GILDA: Was it an English ship?

OTTO: No, Norwegian. I can say, "How do you do?" in Norwegian.

GILDA: We must get to know some Norwegian people immediately, so that you can say "How do you do?" to them.—Where are your pictures?

OTTO: Not unpacked yet. They're at the Carlton.

GILDA: The Carlton! You haven't gone "grand" on me, too, have you?

OTTO: I have, indeed. I've got several commissions to do portraits here in London. The very best people. I only paint the very best people.

GILDA [*almost snappily*]: They have such interesting faces, haven't they?

OTTO [*reproachfully*]: I don't paint their faces, Gilda. Fourth dimensional, that's what I am. I paint their souls.

GILDA: You'd have to be eighth dimensional and clairvoyant to find them.

OTTO: I'm grieved to see that Leo has done little or nothing towards taming your proud revolutionary spirit.

GILDA: He's inflamed it.

OTTO: I know what's wrong with you, my sweet. You're just the concentrated essence of "Love Among the Artists."

GILDA: I think that was unkind.

OTTO: If you were creative yourself you'd understand better. As it is, you know a lot. You know an awful lot. Your critical faculty is first rate. I'd rather have your opinion on paintings or books or plays than anyone else's I know. But you're liable to get sidetracked if you're not careful. Life is for living first and foremost. Even for artists, life is for living. Remember that.

GILDA: You have grown up, haven't you?

OTTO: In the beginning, when we were all in Paris, everything was really very much easier to manage, even our emotional problems. Leo and I were both struggling, a single line was in both our minds leading to success—that's what we were planning for, working like dogs for! You helped us both, jostling us onto the line again when we slipped off, and warming us when we were cold in discouragement. You picked on me to love a little bit more, because you decided, rightly then, that I was the weaker. They were very happy, those days, and glamour will always cling to them in our memories. But don't be misled by them; don't make the mistake of trying to recapture the spirit of them. That's dead, along with our early loves and dreams and quarrels, and all the rest of the foolishness.

GILDA: I think I want to cry again.

OTTO: There's nothing like a good cry.

GILDA: You can't blame me for hating success, when it changes all the—the things I love best.

OTTO: Things would have changed, anyhow. It isn't only

success that does it—it's time and experience and new circumstances.

GILDA [*bitterly*]: Was it the Norwegians that taught you this still wisdom? They must be wonderful people.

OTTO [*gently*]: No, I was alone. I just sat quietly and looked at everything.

GILDA: I see.

OTTO: Would you fancy a little more salad?

GILDA: No, thank you.

OTTO: Then it's high time we started on the cold rice pudding.

GILDA: I see one thing clearly.

OTTO [*smiling*]: What?

GILDA: I'm not needed any more.

OTTO: I thought you were going to say that.

GILDA: It's what you meant me to say, isn't it?

OTTO: We shall always need each other, all three of us.

GILDA: Nonsense! The survival of the fittest—that's what counts.

OTTO: Do have some rice pudding?

GILDA: To hell with you and the rice pudding!

OTTO [*helping himself*]: Hard words. Hard, cruel words!

GILDA: You're so sure of yourself, aren't you? You're both so sure of yourselves, you and Leo. Getting what you want must be terribly gratifying!

OTTO [*unruffled*]: It is.

GILDA [*suddenly smiling*]: Do you remember how I used to rail and roar against being feminine?

OTTO: Yes, dear. You were very noisy about the whole business.

GILDA: I'm suddenly glad about it for the first time. Do you want some jam with that?

OTTO: What sort of jam is it?

GILDA: Strawberry, I think.

OTTO: Of course, I'm used to having dark plum with rice pudding, but I'll make do with strawberry.

GILDA: I'll get it!

[*She goes into the kitchen. The telephone rings. Otto answers it.*]

OTTO [*at telephone*]: Hallo!—Hallo—yes, speaking.—Didn't you recognize my voice?—How absurd! It must be a bad line. —Dinner on the seventh? Yes, I should love to.—You don't mind if I come as Marie Antoinette, do you? I have to go to a fancy dress ball.—Where? Oh, my aunt is giving it—yes, in a bad house, she runs a whole chain of them, you know!—Thank you so much. [*He hangs up the telephone.*]

GILDA [*reëntering*]: I put it into a glass dish. Who was that?

OTTO: Somebody called Brevell, Lady Brevell. She wants Leo to dine on the seventh. I accepted.

GILDA: Good! You can both go. I'm sure she'd be delighted.

OTTO [*sitting down again*]: What! No cream?

GILDA: It was a delusion about the cream. I thought there was a lot, but there isn't a drop.

OTTO: I think you've improved in looks really with the passing of the years.

GILDA: How sweet, Otto! I'm so pleased.

OTTO: Your skin, for instance. Your skin's much better.

GILDA: It ought to be, I've been taking a lot of trouble with it.

OTTO: What sort of trouble?

GILDA: Oh, just having it pushed and rubbed and slapped about.

OTTO: Funny, how much in love with you I was!

GILDA: We'll have a good laugh about it when you've finished your pudding.

OTTO: What's happened to Ernest?

GILDA: He's been away, too, a long way away; he went on a world cruise with a lot of old ladies in straw hats!

OTTO: Dear little Ernest!

GILDA: I saw him a few weeks ago, then he went back to Paris.

OTTO: An odd life. Sterile, don't you think?

GILDA: You've certainly emancipated yourself into a grand complacency.

OTTO: If you're unkind to me, I shall go back to the Carlton.

GILDA: Have you got a suite, or just a common bedroom and bath?

OTTO: Darling, I do love you so very much!

GILDA: A nice comfortable love, without heart throbs.

OTTO: Are you trying to lure me to your wanton bed?

GILDA: What would you do if I did?

OTTO: Probably enjoy it very much.

GILDA: I doubt if I should.

OTTO: Have I changed so dreadfully?

GILDA [*maliciously*]: It isn't you that's changed—it's time and experience and new circumstances!

OTTO [*rising*]: I've finished my supper. It wasn't very good but it sufficed. I should now like a whiskey and soda.

GILDA: It's in that thing over there.

OTTO [*getting it out*]: It is a thing, isn't it? Do you want one?

GILDA: No, I don't think so.

OTTO: Just a little one?

GILDA: All right.

OTTO [*pouring them out*]: If we were bored, we could always go to the pictures, couldn't we?

GILDA: It's too late; we shouldn't get in to anything that's worth seeing.

OTTO: Oh, how disappointing! How very, very, very disappointing!

GILDA: Personally, I'm enjoying myself here.

OTTO [*handing her her drink*]: Are you, indeed?

GILDA: Yes. This measured skirmishing is delightful.

OTTO: Be careful, won't you? I do implore you to be careful!

GILDA: I never was. Why should I start now?

OTTO [*raising his glass*]: I salute your spirit of defiance, my dearest.

GILDA [*raising her glass*]: Yours, too.

OTTO [*shaking his head*]: A bad business; a very bad business.

GILDA: Love among the artists.

OTTO: Love among anybody.

GILDA: Perhaps not love, exactly. Something a little below it and a little above it, but something terribly strong.

OTTO: Meaning this?

GILDA: Of course. What else?

OTTO: We should have principles to hang on to, you know. This floating about without principles is so very dangerous.

GILDA: Life is for living.

OTTO: You accused me of being too sure. It's you who are sure now.

GILDA: Sure of what?

OTTO: Sure that I want you.

GILDA: Don't you?

OTTO: Of course I do.

GILDA: Keep away, then, a minute, and let me look at you all over again.

OTTO: I used to sit on the top deck of that freighter, and shut my eyes and see you standing there, just like you are now.

GILDA: Good old romance, bobbing up again and wrapping up our crudities in a few veils!

OTTO: Shut up! Don't talk like that.

GILDA: I'm not nearly as afraid as you are.

OTTO: You haven't got so much to lose.

GILDA: How do you know? You've forgotten everything about me—the real me. That dim figure you conjured up under your damned tropic stars was an illusion, a misty ghost, scratched out of a few memories, inaccurate, untrue—nothing to do with me in any way. This is me, now! Take a good look and see if you can tell what I have to lose in the game, or to win, either—perhaps you can tell that, too! Can you? Can you?

OTTO: You look so terribly sweet when you're angry.

GILDA: Another illusion. I'm not sweet.

OTTO: Those were only love words. You mustn't be so crushing. How are we to conduct this revivalist meeting without love words?

GILDA: Let's keep them under control.

OTTO: I warn you it's going to be very difficult. You've worked yourself up into a frenzy of sophistication. You've decided on being calculating and disillusioned and brazen, even slightly coarse over the affair. That's all very well, but how long is it going to last? That's what I ask myself. How long is it going to last—this old wanton mood of yours?

GILDA [breaking down]: Don't—don't laugh at me.

OTTO: I must—a little.

GILDA: It's an unfair advantage. You've both got it, and you both use it against me mercilessly.

OTTO: Laugh, too; it's not so serious, really.

GILDA: If I once started, I should never stop. That's a warning.

OTTO: Duly registered.

GILDA: What are we going to do about Leo?

OTTO: Wait and see what he's going to do about us.

GILDA: Haven't you got any shame at all?

OTTO: Just about as much as you have.

GILDA: The whole thing's degrading: completely and utterly degrading.

OTTO: Only when measured up against other people's standards.

GILDA: Why should we flatter ourselves that we're so tremendously different?

OTTO: Flattery doesn't enter into it. We are different. Our lives are diametrically opposed to ordinary social conventions; and it's no use grabbing at those conventions to hold us up when we find we're in deep water. We've jilted them and eliminated them, and we've got to find our own solutions for our own peculiar moral problems.

GILDA: Very glib, very glib indeed, and very plausible.

OTTO: It's true. There's no sense in stamping about and saying how degrading it all is. Of course it's degrading; according to a certain code, the whole situation's degrading and always has been. The Methodists wouldn't approve of us, and the Catholics wouldn't either; and the Evangelists and the Episcopalians and the Anglicans and the Christian Scientists—I don't suppose even the Polynesian Islanders would think very highly of us, but they wouldn't mind quite so much, being so far away. They could all club together—the whole lot of them—and say with perfect truth, according to their lights, that we were loose-living, irreligious, unmoral degenerates, couldn't they?

GILDA [*meekly*]: Yes, Otto, I expect so.

OTTO: But the whole point is, it's none of their business. We're not doing any harm to anyone else. We're not peppering the world with illegitimate children. The only people we could possibly mess up are ourselves, and that's our lookout. It's no use you trying to decide which you love best, Leo or me, because you don't know! At the moment, it's me, because you've been living with Leo for a long time and I've been away. A gay, ironic chance threw the three of us together and tied our lives into a tight knot at the outset. To deny it would be ridiculous, and to unravel it impossible. Therefore, the only thing left is to enjoy it thoroughly, every rich moment of it, every thrilling second——

GILDA: Come off your soap box, and stop ranting!

OTTO: I want to make love to you very badly indeed, please! I've been lonely for a long time without you; now I've come back, and I'm not going to be lonely any more. Believe me, loneliness is a mug's game.

GILDA: The whole thing's a mug's game.

OTTO: You're infinitely lovely to me, darling, and so very necessary. The circle has swung round, and it's my turn again —that's only fair, isn't it?

GILDA: I—I suppose so.

OTTO: If you didn't want me, it would be different, but you do—you do, my dearest dear!—I can see it in your eyes. You want me every bit as much as I want you!

GILDA [*with a little smile*]: Yes, every bit.

OTTO: This is a moment to remember, all right. Scribble it onto your heart; a flicker of ecstasy sandwiched between yesterday and tomorrow—something to be recaptured in the future without illusion, perfect in itself! Don't let's forget this—whatever else happens, don't let's forget this.

GILDA: How easy it all seems in this light.

OTTO: What small perverse meanness in you forbids you to walk round the sofa to me?

GILDA: I couldn't move, if the house was on fire!

OTTO: I believe it is. To hell with the sofa!

[*He vaults over it and takes her in his arms. They stand holding each other closely and gradually subside onto the sofa.*]

OTTO [*kissing her*]: Hvordan staar det til!

GILDA [*blissfully*]: What's that, darling?

OTTO: "How do you do?" in Norwegian.

[*The curtain slowly falls.*]

ACT TWO: SCENE III

THE SCENE *is the same. It is about ten-thirty the next morning.*

As the curtain rises, Miss Hodge shows Ernest Friedman into the room.

MISS HODGE: I will tell madam—miss—madam you're here, sir.

ERNEST: Why so much confusion, Miss Hodge?

MISS HODGE: I was only told last night, sir, that—er, well—that—er——

ERNEST: Oh, I see.

MISS HODGE: It's a bit muddling at first, in a manner of speaking, but I shall get used to it.

ERNEST: I'm sure you will.

[*Miss Hodge goes into the bedroom, and returns again in a moment with very pursed-up lips.*]

MISS HODGE [*coldly*]: She will be in in a moment, sir.

[*Miss Hodge goes into the kitchen and slams the door. Ernest looks after her in some astonishment.*]

[*Gilda enters. She is fully dressed, wearing a hat and coat.*]

GILDA [*with tremendous gaiety*]: Ernest! What a surprise!

ERNEST: What's the matter with Miss Hodge?

GILDA: The matter with her? I don't know—I haven't examined her.

ERNEST: It was foolish of you to tell her you and Leo weren't married.

GILDA: It slipped out; I'd forgotten she didn't know. Have you come from Paris?

ERNEST: Yes, last night. There's been a slight argument going on for weeks.

GILDA: Argument? What kind of an argument?

ERNEST: One of those Holbein arguments.

GILDA: Somebody said it wasn't, I suppose?

ERNEST: Yes, that's it.

GILDA: Was it?

ERNEST: In my humble opinion, yes.

GILDA: Did your humble opinion settle it?

ERNEST: I hope so.

GILDA: Admirable. Quiet, sure, perfect conviction—absolutely admirable.

ERNEST: Thank you, Gilda. Don't imagine that the irony in your tone escaped me.

GILDA: That wasn't irony; it was envy.

ERNEST: It's high time you stopped envying me.

GILDA: I don't think I ever shall.

ERNEST: How's Leo?

GILDA: Not very well.

ERNEST: What's wrong with him?

GILDA: Tummy; he's had an awful night. He didn't close an eye until about five, but he's fast asleep now.

ERNEST: I'm sorry. I wanted to say good-bye to you both.

GILDA: Good-bye?

ERNEST: I'm going back to Paris this afternoon and sailing for America on Wednesday.

GILDA: You do flip about, don't you, Ernest?

ERNEST: Not any more. I've decided to live in New York permanently. I've been angling for a particular penthouse for years and now I've got it.

GILDA: How lovely. Is it very high?

ERNEST: About thirty floors.

GILDA [*gaily*]: Do you want a housekeeper?

ERNEST: Yes, badly. Will you come?

GILDA: Perhaps. [*She laughs.*]

ERNEST: You seem very gay this morning.

GILDA: I'm always gay on Sundays. There's something intoxicating about Sunday in London.

ERNEST: It's excellent about the play. I read all the reviews.

GILDA: Yes, it's grand. It ought to run for years and years and years and years and years!

ERNEST: I suppose Leo's delighted.

GILDA: Absolutely hysterical. I think that's what's upset his stomach. He was always oversensitive, you know; even in Paris in the old days he used to roll about in agony at the least encouragement, don't you remember?

ERNEST: No, I can't say that I do.

GILDA: That's because you're getting a bit "gaga," darling! You've sold too many pictures and made too much money and travelled too much. That world cruise was a fatal mistake. I thought so at the time, but I didn't say anything about it, because I didn't want to upset you. But going round in a troupe, with all those tatty old girls, must have been very, very bad for you. I expected every day to get a wire from somewhere or other saying you'd died of something or other.

ERNEST: Do stop, you're making me giddy.

GILDA: Perhaps you'd like a little Sherry?

ERNEST: No, thank you.

GILDA: It's very good Sherry; dry as a bone!

ERNEST: You seem to me to be in a very strange mood, Gilda.

GILDA: I've never felt better in my life. Ups and downs! My

life is one long convulsive sequence of Ups and Downs. This is an Up—at least, I think it is.

ERNEST: You're sure it's not nervous collapse?

GILDA: I never thought of that; it's a very good idea. I shall have a nervous collapse!

ERNEST: Will you ever change, I wonder? Will you ever change into a quieter, more rational person?

GILDA: Why should I?

ERNEST: What's wrong now?

GILDA: Wrong! What could be wrong? Everything's right. Righter than it's ever been before. God's in His heaven, all's right with the world—I always thought that was a remarkably silly statement, didn't you?

ERNEST: Unreasoning optimism is always slightly silly, but it's a great comfort to, at least, three quarters of the human race.

GILDA: The human race is a let-down, Ernest; a bad, bad let-down! I'm disgusted with it. It thinks it's progressed but it hasn't; it thinks it's risen above the primeval slime but it hasn't —it's still wallowing in it! It's still clinging to us, clinging to our hair and our eyes and our souls. We've invented a few small things that make noises, but we haven't invented one big thing that creates quiet, endless peaceful quiet—something to pull over us like a gigantic eiderdown; something to deaden the sound of our emotional yellings and screechings and suffocate our psychological confusions——

ERNEST [weakly]: I think, perhaps, I would like a glass of Sherry after all.

GILDA [going to the "thing"]: It's all right, Ernest, don't be frightened! You're always a safety valve for me. I think, during the last few years, I've screamed at you more than anyone else in the world. [She hands him the bottle.] Here you are.

ERNEST [*looking at it*]: This is brandy.

GILDA: So it is. How stupid of me. [*She finds the Sherry and two glasses.*] Here we are!

ERNEST [*putting the brandy bottle on the desk*]: I'm not sure that I find it very comfortable, being a safety valve!

GILDA: It's the penalty you pay for being sweet and sympathetic, and very old indeed.

ERNEST [*indignantly*]: I'm not very old indeed!

GILDA: Only in wisdom and experience, darling. [*She pours out Sherry for them both.*] Here's to you, Ernest, and me, too!

[*They both drink.*]

ERNEST: Now, then?

GILDA: Now then, what?

ERNEST: Out with it!

GILDA: Take my advice, my dear; run like a stag—be fleet of foot! Beat it!

ERNEST: Why?

GILDA: I'm a lone woman. I'm unattached. I'm free.

ERNEST: Oh! Oh, are you, really!

GILDA: I'm cured. I'm not a prisoner any more. I've let myself out. This is a day of great exaltation for me.

ERNEST: I'm sure I'm delighted to hear it.

GILDA [*with the suspicion of a catch in her voice*]: I'm not needed any more—I'm going.

ERNEST: Where are you going?

GILDA: I haven't the faintest idea. The world is wide, far too wide and round, too. I can scamper round and round it, like a white rat in a cage!

ERNEST: That will be very tiring.

GILDA: Not so tiring as staying still; at least, I might preserve the illusion that I'm getting somewhere.

ERNEST [*prosaically*]: Have you had a row with Leo?

GILDA: No; I haven't had a row with anyone. I've just seen the light suddenly. I saw it last night. The survival of the fittest, that's the light. Didn't you know?

ERNEST: I think, perhaps, I should understand better if you spoke in Russian.

GILDA: Or Norwegian. There's a fascinating language for you!

ERNEST: I believe there is a very nice nursing home in Manchester Street.

GILDA [*taking a note out of her bag*]: You see this?

ERNEST: Yes.

GILDA: It's for Leo.

ERNEST: To read when he wakes up?

GILDA: Yes. If he ever wakes up.

ERNEST: You haven't poisoned him, have you?

GILDA: No; but he's nearly poisoned me! An insidious, dreary sort of poison; a lymphatic poison, turning me slowly into a cow.

ERNEST [*laughing*]: My poor Gilda!

GILDA [*propping it up against the brandy bottle*]: I shall leave it here.

ERNEST: Pity there isn't a pin cushion.

GILDA: I expect you think I'm being overdramatic?

ERNEST: Not any more than usual.

GILDA: Well, I'm not. I'm perfectly calm inside. Cold as steel.

ERNEST: Can one be exalted and cold as steel at the same time?

GILDA: I can. I can be lots of things at the same time; it becomes a great bore after a while. In the future, I intend to be only one thing.

ERNEST: That being——?

GILDA: Myself, Ernest. My unadulterated self! Myself, without hangings, without trimmings, unencumbered by the winding tendrils of other people's demands——

ERNEST: That was very nicely put.

GILDA: You can laugh at me as much as you like. I give every-body free permission to laugh at me. I can laugh at myself, too, now—for the first time, and enjoy it.

ERNEST: Can you?

GILDA: Yes; isn't it lovely?

ERNEST: I congratulate you.

GILDA: I'm glad you suddenly appeared this morning to say good-bye—very appropriate! It's a day of good-byes—the air's thick with them. You have a tremendous sense of the "right moment," Ernest. It's wonderful. You pop up like a genie out of a bottle, just to be in at the death! You really ought to have been a priest.

ERNEST: Are you really serious? Are you really going?

GILDA: I've never been more serious in my life. Of course I'm going—I've got to learn a few things while there's still time—who knows, I might even learn to be an artist! Just think of that! And even if I can't quite achieve such—such splendour, there are other lessons for me. There's the lesson of paddling my own canoe, for instance—not just weighing down somebody else's and imagining I'm steering it!

ERNEST: Oh, I see. I see it all now.

GILDA: No, you don't—not all; just a little, perhaps, but not all.

ERNEST: Where are you going, really?

GILDA: First, to a hotel, to make a few plans.

ERNEST: You can take over my room at the Carlton, if you like. I'm leaving today.

GILDA [laughing hysterically]: The Carlton! Oh, no, Ernest, not the Carlton!

ERNEST: Why, what's the matter with it?

GILDA: It's too big and pink and grand for me. I want a decayed hotel; gentle and sad and a little bit under the weather.

ERNEST: And afterwards?

GILDA: Paris—no, not Paris—Berlin. I'm very attached to Berlin.

ERNEST: Are you sure you're wise? This is rather—well, rather drastic, isn't it?

GILDA [*quietly*]: I'm quite sure.

ERNEST: I won't try to dissuade you, then.

GILDA: No, don't. It wouldn't do any good. I'm quite determined.

ERNEST: I have an instinctive distrust of sudden impulses.

GILDA: I'll fool you yet! I'll make you eat your damned skepticism!

ERNEST [*smiling*]: Sorry!

GILDA: Good-bye, Ernest. I'm going now.

ERNEST: You'll be very lonely. Aren't you afraid?

GILDA: I can bear it. I've been lonely before.

ERNEST: Not for a long while.

GILDA: Recently, quite—quite recently. Loneliness doesn't necessarily mean being by yourself.

ERNEST [*gently*]: Very well, dear.

GILDA [*suddenly flinging her arms round his neck*]: You're very tender and very kind and I'm tremendously grateful to you! Come on, let's go.

ERNEST: Haven't you got any bags or anything?

GILDA: I've packed a dressing case with all my immediate wants; I shall get everything else new, brand new—— [*She goes quietly to the bedroom door and gets a dressing case, which she has left just behind it.*] I'll drop you off at the Carlton, and take your taxi on.

ERNEST: Is he asleep?

GILDA: Fast asleep. Come on!

[*They go out into the hall. Suddenly Gilda is heard to say,* "*Just a moment, I've forgotten something!*"]

[*She comes quickly back into the room, takes another letter out of her bag and props it up on the desk. Then she goes out.*]

[*The front door is heard to slam very loudly.*]

[*After a moment or two the telephone rings; it goes on ringing until Miss Hodge comes out of the kitchen and answers it.*]

MISS HODGE [*at telephone*]: 'Allo, 'allo!—What?—No, 'e's not—'e's away.—All right!—Not at all.

[*She slams down the telephone and goes back into the kitchen. Otto comes out of the bedroom. He is wearing a dressing gown and pyjamas belonging to Leo, and looks very sleepy. He finds a cigarette and lights it; then goes to the kitchen door.*]

OTTO [*calling*]: Gilda!—Gilda, where are you?

[*Miss Hodge appears. Her face grim with disapproval.*]

MISS HODGE: She's gone h'out.

OTTO [*startled*]: Oh! Did she say where?

MISS HODGE: She did not.

OTTO: What's the time?

MISS HODGE: H'eleven.

OTTO [*pleasantly*]: We met last night on the doorstep: do you remember?

MISS HODGE: Yes, I remember all right.

OTTO: It was very kind of you to let me in.

MISS HODGE: I didn't know you was going to stay all night.

OTTO: I wasn't sure, myself.

MISS HODGE: A pretty thing!

OTTO: I beg your pardon?

MISS HODGE: I said, "A prettty thing" and I meant "A pretty thing"—nice goings on!

OTTO [*amiably*]: Very nice, thank you.

MISS HODGE: I'm a respectable woman.

OTTO: Never mind.

MISS HODGE: I don't mind a little fun every now and then among friends, but I do draw the line at looseness!

OTTO: You're making a mistake, Miss—Miss——?

MISS HODGE: Me name's 'Odge.

OTTO: You're making a mistake, Miss Odge.

MISS HODGE: 'Ow do you mean?

OTTO: You are making a mistake in daring to disapprove of something that has nothing to do with you whatever.

MISS HODGE [astounded]: Well, I never!

OTTO: Please go away, and mind your own business.

[Miss Hodge, with a gasp of fury, flounces off into the kitchen. Otto comes down to the sofa and lies on it with his back towards the door, blowing smoke rings into the air.]

[The door opens and Leo creeps into the room. He can only see the cigarette smoke, Otto's head being hidden by the cushion.]

LEO: Hallo, darling! I couldn't bear it any more, so I've come back.

OTTO [sitting up slowly]: Hello, Leo.

LEO: You!

OTTO: Yes. I couldn't bear it any longer, either, so I've come back.

LEO: Where have you come from?

OTTO: New York.

LEO: When—when did you arrive?

OTTO: Last night.

LEO: Why—why aren't you dressed?

OTTO: I've only just got up.

LEO: You stayed here?

OTTO: Yes.

LEO [slowly]: With Gilda?

OTTO: Yes.

LEO: I see.

OTTO: It wouldn't be any use lying, would it? Pretending I didn't?

LEO: No use at all.

OTTO: I'm not even sorry, Leo, except for hurting you.

LEO: Where is Gilda?

OTTO: She's gone out.

LEO: Out! Why? Where's she gone to?

OTTO: I don't know.

LEO [*turning away*]: How vile of you! How unspeakably vile of you both!

OTTO: It was inevitable.

LEO [*contemptuously*]: Inevitable!

OTTO: I arrived unexpectedly; you were away; Gilda was alone. I love her; I've always loved her—I've never stopped for a minute, and she loves me, too.

LEO: What about me?

OTTO: I told you I was sorry about hurting you.

LEO: Gilda loves me.

OTTO: I never said she didn't.

LEO [*hopelessly*]: What are we to do? What are we to do now?

OTTO: Do you know, I really haven't the faintest idea.

LEO: You're laughing inside. You're thoroughly damned well pleased with yourself, aren't you?

OTTO: I don't know. I don't know that either.

LEO [*savagely*]: You are! I can see it in your eyes—so much triumph—such a sweet revenge!

OTTO: It wasn't anything to do with revenge.

LEO: It was. Of course it was—secretly thought out, planned for ages—infinitely mean!

OTTO: Shut up! And don't talk such nonsense.

LEO: Why did you do it, then? Why did you come back and break everything up for me?

OTTO: I came back to see you both. It was a surprise.

LEO: A rather cruel surprise, and brilliantly successful. You should be very happy.

OTTO [*sadly*]: Should I?

LEO: Perhaps I should be happy, too; you've set me free from something.

OTTO: What?

LEO [*haltingly*]: The—feeling I had for you—something very deep, I imagined it was, but it couldn't have been, could it—now that it has died so easily.

OTTO: I said all that to you in Paris. Do you remember? I thought it was true then, just as you think it's true now.

LEO: It is true.

OTTO: Oh, no, it isn't.

LEO: Do you honestly believe I could ever look at you again, as a real friend?

OTTO: Until the day you die.

LEO: Shut up! It's too utterly beastly—the whole thing.

OTTO: It's certainly very, very uncomfortable.

LEO: Is Gilda going to leave me? To go away with you?

OTTO: Do you want her to?

LEO: Yes, I suppose so, now.

OTTO: We didn't make any arrangement or plans.

LEO: I came back too soon. You could have gone away and left a note for me—that would have been nice and easy for you, wouldn't it?

OTTO: Perhaps it would, really. I don't know that I should have done it, though.

LEO: Why not?

OTTO: If I had, I shouldn't have seen you at all, and I wanted to see you very much.

LEO: You even wanted to see me, hating you like this? Very touching!

OTTO: You're not hating me nearly as much as you think you are. You're hating the situation: that's quite different.

LEO: You flatter yourself.

OTTO: No. I'm speaking from experience. You forget, I've been through just what you're going through now. I thought I hated you with all my heart and soul, and the force of that hatred swept me away onto the high seas, too far out of reach to be able to come back when I discovered the truth.

LEO: The truth!

OTTO: That no one of us was more to blame than the other. We've made our own circumstances, you and Gilda and me, and we've bloody well got to put up with them!

LEO: I wish I could aspire to such a sublime God's eye view!

OTTO: You will—in time—when your acids have calmed down.

LEO: I'd like so very much not to be able to feel anything at all for a little. I'm desperately tired.

OTTO: You want a change.

LEO: It seems as if I'm going to get one, whether I want it or not.

OTTO [laughing]: Oh, Leo, you really are very, very tender!

LEO: Don't laugh! How dare you laugh! How can you laugh?

OTTO: It's a good joke. A magnificent joke.

LEO [bitterly]: A pity Gilda chose just that moment to go out, we could all have enjoyed it together.

OTTO: Like we did before?

LEO: Yes, like we did before.

OTTO: And like we shall again.

LEO [*vehemently*]: No, *never* again—never!

OTTO: I wonder.

[*The telephone rings. Leo goes over mechanically to answer it; he lifts up the receiver, and as he does so he catches sight of the two letters propped up against the brandy bottle. He stares at them and slowly lets the receiver drop onto the desk.*]

LEO [*very quietly*]: Otto.

OTTO: What is it?

LEO: Look.

[*Otto comes over to the desk, and they both stand staring at the letters.*]

OTTO: Gilda!

LEO: Of course.

OTTO: She's gone! She's escaped!

LEO: Funny word to use, "escaped."

OTTO: That's what she's done, all the same, escaped.

LEO: The joke is becoming richer.

OTTO: Escaped from both of us.

LEO: We'd better open them, I suppose.

OTTO [*slowly*]: Yes—yes, I suppose we had.

[*They both open the letters, in silence, and read them.*]

LEO [*after a pause*]: What does yours say?

OTTO [*reading*]: "Good-bye, my clever little dear! Thank you for the keys of the city."

LEO: That's what mine says.

OTTO: I wonder where she's gone?

LEO: I don't see that that matters much.

OTTO: One up to Gilda!

LEO: What does she mean, "keys of the city"?

OTTO: A lot of things.

LEO: I feel rather sick.

OTTO: Have some Sherry?

LEO: That's brandy.

OTTO: Better still. [*He pours out a glass and hands it to Leo.*]

LEO [*quietly*]: Thank you.

OTTO [*pouring one out for himself*]: I feel a little sick, too.

LEO: Do you think she'll come back?

OTTO: No.

LEO: She will—she must—she must come back!

OTTO: She won't. Not for a long time.

LEO [*drinking his brandy*]: It's all my fault, really.

OTTO [*drinking his*]: Is it?

LEO: Yes. I've, unfortunately, turned out to be successful. Gilda doesn't care for successful people.

OTTO: I wonder how much we've lost, with the years?

LEO: A lot. I think, practically everything now.

OTTO [*thoughtfully*]: Love among the artists. Very difficult, too difficult.

LEO: Do you think we could find her?

OTTO: No.

LEO: We could try.

OTTO: Do you want to?

LEO: Of course.

OTTO: Why? What would be the use?

LEO: She might explain a little—a little more clearly.

OTTO: What good would that do? We know why she's gone perfectly well.

LEO: Because she doesn't want us any more.

OTTO: Because she thinks she doesn't want us any more.

LEO: I suppose that's as good a reason as any.

OTTO: Quite.

LEO: All the same, I should like to see her just once—just to find out, really, in so many words——

OTTO [*with sudden fury*]: So many words! That's what's wrong with us! So many words—too many words, masses and masses of words, spewed about until we're choked with them. We've argued and probed and dragged our entrails out in front of one another for years! We've explained away the sea and the stars and life and death and our own peace of mind! I'm sick of this endless game of three-handed, spiritual ping-pong—this battling of our little egos in one another's faces! Sick to death of it! Gilda's made a supreme gesture and got out. Good luck to her, I say! Good luck to the old girl—she knows her onions! [*Otto refills his glass and drains it at a gulp.*]

LEO: You'll get drunk, swilling down all that brandy on an empty stomach.

OTTO: Why not! What else is there to do? Here, have some more as well. [*He refills Leo's glass and hands it to him.*]

LEO: All right! Here goes. [*He drains his glass.*] Now, we start fair. [*He refills both their glasses.*]

OTTO [*raising his glass*]: Gilda! [*He drains it.*]

LEO [*doing the same*]: Gilda! [*He drains it.*]

OTTO: That's better, isn't it? Much, much better.

LEO: Excellent. We shall be sick as dogs!

OTTO: Good for our livers.

LEO: Good for our immortal souls. [*He refills the glasses, and raises his.*] Our Immortal Souls!

OTTO [*raising his*]: Our Immortal Souls!

[*They both drain them to the last drop.*]

LEO: I might have known it!

OTTO: What?

LEO: That there was going to be a break. Everything was running too smoothly, too well. I was enjoying all the small things too much.

OTTO: There's no harm in enjoying the small things.

LEO: Gilda didn't want me to.

OTTO: I know.

LEO: Did she tell you so?

OTTO: Yes, she said she was uneasy.

LEO: She might have had a little faith in me, I think. I haven't got this far just to be sidetracked by a few garlands.

OTTO: That's what I said to her; I said you wouldn't be touched, inside.

LEO: How about you?

OTTO: Catching up, Leo! Popular portraits at popular prices.

LEO: Good work or bad work?

OTTO: Good. An occasional compromise, but essentials all right.

LEO [*with a glint in his eye*]: Let's make the most of the whole business, shall we? Let's be photographed and interviewed and pointed at in restaurants! Let's play the game for what it's worth, secretaries and fur coats and de-luxe suites on transatlantic liners at minimum rates! Don't let's allow one shabby perquisite to slip through our fingers! It's what we dreamed many years ago and now it's within our reach. Let's cash in, Otto, and see how much we lose by it. [*He refills both glasses and hands one to Otto.*] Come on, my boy! [*He raises his glass.*] Success in twenty lessons! Each one more bitter than the last! More and better Success! Louder and funnier Success!

[*They both drain their glasses.*]

[*They put down their glasses, gasping slightly.*]

OTTO [*agreeably*]: It takes the breath away a bit, doesn't it?

LEO: How astonished our insides must be—all that brandy hurtling down suddenly!

OTTO: On Sunday, too.

LEO: We ought to know more about our insides, Otto. We ought to know why everything does everything.

OTTO: Machines! That's what we are, really—all of us! I can't help feeling a little discouraged about it every now and then.

LEO: Sheer sentimentality! You shouldn't feel discouraged at all; you should be proud.

OTTO: I don't see anything to be proud about.

LEO: That's because you don't understand; because you're still chained to stale illusions. Science dispels illusions; you ought to be proud to be living in a scientific age. You ought to be proud to know that you're a minute cog in the vast process of human life.

OTTO: I don't like to think I'm only a minute cog—it makes me sort of sad.

LEO: The time for dreaming is over, Otto.

OTTO: Never! I'll never consent to that. Never, as long as I live! How do you know that science isn't a dream, too? A monstrous, gigantic hoax?

LEO: How could it be? It proves everything.

OTTO: What does it prove? Answer me that!

LEO: Don't be silly, Otto. You must try not to be silly.

OTTO [*bitterly*]: A few facts, that's all. A few tawdry facts torn from the universe and dressed up in terminological abstractions!

LEO: Science is our only hope, the only hope for humanity! We've wallowed in false mysticism for centuries; we've fought and suffered and died for foolish beliefs, which science has proved to be as ephemeral as smoke. Now is the moment to open our eyes fearlessly and look at the truth!

OTTO: What is the truth?

LEO [*irritably*]: It's no use talking to you—you just won't try to grasp anything! You're content to go on being a romantic clod until the end of your days.

OTTO [*incensed*]: What about you? What about the plays you write? Turgid with romance; sodden with true love; rotten with nostalgia!

LEO [*with dignity*]: There's no necessity to be rude about my work—that's quite separate, and completely beside the point.

OTTO: Well, it oughtn't to be. It ought to be absolutely in accord with your cold, incisive, scientific viewpoint. If you're a writer it's your duty to write what you think. If you don't you're a cheat—a cheat and a hypocrite!

LEO [*loftily*]: Impartial discussion is one thing, Otto. Personal bickering is another. I think you should learn to distinguish between the two.

OTTO: Let's have some more brandy.

LEO: That would be completely idiotic.

OTTO: Let's be completely idotic!

LEO: Very well.

[*They both refill their glasses and drain them in silence.*]

OTTO: There's a certain furtive delight in doing something consciously that you know perfectly well is thoroughly contemptible.

LEO: There is, indeed.

OTTO: There isn't much more left. Shall we finish it?

LEO: Certainly.

[*Otto refills both glasses.*]

OTTO [*handing Leo his*]: Now what?

LEO: Now what what?

OTTO [*giggling slightly*]: Don't keep on saying, what, what, what—it sounds ridiculous!

LEO: I wanted to know what you meant by "Now what"?

OTTO: Now what shall we drink to?

LEO [*also giggling*]: Let's not drink to anything—let's just drink!

OTTO: All right. [*He drinks.*]

LEO [*also drinking*]: Beautiful!

OTTO: If Gilda came in now she'd be surprised all right, wouldn't she?

LEO: She'd be so surprised, she'd fall right over backwards!

OTTO: So should we.

[*They both laugh immoderately at this.*]

LEO [*wiping his eyes*]: Oh, dear! Oh, dear, oh, dear, how silly! How very, very silly.

OTTO [*with sudden change of mood*]: She'll never come back. Never.

LEO: Yes, she will—when we're very, very old, she'll suddenly come in—in a Bath chair!

OTTO [*sullenly*]: Damn fool.

LEO [*with slight belligerence*]: Who's a damn fool?

OTTO: You are. So am I. We both are. We were both damn fools in the first place, ever to have anything to do with her.

LEO [*admiringly*]: You're awfully strong, Otto! Much, much stronger than you used to be.

OTTO: I've been all over the world; I've roughed it—that's what's made me strong. Every man ought to rough it.

LEO: That's the trouble with civilized life—it makes you soft. I've been thinking that for a long time. I've been watching myself getting softer and softer and softer—it's awful!

OTTO: You'd soon be all right if you got away from all this muck.

LEO: Yes, I know, but how?

OTTO [*putting his arm around his shoulders*]: Get on a ship, Leo—never mind where it's going! Just get on a ship—a small ship.

LEO: How small?

OTTO: Very small indeed; a freighter.

LEO: Is that what you did?

OTTO: Yes.

LEO: Then I will. Where do very small ships sail from?

OTTO: Everywhere—Tilbury, Hamburg, Havre——

LEO: I'm free! I've suddenly realized it. I'm free!

OTTO: So am I.

LEO: We ought to drink to that, Otto. It's something worth drinking to. Freedom's been lost to us for a long, long time and now we've found it again! Freedom from people and things and softness! We really ought to drink to it.

OTTO: There isn't any more brandy.

LEO: What's that over there?

OTTO: Where?

LEO: On the thing.

OTTO [*going to it*]: Sherry.

LEO: What's the matter with Sherry?

OTTO: All right. [*He brings over the bottle and fills their glasses.*]

LEO [*raising his*]: Freedom!

OTTO [*doing the same*]: Freedom!

[*They both drink.*]

LEO: Very insipid.

OTTO: Tastes like brown paper.

LEO: I've never tasted brown paper.

OTTO: Neither have I.

[*They roar with laughter.*]

LEO: Sherry's a very ludicrous word, isn't it, when you begin to analyze it?

OTTO: Any word's ludicrous if you stare at it long enough. Look at "macaroni."

LEO: That's Italian; that doesn't count.

OTTO: Well, "rigmarole" then, and "neophyte" and "haddock."

LEO: And "wimple"—wimple's the word that gets me down!

OTTO: What is a wimple?

LEO: A sort of mediæval megaphone, made of linen. Guinevere had one.

OTTO: What did she do with it?

LEO [*patiently*]: Wore it, of course. What did you think she did with it?

OTTO: She might have blown down it.

LEO [*with slight irritation*]: Anyhow, it doesn't matter, does it?

OTTO [*agreeably*]: Not in the least. It couldn't matter less. I always thought Guinevere was tedious, wimple or no wimple.

LEO: I'm beginning to float a little, aren't you?

OTTO: Just leaving the ground. Give me time! I'm just leaving the ground——

LEO: Better have some more Sherry.

OTTO: I'm afraid it isn't very good Sherry.

LEO [*scrutinizing the bottle*]: It ought to be good; it's real old Armadildo.

OTTO: Perhaps we haven't given it a fair chance.

[*He holds out his glass; Leo refills it and his own.*]

LEO [*raising his glass*]: Après moi le déluge!

OTTO: Après both of us the deluge!

[*They drain their glasses.*]

LEO: I think I shall sit down now. I'm so terribly sick of standing up.

OTTO: Human beings were never meant to stand up, in the first place. It's all been a grave mistake.

[*They both sit on the sofa.*]

LEO: All what?

OTTO: All this stamping about.

LEO: I feel ever so much happier. I don't feel angry with you or with Gilda or with anybody! I feel sort of at peace, if you know what I mean.

OTTO [*putting his arm around him*]: Yes, I know—I know.

LEO: Keys of the city, indeed!

OTTO: Lot of damned nonsense.

LEO: Too much sense of drama, flouncing off like that——

OTTO: We've all got too much sense of drama, but we won't have any more—from now onwards, reason and realism and clarity of vision.

LEO: What?

OTTO [*very loudly*]: I said "Clarity of vision."

LEO: I wouldn't have believed I could ever feel like this again —so still and calm, like a deep, deep pool.

OTTO: Me, too—a deep pool, surrounded with cool green rushes, with the wind rustling through them——[*This flight of fancy is disturbed by a faint hiccup.*]

LEO [*resting his head on Otto's shoulder*]: Will you forgive me —for—for everything?

OTTO [*emotionally*]: It's I who should ask you that

LEO: I'm glad Gilda's gone, really—she was very wearisome sometimes. I shall miss her, though.

OTTO: We shall both miss her.

LEO: She's the only really intelligent woman I've ever known.

OTTO: Brilliant!

LEO: She's done a tremendous lot for us, Otto. I wonder how much we should have achieved without her?

OTTO: Very little, I'm afraid. Terribly little.

LEO: And now she's gone because she doesn't want us any more.

OTTO: I think she thinks we don't want her any more.

LEO: But we do, Otto—we do——

OTTO: We shall always want her, always, always, always——

LEO [*miserably*]: We shall get over it in time, I expect, but it will take years.

OTTO: I'm going to hate those years. I'm going to hate every minute of them.

LEO: So am I.

OTTO: Thank God for each other, anyhow!

LEO: That's true. We'll get along, somehow—[*his voice breaks*] —together——

OTTO [*struggling with his tears*]: Together——

LEO [*giving way to his, and breaking down completely*]: But we're going to be awfully—awfully—lonely——

[*They both sob hopelessly on each other's shoulders as the curtain slowly falls.*]

ACT THREE: SCENE I

NEARLY *two years have elapsed since Act Two.*

The scene is Ernest Friedman's penthouse in New York. It is an exquisite apartment, luxuriously furnished. Up stage, on the Right, are three windows opening onto a balcony. These are on an angle; below them are double doors leading into the hall. A staircase climbs up the Left-hand side of the room, leading through a curtained archway to the bedrooms, etc. Below the staircase there is a door leading to the servants' quarters.

When the curtain rises it is about eleven-thirty on a summer night. The windows are wide open and beyond the terrace can be seen the many lights of the city. There is a table set with drinks and sandwiches, with, below it, an enormous sofa.

Voices are heard in the hall, and Gilda enters with Grace Torrence and Henry and Helen Carver. The Carvers are a comparatively young married couple, wealthy and well dressed. Grace Torrence is slightly older, a typical Europeanized New York matron. Gilda is elaborately and beautifully gowned. Her manner has changed a good deal. She is much more still and sure than before. A certain amount of vitality has gone from her, but, in its place, there is an aloof poise quite in keeping with her dress and surroundings.

GILDA: Who'd like a highball?
GRACE: We all would. We all need it!

GILDA: People are wrong when they say that the opera isn't what it used to be. It is what it used to be—that's what's wrong with it!

HENRY [*going for the drinks*]: Never again!

GILDA: Is there enough ice there, Henry?

HENRY: Yes, heaps.

HELEN [*wandering out onto the terrace*]: This is the most wonderful view I've ever seen!

HENRY: Next to ours.

HELEN: I like this better; you can see more of the river.

GRACE: You did all this, I suppose, Gilda?

GILDA: Not all of it; just a few extras. Ernest laid the foundations.

GRACE: When's he coming back?

GILDA: Tomorrow.

GRACE [*wandering about the room*]: It's lovely.

GILDA: I'd forgotten you hadn't been here before.

HENRY: Here, Grace. [*He gives her a drink.*] Gilda——

GILDA [*taking one*]: Thanks, Henry.

HENRY: Helen, do you want yours out there?

HELEN: No, I'll come in for it. [*She comes in, takes her drink, and sits down on the sofa.*]

GRACE [*stopping before an antique chair*]: Where did you get this?

GILDA: Italy. We were motoring to Siena, and we stopped at a little village for lunch and there it was—just waiting to be grabbed.

GRACE: You ought to open a shop; with your reputation you'd make a packet!

GILDA: This is my shop, really. I make quite enough, one way and another.

HELEN: But the things in this room aren't for sale, are they?

GILDA: All except the pictures. Those are Ernest's.

GRACE [*laughing*]: Then they are for sale!

GILDA: Perhaps. At a price.

HENRY: And oh, boy, what a price! [*To Helen*]: What was the name of that one he sold Dad?

HELEN: I don't think it had a name.

HENRY: The name of the artist, I mean.

GILDA: Matisse.

HENRY: Well, all I can say is, it ought to have been a double Matisse for that money!

GILDA [*smiling*]: Eleven thousand dollars, wasn't it?

HENRY: It was.

GILDA [*sweetly*]: Your father was very lucky, but then he always has been, hasn't he?

GRACE: Bow, Henry! Or fall down dead—one or the other!

GILDA: Do you want to see over the rest of it, Grace?

GRACE: I do, indeed! I'm taking mental notes, and if any of them come out right, I'll send you a handsome gift.

GILDA: Terrace first? Very nice line in balcony furniture, swing chairs, striped awnings, shrubs in pots——

GRACE: I'd rather die than go near the terrace—it makes me giddy from here.

GILDA: I love being high up.

HELEN: So do I—the higher the better!

GRACE: What floor is this?

GILDA: Thirtieth.

GRACE: I was caught by fire once on the sixth floor; I had to be hauled down a ladder in my nightgown—since then I've always lived on the ground level.

HELEN: What about burglars?

GRACE: I'd rather have fifty burglars than one fire. What would you do here if there was a fire, Gilda? If it started down below, in the elevator shaft or something?

GILDA [*pointing towards the servants' door*]: Very nice line in fire escapes just through that door; perfectly equipped, commodious—there's even a wide enough balustrade to slide down.

GRACE: One day there'll be an earthquake in this city, then all you high livers will come tumbling down!

HENRY: In that case, I'd rather be here than on the ground.

GILDA: Come and see the bedrooms.

GRACE: Higher still?

GILDA: Yes, higher still. You two will be all right, won't you?

HELEN: Of course.

GILDA [*leading the way upstairs*]: Help yourself to another drink, Henry.

HENRY: Thanks. I will.

[*Gilda and Grace disappear through the archway.*]

HENRY [*at table*]: Do you want another?

HELEN: I haven't finished this one yet.

HENRY: Promise me one thing, Helen?

HELEN: What?

HENRY: That you'll never become a professional decorator.

HELEN: Why?

HENRY: I've never met one yet that wasn't hard as nails, and, my God, I've met hundreds!

HELEN: Do you think Gilda's hard?

HENRY: Hard! Look at her eyes. Look at the way she's piloting old Grace round the apartment. Look at the way she snapped me up over Dad's picture!

HELEN: You were rather awful about it.

HENRY: So I should think! Eleven thousand bucks for that daub! I've only found three people who could tell me what it was supposed to be, and they all told me different.

HELEN: Art's not in your line, Henry.

HENRY: You bet your sweet life it isn't—not at that price!

HELEN: I like modern painting. I think it's thrilling.

HENRY: Bunk.

HELEN [*with superiority*]: That's what everybody always says about new things. Look at Wagner.

HENRY: What's Wagner got to do with it?

HELEN: When first his music came out everyone said it was terrible.

HENRY: That's jake with me!

HELEN [*laughing patronizingly*]: It's silly to laugh at things just because you don't understand them.

HENRY: You've been around too much lately, Helen; you ought to stay home more.

HELEN: If it hadn't been for Gilda, I don't know what I'd have done all winter.

HENRY: If it hadn't been for us, I don't know what she'd have done all winter! You could have fixed our apartment just as well as she did. What do we want with all that Spanish junk?

HELEN: It isn't junk; it's beautiful! She's got the most wonderful taste, everybody knows she has.

HENRY: It's a racket, Helen! The whole thing is a racket.

HELEN: I don't know what's the matter with you tonight.

HENRY: The evening's been a flop. The opera was lousy, and now we've been dragged up here instead of going to the Casino. Just because Gilda's sniffed a bit of business.

[*There is a ring at the door bell.*]

HELEN: Do you really think she only got Grace up here to sell her something?

HENRY: I do.

HELEN: Oh, Henry!

HENRY: Don't you?

HELEN: No, of course I don't. They've got a lot of money; they don't need to go on like that.

HENRY: That's how they made the money. Ernest's been palming off pictures on people for years.

HELEN: I don't see why he shouldn't, if they're willing to buy them. After all, everybody sells something; I mean——

[*The door bell rings again.*]

HENRY: Don't they keep any servants?

HELEN: I expect they've gone to bed.

HENRY: I'd better answer the door, I suppose.

HELEN: Yes, I think you had.

[*Henry goes off. Helen does up her face. There is the sound of voices in the hall. Henry reënters, followed by Otto and Leo, both attired in very faultless evening dress.*]

HENRY: Mrs. Friedman's upstairs—I'll call her.

LEO: No, don't trouble to do that; she'll be down soon, won't she?

HENRY: Yes, she's only showing Mrs. Torrence over the apartment.

OTTO: Torrence—Torrence! How very odd! I wonder if that's the same Mrs. Torrence we met in the Yoshiwara?

LEO: Very possibly.

HENRY: This is my wife, Mrs. Carver. I'm afraid I don't know your names.

LEO: My name is Mercuré.

HELEN [*shaking hands*]: How do you do, Mr. Mercuré?

OTTO: And mine is Sylvus.

HELEN [*shaking hands again*]: How do you do, Mr. Sylvus?

LEO [*turning abruptly to Henry and shaking his hand*]: How do you do, Mr. Carver?

OTTO [*doing the same with some violence*]: How do you do, Mr. Carver?

HENRY: Would you care for a drink?

LEO: Passionately.

HENRY [*coldly*]: They're over there. Help yourself.

HELEN [*while they are helping themselves*]: Are you old friends of Mrs. Friedman's?

OTTO [*over his shoulder*]: Yes, we lived with her for years.

HELEN [*gasping slightly*]: Oh!

[*There is silence for a moment. Otto and Leo settle themselves comfortably in chairs.*]

LEO [*raising his glass*]: Here's to you, Mr. and Mrs. Carver.

OTTO [*also raising his glass*]: Mr. and Mrs. Carver.

HENRY [*automatically raising his glass*]: Here's luck!

[*There is another silence.*]

LEO [*conversationally*]: I once knew a man called Carver in Sumatra.

HELEN: Really?

LEO: He had one of the longest beards I've ever seen.

OTTO [*quickly*]: That was Mr. Eidelbaum.

LEO: So it was! How stupid of me.

OTTO [*apologetically*]: We've travelled so much, you know, we sometimes get a little muddled.

HELEN [*weakly*]: Yes, I expect you do.

LEO: Have you been married long?

HENRY: Two years.

LEO: Oh dear Oh dear Oh dear Oh dear Oh dear.

HENRY: Why? What of it?

OTTO: There's something strangely and deeply moving about young love, Mr. and Mrs. Carver.

LEO: Youth at the helm.

OTTO: Guiding the little fragile barque of happiness down the river of life. Unthinking, unknowing, unaware of the perils that lie in wait for you, the sudden tempests, the sharp jagged rocks beneath the surface. Are you never afraid?

HENRY: I don't see anything to be afraid of.

LEO [*fondly*]: Foolish headstrong boy.

OTTO: Have you any children?

HENRY [*sharply*]: No, we have not.

LEO: That's what's wrong with this century. If you were living in Renaissance Italy you'd have been married at fourteen and by now you'd have masses of children and they'd be fashioning things of great beauty. Wouldn't they, Otto?

OTTO: Yes, Leo, they would.

LEO: There you are, you see!

OTTO: The tragedy of the whole situation lies in the fact that you don't care, you don't care a fig, do you?

HELEN [*stiffly*]: I really don't understand what you mean.

[*Conversation again languishes.*]

LEO: You've been to Chuquicamata, I suppose?

HENRY: Where?

LEO: Chuquicamata. It's a copper mine in Chile.

HENRY: No, we haven't. Why?

LEO [*loftily*]: It doesn't matter. It's most unimportant.

HENRY: Why do you ask?

LEO [*magnanimously*]: Please don't say any more about it— it's perfectly all right.

HENRY [*with irritation*]: What are you talking about?

LEO: Chuquicamata.

OTTO [*gently*]: A copper mine in Chile.

HELEN [*to relieve the tension*]: It's a very funny name. [*She giggles nervously.*]

LEO [*coldly*]: Do you think so?

HELEN [*persevering*]: Is it—is it an interesting place?

LEO: I really don't remember; I haven't been there since I was two.

OTTO: I've never been there at all.

HELEN [*subsiding*]: Oh!

LEO [*after another pause*]: Is Mrs. Torrence a nice woman?

HENRY: Nice! Yes, very nice.

LEO [*with a sigh of relief*]: I'm so glad.

OTTO: One can't be too careful, you know—people are so deceptive.

LEO [*grandiloquently*]: It's all a question of masks, really; brittle, painted masks. We all wear them as a form of protection; modern life forces us to. We must have some means of shielding our timid, shrinking souls from the glare of civilization.

OTTO: Be careful, Leo. Remember how you upset yourself in Mombasa!

LEO: That was fish.

[*Helen and Henry exchange startled glances. Gilda and Grace reappear through the archway and come down the stairs. Otto and Leo and Henry rise to their feet.*]

GILDA [*as they come down*]: . . . and the terrace is lovely in the summer, because, as it goes right round, there's always somewhere cool to sit——

[*She reaches the foot of the stairs and sees Otto and Leo. She puts her hand onto the balustrade just for a second, to steady herself; then she speaks. Her voice is perfectly calm.*]

GILDA: Hallo!

LEO: Hallo, Gilda.

OTTO: We've come back.

GILDA [*well under control*]: Yes—yes, I see you have. This is Mrs. Torrence. Grace, these are two old friends of mine—Leo Mercuré and Otto Sylvus.

GRACE [*shaking hands*]: Oh—how do you do.

LEO [*shaking hands*]: You must forgive our clothes but we've only just come off a freight boat.

OTTO: A Dutch freight boat. The food was delicious.

GILDA: I see you both have drinks. Henry, mix me one, will you?

HENRY: Certainly.

GILDA [*in an empty voice*]: This is the most delightful surprise. [*To Grace*]: Do you know, I haven't seen either of them for nearly two years.

GRACE: Gilda has been showing me this perfectly glorious apartment. Don't you think it's lovely?

OTTO [*looking around*]: Artistically too careful, but professionally superb.

GILDA [*laughing lightly*]: Behave yourself, Otto!

LEO: Where's darling little Ernest?

GILDA: Chicago.

HENRY: Here's your drink, Gilda. [*He hands it to her.*]

GILDA: Thank you.

GRACE [*sinking into a chair*]: Where did you come from on your freight boat, Mr. Mercuré?

LEO: Manila.

OTTO: It was very hot in Manila.

LEO: It was also very hot in Singapore.

GILDA [*drily*]: It always is, I believe.

OTTO: It was cooler in Hong Kong; and in Vladivostok it was downright cold!

LEO: We had to wear mittens.

HELEN: Was all this a pleasure trip?

LEO: Life is a pleasure trip, Mrs. Carver; a Cheap Excursion.

OTTO: That was very beautifully put, Leo. I shall always remember it.

[*Henry and Helen's faces set in disapproval. Grace looks slightly bewildered.*]

GRACE [*with a little social laugh*]: Well, life certainly hasn't been a cheap excursion for me! Every day it gets more and more expensive. Everyone here has had the most dreadful winter. I was in Europe, of course, but they were feeling it there, too, very badly. Paris, particularly. Paris seemed to have lost its vitality; it used to be much more gay, somehow——

OTTO: I once had a flat in Paris. It was really more a studio than a flat, but I had to leave it.

GRACE: They pulled it down, I suppose. They're pulling down everything in Paris, now.

OTTO: They pulled it down to the ground; it was a small edifice and crumbled easily.

GRACE: It's sad, isn't it, to think of places where one has lived not being there any more?

LEO: I remember a friend of mine called Mrs. Purdy being very upset once when her house in Dorset fell into the sea.

GRACE [*startled*]: How terrible!

LEO: Fortunately Mr. Purdy happened to be in it at the time.

OTTO: In my case, of course, it was more like an earthquake than anything else, a small but thorough earthquake with the room trembling and the chandelier swinging and the ground opening at my feet.

GRACE: Funny. We were talking about earthquakes just now.

LEO: I've never been able to understand why the Japanese are such a cheerful race. All that hissing and grinning on the brink of destruction.

OTTO: The Japanese don't mind destruction a bit; they like it, it's part of their upbringing. They're delighted with death. Look at the way they kill themselves on the most whimsical of pretexts.

LEO: I always thought Madame Butterfly was over-hasty.

OTTO: She should have gone out into the world and achieved an austere independence. Just like you, Gilda.

GILDA: Don't talk nonsense. [*To Grace*]: They both talk the most absurd nonsense; they always have, ever since I've known them. You mustn't pay any attention to them.

OTTO: Don't undermine our social poise, Gilda, you—who have so much!

GILDA [*sharply*]: Your social poise is nonexistent.

LEO: We have a veneer, though; it's taken us years to acquire; don't scratch it with your sharp witty nails—*darling!*

[*Everybody jumps slightly at the word "darling."*]

GILDA: Have you written any new plays, Leo? Have you painted any new pictures, Otto? You must both come to lunch one day and tell me all about yourselves.

LEO: That would be delightful. Just the three of us.

OTTO: Should old acquaintance be forgot.

LEO: Close harmony.

GILDA: You'll have to forgive me if I'm not quite as helpful to you as I used to be. My critical faculties aren't as strong as they once were. I've grown away, you see.

LEO: How far have you grown away, my dear love? How lonely are you in your little box so high above the arena? Don't you ever feel that you want to come down in the cheap seats again, nearer to the blood and the sand and the warm smells, nearer to Life and Death?

GILDA: You've changed, Leo! You used to be more subtle.

OTTO: You've changed, too, but we expected that.

HELEN [*social poise well to the fore*]: It's funny how people alter; only the other day in the Colony a boy that I used to know when he was at Yale walked up to my table, and I didn't recognize him!

LEO: Just fancy!

OTTO: Do you know, I have an excellent memory for names, but I cannot for the life of me remember faces. Sometimes I look at Leo suddenly and haven't the faintest idea who he is.

LEO [*quickly*]: I can remember *things*, though, very clearly, and past conversations and small trivial incidents. Some trick of the light, some slight movement, can cause a whole flock of irrelevant memories to tumble into my mind—just unattached fragments, which might have been significant once but which don't seem to mean anything any more. Trees in a quiet London square, for instance—a green evening dress, with earrings to match—two notes propped up against a brandy bottle—odd, isn't it?

GILDA: Not particularly odd. The usual litter of an over-sentimental mind.

OTTO: Be careful, Gilda. An ugly brawl is imminent.

GILDA: I'm not afraid.

OTTO: That's brave, when you have so much to lose. [*He glances comprehensively round the room.*]

GILDA [*quietly*]: Is that a threat?

OTTO: We've come back. That should be threat enough!

GILDA [*rising, with a strange smile*]: There now! That's what happens when ghosts get into the house. They try to frighten you with their beckoning fingers and clanking chains, not knowing that they're dead and unable to harm you any more. That's why one should never be scared of them, only sorry for them. Poor little ghosts! It must be so uncomfortable, wandering through empty passages, feeling they're not wanted very much.

LEO [*to Grace*]: You see, Gilda can talk nonsense too.

OTTO [*reprovingly*]: That wasn't nonsense, Leo; that was a flight of fancy, tinged with the macabre and reeking with allegory—a truly remarkable achievement!

LEO: It certainly requires a vivid imagination to describe this apartment as an empty passage.

GILDA [*laughing a trifle wildly*]: Stop it, both of you! You're behaving abominably!

OTTO: We're all behaving abominably.

LEO: The veneer is wearing thin. Even yours, Gilda.

GRACE: This, really, is the most extraordinary conversation I've ever heard.

OTTO: Fascinating, though, don't you think? Fascinating to lift the roofs a fraction and look down into the houses.

GILDA: Not when the people inside know you're looking: not when they're acting for you and strutting about and showing off!

LEO: How does it feel to be so secure, Gilda? Tell us about it?

GILDA [*ignoring him*]: Another drink, Henry?

HENRY: No, thanks.

HELEN [*rising*]: We really ought to be going now.

GILDA: Oh, I'm so sorry!

LEO: Watch the smooth wheels going round!

OTTO: Reach for a Murad!

GRACE [*also rising*]: I'm going too, Gilda. Can I drop anybody?

HENRY: No, thanks, our car's outside.

GRACE: Good-night, Mr. Mercuré.

LEO [*shaking hands*]: Good-night.

GRACE [*shaking hands with Otto*]: Good-night. Can I drop you anywhere?

OTTO: No, thank you; we're staying a little longer.

GILDA: No! Go now, Otto, please. Both of you, go with Grace. I'm terribly tired; you can telephone me first thing in the morning.

LEO: We want to talk to you.

GILDA: Tomorrow, you can talk to me tomorrow; we can all talk for hours.

LEO: We want to talk now.

GILDA: I know you do, but I tell you, I'm tired—dreadfully tired. I've had a very hard day—— [*She winks at them violently.*]

OTTO [*grinning*]: Oh, I see.

HELEN [*at the door*]: Come on, Henry! Good-night, Gilda darling; it's been a lovely evening.

[*She bows to Otto and Leo, and goes out. Grace looks at Otto and Leo and Gilda, and then with great tact ioins Henry at the door.*]

GRACE [*to Otto*]: My car's there, if you are coming now. Good-night, Gilda—ring for the elevator, Henry——

[*She goes out with Henry.*]

GILDA [*hurriedly, in a whisper*]: It was awful of you to behave like that! Why couldn't you have waited quietly until they'd gone?

LEO [*also in a whisper*]: They wouldn't go—they were going to stay for ever and ever and ever!

[*Gilda runs over to her bag, which is lying on a chair, and takes a latchkey out of it.*]

GILDA: Go, now, both of you! Go with Grace. She'll gossip all over the town if you don't. Here's the key; come back in ten minutes.

OTTO: Intrigue, eh? A nice state of affairs.

LEO: Good old Decameron!

GILDA [*shoving the key into his hand*]: Go on, quickly! Get a taxi straight back——

[*They both kiss her lightly on the lips and go out.*]

[*Gilda stands still, staring after them until she hears the door slam. Her eyes are filled with tears. She strides about the room in great agitation, clasping and unclasping her hands. She stops in front of a table on which is someone's unfinished drink. She drinks it thoughtfully, frowning and tapping her foot nervously on the ground.*]

[*Suddenly, she bangs down the glass, snatches up her cloak and bag, switches off all the lights, and runs out through the door leading to the fire escape.*]

[*Curtain.*]

ACT THREE: SCENE II

THE SCENE *is the same, and it is the next morning.*

The windows are wide open, and sunlight is streaming into the room.

As the curtain rises, Matthew crosses over from the servants' quarters, door Left, and goes into the hall. Matthew is black but comely. He wears a snow-white coat and dark trousers and is very smart indeed.

Ernest enters from the hall, carrying a suitcase.

Matthew follows him, staggering under three or four large canvases in a wooden crate.

ERNEST: Put them down there for the moment, Matthew, and get me some coffee.

MATTHEW: Yes, sir. [*He rests the canvases against the wall.*]

ERNEST [*taking off his hat and coat*]: Is Mrs. Friedman awake?

MATTHEW: She hasn't rung yet, sir.

ERNEST: All right. Get me the coffee as quickly as you can.

MATTHEW: It's all ready, sir.

[*He goes off Left. Ernest wanders out onto the terrace and then in again. He picks up a newspaper off the table, glances at it and throws it down again. He is obviously irritable. Matthew reënters with a breakfast tray, which he places on a small table.*]

MATTHEW: Perhaps you'd like to have it out on the terrace, sir?

ERNEST: No. This'll do.

MATTHEW: Did you have a good trip, sir?

ERNEST [*sitting down at the table*]: No, I did not.

MATTHEW: Very good, sir.

[*He goes out. Ernest pours himself some coffee. While he is doing so, Otto and Leo come down the stairs. They are both wearing Ernest's pyjamas and dressing gowns, which are considerably small for them. Their feet are bare.*]

LEO [*as they reach the bottom of the stairs*]: Good-morning, Ernest!

ERNEST [*flabbergasted*]: God bless my soul!

OTTO [*kissing him*]: He will, Ernest. He couldn't fail to!

LEO [*also kissing him*]: Dear little Ernest!

ERNEST: Where—where in heaven's name have you come from?

OTTO: Manila.

LEO [*grinning*]: It was very hot in Manila.

OTTO: Aren't you pleased to see us?

ERNEST: Have you been staying here?

LEO: Of course.

ERNEST: Since when?

OTTO: Last night.

ERNEST: Where did you sleep?

LEO: Upstairs.

ERNEST: What! Where's Gilda?

OTTO: We don't know. She's disappeared.

ERNEST: Disappeared! What on earth do you mean?

OTTO: What I say. She's disappeared.

LEO: Disappeared! Gone. She fluttered out into the night like a silly great owl.

OTTO: We arrived when she was entertaining a few smart friends, and she pressed a latchkey into our hands and told us to come back later; and when we came back later, she wasn't here. So we waited a little while, and then we went to bed.

LEO: We were very tired.

ERNEST: It's fantastic, the whole thing! Ridiculous.

LEO: Do you think we could have some coffee?

ERNEST: Yes, you can have some coffee, if you want it. [*He rings a little bell on the table and slams it down again irritably.*]

OTTO: I do hope you're not going to be disagreeable, Ernest. After all, you haven't seen us for ages.

ERNEST: Disagreeable! What do you expect me to be? I arrive home after twenty hours in the train to find Gilda gone, and you both staying in the house uninvited and wearing my pyjamas.

LEO: We'll take them off at once, if you like.

ERNEST: You won't do any such thing!

[*Matthew enters and stands stricken with astonishment.*] Two more cups, Matthew.

MATTHEW: Yes, sir. [*He goes out, staring.*]

ERNEST: Had you warned Gilda that you were coming?

OTTO: No. We just arrived—it was a surprise.

ERNEST [*suddenly*]: What do you want?

LEO: Why do you ask that?

ERNEST: I want to know. Why have you come? What do you want?

OTTO: We want Gilda, of course!

ERNEST: Have you gone out of your mind?

LEO: Not at all. It's quite natural. We've always wanted Gilda.

ERNEST: Are you aware that she is my wife?

OTTO [*turning away*]: Oh, don't be so silly, Ernest!

ERNEST: Silly! How dare you!

LEO: You're a dear old pet, Ernest, and we're very, very fond of you and we know perfectly well that Gilda could be married to you fifty times and still not be your wife.

[*Matthew comes in with two cups.*]

MATTHEW: Do you want some fresh coffee, sir?

ERNEST [*mechanically, staring at them*]: No—no, there's enough here.

MATTHEW [*to Otto*]: Can I get you some grapefruit, sir? Or an egg?

OTTO: No, thank you.

MATTHEW [*to Leo*]: For you, sir?

LEO: No, thank you.

ERNEST: That will do, Matthew.

MATTHEW: Yes, sir. [*He goes out.*]

ERNEST: Do you seriously imagine that you have the slightest right to walk into my house like this and demand my wife?

OTTO: Do stop saying "my wife" in that complacent way, Ernest; it's absurd!

LEO: We know entirely why you married Gilda; and if we'd both been dead it would have been an exceedingly good arrangement.

ERNEST: You are dead, as far as she's concerned.

OTTO: Oh, no, we're not! We're very much alive.

LEO: I fear your marriage is on the rocks, Ernest.

ERNEST: This is one of the most superb exhibitions of brazen impertinence I've ever encountered.

OTTO: It's inconvenient, I do see that. It may quite possibly inconvenience you very much.

LEO: But no more than that; and you know it as well as we do.

ERNEST [*with admirable control*]: Aren't you taking rather a lot for granted?

OTTO: Only what we know.

ERNEST: I won't lose my temper with you, because that would be foolish——

OTTO: And ineffective.

ERNEST: But I think you had better put on whatever clothes

you came in, and go away. You can come back later, when you're in a more reasonable frame of mine.

LEO: We're in a perfectly reasonable frame of mind, Ernest. We've never been more reasonable in our lives; nor more serenely determined.

ERNEST [*with great calmness*]: Now look here, you two. I married Gilda because she was alone, and because for many, many years I have been deeply attached to her. We discussed it carefully together from every angle, before we decided. I know the whole circumstances intimately. I know exactly how much she loved you both; and also, I'm afraid, exactly how little you both loved her. You practically ruined her life between you, and you caused her great unhappiness with your egotistical, casual passions. Now you can leave her alone. She's worked hard and made a reputation for herself. Her life is fully occupied; and she is completely contented. Leave her alone! Go away! Go back to Manila or wherever you came from—and leave her alone!

LEO: Admirable, Ernest! Admirable, but not strictly accurate. We love her more than anyone else in the world and always shall. She caused us just as much unhappiness in the past as we ever caused her. And although she may have worked hard, and although her life is so fully occupied, she is far from being contented. We saw her last night and we know.

OTTO: She could never be contented without us, because she belongs to us just as much as we belong to her.

ERNEST: She ran away from you.

LEO: She'll come back.

[*The front door bell rings.*]

OTTO: She has come back!

[*There is silence while Matthew crosses from the servants' door to the hall.*]

LEO: Coffee! That's the thing—nice, strong coffee! [*He pours some out for himself.*]

OTTO [*doing the same*]: Delicious!

ERNEST [*rising, and flinging down his napkin*]: This is insupportable!

LEO: Peculiar and complicated, I grant you, and rather exciting, but not insupportable.

[*Gilda enters, followed by Matthew, who looks utterly bewildered. She is wearing a dark day coat and hat over her evening dress, and carrying a brown paper parcel that is obviously her evening cloak. She sees the three of them and smiles.*]

GILDA: I might have known it!

MATTHEW: Shall I take your parcel, ma'am?

GILDA: Yes, give it to Nora, Matthew; it's my evening cloak.

MATTHEW: Yes, ma'am.

[*He goes off, Left, with it; while Gilda takes off her hat and coat and fluffs out her hair.*]

GILDA: I borrowed this coat and hat from the telephone operator at the Ritz: remind me to return it some time this morning, Ernest. [*She comes over and kisses him absently.*] This is all very awkward, isn't it? I am so sorry. The very first minute you get home, too. It's a shame! [*To Otto and Leo*]: Did you stay here all night?

LEO: Yes, we did.

GILDA: I wondered if you would.

OTTO: Why did you sneak off like that?

GILDA [*coolly*]: I should have thought the reason was obvious enough.

LEO: It was very weak of you.

GILDA: Not at all. I wanted time to think. Give me some coffee, Ernest—no, don't ring for another cup; I'll have yours. I couldn't bear to see Matthew's eyes popping out at me any more! [*She pours out some coffee and sits down and surveys the three of them.*]

GILDA [*blandly*]: Now then!

LEO: Now then *indeed!*

GILDA: What's going to happen?

OTTO: Social poise again. Oh, dear! Oh, dear, oh, dear!

GILDA: You know you both look figures of fun in those pyjamas!

ERNEST: I don't believe I've ever been so acutely irritated in my whole life.

LEO: It is annoying for you, Ernest, I do see that! I'm so sorry.

OTTO: Yes, we're both sorry.

ERNEST: I think your arrogance is insufferable. I don't know what to say. I don't know what to do. I'm very, very angry. Gilda, for heaven's sake, tell them to go!

GILDA: They wouldn't. Not if I told them until I was black in the face!

LEO: Quite right.

OTTO: Not without you, we wouldn't.

GILDA [*smiling*]: That's very sweet of you both.

LEO [*looking at her sharply*]: What are you up to?

OTTO: Tell us, my little dear, my clever little dear! Tell us what you're up to.

GILDA: What have you been saying to Ernest?

LEO: Lots of things.

ERNEST: They've been extremely offensive, both of them.

GILDA: In what way?

ERNEST: I'd rather not discuss it any further.

GILDA: I believe you've got a little fatter, Otto.

LEO: He eats too much rice.

GILDA: You look very well, though.

OTTO [*raising his eyebrows slightly*]: Thank you.

GILDA: So do you, Leo. The line in between your eyes is deeper, but you seem very healthy.

LEO: I am.

GILDA: You were always very strong, constitutionally. Strong as an ox! Do you remember that, Ernest?

ERNEST [*irritably*]: What?

GILDA [*smiling*]: Nothing. It doesn't matter.

LEO: Stop pulling our ears and stroking us, Gilda, and tell us your secret. Tell us why you're so strange and quiet—tell us what you're up to.

GILDA: Don't you know? I've given in!

LEO [*quickly*]: What!

GILDA [*quietly and very distinctly*]: I've given in. I've thrown my hand in! The game's over.

ERNEST: Gilda! What do you mean?

GILDA: What I say.

ERNEST: You mean—you can't mean that——

GILDA [*gently*]: I mean I'm going away from you, Ernest. Some things are too strong to fight against; I've been fighting for two years and it's no use. I'm bored with the battle, sick to death of it! So I've given in.

ERNEST: You're—you're insane! You can't be serious.

GILDA: I'm not serious! That's what's so dreadful. I feel I ought to be but I'm not—my heart's bobbing up and down inside me like a parrot in a cage! It's shameful, I know, but I can't help it—— [*She suddenly turns on Otto and Leo*]: And you two—you two sitting there with the light of triumph in your eyes!—Say something, can't you! Say something, for God's sake, before I slap your smug little faces!

LEO: I knew it. I knew it last night!

OTTO: We both knew it! We laughed ourselves to sleep.

ERNEST: Gilda, pull yourself together! Don't be a fool—pull yourself together!

GILDA: Don't get excited, Ernest. It doesn't matter to you as much as all that, you know.

ERNEST: You're crazy! You're stark staring mad!

GILDA [*ecstatically*]: I am, I am! I'm mad with joy! I'm mad with relief! I thought they really had forgotten me; that they really were free of me. I thought that they were never coming back, that I should never see them again; that my heart would be heavy and sick and lonely for them until I died!

LEO: Serve you right for leaving us! Serve you damn well right!

GILDA: Be quiet! Shut your trap, my darling! I've got to explain to Ernest.

ERNEST: I don't want to hear your explanations. I don't want to hear any more——

OTTO: Try and stop her, that's all! Just try and stop her! She's off, she's embarked on a scene. Oh, dear love, this is highly delectable! The old girl's on the war path!

GILDA: Be quiet, I tell you! Don't crow! Don't be so mean.

ERNEST: I don't want to hear any more, I tell you!

GILDA: You've got to. You must! There's so much I have to say. You must listen. In fairness to yourself and to all of us, you must listen.

ERNEST: You're being unbelievably vulgar! I'm ashamed of you.

GILDA: I'm ashamed of many things, but not of this! This is real. I've made use of you, Ernest, and I'm ashamed of that, and I've lied to you. I'm ashamed of that, too; but at least I didn't know it: I was too busy lying to myself at the same time. I took refuge in your gentle, kind friendship, and tried to pretend to myself that it was enough, but it wasn't. I've talked and laughed and entertained your friends; I've been excellent company and very efficient. I've worked hard and bought things and sold things, all the time pretending that my longing for these two was fading! But it wasn't. They came back last night, looking very sleek and sly in their newly pressed suits, and the moment I saw them, I knew; I knew it was no good pretending any more. I fought against it, honestly I did! I ran away from them, and walked about the streets and sat in Childs weeping into glasses of milk. Oh, Ernest, you've understood such a lot, understand just this much more, and try to forgive me—because I can't possibly live without them, and that's that!

ERNEST [*with icy calm*]: I gather that the fact that I'm your husband is not of the faintest importance to you?

GILDA: It's never been anything more than a comfortable sort of arrangement, has it?

ERNEST: Apparently not as comfortable as I imagined.

GILDA: Exquisitely comfortable, Ernest, and easy-going and very, very nice; but those things don't count in a situation like this, you must see that!

ERNEST: I see a ruthless egotism, an utter disregard for any-one's feelings but your own. That's all I can see at the moment.

LEO: You should see more, Ernest, you really should. The years that you've known us should have taught you that it's no use trying to make any one of us toe the line for long.

ERNEST: Gilda is different from you two, she always has been.

GILDA: Not different enough.

ERNEST: You let her down utterly. You threw away everything she gave you. It was painful to watch her writhing in the throes of her own foolish love for you. I used to love you both too. You were young and gay, and your assurance wasn't set and un-becoming as it is now. But I don't love you any more. I'm not even fond of you. You set every instinct that I have on edge. You offend my taste. When Gilda escaped from you I tried to make her happy and contented, quietly, without fuss.

OTTO: She could never be happy without fuss. She revels in it.

ERNEST: Superficially, perhaps, but not really. Not deep down in her heart.

LEO: What do you know of her heart?

GILDA: Cruel little cat.

OTTO: Shut up!

LEO: She's chosen to come back to us. She just said so. How do you account for that?

ERNEST: The sight of you has revived her old idiotic infatuation for you, but only for a little. It won't last. She knows too much now to be taken in by you again.

GILDA: You're wrong, Ernest. You're wrong.

ERNEST: Your lack of balance verges on insanity.

OTTO: Do you know that was downright rude!

GILDA: Why go on talking? Talking isn't any good. Look at me, Ernest. Look at me! Can't you see what's happened?

ERNEST: You're a mad woman again.

GILDA: Why shouldn't I be a mad woman? I've been sane and still for two years. You were deceived by my dead behaviour because you wanted to be. It's silly to go on saying to yourself that I'm different from Otto and Leo just because you want to believe it. I'm not different from them. We're all of a piece, the three of us. Those early years made us so. From now on we shall have to live and die our own way. No one else's way is any good, we don't fit.

ERNEST: No, you don't, you don't and you never will. Your values are false and distorted.

GILDA: Only from your point of view.

ERNEST: From the point of view of anyone who has the slightest sense of decency.

LEO: We have our own decencies. We have our own ethics. Our lives are a different shape from yours. Wave us good-bye, Little Ernest, we're together again.

GILDA: Ernest, Ernest, be friendly. It can't hurt you much.

ERNEST: Not any more. I've wasted too much friendship on all of you, you're not worth it.

OTTO: There's a lot of vanity in your anger, Ernest, which isn't really worthy of your intelligence.

ERNEST [*turning to him*]: Don't speak to me, please!

LEO: Otto's perfectly right. This behaviour isn't worthy of your intelligence. If you were twisted up inside and really unhappy it would be different; but you're not, you're no more than offended and resentful that your smooth habits should be tampered with——

ERNEST [*losing control*]: Hold your tongue!—I've had too much of your effrontery already!

GILDA [*peaceably*]: Once and for all, Ernest, don't be bitter and so dreadfully outraged! Please, please calm down and you'll find it much easier to understand.

ERNEST: You overrate my capacity for understanding! I don't understand; the whole situation is revolting to me. I never shall understand; I never could understand this disgusting three-sided erotic hotch-potch!

GILDA: Ernest!

LEO: Why, good heavens! King Solomon had a hundred wives and was thought very highly of. I can't see why Gilda shouldn't be allowed a couple of gentlemen friends.

ERNEST [*furiously*]: Your ill-timed flippancy is only in keeping with the rest of your execrable taste!

OTTO: Certain emotions transcend even taste, Ernest. Take anger, for example. Look what anger's doing to you! You're blowing yourself out like a frog!

ERNEST [*beside himself*]: Be quiet! Be quiet!

LEO [*violently*]: Why should we be quiet! You're making enough row to blast the roof off! Why should you have the monopoly of noise? Why should your pompous moral pretensions be allowed to hurtle across the city without any competition? We've all got lungs; let's use them! Let's shriek like mad! Let's enjoy ourselves!

GILDA [*beginning to laugh*]: Stop it, Leo! I implore you!—This is ludicrous! Stop it—stop it——

ERNEST [*in a frenzy*]: It is ludicrous! It's ludicrous to think that I was ever taken in by any of you—that I ever mistook you for anything but the unscrupulous, worthless degenerates that you are! There isn't a decent instinct among the lot of you. You're shifty and irresponsible and abominable, and I don't wish to set eyes on you again—as long as I live! Never! Do you hear me? Never—never—never! [*He stamps out of the room, quite beside himself with fury; on his way into the hall he falls over the package of canvases.*]

This is too much for Gilda and Otto and Leo; they break down utterly and roar with laughter. They groan and weep with laughter; their laughter is still echoing from the walls as—

THE CURTAIN FALLS

CAVALCADE

SCENES

PART ONE

Scene I: SUNDAY, DECEMBER 31ST, 1899	Drawing-room
Scene II: SATURDAY, JANUARY 27TH, 1900	Dockside
Scene III: FRIDAY, MAY 18TH, 1900	Drawing-room
Scene IV: FRIDAY, MAY 18TH, 1900	Theatre
Scene V: MONDAY, JANUARY 21ST, 1901.	Kitchen
Scene VI: SUNDAY, JANUARY 27TH, 1901	Park
Scene VII: SATURDAY, FEBRUARY 2ND, 1901	Drawing-room
Scene VIII: THURSDAY, MAY 14TH, 1903	Ball-room

PART TWO

Scene I: SATURDAY, JUNE 16TH, 1906	Bar Parlour
Scene II: SATURDAY, JUNE 16TH, 1906	Street
Scene III: WEDNESDAY, MARCH 10TH, 1909	Restaurant, Private Room
Scene IV: MONDAY, JULY 25TH, 1910	Seaside
Scene V: SUNDAY, APRIL 14TH, 1912	Ship
Scene VI: TUESDAY, AUGUST 4TH, 1914	Drawing-room
Scene VII: 1914–1915–1916–1917–1918	Marching
Scene VIII: TUESDAY, OCTOBER 22ND, 1918	Restaurant
Scene IX: TUESDAY, OCTOBER 22ND, 1918	Railway Station
Scene X: MONDAY, NOVEMBER 11TH, 1918	Drawing-room
Scene XI: MONDAY, NOVEMBER 11TH, 1918	Trafalgar Square

PART THREE

Scene I: TUESDAY, DECEMBER 31ST, 1929	Drawing-room
Scene II: TUESDAY, 1930	CHAOS

PART ONE: SCENE I

Principals—1899: JANE MARRYOT [*aged 31*], ROBERT MARRYOT [*aged 35*], ELLEN [*aged 25*], BRIDGES [*aged 40*].

SCENE: *The drawing-room of a London house. The room is charmingly furnished in the taste of the period. There are two windows at the back with a small balcony in front of each of them; apart from this structural necessity the decoration and furniture, etc., can be left to the discretion of the designer.*

TIME: *About* 11.45 *p. m. Sunday, December 31st, 1899.*

When the curtain rises, Ellen, the parlourmaid, is discovered setting the table with a light supper consisting of sandwiches and cake. She is a pleasant-looking woman of twenty-five.

Enter Bridges, the butler, with a bottle of champagne in a bucket of ice. He is older than Ellen, about forty, with iron-grey hair.

ELLEN: They won't need champagne if they've got 'ot punch, will they?

BRIDGES: You never know; best to be on the safe side.

ELLEN: How was Cook when you come up?

BRIDGES: Running round that kitchen like a cat on a griddle; New Year's Eve's gone to 'er 'ead, and no mistake.

ELLEN: She's been queer all day, she says she feels like as if it was the end of everything. So do I, for that matter.

BRIDGES: Don't start all that over again.

ELLEN: Oh, Alfred!

BRIDGES: What?

ELLEN: I can't bear to think what it's going to be like when you've gone.

BRIDGES: Well, don't.

ELLEN: I can't 'elp it.

BRIDGES: It's no use upsetting yourself; think of the missus, think of all the other soldiers' wives. You're in the same boat as wot they are.

ELLEN: You was never cut out for a soldier.

BRIDGES: Never mind what I was cut out for. I am one now.

ELLEN: What's going to 'appen to me and Fanny if anything 'appens to you?

BRIDGES [*putting his hands on Ellen's shoulders*]: Look 'ere, old girl, you married me for better or for worse, didn't you?

ELLEN: Yes, but——

BRIDGES: Well, if this turns out to be worse, so much the worse, see? And if it turns out to be better——

ELLEN: So much the better—yes, a fat lot of comfort that is.

BRIDGES: Look at the missus, with a brother out there ever since the beginning, and now 'er 'usband going, and two growing boys to look after.

ELLEN: What's the war for, anyhow? Nobody wanted to 'ave a war.

BRIDGES: We've got to 'ave wars every now and then to prove we're top-dog——

ELLEN: This one don't seem to be proving much.

BRIDGES: 'Ow can you tell sitting at 'ome 'ere safe and sound? 'Ow can you tell what our brave boys are suffering out there in darkest Africa, giving their life's blood for their Queen and country?

ELLEN: Africa looks very sunny and nice in the *Illustrated London News*.

BRIDGES: If this wasn't New Year's Eve, I'd lose my temper, and that's a fact.

ELLEN: Well, it wouldn't be the first time. You'd better go and get the 'ot punch, they'll be in in a minute.

BRIDGES: You mark my words, Ellen, if we didn't go out and give them Boers wot for, they'd be over 'ere wreakin' 'avoc and carnage before you could say Jack Robinson.

ELLEN: Oh, get along with you.

[*Bridges goes out.*]

[*Ellen puts the finishing touches to the table and then, going to the windows, she pulls back the curtains.*]

[*Enter Jane Marryot. She is a handsome woman of about thirty-one. She is wearing an evening gown and cloak.*]

[*Enter Robert, Jane's husband, following her. He is older, about thirty-five, also in evening dress.*]

JANE [*throwing off her cloak*]: I thought we should never get here in time. I'm sure that cabby was tipsy, Robert. How nice the table looks, Ellen. Where did those flowers come from?

ELLEN: They're from Bridges and me, ma'am, with our very best wishes, I'm sure.

JANE: Thank you, Ellen, very much indeed.

ROBERT: A charming thought, Ellen. Thank you both.

ELLEN: Not at all, sir—it's—it's a pleasure indeed.

[*Ellen withdraws from the room covered with respectful embarrassment.*]

[*Jane smiles at Robert.*]

JANE: Small things are so infinitely touching, aren't they? I feel I want to cry. Just a few gentle tears to usher in the new century.

ROBERT: Do, by all means, dearest: this evening was planned sentimentally.

JANE: Just the two of us saying, "Hail and Farewell."

ROBERT: Not farewell quite yet.

JANE: Soon—dreadfully soon.

ROBERT: You looked so beautiful at dinner.

JANE: Did I, Robert?

ROBERT: You look so beautiful now.

JANE: Do I, Robert?

ROBERT: I expect it's only that dress, really. Very deceiving.

JANE: Yes, Robert.

ROBERT: And that ornament in your hair.

JANE: Yes, Robert.

ROBERT: And the fact that I love you so dearly.

JANE: After so long. How can you?

ROBERT: Perhaps you're hideous and ill-dispositioned and tedious, really, and I never knew.

JANE: Perhaps.

ROBERT: Well, it's too late now. I'm set in the habit of loving you. I shall never know the truth.

JANE: I wonder if the boys are asleep.

ROBERT: Snoring, I expect.

JANE: Oh, no, Robert; not snoring. They both have perfect tonsils. Doctor Harrison said so.

ROBERT: Inherited from their mother, dear. You have the most exquisite tonsils in the world.

JANE: You're in a very facetious mood, Robert. It shocks me a little. This should be a solemn occasion. Your bow is crooked, too, and you look raffish.

ROBERT: Raffish?

JANE [*suddenly running into his arms*]: Oh, my darling, my darling, why must you leave me? I shall miss you so.

ROBERT [*smiling and holding her tenderly*]: The Bugle Call, dear, the Red, White and Blue——

Britons never, never, never shall be slaves.

JANE: Don't tease me—not about that. What does it matter about the Boers—it can't matter, really.

ROBERT [*seriously*]: It matters about Jim, doesn't it? He's out there.

JANE: Yes, I know, I know, but——

ROBERT: But what?

JANE [*leaving his embrace*]: I'm sorry, dear. I was nearly behaving badly.

ROBERT: You couldn't behave badly.

JANE [*lightly*]: Give him my love if you ever see him, if he's alive.

ROBERT: Of course he's alive. They're all alive. They're bound to be relieved soon.

JANE: Everyone has been saying that for weeks.

ROBERT: Baden Powell's a fine man.

JANE: How long will it last, the war, I mean?

ROBERT: It can't last more than a few months.

JANE: Perhaps it will be over before you get there.

ROBERT: Perhaps.

JANE: I suppose you'd hate that. Wouldn't you?

ROBERT: Bitterly.

JANE: Thank Heaven for one thing. The boys are too young. They won't have to fight; Peace and Happiness for them. Oh, please God, Peace and Happiness for them, always. [*She leans against the window and looks out.*]

[*Enter Bridges with a bowl of punch, followed by:*

[*Ellen entering, carrying a tray of punch glasses and almonds and raisins.*]

BRIDGES: It's started, sir. Just twelve o'clock now.

ROBERT: Open the windows quick.

[*Robert takes the punch from Bridges and fills two glasses.*]

[*Bridges opens the windows wide.*]

[*Outside can be heard the growing noise of sirens and chimes of bells.*]

[*Ellen and Bridges are about to go.*]

JANE [*suddenly*]: Stay and drink with us, won't you? Robert, two more glasses.

BRIDGES: Thank you very much, ma'am.

ELLEN: Thank you, ma'am.

ROBERT [*pouring them two glasses of punch*]: Here you are, Jane, Ellen, Bridges. 1900—1900.

JANE: 1900.

ELLEN and BRIDGES [*together*]: 1900.

[*Suddenly Jane hears a sound upstairs. She puts down her glass hurriedly and:*

[*Jane runs out of the room.*]

ELLEN: It sounded like Master Joe.

ROBERT [*going to the door and calling after Jane*]: Dearest, bring them down here. Bring them both down. [*Coming slowly back into the room, smiling*] How very impolite of the twentieth century to waken the children.

[*The lights fade as the noise of chimes and sirens grows louder.*]

NOTE ON PART I

*In the interim of darkness between Scenes 1
and 2, 2 and 3, 3 and 4, newsboys are heard
shouting latest news from the front.*

PART ONE: SCENE II

Principals: ROBERT, JANE, ELLEN, BRIDGES.

SCENE: *A Dockside.*
TIME: *About twelve noon, Saturday, January 27th,* 1900.

Before the stage becomes visible to the audience, down stage on the left Bridges and Ellen appear in a pool of light. Bridges is wearing the uniform of a Private in the C.I.V. Ellen is gaily dressed, but weeping.

BRIDGES: Be brave, old woman.

ELLEN: Oh, Alfred, Alfred, my 'eart's breaking.

BRIDGES: There, there—I'll soon be back—you see.

ELLEN: I can't bear it.

BRIDGES: Think of the missus—you'll 'ave to look after 'er, you know.

ELLEN: I can't think of anything but you going out among all them awful Boers and lying bleeding yer 'eart out on the battlefield.

BRIDGES: That's a cheerful outlook, I will say.

ELLEN: And Fanny 'aving no father and me being widowed for life.

BRIDGES: You're getting morbid, you know. Fanny'll be all right, and so will you and so will I. She was right as rain when I kissed her good-bye. See her laugh, eh?

ELLEN: She didn't mean to laugh; she's too young to understand.

BRIDGES: All the better, I say. I could do with a bit of a smile from you, now you mention it.

ELLEN: All right—I'll try.

BRIDGES: That's a girl—— [*He kisses her as*]:

[*The lights fade on them and a steamer siren sounds loudly.*]

[*Down stage on the right Robert and Jane appear in a pool of light.*]

[*Robert is in the uniform of a C.I.V. officer.*]

[*Jane is quietly dressed.*]

ROBERT: I think I'd better be getting aboard.

JANE: It's come at last, hasn't it—this moment?

ROBERT: You'll be very brave, won't you?

JANE: Take care of yourself, my dearest.

ROBERT: I shall probably be seasick.

JANE: Lie down flat on every possible occasion.

ROBERT: I'll try to remember.

JANE: Bridges will look after you.

ROBERT: Perhaps he'll be lying down flat, too.

JANE: You mustn't worry about me being unhappy when you've gone. I'm going to keep myself very busy. Lady Brandon is organizing an enormous relief fund matinée in February. She asked me to help her, and there'll be lots of other things, too. I shan't give myself time to feel anything except just very proud.

ROBERT: I'll write and telegraph whenever it's possible.

[*Pause.*]

JANE: This is horrid, isn't it?

ROBERT: I really must go.

JANE: Not just for a minute.

ROBERT: I'm going to kiss you once more now, and then I want you to turn away and go on talking, so that you won't see me actually leave you.

JANE [*in a stifled voice*]: Very well, my darling.

[*Robert kisses her lingeringly.*]

[*Turning away and talking rapidly*]: Edward and Joe were terribly anxious to come, too, but I'm glad I didn't bring them really. Joe gets over-excited so easily, and he's had a very bad cold, anyhow. Edward could have come, I suppose, really, but that would have upset Joe so dreadfully, being left alone. Take care of yourself, my own dear—you're not here any more, so I can break down a little—I felt you go when I said about Joe being over-excited—Robert—Robert——

[*Robert has disappeared into the surrounding darkness. As she turns the lights go up and Robert is seen threading his way through the crowd to the ship's gangway. Bridges is waiting for him, and they go aboard together. Jane walks over to Ellen, who is sobbing bitterly, and puts her arms round her. The crowd is cheering wildly, although several mothers and sweethearts and wives are weeping.*]

[*The steamer gives a short blast on its siren.*]

[*A band strikes up "Soldiers of the Queen."*]

[*The decks of the ship are lined with waving soldiers.*]

[*The gangway is pulled away. Slowly the ship begins to move as:*]

[*The lights fade.*]

PART ONE: SCENE III

Principals: JANE MARRYOT, MARGARET HARRIS, EDITH HARRIS [*aged* 10], EDWARD [*aged* 12], JOE [*aged* 8], ELLEN

SCENE: *The Same as Scene I.*

TIME: *About five o'clock on the afternoon of Friday, May* 18*th,* 1900.

When the lights go up Edward and Joe Marryot and Edith Harris are discovered playing soldiers on the floor. Edward is aged twelve, Joe eight, and Edith Harris about ten.

JOE [*shooting off a cannon*]: Bang—bang, bang, bang.

EDITH [*giving a little squeak*]: Oh—oh, dear!

EDWARD: How many?

EDITH: Seven.

EDWARD [*curtly*]: Good! You'd better retreat.

EDITH: I don't know how.

JOE: I'm going to shoot again.

EDITH: I do wish you wouldn't. I've only got fourteen left.

JOE [*yelling*]: Bang, bang, bang! Dirty old Kruger—dirty old Kruger——

EDWARD: Shut up! How dare you fire without orders.

JOE [*saluting*]: I'm sorry, Bobs.

EDITH: Edward.

EDWARD: What?

EDITH: Need I always be the Boers?

EDWARD: Yes.

EDITH: Why?

JOE: Because you're a girl—only a girl. Bang, bang, bang!

EDITH [*struggling with her cannon and ammunition*]: I'll teach you, you mean little pig! Bang, bang, bang! There! Bang——

[*The cannon sticks, so Edith throws it at Joe's battalion, annihilating about fifty soldiers.*]

JOE [*yelling*]: It's not fair.

EDWARD: Be quiet. Edith, that was cheating.

EDITH [*in tears*]: I'm sick of being the Boers—I'll never be the Boers again, never as long as I live!

[*The door opens.*]

[*Enter Jane, looking obviously worried and nervy.*]

[*Enter Margaret Harris, following Jane. She is a nicely dressed woman of about thirty.*]

JANE: Children, why on earth are you making such an awful noise? I heard you right down in the hall. Edith, what's the matter? Joe, be quiet.

EDWARD: Edith doesn't like being the Boers—she's mutinied.

JANE: So I should think.

JOE: Bang, bang, bang!

[*Joe throws Edith's cannon back at her and hits her on the knee.*]

[*Edith screams.*]

[*Jane slaps Joe sharply.*]

JANE: You're a naughty, wicked little boy. You go upstairs this minute.

[*Margaret rushes to Edith and proceeds to comfort her.*]

MARGARET: Edith, don't cry—it couldn't have hurt you so very much.

JANE: I can't bear it. Go away, all of you. Edward, take Joe away.

EDWARD: Sorry, mum.

JANE: Can't you play any other game but soldiers, soldiers— soldiers hurting each other—killing each other? Go away from me—go away—go away—go away——

[*Margaret, seeing that Jane is in a bad state of nerves, bustles all three children out of the room.*]

MARGARET: Go along, all of you. Edith, I'm ashamed of you, making such a fuss. It's only a tiny little scratch. Go upstairs and ask nurse to put some Pommade Devigne on it. Go along, now.

[*Exeunt Edith, Edward and Joe.*]

[*Margaret shuts the door after the children and comes back to Jane.*]

[*Jane is wearily removing her hat in front of a mirror.*]

[*A barrel organ in the street strikes up "Soldiers of the Queen."*]

JANE: There's no escape anywhere, is there?

MARGARET: Shall I throw him something?

JANE: Make him go away.

[*Margaret goes to the window and out on to the balcony.*]

MARGARET: Hi! Hi!

[*The organ stops.*]

Will you please go away further down the street? [*Throwing some money out and returning into the room.*] He's moving off. Do sit down, Jane dear, you've been standing up all the afternoon.

JANE [*sitting down*]: Will these days never end?

[*The barrel organ starts again, but much further off.*]

MARGARET: News will come soon.

JANE: I don't believe I shall see either of them ever again.

MARGARET: Don't give way to despair, Jane. It's foolish. You must have courage.

JANE: It's much easier to be brave when there's something to hear, something definite; this long suspense, these dragging, dragging weeks of waiting are horrible. The two people I love best in the world, so remote from me, beyond reach of my love, probably suffering—it's dreadful, dreadful——

MARGARET: Mafeking is bound to be relieved within the next few days, all the papers say so.

JANE: They've been saying so for months—meanwhile Jim is dying there slowly, by inches, starvation and disease and horror. I can't bear to think of it and yet I can't stop thinking. I wake at night and see his face, as he was when he was a little boy. He was always awfully plucky, my little brother, and so very, very dear to me. [*She breaks down.*]

[*Enter Ellen with tea. She places it on the table and looks enquiringly at Margaret.*]

[*Margaret shakes her head.*]

MARGARET: No news yet, Ellen. We've been standing outside the Mansion House for hours, and then we went to Fleet Street to the newspaper offices.

ELLEN [*to Jane*]: Have a nice cup of tea, ma'am, it'll make you feel better.

JANE: Thank you, Ellen.

ELLEN: There ain't no cause to worry about the master, ma'am; he's all right. I feel it in me bones. You see, he's got my Alfred with 'im, and if anything 'appened to either of them we'd be bound to 'ear from one of them, if you know what I mean.

JANE: You must be fearfully worried, too, Ellen.

ELLEN: Well, on and off, I am, but I say to myself—no news is good news, and what must be must be, and you'd never believe how it cheers me up. [*Ellen goes out.*]

MARGARET: Poor Ellen!

[*A newsboy runs by, shouting.*]

JANE [*jumping up*]: Quick! Quick! Give me a halfpenny. [*Jane rushes on to the balcony and leans over.*] What is it, Ellen—what is it?

[*Ellen apparently answers "nothing much," and Jane returns wearily.*]

Ellen's up those area steps like lightning every time a paper boy passes. No news is good news. What must be must be. Oh, God!

[*Margaret gets up with an air of determination.*]

MARGARET: Now, look here, Jane. I'm going now, and I shall be back at a quarter to seven.

JANE: A quarter to seven—why?

MARGARET: We're going out to dine at a restaurant and we're going to a theatre.

JANE: A restaurant! A theatre! I couldn't!

MARGARET: You could and you will—it's senseless sitting at home all by yourself fretting and worrying, and it doesn't do any good. I'll get Ronnie James to take us, and if he can't, we'll go by ourselves, and I don't care what people say. We'll go to something gay—they say "Mirabelle" is very good.

JANE: I can't, Margaret—it's very sweet of you, but I really can't.

MARGARET: I am now going home to have a bath and put on

my new Redfern model, and I shall be back at a quarter to seven.

JANE: Margaret—no, really, I——

MARGARET [*kissing Jane*]: Don't argue—just do what you're told.

JANE: I haven't anything to wear.

MARGARET: Nonsense! You have your blue "Worth" and if that won't do, put on your presentation gown, feathers and all!

JANE: Margaret, don't be so silly.

MARGARET: I mean it—it's a gesture. Robert and Jim would hate to think of you weeping and wailing. They're being gallant enough. We'd better try and be gallant, too. We'll dine at the Café Royal.

JANE: Margaret!

MARGARET: Be ready at a quarter to seven.

[*Margaret goes out.*]

[*Jane makes a movement to call Margaret back and then subsides into her chair.*]

[*Suddenly directly under the window another barrel organ strikes up "Soldiers of the Queen."*]

[*Jane jumps up and runs to the window.*]

JANE [*on balcony*]: Go on, then—play louder—play louder! Soldiers of the Queen—wounded and dying and suffering for the Queen! Play louder, play louder!

[*She comes back into the room laughing hysterically and proceeds to kick the children's toy soldiers all over the room; finally collapsing on to the sofa in a storm of tears as:*]

[*The lights fade.*]

PART ONE: SCENE IV

Principals: JANE, MARGARET, MIRABELLE, ADA, EDGAR, TOM
JOLLY, SIX C.I.V. GIRLS, CHORUS, STAGE MANAGER.

SCENE: *A theatre.*
TIME: *About 9 p.m. Friday, May 18th, 1900.*

*Before the lights go up, a spotlight illuminates Jane and Mar-
garet in evening cloaks and gowns sitting in a stage box left. When
the lights go up, it is seen that they are watching a typical musical
comedy of the period.*
    *A Sextette of ample girls are singing a song called "The Girls
of the C.I.V.", dressed rakishly in C.I.V. uniforms.*

> We're the girls of the C.I.V.
> Form fours, get in line, one two three.
> For our bravery is such
> That the Boers won't like it much
> When we chase them across the veldt and
>   teach them double Dutch.
> We're the girls of the C.I.V.
> And we're out for a lark and a spree
> In our uniforms so stunning
> We shall soon have Kruger running
> From the girls of the C.I.V.

*The Scene on the stage is excessively rural, with apple blossom
predominating. When the girls have finished their number, they
bounce off and:*
    *The leading lady, Mirabelle, enters. She is in reality a Princess,
but has disguised herself as a farm girl in order that she might con-*

ceivably find a young man to love her for herself alone. Her costume
is charming but slightly inappropriate for manual labour.

She is met down stage by Lieut. Edgar Tyrell, R. N., a wooden
young man with an excellent tenor voice.

EDGAR [*saluting*]: We meet again.

MIRABELLE [*curtseying*]: Yes, indeed.

EDGAR: It seems a sin that beauty so rare should be hidden for
ever in this small country village.

MIRABELLE: Flatterer!

EDGAR: No, no, I mean it.

MIRABELLE: You are a sailor, sir, and I have been warned about
sailors.

EDGAR: What have they told you?

MIRABELLE: That sailors are fickle, and that when they have
loved a maid they sail away and leave her lonely.

EDGAR: Do you believe that?

MIRABELLE: I hardly know.

EDGAR: Dearest, dearest Mirabelle—my heart is at your feet.

MIRABELLE [*gaily*]: Pick it up, sir, pick it up.

EDGAR: Ah, do not tease me. Look into my eyes—can you not
see the lovelight shining there?

MIRABELLE: I know nothing of love.

EDGAR: Let me teach you.

MIRABELLE: I know nothing of life.

MIRABELLE WALTZ

Lover of My Dreams

SHE: A simple country maid am I,
        As innocent as any flower.
        The great big world has pass'd me by,
        No lover comes my way to greet me shyly in my bower.

HE: Oh, say not so!
Such modesty enchants me:
Could I but stay to while away with you a happy hour.

SHE: It must be Spring that fills my heart to over-flowing,
Ah, whither am I going?
What is the voice that seems to say:
Be kind to love, don't let him call to you unknowing.

HE: If true love comes to you don't turn your face away.

SHE: Maybe 'tis something in the air;
For Spring is made for lovers only.

HE: Live for the moment and take care
Lest love should fly and leave us lonely.

BOTH: Ah, if love should leave us lonely.

Refrain

SHE: All my life I have been waiting
Dreaming ages through;
Until to-day I suddenly discover
The form and face of he who is my lover.
No more tears and hesitating;
Fate has sent me you.
Time and tide can never sever
Those whom love has bound forever,
Dear lover of my Dreams come true.

HE: All my life I have been waiting,

SHE: All my life I have been waiting,

HE: Dreaming ages through;

SHE: Dreaming ages through;

HE: Until to-day I suddenly discover

SHE: Until to-day I suddenly discover

HE: The form and face of she who is my lover.

SHE: The form and face of he who is my lover.

HE: No more tears and hesitating;
SHE: No more tears and hesitating;
HE: Fate has sent me you—Time and tide can never sever,
SHE: Fate has sent me you and tide can never sever
HE: Those whom love has bound for ever,
SHE: Those whom love has bound for ever,
HE: Dear lover of my Dreams come true,
SHE: Dear lover of my Dreams come true,
BOTH: Dear lover of my
        Dreams come true,
        Dear lover of my Dreams come true,
        Dear lover of my Dreams come true.

[*Enter Tom Jolly, comedian. He is dressed as a common sailor.*
[*Enter Ada with Tom (soubrette). She is dressed as a dairymaid.*]

TOM: If I make a noise like a cow—would you kiss me?
ADA [*laughing*]: Perhaps.
TOM: Moo—moo. [*He tries to kiss her.*]
ADA: No, no! I'm frightened of bulls.
TOM: If I make a noise like a sheep—then?
ADA: Who knows!
TOM: Baa, baa, baa——
ADA: No, no—no good at all.
TOM: I'll sing, then. Sailing, sailing, over the bounding main!
ADA: I'll kiss you now. I love donkeys!

FUN OF THE FARM

Verse

ADA: Tho' sailors are so brave and bold,
       It really must be dreadfully cold
       To sail across the sea.

TOM: I quite agree,
     I quite agree,
  I'm sick of the ocean wild and free,
  Heigho, heigho, this is the place for me.

ADA: Now I am weary of the town
  And feel inclined to settle down
    A milk pail on my arm.

TOM: I feel afraid,
     A London maid
  Would never know how the eggs are laid.

ADA: I'd find a cow
   And milk 'til the pail was full,

TOM: I'd shear the sow
   And probably milk the bull.

BOTH: You must agree
     That it would be
  The height of true rusticity
  If you and I should settle on a farm.

Refrain

BOTH: Oh, the Fun of the Farmyard,
    The roosters are crowing,
    The cattle are lowing,
  The turkeys go gobbly gobbly goo;
  This really is an alarm yard.

ADA: Like little Bo-Peep,
     I lose my sheep,
  And cannot find them anywhere.

TOM: I ought to be shot,
     For I forgot
  To coax the horse to meet the mare.

BOTH:	Who left the canary
	Locked up in the dairy?
ADA:	Cheep, cheep, cheep, cheep,
TOM:	Snort, snort, snort, snort,
ADA:	Moo, moo, moo, moo,
TOM:	Cock a doodle doodle do!
BOTH:	Oh, dear, far from being a calm yard,
	Quack, quack, quack, quack,
	All the fun of the farm.

TOM: Tell me something, Ada.

ADA: What?

TOM: You're no dairymaid, are you?

ADA: Mr. Inquisitive.

TOM: What are you?

ADA [*curtseying*]: Lady's maid to the Princess Mirabelle.

[*Mirabelle enters, unobserved, at the back.*]

TOM: The Princess! Then he'll win his bet, after all.

ADA: Who? What bet?

TOM: Lieutenant Edgar. All the officers of the ship wagered him that he would not win the hand of the Princess Mirabelle. He said he'd marry her if she was ugly as sin; he needs the money.

[*Edgar enters.*]

EDGAR: What are you doing here, Tom?

TOM: Just farming! [*Laugh.*]

MIRABELLE: Stop!

[*Enter full Chorus.*]

FINALE

CHORUS:	What is—what is the matter here?
MIRABELLE:	Kind friends, you heard my call,
	And so I thank you all
	For while you chatter here
	My heart has been betrayed.

EDGAR: Ah, no—not so.
            What foolish words you scatter here.
            'Tis naught but your pride that's hurt
            I am afraid.
CHORUS: Who can he be,
            'Tis plain to see,
                He seems to know her well.
            Who is this man
            Who dares offend
                The Princess Mirabelle?
MIRABELLE: You've lied to me and cheated me.
ADA: Madame, don't let him see
            Your poor heart breaking.
EDGAR: Whate'er the future be,
            True love you are mistaking.

WALTZ REFRAIN FINALE

All my life I have been dreaming,
Now my dreams must die.
Within my heart I felt a song awaken,
And now I find a melody forsaken.
All your vows were base and scheming,
All our Love's a lie.
Cruelly you would deceive me,
All I say to you is . . .

[*Enter Stage Manager, who raises his hand for silence.*]
STAGE MANAGER: Ladies and gentlemen—Mafeking has been
relieved.
[*Jane in her box utters a cry of relief.*]
[*The players on the stage cheer wildly and the lights fade.*]

[*The cheering is heard through the darkness; when the lights come up the audience is discovered cheering, waving hats and handkerchiefs, and programmes are fluttering from the crowded balconies; some of the audience join hands and sing "Auld Lang Syne." The lights fade.*]

PART ONE: SCENE V

Principals: MRS. SNAPPER, COOK, ANNIE, ELLEN, BRIDGES, CABBY.

SCENE: *The kitchen of a London house. It is a typical basement kitchen. There is a door at the back opening on to the area steps, also two windows. Another door communicating with the upper parts of the house, and a small door leading into the scullery.*

TIME: *About 5 p.m. Monday, January 21st, 1901.*

When the lights go up Cook is making ~~ast in front of the range.
Mrs. Snapper [Ellen's mother] is sitting on a chair beside a mailcart in which reposes [mercifully invisible to the audience] the infant Fanny.
Annie, a scullery-maid, stands about with her mouth open, obviously in a state of considerable excitement, occasionally putting ineffective finishing touches to the table.

COOK: 'Ere, Annie, 'old this fork a minute, or we'll have to call the Fire Brigade to put my face out.
[*Annie takes the fork.*]
[*Cook fans herself with her apron.*]

MRS. S.: I once knew a woman whose front 'air caught fire when she was making toast, and before you could count ten the 'ole room was ablaze. They'd never 'ave been able to recognize her remains if it 'adn't been for 'er cameo brooch.

COOK: They must 'ave known who she was. [*Coming over to the mail-cart*]: And 'ow's her ladyship—who's a lovely girl, eh? Don't burn that toast, Annie. [*She clicks her tongue at the infant Fanny.*] Yer dad's comin' 'ome, ducks, safe and sound. [*She chants in order to entertain Fanny.*] Safe and sound, safe and sound.

MRS. S.: I only 'ope 'e is safe and sound, I'm sure.

COOK: The telegram said 'e was.

MRS. S.: Maybe it was a lie to spare Ellen's feelings.

COOK: You're a cheerful one, I must say.

MRS. S.: When I was a girl a friend of mine's 'usband come back unexpected from the Crimea with no legs at all.

[*This is too much for Annie, who drops the toast and goes off into snuffles of laughter.*]

COOK: Stop it, Annie—now look what you've done—cut another piece, quick, they'll be 'ere in a minute.

MRS. S.: I do 'ope Ellen didn't cry at the station, it does make her nose so red.

COOK: Alfred will be so pleased to see 'er 'e won't mind if it's red or blue. Come on, Annie, 'urry.

ANNIE: 'Ere they are.

COOK: 'Ere, quick! The rosette for baby. [*She rushes to the dresser and snatches up a red, white, and blue rosette.*] You pin it on 'er, Mrs. Snapper, while I tidy me 'air.

ANNIE [*at window*]: They've come in a cab. Oo-er!

[*There is a great air of tension and excitement in the kitchen, while Ellen's and Bridges' legs appear down the area steps.*]

[*The Cabby follows with Bridges' kit-bag, which is dumped in the passage.*]

[*Bridges enters first, looking very hale and hearty.*]

BRIDGES [*entering*]: You settle the cab, Ellen, I want to see my love-a-duck. 'Allo, Cook—'allo, Ma—where's my girl? [*He kisses Cook and Mrs. Snapper, and then puts his head inside the pram.*] 'Allo, Fanny. Coo, 'aven't you grown. Ma, you 'aven't 'arf bin feedin' 'er up. [*He makes delighted gurgling noises and prods the baby with his finger.*] See 'er laugh—she knows 'er dad. [*He puts his head inside again, apparently kissing her heartily.*]

[*Ellen comes in flushed and happy.*]

ELLEN: I thought that train would never come—an whole hour I waited—an' all the people yellin' and screamin'. 'Ere, Alfred, take yer great 'ead out of that pram, you'll frighten 'er.

BRIDGES [*withdrawing*]: She knows me, that's wot—she knows 'er old dad. Look at 'er rosette and all, smart as my eye. [*He turns and sees Annie.*] 'Ere, who's this? We 'aven't 'ad the pleasure.

ELLEN: This is Annie.

BRIDGES: 'Ullo, Annie.

ANNIE [*giggling*]: Welcome 'ome, Mr. Bridges.

[*Annie and Bridges shake hands.*]

BRIDGES [*putting his arm round Mrs. Snapper*]: Well, Ma, 'ow's everything?

MRS. S.: I mustn't grumble.

BRIDGES: So I should just think not. I got a surprise for you.

MRS. S.: What is it?

BRIDGES: Ellen knows; I told 'er in the cab. Tell 'er, Ellen.

ELLEN: No, you. Go on.

BRIDGES: Well, you know I said in my letters about a lad called Smart—'Erbert Smart.

COOK: Yes, Ellen read your letters aloud.

BRIDGES: Not all of 'em, I 'ope.

ELLEN: Get on with you, you never let yourself go further than a P.S. and a couple of crosses.

BRIDGES: Well, 'Erbert Smart's got a pub, see, and he's staying out in Africa, and I've bought it from 'im cheap, see? So much a year until it's paid off. We always wanted to 'ave somewhere of our own, and you can come and live with us, Ma—'ow's that suit?

MRS. S.: A pub—is it a respectable pub?

BRIDGES: All depends 'ow you behave, Ma, you know what you are when you've 'ad a couple.

MRS. S. [*sniggering*]: Oh, Alfred, 'ow can you?

BRIDGES: Well, what d'you think about it?

MRS. S.: It sounds lovely—but 'ow about them upstairs?

BRIDGES: That's all right. I took the master into me confidence. He wished me luck.

MRS. S. [*breaking down*]: Oh, dear, I can 'ardly believe it, not 'aving to live alone any more—oh, dear!

BRIDGES: 'Ere, cheer up, Ma. Come on, 'ave a cup of tea. There ain't nothing to cry about. Let's all 'ave tea, for God's sake. Come on, Cook, me old girl—'ow'd you like to be a barmaid, eh?

[*They all sit down to tea, a grand tea with eggs and shrimps. Everybody is talking at once.*]

[*Suddenly the cry of a Newsboy outside cuts through their conversation.*]

BRIDGES: What's 'e yelling about?

COOK [*giving Annie a halfpenny*]: 'Ere, Annie, go and get one, quick.

[*Annie runs out of the area steps.*]

[*There is silence in the kitchen.*]

BRIDGES: What's up? What's the matter?

ELLEN: It isn't anything to concern us.

COOK: Ellen, 'ow can you—it concerns the whole country.

[*Annie comes clattering back with the paper.*]

[*Bridges snatches paper from Annie and reads it.*]

BRIDGES [*reading*]: Whew! The Queen—it says she's sinking!

MRS. S.: There now—I told you so.

COOK [*taking paper*]: Let's 'ave a look.

ANNIE: She's very old, ain't she?

COOK: Be quiet, Annie. What's that got to do with it?

ANNIE: Well, I never seen 'er.

BRIDGES: I 'ave—driving along Birdcage Walk once—years ago. Coo! England won't 'arf seem funny without the Queen!

[*The lights fade out.*]

PART ONE: SCENE VI

Principals: ROBERT, JANE, MARGARET, EDITH, EDWARD, JOE.

SCENE: *Kensington Gardens. There is a row of high railings down stage so that the audience can see through them the trees and shrubs and seats and people and dogs.*

TIME: *About noon, Sunday, January 27th, 1901.*

During the course of this scene there should be no word spoken. Everyone is in black and they walk slowly as though perpetually conscious of the country's mourning. Even the children are in black and one Woman leading a large brown dog has tied an enormous black crêpe bow on to his collar.

Robert and Jane walk slowly from the left, followed by Edward and Joe.

Margaret Harris and Edith come from right.

They all meet and carry on a subdued conversation for a moment centre, and then part and go their different ways as:

The lights fade on the scene.

PART ONE: SCENE VII

Principals: JANE, MARGARET, EDWARD, JOE, EDITH, ELLEN, BRIDGES, COOK, ANNIE.

SCENE: *Drawing-room of a London House.*
TIME: *About noon, Saturday, February 2nd, 1901.*

When the lights go up, the children, Edward, Joe and Edith, all in black, are discovered out on the balcony.
Margaret and Jane are seated on the sofa.
There is a small table beside Margaret and Jane on which there is hot cocoa and cake.

JOE [*on balcony*]: Mum, mum, there's a policeman on a lovely white horse!

JANE: Don't jump about, darling, and get hot and excited. Edward, keep Joe as quiet as possible.

EDWARD: All right, mum.

JANE: More cocoa, Margaret?

MARGARET: No, thank you, dear.

JANE: I feel listless and sad, as though her death were a personal grief. Strange, isn't it?

MARGARET: I think everyone feels that. [*She rises and goes to the window.*] All those crowds and crowds of people; they've been waiting for hours so patient and quiet. There's hardly a sound.

JOE [*running in*]: Mum, could I ever be a policeman?

JANE: Perhaps, darling—if you're good.

JOE: Are all policemen good?

JANE: Yes, dear, as good as gold.

JOE: Why did Queen Victoria die, mum?

JANE: Because she was a very old lady, and very tired.

JOE: Could I have another piece of cake?

JANE: You won't be able to eat any luncheon.

JOE: I'd rather have the cake.

JANE [*smiling*]: Very well, then—a small piece. Take some out to Edward and Edith.

JOE: Thanks, mum. [*Joe dashes out on to the balcony with the cake.*]

MARGARET: How proud you must feel, Jane. All your troubles are over—Robert's home, Jim's home. Robert has a V.C.

JANE: Jim ought to have a V.C. too. All those dreadful months.

EDWARD [*rushing in*]: They're coming! They're coming! Quick—quick!

JANE [*rising*]: Run and fetch Ellen and Bridges and Cook.

[*Edward tears out of the room.*]

[*Joe rushes in.*]

JOE: Mum, please come out. I dropped a bit of cake. I couldn't help it—Edward pushed me.

[*Jane goes out and looks over.*]

[*An intelligible voice is heard below.*]

JANE [*leaning over*]: I'm very sorry, it was an accident.

[*The voice mumbles something.*]

He didn't throw it—he dropped it. It was an accident. [*She comes in again.*] Did you throw it, Joe, on purpose?

[*Joe hangs his head.*]

You're a very naughty little boy indeed, and I've a very good mind not to let you see the procession at all.

[*Edith comes in.*]

[*Following Edith are Edward, Ellen, Bridges, Cook, and Annie, very smartened up.*]

EDWARD: Mum, will father be riding in the beginning part or the end part?

JANE: The beginning, I think. Cook, you'd better come out here, Annie, too. Ellen, look after them, will you? Bridges, oughtn't you to be wearing a coat, it's very cold?

BRIDGES: I'm all right, thank you, ma'am. Warm as toast.

EDWARD [*on balcony*]: Here they come—quickly, mum!

[*Everybody crowds out on to the two balconies.*]

[*There is dead silence and then far away the solemn music of the Dead March is heard. As it draws nearer the children jump about excitedly.*]

JOE [*suddenly*]: Look, look—there's father—there's father!

JANE: Shhh! Joe, be quiet—keep still.

[*The procession continues. Suddenly there is an outburst of cheering from the crowd which is instantly subdued.*]

That's Lord Roberts. He held up his hand to stop them cheering.

JOE: Is that Bobs, mum—is that Bobs?

EDWARD: Look, look—one-armed Giffard. Oh, mother, look——

JANE: Shhh! Now then, Joe, Edward, stand absolutely still—to attention, like father showed you.

[*The Boys stand rigid with their hands to their sides.*]

[*Bridges stands rigid with his hands to his sides, on the other balcony.*]

[*The music swells as the band passes directly underneath them. As it begins to die away Cook bursts into tears.*]

JANE: Five kings riding behind her.

JOE: Mum, she must have been a very little lady.

[*The lights fade.*]

PART ONE: SCENE VIII

Principals: ROBERT, JANE, DUCHESS OF CHURT, MAJOR DOMO.

SCENE: *The Grand Staircase of a London house. The head of the staircase is down stage. The stairs descending downwards and out of sight. Behind the well of the staircase can be seen, between columns, the beautifully decorated ballroom in which an orchestra is playing the popular waltzes of the day and people are dancing. The Ball is in full swing.*

TIME: *About 11 p.m. Thursday, May 14th, 1903.*

When the lights go up, the full splendour of a typical Edwardian Ball should, if possible, burst upon the audience.

On the right and left of the staircase a balustraded balcony leads to the ballroom at the entrance of which Footmen stand with programmes to hand to the guests.

The Duchess of Churt stands near the head of the stairs.

Near the Duchess of Churt stands the Major Domo, who announces each guest in stentorian tones.

There is a steady babel of conversation and music, but above it all can be heard the names of guests as they are announced. One by one, or sometimes escorted, come the great beauties of the day. They are all received by the Duchess and then make their way towards the ballroom. Finally the Major Domo announces: "Sir Robert and Lady Marryot" and:

Robert and Jane appear, Robert with full decorations, and Jane in an elaborate ball gown. As they are received by their hostess:

The lights fade and the curtain falls.

PART TWO: SCENE I

Principals: JANE, EDWARD [*aged* 18], ELLEN, FANNY [*aged* 7],
MRS. SNAPPER, GEORGE, FLO, BRIDGES.

SCENE: *The Bar Parlour of a London pub.*
TIME: *About 5 p.m. Saturday, June 16th, 1906.*

*When the curtain rises High Tea is just over. Seated round the
table are Jane, Edward, Mrs. Snapper, Flo and George Grainger.
Flo and George are very smartly got up. Ellen is seated at the piano
with her back to the room. Fanny [aged 7] is dancing. When the
dance is finished everyone applauds.*

JANE: She dances beautifully, Ellen. Come here, dear.
[*Fanny goes to her.*]
I knew you when you were a little tiny baby.

FLO: She's a born dancer, if you ask me—haighly talented,
haighly.

ELLEN [*leaving the piano*]: She certainly does love it. On the
go all day she is, jigging about.

MRS. S.: Can I press you to another cup, your ladyship?

JANE: No, thank you, we really must be going in a moment.

FLO [*to Edward*]: 'Ow was Hoxford when you left it, Mr.
Marryot?

145

EDWARD: Awfully nice.

FLO: I've never been there mayself, but George 'as, haven't you, George?

GEORGE: Oh, yes, nice place, Oxford. Very antique—if you know what I mean.

ELLEN: I'm so glad to 'ear the master, Sir Robert, is well.

JANE: He was so sorry not to be able to come down, but as you know, he's a very busy man these days. He wished very specially to be remembered to you and your husband. He'll be sorry to hear that he's ill.

GEORGE: Ill! Alf ill! What's wrong with him?

[*Mrs. Snapper nudges George violently.*]

[*Ellen speaks hurriedly.*]

ELLEN: Before you and Flo come, George, I was explaining to 'er ladyship about poor Alfred's bad leg.

GEORGE: Bad leg?

MRS. S. [*frowning at George*]: Yes, very bad—'e's been in 'orrible agony since Sunday.

GEORGE: Where is 'e?

ELLEN: Upstairs in bed.

GEORGE: I'll pop up and see 'im.

ELLEN: He's asleep now.

FLO: 'Ow did 'e come to 'ave the haccident?

MRS. S. [*firmly and with great emphasis*]: Cycling, Flo. He was cycling and 'e fell orf.

FLO: I didn't know 'e 'ad a cycle.

MRS. S.: 'E 'asn't any more.

JANE [*rising*]: Well, you will tell him how sorry we were not to have seen him, won't you? And I do hope he'll soon be quite well again. Come along, Edward. We really must go now.

EDWARD [*rising*]: All right, Mother.

ELLEN: It was so kind of you, ma'am, to come all this way to see us and to bring Fanny that lovely doll, and everything. Fanny, come and say good-bye to 'er ladyship.

[*Fanny makes an abortive effort at a curtsey.*]

[*Jane bends down and kisses Fanny.*]

JANE: Good-bye, Fanny. [*To Mrs. Snapper*]: Good-bye, Mrs. Snapper. [*She shakes hands.*] Good-bye. [*She bows to Flo and George.*]

FLO: Pleased to 'ave made your acquaintance, I'm sure.

JANE [*to Ellen*]: Good-bye, Ellen, it's been delightful seeing you again, and to find you well and happy. Don't fail to remember me to Bridges; my husband and I miss you both still, it seems only yesterday that you were with us.

ELLEN: We miss you, too, ma'am.

JANE: Time changes many things, but it can't change old friends, can it?

ELLEN [*emotionally*]: No, ma'am. Oh, no, ma'am.

[*Edward, who has been saying his good-bye to Mrs. Snapper and Flo and George, joins Jane.*]

EDWARD: Good-bye, Ellen. Good luck.

ELLEN: Good-bye, Master Edward. Thank you for coming——

[*Jane and Edward are about to leave when the street door bursts open and:*

[*Bridges staggers into the room. He looks unkempt and unshaven, and is obviously drunk.*]

[*There is a moment of horrible silence.*]

[*Bridges sees Jane and Edward and pulls up short.*]

ELLEN [*in agonised tones*]: Oh, Alfred!

BRIDGES: Ow! So that's why you wash trying to get me out of the way——

MRS. S.: Alfred Bridges, be'ave yourself and take yer 'at orf.

BRIDGES [*bowing low to Jane*]: Pleashed to see you again,

milady, I'm shure—welcome to our 'ovel. [*He lurches toward Jane.*]

[*Jane makes an instinctive movement away from Bridges.*]

[*Bridges draws himself up unsteadily.*]

Ow! I shee—proud and 'aughty, are we——

ELLEN [*wildly*]: Alfred, stop it! Stop it!

JANE [*suddenly coming forward and taking both Ellen's hands in hers*]: Ellen—dear Ellen—I'm so very, very sorry, and I quite understand. Please don't be upset and let me come and see you again soon.

[*Jane goes out with Edward.*]

[*Again there is silence.*]

[*Ellen bursts into hopeless sobbing.*]

MRS. S.: You drunken great brute!

BRIDGES: Shut yer mouth. You mind yours and I'll mind mine.

GEORGE: Look 'ere, 'ole man, you'd better come up and 'ave a lie down. [*He takes Bridges' arm.*]

BRIDGES [*pushing George away*]: Leave me alone. Lot of shnobs —that's wot—lot of bloody shnobs. I'm not good enough to be 'ome when the quality comes. Ow, no—we'll see who'sh good enough.

ELLEN [*wailing*]: Oh, oh, oh! I'll never be able to raise me 'ead again—never—never——

BRIDGES: 'Oo give Fanny that doll? 'Er noble ladyship?

MRS. S. [*stepping forward*]: You let the child alone.

BRIDGES [*pushing Mrs. Snapper so hard that she falls against the table*]: I can buy me own child a doll, can't I? Don't want any bloody charity 'ere. [*He snatches the doll from Fanny and pitches it into the fire.*]

[*Fanny screams.*]

[*Flo makes a dart at the fireplace and finally gets the doll out.*]

[*Fanny continues to scream.*]

[*Ellen goes for Bridges.*]

[*Bridges hits Ellen.*]

[*Flo and George grab Bridges and push him out of the room.*]

[*Ellen, sobbing, takes Fanny in her arms.*]

[*Mrs. Snapper sinks into a chair.*]

ELLEN: She was right—she was right. Time changes many things——

[*The lights fade.*]

PART TWO: SCENE II

Principals: FANNY, FLO.

SCENE: *A London street. The exterior of the public house—the bar parlour of which was the preceding scene—is down stage left. There is a street leading away into darkness up left, and another turning a corner up right. A wedge of houses separates the two streets. There are people at most of the windows of the houses. Down stage right are more houses.*

TIME: *About* 10 *p.m. Saturday, June* 16*th,* 1906.

The centre of the stage is crowded with people and barrows lit by naphtha flares. There is another pub up right from which comes the sound of a penny-in-the-slot piano and the sound of singing and laughter. Everyone is moving about and talking. Women with caps and shawls and string bags are shopping at the booths. Some sailors come out of the left pub with two flashily-dressed girls and roll across to the pub opposite, into which they disappear. A policeman walks through the crowd and goes off. A German band assembles

*down stage left and begins to play, effectively drowning the noise of
three Coster youths playing mouth-organs. A few Costers in pearlies
start dancing, a ring is made round them, and people applaud and
yell from the windows. A Salvation Army band marches on right
and proceeds to play and sing hymns, against the German band. A
few people make a ring round them and begin singing.*

Fanny comes out of the pub left and begins to dance by herself.

*Some of the crowd laugh and those who are dancing stop and
applaud her. A Coster darts forward and puts his pearly cap on
Fanny's head.*

*Bridges comes reeling out of the pub—sees Fanny, and tries to
grab hold of her. He is prevented by the crowd and*

Bridges is pushed off the stage up right.

*Suddenly from just where Bridges has gone there comes a shout
and then an agonising scream. The policeman runs across in the
direction of the noise. All the crowd, scenting a street accident, surge
off, including the German band.*

Exeunt crowd and German band.

Flo comes flying out of the pub and

Flo disappears with the crowd.

*Fanny continues to dance in pool of light shed by a street lamp,
to the rather dismal music of the Salvation Army.*

Flo comes rushing back and hammers on the door of the pub.

FLO: Ellen! Ellen! It's Alfred—'e's been run over—'e's dead.
Ellen! Ellen!

[*The lights fade.*]

PART TWO: SCENE III

Principals: EDWARD [*aged* 21], JOE [*aged* 17], TIM BATEMAN, DOUGLAS FINN, LORD MARTLET [*Chubby*], MARION CHRISTIE, NETTA LAKE [*pianist*], ROSE DARLING [*Ada in "Mirabelle"*], CONNIE CRAWSHAY, DAISY DEVON.

SCENE: *Private room in a popular London restaurant. A supper table set for ten is on one side of the stage. There is a sofa up at the back and another down stage right, and an upright piano.*

TIME: *About 1 a.m. Wednesday, March 10th, 1909.*

Round the table are seated Edward [twenty-one], Tim Bateman, Douglas Finn, Marion Christie, Netta Lake, and Rose Darling.

On the sofa up stage in a more or less amorous attitude are seated Lord Martlet [Chubby] and Daisy Devon.

On the down stage sofa is seated Joe [aged seventeen] with Connie Crawshay, a very fat blonde.

Everyone is very gay. They are all in evening dress. The men in white ties and the women elaborately and slightly theatrically fashionable.

Joe is obviously the youngest present and appears well on the way to being very drunk.

ROSE [*rising, with a glass of champagne in her hand*]: I want to propose a toast—to our host!

EVERYONE: Hear, hear! [*Etc.*]

MARION: A lovely little toastie to our lovely little hostie.

ROSE: Health, wealth and happiness to our Eddie!

EVERYONE [*repeating*]: Health, wealth and happiness! Eddie! [*Etc. They clink glasses.*]

CONNIE [*to Joe*]: Here, sit up. They're drinking your brother's health.

JOE [*rising unsteadily*]: Hear, hear—a thousand times hear, hear!

[*They all sing "For he's a jolly good fellow," which tails off into cries for "speech."*]

EDWARD [*rising*]: Ladies and gentlemen——

JOE [*loudly*]: Hurray!

EDWARD: Shut up, Joe.

JOE: I won't shut up. Connie agrees with me, don't you, Connie?

CONNIE: Yes, dear, completely, dear. Shut up, dear.

JOE: Good old Connie. [*He subsides on Connie's lap.*]

EDWARD [*continuing*]: First of all, in response to your charming toast, I want to apologise for the presence here to-night of my scrubby little brother Joe.

[*Laughter.*]

JOE: Here—I say!

[*Connie puts her hand over Joe's mouth.*]

EDWARD: He is a crawling, loathsome little creature, as you see, and he really ought not to be here at all, but in his little cot at Eton. I felt, however, that as his elder brother, it was my duty to show him how grown-up people behave. Bring him over here, Connie—he must be christened in Clicquot.

CONNIE: He's almost confirmed in it already.

[*Connie drags Joe over to the table where, protesting loudly, he is anointed by Edward with champagne.*]

JOE: I must speak now. I want to speak.

CONNIE: Let him speak, dear, he's having a lovely time.

JOE: Ladies and gentlemen—I have always looked up to my elder brother Edward. He has always been my ideal of what a great big gas-bag should be, and I take this opportunity of asking Connie to marry me.

[*Laughter.*]

CONNIE: Oh, isn't he sweet!

ROSE: You can't have Connie, Joe, she's married already; you'd better choose me. I'm a widow.

[*Everybody chants "The Merry Widow" waltz for a moment.*]

JOE: But I love Connie.

CONNIE: Very well, dear, come back to the sofa, dear. [*She leads Joe back.*]

EDWARD [*to Lord Martlet*]: Chubby, come out of that corner, you've been there long enough.

DAISY [*coming down*]: Quite long enough. This takes me back to the old days of private hansoms. [*She fans herself.*] Give me a drink, somebody.

MARION [*gloomily*]: I was once sick in a private hansom.

ROSE: That must have been lovely, dear; tell us about it.

MARION: Well, it was the two hundredth performance of "Floradora."

ROSE: By God, she's going to!

MARION: And they suddenly put me in the sextette without a rehearsal, and I suppose the excitement went to my stomach.

ROSE: I was in "Mirabelle" then, with poor old Laura Marsden.

EDWARD: "Mirabelle"! I was taken to see that. Mother was there on Mafeking night. She took me a few weeks later to a matinée.

MARION: *Taken* to see it, were you! That dates us a bit.

EDWARD: I remember now. You were Ada——

ROSE: Yes, I was Ada.

MARION: And Laura Marsden was Mirabelle, and Mikey Banks was Tom. What a cast that was!

TIM: What happened to Laura Marsden?

ROSE: She died. [*She makes a significant drinking gesture.*]

TIM: Oh, I see.

ROSE: Nine years ago. Give me another drink, or I shall get reminiscent like Marion.

[*Netta goes over to the piano and starts thumping the Mirabelle waltz.*]

Oh, shut up!

EDWARD: Sing it, Rose.

ROSE: I can't—haven't got any voice.

EVERYONE: Come on, Rose—sing it. Come on, you're among friends.

ROSE: I can't sing it like Laura used to. [*She sings the refrain of the waltz, occasionally forgetting a word or two.*]

[*Everybody applauds.*]

MARION: They do take you back, don't they, those old tunes.

[*Netta strikes up "Keep off the Grass."*]

[*The girls sing it together.*]

[*None of the men are really old enough to remember it.*]

CHUBBY: Play something we all know.

[*Netta starts "Mary" from "Miss Gibbs."*]

[*Everyone joins in. They all go into "The Merry Widow" waltz and sing it lustily as*

[*The lights fade.*]

PART TWO: SCENE IV

Principals: JANE, ROBERT, JOE, MARGARET, ELLEN, FANNY, MRS. SNAPPER, FLO, GEORGE, 1ST WOMAN, 2ND WOMAN, UNCLE GEORGE, UNCLE DICK.

SCENE: *The beach of a popular seaside resort.*

TIME: *About 6 p.m. Monday, July 25th, 1910.*

The Parade runs along the back about 10 feet above stage level.

Down stage left a bandstand on the same level as the Parade juts out on to the beach. On the right the high supports of a swimming enclosure.

There are bathing machines and huts and deck chairs—in fact, all the paraphernalia of a popular seaside town in July.

The beach is crowded with people, some paddling, some playing games, and a lot clustered round an open-air stage, listening to Uncle George's concert party.

The Concert Party consists of six men: Uncle Dick, Uncle Bob, Uncle Harry, Uncle Jim, Uncle Jack and Uncle George himself. They are all dressed in straw hats, coloured blazers and rather grubby white flannel trousers.

People are constantly passing to and fro along the Parade, and leaning on the railing, looking down on to the beach.

When the curtain rises Uncle George is singing "Put a little bit away for a rainy day." He finishes with a great flourish, then steps forward.

UNCLE GEORGE: Ladies and gentlemen and kiddies—I am very happy to announce that the winner of this week's Song and Dance Competition is little Miss Fanny Bridges.

[*Everyone applauds.*]
And it gives me great pleasure to present her with this handsome prize as a souvenir of Uncle George and his merry men. Come on up, my dear.

[*Ellen (in black) hoists Fanny up from the front row.*]

[*Fanny is hoisted up by Ellen. She is wearing a white dress with a black sash.*]

[*Uncle George kisses Fanny and presents her with a box of chocolates.*]

[*The audience clap and one little girl is led away yelling, apparently an unsuccessful competitor.*]

UNCLE GEORGE: And now, to conclude this programme Uncle Dick will sing "Take me back to Yorkshire."

[*Uncle Dick rises and sings.*]

[*All the rest join in the chorus, and then, after perfunctory applause, the crowd round the booth disperses.*]

[*Uncle George and his Merry Men pack up their props and disappear in due course up the steps on to the Parade.*]

[*Exeunt Uncle George and his Merry Men.*]

[*Ellen and Fanny walk across the beach with Mrs. Snapper, Flo, and George. They meet Margaret Harris, Jane and Joe.*]

JANE: Why, it can't be—Ellen—what a surprise!

[*They shake hands.*]

ELLEN: Oh, ma'am—I'd no idea—fancy you being here!

JANE: Margaret, Joe, you remember Ellen, don't you?

MARGARET [*shaking hands*]: Of course! yes—how do you do, Ellen?

JOE: Hullo, Ellen.

ELLEN: You remember mother—Mrs. Snapper—and Flo and George, my cousins by marriage?

JANE: Yes, indeed.

MRS. S.: Delighted, I'm sure.

[*Everyone shakes hands and talks politely.*]

ELLEN: Well, Master Joe, 'ow you 'ave grown. Quite the young man about town! How's Master Edward?

JOE: He's here. He and Edith have been to a concert on the pier. They'll be along soon.

ELLEN [*to Jane*]: I got your letter, ma'am, when my Alfred died; it was kind of you to write.

JANE: How is your business going?

ELLEN: Oh, very well, really. I've managed to save quite a bit one way and another, and now I've closed the 'ole place for a month so as to give Fanny a holiday. She goes to dancing school now. She's going on the stage.

MARGARET: Surely she's very young.

MRS. S.: She's set on it—plain set on it.

[*Robert comes down on to the beach. He has grey hair now and looks very distinguished.*]

ROBERT: Jane—there you are—Why, Ellen! [*He shakes hands.*]

[*All the introductions start all over again.*]

[*Two elderly women pass in front of them, talking.*]

1ST WOMAN: She went on board the ship dressed as a boy, and that's how the Captain recognised them.

2ND WOMAN: 'Er 'air probably come down under 'er cap.

1ST WOMAN: I don't know 'ow she managed at meals. She couldn't wear 'er cap then.

2ND WOMAN: It's Mrs. Crippen that gets on my mind, poor dear, being all chopped up into little tiny pieces——

[*They pass on and up the steps.*]

[*Meanwhile the Marryots and Ellen are parting company.*]

ELLEN: It's been lovely seeing you again, ma'am, and you, too, Mrs. Harris. I expect your Edith has grown into a great big girl by now. I remember her when she was ever so small. [*To Robert*]: Good-bye, sir—good-bye, Master Joe.

ROBERT: Good-bye, Ellen.

JOE: Good-bye.

JANE: You must come and see us one day—bring Fanny to tea.

ELLEN: Thank you, ma'am—I'd like to see the 'ouse again. I was very 'appy there——

[*The Marryots and Margaret go off.*]

[*Mrs. Snapper, Ellen and Fanny rejoin Flo and George, who have been standing waiting for them a little way off.*]

[*The band, having assembled, breaks into a gay march.*]

[*A man walks along with a tray of pink rock, yelling.*]

[*All dialogue is drowned in the noise of the band. Several children dodge in and out, playing Tag. One child falls down and screams. Suddenly there is the noise of an aeroplane. Everyone screams and surges down to the beach, staring upwards. The band stops abruptly and cranes out of the bandstand. People half dressed rush out of bathing machines. Somebody starts cheering—then everyone takes it up. The aeroplane noise grows fainter. The band strikes up again. A troop of Boy Scouts with a very sour six-piece band march along the Parade. Suddenly there is a roll of thunder. Everyone looks up apprehensively, people on the beach begin to collect their children and belongings. It starts to rain, gently at first, then develops into a downpour. People put their coat collars up and run. Several umbrellas go up, then more, until the whole beach becomes a sea of umbrellas. Gradually everyone scurries off. The bandstand has by now let down its weather blinds. One fat old woman is left asleep in a deck chair. A tremendous roll of thunder wakes her abruptly and she struggles to get up, and falls back into the chair, which collapses.*]

PART TWO: SCENE V

Principals: EDWARD, EDITH.

SCENE: *The deck of an Atlantic liner. This is quite a small inset scene. The rail of the Promenade Deck faces the audience. Behind it can be seen the lighted windows of the lounge. Above can be seen vaguely the Boat Deck, with ventilators and a funnel silhouetted against the stars.*

TIME: *About 7 p. m. Sunday, April 14th, 1912.*

Edward and Edith, he in dinner-jacket, she in evening dress, are leaning on the rail.

EDITH: It's too big, the Atlantic, isn't it?

EDWARD: Far too big.

EDITH: And too deep.

EDWARD: Much, much too deep.

EDITH: I don't care a bit, do you?

EDWARD: Not a scrap.

EDITH: Wouldn't it be awful if a magician came to us and said: "Unless you count accurately every single fish in the Atlantic you die to-night"?

EDWARD: We should die to-night.

EDITH: How much would you mind—dying, I mean?

EDWARD: I don't know really—a good deal, I expect.

EDITH: I don't believe I should mind so very much now. You see, we could never in our whole lives be happier than we are now, could we?

EDWARD: Darling, there *are* different sorts of happiness.

EDITH: This is the best sort.

EDWARD [*kissing her*]: Sweetheart!

EDITH: Don't, darling, we don't want any more of the stewards to know we're on our honeymoon.

EDWARD: Why not? It gives them so much vicarious pleasure. Most of them have forgotten what it was like.

EDITH: Are all honeymoons like this?

EDWARD [*firmly*]: Exactly.

EDITH: Oh, Edward—that's rather disheartening, isn't it? I do so want this to be unique.

EDWARD: It is, for us.

EDITH: Did you ever think when we were children, going to the pantomime, and going to the Zoo, and playing soldiers, that we should ever be married?

EDWARD: Of course I didn't.

EDITH: Was I nice as a child?

EDWARD: Horrible!

EDITH: So were you, and so was Joe—vile. You always used to take sides against me.

EDWARD: And yet we all liked one another really.

EDITH: I think I liked Joe better than you, but then he was younger and easier to manage. Dear Joe, he was awfully funny at the wedding, wasn't he?

EDWARD: Ribald little beast!

EDITH: He has no reverence, I'm afraid.

EDWARD: Absolutely none.

EDITH: He's passing gallantly through the chorus-girl phase now, isn't he?

EDWARD: Gallantly but not quickly.

EDITH: Well, darling, you took your time over it.

EDWARD: Now then, Edith——

EDITH: You had several affairs before you married me, didn't you?

EDWARD: Light of my life, shut up!

EDITH: You'd be awfully cross if *I* had, wouldn't you?

EDWARD: Had what?

EDITH: Affairs—love affairs—before you.

EDWARD: Did you?

EDITH: Hundreds.

EDWARD: Liar!

EDITH: I rather wish I had, really. Perhaps I should have learnt some tricks to hold you with when you begin to get tired of me.

EDWARD: I never shall, tricks or no tricks.

EDITH: Yes, you will one day. You're bound to; people always do. This complete loveliness that we feel together now will fade, so many years and the gilt wears off the gingerbread, and just the same as the stewards, we shall have forgotten what it was like.

EDWARD [*seriously*]: Answer me one thing truly, dearest. Have you ever seen gingerbread with gilt on it?

EDITH: Never!

EDWARD: Then the whole argument is disposed of. Anyhow, look at father and mother; they're perfectly happy and devoted, and they always have been.

EDITH: They had a better chance at the beginning. Things weren't changing so swiftly; life wasn't so restless.

EDWARD: How long do you give us?

EDITH: I don't know—and Edward—[*she turns to him*] I don't care. This is our moment—complete and heavenly. I'm not afraid of anything. This is our own, for ever.

[*Edward takes Edith in his arms and kisses her.*]

EDWARD: Do you think a nice warming glass of sherry would make it any more heavenly?

EDITH: You have no soul, darling, but I'm very attached to you. Come on——

[*Edith takes up her cloak which has been hanging over the rail, and they walk away. The cloak has been covering a life-belt, and when it is withdrawn the words "S. S. Titanic" can be seen in black letters on the white.*]

[*The lights fade into complete darkness, but the letters remain glowing as*

[*The orchestra plays very softly and tragically "Nearer, My God, to Thee."*]

PART TWO: SCENE VI

Principals: JANE, ROBERT, JOE, MARGARET.

SCENE: *The drawing-room of a London house. The room is dark; the blinds are down over the windows.*
TIME: *About 11:16 p. m. Tuesday, August 4th, 1914.*

There is the sound of voices outside.
Enter Jane and Margaret, both in travelling clothes.
Jane turns on the lights and the room is seen to be enshrouded in dust-sheets.

JANE [*shuddering*]: Why is it that a house that's been shut up for a little while feels so awful? [*She goes to the windows, pulls up the blinds, and opens the windows wide.*] There! That's better. It's stifling.

MARGARET [*taking off her hat and coat*]: That was definitely the most uncomfortable journey I've ever experienced.

[*Joe rushes in. He still has his hat and coat on.*]

JOE: Mum, have you got any change? Father and I have both run out.

MARGARET: I have—here—[*she fumbles in her bag*]. How much d'you want?

JOE: Four bob.

MARGARET: There's half-a-crown and two shillings.

JOE: Thanks, Aunt Margaret. [*Joe goes out again.*]

JANE: Help me with these dust-sheets, Margaret. Put them anywhere. We'll get a char in to-morrow to clean up.

[*They proceed to pull the dust-sheets off the furniture.*] I shall never go on a holiday again, ever. It's horrid when you're there, and much worse when you come back.

MARGARET: Still it's better to be here in London if anything's going to happen.

JANE: It's going to happen all right. I'm afraid there's no doubt about it, now.

MARGARET [*glancing out of the window*]: There seem to be lots more people in the streets than usual—where on earth do they all come from?

[*Joe comes in, this time without his hat and coat.*]

JOE: Well, that's that!

JANE: Where's father?

JOE: Groping about in the wine cellar like an angry old beetle. He says strong drink is essential in a crisis.

JANE: We must have something to eat, too. I wonder if there is anything.

JOE: There's a strong bit of cold tongue in the larder. I just put my head in and it sang the Marseillaise.

JANE: There must be some biscuits, or something. [*Jane goes out hurriedly.*]

JOE [*to Margaret*]: Cigarette? [*He offers her his case.*]

MARGARET [*taking one*]: Thank you, Joe.

JOE [*lighting them*]: This is pretty thrilling, isn't it?

MARGARET: Yes, I suppose so. I must really go and help Jane. [*Margaret runs out, almost colliding with*
[*Robert, who is entering with two bottles and some glasses.*]

ROBERT: I could only find hock and port, and port's far too heavy at this time of night; so we'll have to drink to the downfall of Germany in their own damned wine.

JOE: I rather like Germans, don't you, Father?

ROBERT: Enormously. Move these things off the table, and help me open the bottles.

JOE [*doing so*]: Got a corkscrew?

ROBERT: In my left pocket.

[*Joe gropes for the corkscrew while*
[*Robert puts the bottles and glasses on the table.*]

JOE [*wrestling with a bottle*]: If there is a war, how long do you think it will last?

ROBERT: Three months, at the outside.

JOE: I suppose we shall win, shan't we?

ROBERT: Yes—we shall win.

JOE [*hopefully*]: Maybe it will last six months.

ROBERT: Leaving everything else aside, that would be economically quite impossible. Have you any idea of what a war costs, Joe, in actual money?

JOE: Hell of a lot, I should think.

ROBERT: You're quite right. And the Germans can afford it even less than we can. And then there's Russia.

JOE: Good old Russia!

ROBERT: And France and Italy and America.

JOE: And Japan and China and Finland—why, by God! we've got 'em licked before we start.

ROBERT: Don't be silly, Joe.

JOE: Are you glad you left the Army, Father, or sorry?

ROBERT: Absolutely delighted.

JOE: Will you go back again?

ROBERT: I expect so.

JOE: How will you feel about that?

ROBERT: Absolutely delighted.

JOE: I suppose I shall have to do something about it, too.

ROBERT: Do you want to?

JOE: Terribly.

ROBERT: Why?

JOE: I don't know. It's—it's sort of exciting, isn't it?

ROBERT: Yes, but don't set your hopes too high, Joey—it takes a lot of training to make a soldier. It will all be over before you get far.

JOE: I wish Edward hadn't been drowned, we could have started off together.

ROBERT [after a slight pause]: Don't be too impulsive and patriotic and dashing, Joey. Think of your mother. Think of me, too, you're all we've got left. [Robert abruptly puts down the bottle he is holding and goes out on to the balcony.]

[Joe stands staring after Robert thoughtfully.]

[*Jane enters carrying a tray.*]

[*Margaret enters following Jane, with some plates.*]

JANE: We found some potted meat and biscuits and Worcester Sauce; and the tongue doesn't look too bad.

JOE [*taking the tray from Jane*]: It isn't its looks I object to, it's its personality. [*Joe puts the tray on the table.*]

[*A newsboy runs by outside, shouting.*]

[*Robert shouts from the balcony and goes hurriedly from the room.*]

[*Joe, Jane and Margaret stand stock still, waiting.*]

[*Robert returns with the paper.*]

ROBERT: We're at war, my dears.

JOE [*grabbing the paper*]: Let me see—let me see——

MARGARET: Listen—listen!

[*From far away comes the sound of cheering.*]

[*Margaret runs out on the balcony for a moment, and then returns.*]

[*Jane sinks down on a chair.*]

JANE: It's very hot, isn't it?

JOE: Don't look sad, mum. It won't last long; Father says it can't possibly; and it's terribly exciting.

JANE: I didn't mean to look sad; I feel rather tired.

JOE [*handing Jane a glass of wine*]: Here, mum dear—have a nice sozzle. We ought all to get drunk really, and go roaring about the streets——

JANE: Edward missed this, anyhow. At least he died when he was happy, before the world broke over his head.

ROBERT: Don't take that view, dearest, it's foolish. We've had wars before without the world breaking.

JANE: My world isn't very big.

[*A group of people pass along under the balcony laughing and cheering. Some of them start singing the Marseillaise and the others down them with Rule Britannia.*]

[*Jane gets up suddenly.*]

JANE: Drink to the war, then, if you want to. I'm not going to. I can't! Rule Britannia! Send us victorious, happy and glorious! Drink, Joey, you're only a baby, still, but you're old enough for war. Drink like the Germans are drinking, to Victory and Defeat, and stupid, tragic sorrow. But leave me out of it, please! [*Jane goes abruptly from the room.*]

[*The lights fade.*]

PART TWO: SCENE VII

ABOVE *the proscenium* 1914 *glows in lights. It changes to* 1915-1916, 1917 *and* 1918. *Meanwhile, soldiers march uphill endlessly. Out of darkness into darkness. Sometimes they sing gay songs, sometimes they whistle, sometimes they march silently, but the sound of their tramping feet is unceasing. Below the vision of them brightly-dressed, energetic women appear in pools of light, singing stirring recruiting songs—"Sunday I walk out with a soldier," "We don't want to lose you," etc., etc. With* 1918 *they fade away, as also does the vision of the soldiers, although the soldiers can still be heard very far off, marching and singing their songs.*

PART TWO: SCENE VIII

Principals: JOE, FANNY.

SCENE: *A restaurant.*

TIME: *About* 7.30 *p.m. Tuesday, October 22nd,* 1918.

Joe and Fanny are seated at a table; they have just finished dinner.

Joe is in officer's uniform.

Fanny is in very charming day clothes. She is now nineteen and extremely attractive.

JOE [*pouring some champagne into Fanny's glass*]: Have some more.

FANNY: Darling, I shall be tight. You don't want me to fall down during my first number, do you?

JOE: How much do you love me?

FANNY: Now, then, dear, we've had all this out before.

JOE: Will you send me a telegram to Dover?

FANNY: Of course I will. I promised, didn't I?

JOE: Once you get into the theatre, with all those changes, you might forget.

FANNY: I'll send Maggie out with it.

JOE: Dear old Maggie. Say good-bye to her for me, won't you?

FANNY: Aren't you coming down to talk to me while I make up?

JOE: No, I promised to go home. Mother's waiting for me.

FANNY: I shall have to give it to you now, then.

JOE: What?

FANNY: Just a little something I had made for you.

JOE: Oh, Fanny—what is it?

FANNY: Hold on a minute, dear. It's in my bag. [*She searches in her bag and produces a small packet.*] Here—with my love.

JOE [*opening it*]: Oh, it's lovely.

FANNY: It's nothing really. Just a little souvenir of all the fun we've had.

JOE: You are a darling——

FANNY [*grabbing it from Joe*]: Here, silly, you've missed the whole point. It opens—there. [*Fanny opens the little locket and discloses a minute photograph of herself.*]

JOE [*taking it*]: It will be with me always, to the end of my days.

FANNY: You won't want it that long.

JOE: I almost wish I didn't love you quite so awfully. It makes going back much worse.

FANNY: I shall miss you dreadfully.

JOE: It has been fun, hasn't it?

FANNY: Lovely.

JOE: You don't regret it—any of it?

FANNY: Not a moment of it.

JOE: How wonderful you are. Do you really love me, I wonder, deep down inside, I mean?

FANNY: Yes, I think so.

JOE: Enough to marry me?

FANNY: Yes, but I wouldn't.

JOE: Why not?

FANNY: It would be too difficult. We shouldn't be happy married. Your mother wouldn't like it.

JOE: She'd be all right.

FANNY: Don't let's talk about it now. Let's wait until you come back.

JOE: Very well.

[*There is silence for a moment.*]

[*Fanny puts her hand on Joe's across the table.*]

FANNY: Listen, dear. I love you and you love me, and I've got to go now or I shall be late; and you've got to go, too, but I'm not going to say good-bye. We've had fun, grand fun, and I don't want you to forget me, that's why I gave you the locket. Please keep it close to you, Joey—darling Joey. [*Fanny goes as*

[*The lights fade.*]

PART TWO: SCENE IX

Principals: JANE, JOE.

SCENE: *A railway station. The station is foggy and very dimly lit on account of air raids. The ticket barrier can be vaguely discerned and beyond it, the back of a train. Just above the barrier a lamp shines downwards partially illuminating a recruiting poster. On the right is an empty platform, but there are people moving about on it, and several Red Cross orderlies and nurses. There is a crowd of people, mostly women, clustered around the left barrier—occasionally a door in the train opens and a shaft of light falls on to the platform.*
TIME: *About 11 p.m. Tuesday, October 22nd, 1918.*

A crowd of soldiers comes on from the left, wearing full equipment. They are greeted by some of the women. Presently a Sergeant enters, and after their good-byes have been said, the Sergeant gets them in line and marches them through on to the platform, where they can be seen getting into the train.
Jane and Joe come on from the left.

JOE [*breathlessly*]: Whew: I thought we were going to miss it, didn't you, mum?
JANE: Yes.
JOE: Not much time for long good-byes, darling.
JANE: I know. I'm glad, really—aren't you?
JOE: Yes. I never know what to say.
JANE: I'm almost hardened to it by now. This has happened so often.
JOE: Dearest mum, you are marvellous. You never make a fuss.

JANE: Don't be too sweet to me, Joey, I don't want to disgrace you, to behave badly.

JOE: You couldn't behave badly.

JANE: How funny! Do you know that Robert said that to me years and years ago. I must be very dull and unimaginative to be so reserved. It was the Boer War, then. This is very, very different.

[*A whistle blows.*]

[*Joe takes Jane in his arms.*]

JOE: Good-bye, darling.

JANE: Good-bye, darling—take care of yourself.

[*Joe rushes through the barrier and jumps into the train just as it starts to move.*]

[*Jane stands under the lamp looking after him.*]

[*Two or three of the women at the barrier burst into loud sobbing, some soldiers in the train start singing. A big steaming locomotive comes slowly to a standstill at the right-hand platform. Almost immediately Red Cross Orderlies begin to walk off the platform carrying wounded men on stretchers.*]

[*Jane stands watching them; her face is quite expressionless. Then with a trembling hand she takes a cigarette out of her bag and lights it.*]

[*The lights fade.*]

PART TWO: SCENE X

Principals: JANE, ELLEN, GLADYS [*a parlourmaid*].

SCENE: *The drawing-room of a London house. The decoration of the room has changed slightly with the years, but not to any marked extent. It looks very much the same as it has always looked.*

TIME: *About 11 a.m. Monday, November 11th, 1918.*

As the lights go up on the scene, a Parlourmaid shows Ellen into the room. Ellen has certainly changed with the years. She is very well dressed, almost smart.

GLADYS: Her Ladyship will be down in a moment, madam.

ELLEN: Thanks.

[*Gladys goes out.*]

[*Ellen wanders about the room. There is a photograph of Edward on the table, and also one of Joe. She looks at them both and sighs.*]

[*Jane enters. She is dressed in street clothes.*]

JANE: Ellen! Gladys said Mrs. Bridges, but I couldn't believe it was you.

ELLEN: I just thought I'd call. It's rather important, as a matter of fact.

JANE: Do sit down. I'm delighted to see you again.

ELLEN: Thanks. [*She sits down.*]

JANE: How's Fanny?

ELLEN: Oh, very well. She's in "Over the Moon," now, you know.

JANE: Yes. I went the other night. She was splendid. I felt very proud to know her.

ELLEN: It's about her I've come to see you, really.

JANE: Oh! Well?

ELLEN: It's—it's—er—rather difficult.

JANE: What is it? What on earth is the matter?

ELLEN: About her and Master—her and Joe.

JANE: Joe?

ELLEN: Yes. They've been—well—er—to put it frankly, if you know what I mean, they've been having an affair.

JANE: My Joe?

ELLEN: Yes—your Joe. His last two leaves he spent a lot of time with Fanny.

JANE [*slowly*]: Oh, I see.

ELLEN: I wouldn't have come to see you about it at all, only I think Fanny's very upset about it, and now that the war's over —or almost over, that is—and he'll be coming home—I thought——

JANE [*coldly*]: What did you think?

ELLEN: Well, I thought they ought to get married.

JANE: Does Fanny want to marry him?

ELLEN: No—er—not exactly. That is—I haven't talked about it to her. She doesn't know I know.

JANE: How do you know?

ELLEN: I found a letter from him——

JANE: And you read it?

ELLEN: Yes—it's here. I've brought it with me. [*She fumbles in her bag.*]

JANE: I don't wish to see it, thank you.

ELLEN: I only brought it because——

JANE [*cutting Ellen short*]: Is Fanny in any sort of trouble?

ELLEN: Oh, no. Nothing like that.

JANE [*rising*]: Then I think we'd better leave it until Joe comes home. Then he and Fanny can decide what they wish to do.

ELLEN [*also rising*]: I—I didn't mean to upset you.

JANE: I'm not in the least upset.

ELLEN: It's been on my mind—it's been worrying me to death.

JANE: I think you should have spoken to Fanny before you came to me. I never interfere with my son's affairs.

ELLEN: Well, I'm sure I'm very sorry.

JANE: Please don't let's discuss it any further. Good-bye, Ellen.

ELLEN: I suppose you imagine my daughter isn't good enough to marry your son; if that's the case I can assure you you're very much mistaken. Fanny's received everywhere; she knows all the best people.

JANE: How nice for her; I wish I did.

ELLEN: Things aren't what they used to be, you know—it's all changing.

JANE: Yes, I see it is.

ELLEN: Fanny's at the top of the tree now; she's having the most wonderful offers.

JANE: Oh, Ellen!

ELLEN: What is it?

JANE: I'm so very, very sorry.

ELLEN: I don't know what you mean.

JANE: Yes, you do—inside, you must. Something seems to have gone out of all of us, and I'm not sure I like what's left. Good-bye, Ellen.

[*Gladys enters with a telegram.*]

[*Jane takes telegram.*]

Excuse me, will you. [*She opens it and reads it, and then says in a dead voice.*] There's no answer, Gladys.

GLADYS [*excitedly*]. It's all over, milady—it's eleven o'clock —the maroons are going off.

JANE: Thank you, Gladys, that will do.

GLADYS: Yes, milady. [*Gladys goes out.*]

[*Jane stands holding the telegram. She sways slightly.*]

ELLEN: What is it? What's happened? Oh, my God!

JANE: You needn't worry about Fanny and Joe any more, Ellen. He won't be able to come back after all because he's dead. [*She crumples up and falls to the ground.*]

[*Maroons can be heard in the distance and people cheering.*]

[*The lights fade.*]

PART TWO: SCENE XI

Principal: JANE.

SCENE: *Trafalgar Square.*
TIME: 11 *p.m. Monday, November* 11*th,* 1918.

Before the scene begins Jane appears far up stage in a pool of light. Her hat has been pushed on to one side, her clothes look dishevelled, and her handbag hangs on her arm wide open. Twined round her neck and over her hat are coloured paper streamers. She holds in her left hand a large painted wooden rattle, in her right hand a red, white, and blue paper squeaker. Her face is dead white and quite devoid of expression.

The lights go up.

Jane can be seen threading her way like a sleep-walker through dense crowds of cheering, yelling people. They push her and jostle her. One man blows a long squeaking paper tongue into her face. There is a motor bus festooned with people and a Rolls Royce and one or two taxis and a hansom cab, all equally burdened with screaming humanity. They move at a snail's pace. Jane finally arrives down stage under a lamp-post in the centre. She stands there cheering wildly, with the tears rolling down her face. The lights dim and the yelling crowds fade away. Jane is left, still cheering and occasionally brandishing the rattle and blowing the squeaker. But she can't be heard at all because the full strength of the orchestra is playing "Land of Hope and Glory."

PART THREE: SCENE I

Principals: ROBERT, JANE, MARGARET.

SCENE: *Drawing-room of a London house.*
TIME: 11.45 *p.m. Tuesday, December 31st,* 1929.

*Margaret and Jane, both old women, are sitting by the fire.
Margaret is very made up, with dyed hair. Jane's hair is white.
Margaret is wearing a coloured evening gown. Jane is in black.*

MARGARET: I assure you he's the most marvellous man I've
ever met. I'd never go to another doctor in the world. He has
the most wonderful touch—he's completely cured me, and anyhow the hotel is divine. It's really more a Hydro really, although,
thank God, not in the English sense. You can eat what you like
and do what you like——
JANE: And what do you like?
MARGARET [*laughing*]: Enjoying myself.
JANE: And you do.
MARGARET: Certainly I do.
JANE: Good!
MARGARET: Jane, dear, you really are hopeless.
JANE: I refuse to be jostled, Margaret. I'm perfectly comfort-
able where I am, without going gallivanting about the Con-
tinent taking cures for ailments I haven't got.

MARGARET: How do you know you haven't got any ailments?

JANE: Because I'm sane and active, and as strong as a horse. So is Robert. We've both outstayed our welcome, that's the only thing that's wrong with us.

MARGARET: I don't see any sense in sitting waiting for the grave.

JANE: I'm not waiting for anything. I have a perfectly good time. You're not the only one who enjoys yourself. I go to the Opera. I go to theatres, I go to the Zoo, and, I must say, so far I've found the Zoo infinitely the most entertaining.

MARGARET: Dearest Jane—you really are amazing!

[*Robert enters. His hair is also white, but he is otherwise hale and hearty.*]

ROBERT: It's nearly time.

MARGARET: Good heavens, I must fly. I wouldn't interfere with your little ritual for the world.

JANE: You wouldn't interfere—you're an old friend.

MARGARET [*kissing Jane*]: That's very sweet, Jane, but all the same I must go. I promised I'd be at the Embassy at eleven-thirty. Good-night, dear. Good-night, Robert. No, don't see me down— the car's outside, isn't it?

ROBERT: Yes, it's been there for a long while.

MARGARET: Happy New Year to you both. Remember you're both dining with me on Thursday.

ROBERT: Good-night, Margaret—same to you.

[*Margaret goes out.*]

[*Robert goes over to Jane.*] Did Franklin bring the champagne up?

JANE: Yes, it's by the table.

ROBERT: Good!

JANE: Well, Robert—here we go again.

ROBERT: I believe you laugh at me inside—for my annual sentimental outburst.

JANE: No dear, I don't laugh at you.

ROBERT: One more year behind us.

JANE: One more year before us.

ROBERT: Do you mind?

JANE: Oh, no—everything passes—even time.

ROBERT: It seems incredible, doesn't it? Here we are in this same room!

JANE: Yes. I've hated it for years.

ROBERT: Do you want to move?

JANE: Of course not.

ROBERT: We might have some new curtains.

JANE: We have, dear.

ROBERT: Good God, so we have! I never noticed.

JANE: They've only been up a week.

ROBERT: They look very nice.

JANE: Dear Robert. [*She pats Robert's hand.*] What toast have you in mind for to-night—something gay and original, I hope?

ROBERT: Just our old friend—the future. The Future of England.

JANE: It's starting—the champagne, quick!

[*Robert gets a champagne bottle out of the bucket and struggles with it.*]

[*Jane opens the window.*]

ROBERT: I can't get the damned thing open.

JANE: Let me try.

ROBERT [*doing it*]: There!

[*Jane holds the glasses.*]

[*Robert fills the glasses.*]

[*Meanwhile the chimes and sirens are beginning outside.*]

JANE [*holding up her glass*]: First of all, my dear, I drink to you. Loyal and loving always. [*She drinks.*] Now, then, let's couple the Future of England with the past of England. The glories and victories and triumphs that are over, and the sorrows that are over, too. Let's drink to our sons who made part of the pattern and to our hearts that died with them. Let's drink to the spirit of gallantry and courage that made a strange Heaven out of unbelievable Hell, and let's drink to the hope that one day this country of ours, which we love so much, will find dignity and greatness and peace again.

[They both lift their glasses and drink as
[The lights fade.]

PART THREE: SCENE II

Principals: ROBERT, JANE, FANNY, MARGARET, ELLEN, FULL COMPANY

SCENE: *A Night Club.*
TIME: *Evening*—1930.
This Scene begins with a night club in which Fanny is singing, seated on a piano. The decoration is angular and strange, and the song she is singing is oddly discordant.

TWENTIETH CENTURY BLUES

Verse
Why is it that civilised humanity
Must make the world so wrong?
In this hurly burly of insanity
Your dreams cannot last long.
We've reached a headline—
The Press headline—every sorrow,
Blues value is News value to-morrow.

Refrain

Blues, Twentieth Century Blues, are getting me down.
Who's escaped those weary Twentieth Century Blues?
Why, if there's a God in the sky, why shouldn't he grin?
High above this dreary Twentieth Century din,
In this strange illusion,
Chaos and confusion,
People seem to lose their way.
What is there to strive for,
Love or keep alive for? Say—
Hey, hey, call it a day.
Blues, nothing to win or to lose.
It's getting me down.
Blues, I've got those weary Twentieth Century Blues.

[*When the song is finished, people rise from table and dance without apparently any particular enjoyment; it is the dull dancing of habit. The lights fade away from everything but the dancers, who appear to be rising in the air. They disappear and down stage left six "incurables" in blue hospital uniform are sitting making baskets. They disappear and Fanny is seen singing her song for a moment, then far away up stage a jazz band is seen playing wildly. Then down stage Jane and Robert standing with glasses of champagne held aloft, then Ellen sitting in front of a Radio loud speaker; then Margaret dancing with a young man. The visions are repeated quicker and quicker, while across the darkness runs a Riley light sign spelling out news. Noise grows louder and louder. Steam rivets, loud speakers, jazz bands, aeroplane propellers, etc., until the general effect is complete chaos.*]

[*Suddenly it all fades into darkness and silence and away at the back a Union Jack glows through the blackness.*]

[*The lights slowly come up and the whole stage is composed of massive tiers, upon which stand the entire Company. The Union Jack flies over their heads as they sing "God Save the King."*]

THE END

PRIVATE
LIVES

CHARACTERS

AMANDA PRYNNE

VICTOR PRYNNE, *her husband*

LOUISE, *a maid*

SIBYL CHASE

ELYOT CHASE, *her husband*

ACT ONE

The Terrace of a Hotel in France. Summer evening.

ACT TWO

Amanda's flat in Paris. A few days later. Evening.

ACT THREE

The same. The next morning.

Time: THE PRESENT

ACT ONE

THE SCENE *is the terrace of a hotel in France. There are two French windows at the back opening on to two separate suites. The terrace space is divided by a line of small trees in tubs, and, down-stage, running parallel with the footlights, there is a low stone balustrade. Upon each side of the line of tree tubs is a set of suitable terrace furniture, a swinging seat, two or three chairs, and a table. There are orange and white awnings shading the windows, as it is summer.*

When the curtain rises it is about eight o'clock in the evening. There is an orchestra playing not very far off. Sibyl Chase opens the windows on the Right, and steps out on to the terrace. She is very pretty and blonde, and smartly dressed in travelling clothes. She comes down stage, stretches her arms wide with a little sigh of satisfaction, and regards the view with an ecstatic expression.

SIBYL [*calling*]: Elli, Elli dear, do come out. It's so lovely.

ELYOT [*inside*]: Just a minute.

[*After a pause Elyot comes out. He is about thirty, quite slim and pleasant looking, and also in travelling clothes. He walks right down to the balustrade and looks thoughtfully at the view. Sibyl stands beside him, and slips her arm through his.*]

ELYOT: Not so bad.

SIBYL: It's heavenly. Look at the lights of that yacht reflected in the water. Oh dear, I'm so happy.

ELYOT [*smiling*]: Are you?

SIBYL: Aren't you?

ELYOT: Of course I am. Tremendously happy.

SIBYL: Just to think, here we are, you and I, married!

ELYOT: Yes, things have come to a pretty pass.

SIBYL: Don't laugh at me, you mustn't be *blasé* about honeymoons just because this is your second.

ELYOT [*frowning*]: That's silly.

SIBYL: Have I annoyed you by saying that?

ELYOT: Just a little.

SIBYL: Oh, darling, I'm so sorry. [*She holds her face up to his.*] Kiss me.

ELYOT [*doing so*]: There.

SIBYL: Ummm, not so very enthusiastic.

ELYOT [*kissing her again*]: That better?

SIBYL: Three times, please, I'm superstitious.

ELYOT [*kissing her*]: You really are very sweet.

SIBYL: Are you glad you married me?

ELYOT: Of course I am.

SIBYL: How glad?

ELYOT: Incredibly, magnificently glad.

SIBYL: How lovely.

ELYOT: We ought to go in and dress.

SIBYL: Gladder than before?

ELYOT: Why do you keep harping on that?

SIBYL: It's in my mind, and yours too, I expect.

ELYOT: It isn't anything of the sort.

SIBYL: She was pretty, wasn't she? Amanda?

ELYOT: Very pretty.

SIBYL: Prettier than I am?

ELYOT: Much.

SIBYL: Elyot!

ELYOT: She was pretty and sleek, and her hands were long and slim, and her legs were long and slim, and she danced like an angel. You dance very poorly, by the way.

SIBYL: Could she play the piano as well as I can?

ELYOT: She couldn't play the piano at all.

SIBYL [*triumphantly*]: Aha! Had she my talent for organisation?

ELYOT: No, but she hadn't your mother either.

SIBYL: I don't believe you like mother.

ELYOT: Like her! I can't bear her.

SIBYL: Elyot! She's a darling, underneath.

ELYOT: I never got underneath.

SIBYL: It makes me unhappy to think you don't like mother.

ELYOT: Nonsense. I believe the only reason you married me was to get away from her.

SIBYL: I married you because I loved you.

ELYOT: Oh dear, oh dear, oh dear, oh dear!

SIBYL: I love you far more than Amanda loved you. I'd never make you miserable like she did.

ELYOT: We made each other miserable.

SIBYL: It was all her fault, you know it was.

ELYOT [*with vehemence*]: Yes, it was. Entirely her fault.

SIBYL: She was a fool to lose you.

ELYOT: We lost each other.

SIBYL: She lost you, with her violent tempers and carryings on.

ELYOT: Will you stop talking about Amanda?

SIBYL: But I'm very glad, because if she hadn't been uncontrolled, and wicked, and unfaithful, we shouldn't be here now.

ELYOT: She wasn't unfaithful.

SIBYL: How do you know? I bet she was. I bet she was unfaithful every five minutes.

ELYOT: It would take a far more concentrated woman than Amanda to be unfaithful every five minutes.

SIBYL [*anxiously*]: You do hate her, don't you?

ELYOT: No, I don't hate her. I think I despise her.

SIBYL [*with satisfaction*]: That's much worse.

ELYOT: And yet I'm sorry for her.

SIBYL: Why?

ELYOT: Because she's marked for tragedy; she's bound to make a mess of everything.

SIBYL: If it's all her fault, I don't see that it matters much.

ELYOT: She has some very good qualities.

SIBYL: Considering what a hell she made of your life, I think you are very nice about her. Most men would be vindictive.

ELYOT: What's the use of that? It's all over now, such a long time ago.

SIBYL: Five years isn't very long.

ELYOT [*seriously*]: Yes it is.

SIBYL: Do you think you could ever love her again?

ELYOT: Now then, Sibyl.

SIBYL: But could you?

ELYOT: Of course not, I love you.

SIBYL: Yes, but you love me differently; I know that.

ELYOT: More wisely perhaps.

SIBYL: I'm glad. I'd rather have that sort of love.

ELYOT: You're right. Love is no use unless it's wise, and kind, and undramatic. Something steady and sweet, to smooth out your nerves when you're tired. Something tremendously cosy; and unflurried by scenes and jealousies. That's what I want, what I've always wanted really. Oh my dear, I do hope it's not going to be dull for you.

SIBYL: Sweetheart, as tho' you could ever be dull.

ELYOT: I'm much older than you.

SIBYL: Not so very much.

ELYOT: Seven years.

SIBYL [*snuggling up to him*]: The music has stopped now and you can hear the sea.

ELYOT: We'll bathe to-morrow morning.

SIBYL: I mustn't get sunburnt.

ELYOT: Why not?

SIBYL: I hate it on women.

ELYOT: Very well, you shan't then. I hope you don't hate it on men.

SIBYL: Of course I don't. It's suitable to men.

ELYOT: You're a completely feminine little creature, aren't you?

SIBYL: Why do you say that?

ELYOT: Everything in its place.

SIBYL: What do you mean?

ELYOT: If you feel you'd like me to smoke a pipe, I'll try and master it.

SIBYL: I like a man to be a man, if that's what you mean.

ELYOT: Are you going to understand me, and manage me?

SIBYL: I'm going to try to understand you.

ELYOT: Run me without my knowing it?

SIBYL [*withdrawing slightly*]: I think you're being a little unkind.

ELYOT: No, I don't mean to be. I was only wondering.

SIBYL: Well?

ELYOT: I was wondering what was going on inside your mind, what your plans are really?

SIBYL: Plans? Oh, Elli!

ELYOT: Apart from loving me and all that, you must have plans.

SIBYL: I haven't the faintest idea what you're talking about.

ELYOT: Perhaps it's subconscious then, age-old instincts working away deep down, mincing up little bits of experience for future use, watching me carefully like a little sharp-eyed, blonde kitten.

SIBYL: How can you be so horrid.

ELYOT: I said Kitten, not Cat.

SIBYL: Kittens grow into cats.

ELYOT: Let that be a warning to you.

SIBYL [*slipping her arm through his again*]: What's the matter, darling; are you hungry?

ELYOT: Not a bit.

SIBYL: You're very strange all of a sudden, and rather cruel. Just because I'm feminine, it doesn't mean that I'm crafty and calculating.

ELYOT: I didn't say you were either of those things.

SIBYL: I hate these half masculine women who go banging about.

ELYOT: I hate anybody who goes banging about.

SIBYL: I should think you needed a little quiet womanliness after Amanda.

ELYOT: Why will you keep on talking about her?

SIBYL: It's natural enough, isn't it?

ELYOT: What do you want to find out?

SIBYL: Why did you really let her divorce you?

ELYOT: She divorced me for cruelty, and flagrant infidelity. I spent a whole week-end at Brighton with a lady called Vera Williams. She had the nastiest looking hair brush I have ever seen.

SIBYL: Misplaced chivalry, I call it. Why didn't you divorce her?

ELYOT: It would not have been the action of a gentleman, whatever that may mean.

SIBYL: I think she got off very lightly.

ELYOT: Once and for all will you stop talking about her.

SIBYL: Yes, Elli dear.

ELYOT: I don't wish to see her again or hear her name mentioned.

SIBYL: Very well, darling.

ELYOT: Is that understood?

SIBYL: Yes, darling. Where did you spend your honeymoon?

ELYOT: St. Moritz. Be quiet.

SIBYL: I hate St. Moritz.

ELYOT: So do I, bitterly.

SIBYL: Was she good on skis?

ELYOT: Do you want to dine downstairs here, or at the Casino?

SIBYL: I love you, I love you, I love you.

ELYOT: Good, let's go in and dress.

SIBYL: Kiss me first.

ELYOT [*kissing her*]: Casino?

SIBYL: Yes. Are you a gambler? You never told me.

ELYOT: Every now and then.

SIBYL: I shall come and sit just behind your chair and bring you luck.

ELYOT: That will be fatal.

[*They go off into their suite. There is a slight pause and then Victor Prynne enters from the Left suite. He is quite nice looking, about thirty or thirty-five. He is dressed in a light travelling suit. He sniffs the air, looks at the view, and then turns back to the window.*]

VICTOR [*calling*]: Mandy.

AMANDA [*inside*]: What?

VICTOR: Come outside, the view is wonderful.

AMANDA: I'm still damp from the bath. Wait a minute——

[*Victor lights a cigarette. Presently Amanda comes out on to the terrace. She is quite exquisite with a gay face and a perfect figure. At the moment she is wearing a negligee.*]
I shall catch pneumonia, that's what I shall catch.

VICTOR [*looking at her*]: God!

AMANDA: I beg your pardon?

VICTOR: You look wonderful.

AMANDA: Thank you, darling.

VICTOR: Like a beautiful advertisement for something.

AMANDA: Nothing peculiar, I hope.

VICTOR: I can hardly believe it's true. You and I, here alone together, married!

AMANDA [*rubbing her face on his shoulder*]: That stuff's very rough.

VICTOR: Don't you like it?

AMANDA: A bit hearty, isn't it?

VICTOR: Do you love me?

AMANDA: Of course, that's why I'm here.

VICTOR: More than——

AMANDA: Now then, none of that.

VICTOR: No, but do you love me more than you loved Elyot?

AMANDA: I don't remember, it's such a long time ago.

VICTOR: Not so very long.

AMANDA [*flinging out her arms*]: All my life ago.

VICTOR: I'd like to break his damned neck.

AMANDA [*laughing*]: Why?

VICTOR: For making you unhappy.

AMANDA: It was mutual.

VICTOR: Rubbish! It was all his fault, you know it was.

AMANDA: Yes, it was, now I come to think about it.

VICTOR: Swine!

AMANDA: Don't be so vehement, darling.

VICTOR: I'll never treat you like that.

AMANDA: That's right.

VICTOR: I love you too much.

AMANDA: So did he.

VICTOR: Fine sort of love that is. He struck you once, didn't he?

AMANDA: More than once.

VICTOR: Where?

AMANDA: Several places.

VICTOR: What a cad.

AMANDA: I struck him too. Once I broke four gramophone records over his head. It was very satisfying.

VICTOR: You must have been driven to distraction.

AMANDA: Yes, I was, but don't let's talk about it, please. After all, it's a dreary subject for our honeymoon night.

VICTOR: He didn't know when he was well off.

AMANDA: Look at the lights of that yacht reflected in the water. I wonder whose it is.

VICTOR: We must bathe to-morrow.

AMANDA: Yes. I want to get a nice sunburn.

VICTOR [*reproachfully*]: Mandy!

AMANDA: Why, what's the matter?

VICTOR: I hate sunburnt women.

AMANDA: Why?

VICTOR: It's somehow, well, unsuitable.

AMANDA: It's awfully suitable to me, darling.

VICTOR: Of course if you really want to.

AMANDA: I'm absolutely determined. I've got masses of lovely oil to rub all over myself.

VICTOR: Your skin is so beautiful as it is.

AMANDA: Wait and see. When I'm done a nice crisp brown, you'll fall in love with me all over again.

VICTOR: I couldn't love you more than I do now.

AMANDA: Oh, dear. I did so hope our honeymoon was going to be progressive.

VICTOR: Where did you spend the last one?

AMANDA [*warningly*]: Victor.

VICTOR: I want to know.

AMANDA: St. Moritz. It was very attractive.

VICTOR: I hate St. Moritz.

AMANDA: So do I.

VICTOR: Did he start quarrelling with you right away?

AMANDA: Within the first few days. I put it down to the high altitudes.

VICTOR: And you loved him?

AMANDA: Yes, Victor.

VICTOR: You poor child.

AMANDA: You must try not to be pompous, dear. [*She turns away*.]

VICTOR [*hurt*]: Mandy!

AMANDA: I don't believe I'm a bit like what you think I am.

VICTOR: How do you mean?

AMANDA: I was never a poor child.

VICTOR: Figure of speech, dear, that's all.

AMANDA: I suffered a good deal, and had my heart broken. But it wasn't an innocent girlish heart. It was jagged with sophistication. I've always been sophisticated, far too knowing. That caused many of my rows with Elyot. I irritated him because he knew I could see through him.

VICTOR: I don't mind how much you see through me.

AMANDA: Sweet. [*She kisses him*.]

VICTOR: I'm going to make you happy.

AMANDA: Are you?

VICTOR: Just by looking after you, and seeing that you're all right, you know.

AMANDA [*a trifle wistfully*]: No, I don't know.

VICTOR: I think you love me quite differently from the way you loved Elyot.

AMANDA: Do stop harping on Elyot.

VICTOR: It's true, though, isn't it?

AMANDA: I love you much more calmly, if that's what you mean.

VICTOR: More lastingly?

AMANDA: I expect so.

VICTOR: Do you remember when I first met you?

AMANDA: Yes. Distinctly.

VICTOR: At Marion Vale's party.

AMANDA: Yes.

VICTOR: Wasn't it wonderful?

AMANDA: Not really, dear. It was only redeemed from the completely commonplace by the fact of my having hiccoughs.

VICTOR: I never noticed them.

AMANDA: Love at first sight.

VICTOR: Where did you first meet Elyot?

AMANDA: To hell with Elyot.

VICTOR: Mandy!

AMANDA: I forbid you to mention his name again. I'm sick of the sound of it. You must be raving mad. Here we are on the first night of our honeymoon, with the moon coming up, and the music playing, and all you can do is to talk about my first husband. It's downright sacrilegious.

VICTOR: Don't be angry.

AMANDA: Well, it's very annoying.

VICTOR: Will you forgive me?

AMANDA: Yes; only don't do it again.

VICTOR: I promise.

AMANDA: You'd better go and dress now, you haven't bathed yet.

VICTOR: Where shall we dine, downstairs here, or at the Casino?

AMANDA: The Casino is more fun, I think.

VICTOR: We can play Boule afterwards.

AMANDA: No, we can't, dear.

VICTOR: Don't you like dear old Boule?

AMANDA: No, I hate dear old Boule. We'll play a nice game of Chemin de fer.

VICTOR [*apprehensively*]: Not at the big table?

AMANDA: Maybe at the biggest table.

VICTOR: You're not a terrible gambler, are you?

AMANDA: Inveterate. Chance rules my life.

VICTOR: What nonsense.

AMANDA: How can you say it's nonsense? It was chance meeting you. It was chance falling in love; it's chance that we're here, particularly after your driving. Everything that happens is chance.

VICTOR: You know I feel rather scared of you at close quarters.

AMANDA: That promises to be very embarrassing.

VICTOR: You're somehow different now, wilder than I thought you were, more strained.

AMANDA: Wilder! Oh Victor, I've never felt less wild in my life. A little strained, I grant you, but that's the newly married atmosphere; you can't expect anything else. Honeymooning is a very overrated amusement.

VICTOR: You say that because you had a ghastly experience before.

AMANDA: There you go again.

VICTOR: It couldn't fail to embitter you a little.

AMANDA: The honeymoon wasn't such a ghastly experience really; it was afterwards that was so awful.

VICTOR: I intend to make you forget it all entirely.

AMANDA: You won't succeed by making constant references to it.

VICTOR: I wish I knew you better.

AMANDA: It's just as well you don't. The "woman"—in italics —should always retain a certain amount of alluring feminine mystery for the "man"—also in italics.

VICTOR: What about the man? Isn't he allowed to have any mystery?

AMANDA: Absolutely none. Transparent as glass.

VICTOR: Oh, I see.

AMANDA: Never mind, darling; it doesn't necessarily work out like that; it's only supposed to.

VICTOR: I'm glad I'm normal.

AMANDA: What an odd thing to be glad about. Why?

VICTOR: Well, aren't you?

AMANDA: I'm not so sure I'm normal.

VICTOR: Oh, Mandy, of course you are, sweetly, divinely normal.

AMANDA: I haven't any peculiar cravings for Chinamen or old boots, if that's what you mean.

VICTOR [*scandalised*]: Mandy!

AMANDA: I think very few people are completely normal really, deep down in their private lives. It all depends on a combination of circumstances. If all the various cosmic thingummys fuse at the same moment, and the right spark is struck, there's no knowing what one mightn't do. That was the trouble with Elyot and me, we were like two violent acids bubbling about in a nasty little matrimonial bottle.

VICTOR: I don't believe you're nearly as complex as you think you are.

AMANDA: I don't think I'm particularly complex, but I know I'm unreliable.

VICTOR: You're frightening me horribly. In what way unreliable?

AMANDA: I'm so apt to see things the wrong way round.

VICTOR: What sort of things?

AMANDA: Morals. What one should do and what one shouldn't.

VICTOR [*fondly*]: Darling, you're so sweet.

AMANDA: Thank you, Victor, that's most encouraging. You really must have your bath now. Come along.

VICTOR: Kiss me.

AMANDA [*doing so*]: There, dear, hurry now, I've only got to slip my dress on and then I shall be ready.

VICTOR: Give me ten minutes.

AMANDA: I'll bring the cocktails out here when they come.

VICTOR: All right.

AMANDA: Go along now, hurry.

[*They both disappear into their suite. After a moment's pause Elyot steps carefully on to the terrace carrying a tray upon which are two champagne cocktails. He puts the tray down on the table.*]

ELYOT [*calling*]: Sibyl.

SIBYL [*inside*]: Yes.

ELYOT: I've brought the cocktails out here, hurry up.

SIBYL: I can't find my lipstick.

ELYOT: Never mind, send down to the kitchen for some cochineal.

SIBYL: Don't be so silly.

ELYOT: Hurry.

[*Elyot saunters down to the balustrade. He looks casually over on to the next terrace, and then out at the view. He looks up at the moon and sighs, then he sits down in a chair with his back towards the line of tubs, and lights a cigarette. Amanda steps gingerly on to her terrace carrying a tray with two champagne cocktails on it. She is wearing a charmingly simple evening gown, her cloak is flung over her right shoulder. She places the tray carefully on the table, puts her cloak over the back of a chair, and sits down with her back towards Elyot. She takes a small mirror from her handbag, and scrutinizes her face in it. The orchestra downstairs strikes up a new melody. Both Elyot and Amanda give a little start. After a moment, Elyot pensively begins to hum the tune the band is playing. It is a*

*sentimental, romantic little tune. Amanda hears him, and clutches
at her throat suddenly as though she were suffocating. Then she
jumps up noiselessly, and peers over the line of tubs. Elyot, with his
back to her, continues to sing obliviously. She sits down again, re-
laxing with a gesture almost of despair. Then she looks anxiously
over her shoulder at the window in case Victor should be listening,
and then, with a little smile, she takes up the melody herself, clearly.
Elyot stops dead and gives a gasp, then he jumps up, and stands
looking at her. She continues to sing, pretending not to know that he
is there. At the end of the song, she turns slowly, and faces him.*]

AMANDA: Thoughtful of them to play that, wasn't it?

ELYOT [*in a stifled voice*]: What are you doing here?

AMANDA: I'm on honeymoon.

ELYOT: How interesting, so am I.

AMANDA: I hope you're enjoying it.

ELYOT: It hasn't started yet.

AMANDA: Neither has mine.

ELYOT: Oh, my God!

AMANDA: I can't help feeling that this is a little unfortunate.

ELYOT: Are you happy?

AMANDA: Perfectly.

ELYOT: Good. That's all right, then, isn't it?

AMANDA: Are you?

ELYOT: Ecstatically.

AMANDA: I'm delighted to hear it. We shall probably meet
again sometime. Au revoir! [*She turns.*]

ELYOT [*firmly*]: Good-bye.

[*She goes indoors without looking back. He stands gazing after
her with an expression of horror on his face. Sibyl comes brightly
on to the terrace in a very pretty evening frock.*]

SIBYL: Cocktail, please. [*Elyot doesn't answer.*] Elli, what's the
matter?

ELYOT: I feel very odd.

SIBYL: Odd, what do you mean? Ill?

ELYOT: Yes, ill.

SIBYL [*alarmed*]: What sort of ill?

ELYOT: We must leave at once.

SIBYL: Leave!

ELYOT: Yes, dear. Leave immediately.

SIBYL: Elli!

ELYOT: I have a strange foreboding.

SIBYL: You must be mad.

ELYOT: Listen, darling. I want you to be very sweet, and patient, and understanding, and not be upset, or ask any questions, or anything. I have an absolute conviction that our whole future happiness depends upon our leaving here instantly.

SIBYL: Why?

ELYOT: I can't tell you why.

SIBYL: But we've only just come.

ELYOT: I know that, but it can't be helped.

SIBYL: What's happened, what has happened?

ELYOT: Nothing has happened.

SIBYL: You've gone out of your mind.

ELYOT: I haven't gone out of my mind, but I shall if we stay here another hour.

SIBYL: You're not drunk, are you?

ELYOT: Of course I'm not drunk. What time have I had to get drunk?

SIBYL: Come down and have some dinner, darling, and then you'll feel ever so much better.

ELYOT: It's no use trying to humour me. I'm serious.

SIBYL: But darling, please be reasonable. We've only just arrived; everything's unpacked. It's our first night together. We can't go away now.

ELYOT: We can have our first night together in Paris.

SIBYL: We shouldn't get there until the small hours.

ELYOT [*with great effort at calmness*]: Now please, Sibyl, I know it sounds crazy to you, and utterly lacking in reason and sense, but I've got second sight over certain things. I'm almost psychic. I've got the most extraordinary sensation of impending disaster. If we stay here something appalling will happen. I know it.

SIBYL [*firmly*]: Hysterical nonsense.

ELYOT: It isn't hysterical nonsense. Presentiments are far from being nonsense. Look at the woman who cancelled her passage on the *Titanic*. All because of a presentiment.

SIBYL: I don't see what that has to do with it.

ELYOT: It has everything to do with it. She obeyed her instincts, that's what she did, and saved her life. All I ask is to be allowed to obey my instincts.

SIBYL: Do you mean that there's going to be an earthquake or something?

ELYOT: Very possibly, very possibly indeed, or perhaps a violent explosion.

SIBYL: They don't have earthquakes in France.

ELYOT: On the contrary, only the other day they felt a distinct shock at Toulon.

SIBYL: Yes, but that's in the South where it's hot.

ELYOT: Don't quibble, Sibyl.

SIBYL: And as for explosions, there's nothing here that can explode.

ELYOT: Oho, isn't there.

SIBYL: Yes, but Elli——

ELYOT: Darling, be sweet. Bear with me. I beseech you to bear with me.

SIBYL: I don't understand. It's horrid of you to do this.

ELYOT: I'm not doing anything. I'm only asking you, imploring you to come away from this place.

SIBYL: But I love it here.

ELYOT: There are thousands of other places far nicer.

SIBYL: It's a pity we didn't go to one of them.

ELYOT: Now, listen, Sibyl——

SIBYL: Yes, but why are you behaving like this, why, why, why?

ELYOT: Don't ask why. Just give in to me. I swear I'll never ask you to give in to me over anything again.

SIBYL [*with complete decision*]: I won't think of going to-night. It's utterly ridiculous. I've done quite enough travelling for one day, and I'm tired.

ELYOT: You're as obstinate as a mule.

SIBYL: I like that, I must say.

ELYOT [*hotly*]: You've got your nasty little feet dug into the ground, and you don't intend to budge an inch, do you?

SIBYL [*with spirit*]: No, I do not.

ELYOT: If there's one thing in the world that infuriates me, it's sheer wanton stubbornness. I should like to cut off your head with a meat axe.

SIBYL: How dare you talk to me like that, on our honeymoon night.

ELYOT: Damn our honeymoon night. Damn it, damn it, damn it!

SIBYL [*bursting into tears*]: Oh, Elli, Elli——

ELYOT: Stop crying. Will you or will you not come away with me to Paris?

SIBYL: I've never been so miserable in my life. You're hateful and beastly. Mother was perfectly right. She said you had shifty eyes.

ELYOT: Well, she can't talk. Hers are so close together, you couldn't put a needle between them.

SIBYL: You don't love me a little bit. I wish I were dead.

ELYOT: Will you or will you not come to Paris?

SIBYL: No, no I won't.

ELYOT: Oh, my God! [*He stamps indoors.*]

SIBYL [*following him, wailing*]: Oh, Elli, Elli, Elli——

[*Victor comes stamping out of the French windows on the left, followed by Amanda.*]

VICTOR: You were certainly right when you said you weren't normal. You're behaving like a lunatic.

AMANDA: Not at all. All I have done is to ask you a little favour.

VICTOR: Little favour indeed.

AMANDA: If we left now we could be in Paris in a few hours.

VICTOR: If we crossed Siberia by train we could be in China in a fortnight, but I don't see any reason to do it.

AMANDA: Oh, Victor darling—please, please—be sensible, just for my sake.

VICTOR: Sensible!

AMANDA: Yes, sensible. I shall be absolutely miserable if we stay here. You don't want me to be absolutely miserable all through my honeymoon, do you?

VICTOR: But why on earth didn't you think of your sister's tragedy before?

AMANDA: I forgot.

VICTOR: You couldn't forget a thing like that.

AMANDA: I got the places muddled. Then when I saw the Casino there in the moonlight, it all came back to me.

VICTOR: When did all this happen?

AMANDA: Years ago, but it might just as well have been yesterday. I can see her now lying dead, with that dreadful expression on her face. Then all that awful business of taking the body home to England. It was perfectly horrible.

VICTOR: I never knew you had a sister.

AMANDA: I haven't any more.

VICTOR: There's something behind all this.

AMANDA: Don't be silly. What could there be behind it?

VICTOR: Well, for one thing, I know you're lying.

AMANDA: Victor!

VICTOR: Be honest. Aren't you?

AMANDA: I can't think how you can be so mean and suspicious.

VICTOR [*patiently*]: You're lying, Amanda. Aren't you?

AMANDA: Yes, Victor.

VICTOR: You never had a sister, dead or alive?

AMANDA: I believe there was a stillborn one in 1902.

VICTOR: What is your reason for all this?

AMANDA: I told you I was unreliable.

VICTOR: Why do you want to leave so badly?

AMANDA: You'll be angry if I tell you the truth.

VICTOR: What is it?

AMANDA: I warn you.

VICTOR: Tell me. Please tell me.

AMANDA: Elyot's here.

VICTOR: What!

AMANDA: I saw him.

VICTOR: When?

AMANDA: Just now, when you were in the bath.

VICTOR: Where was he?

AMANDA [*hesitatingly*]: Down there, in a white suit. [*She points over the balustrade.*]

VICTOR [*sceptically*]: White suit?

AMANDA: Why not? It's summer, isn't it?

VICTOR: You're lying again.

AMANDA. I'm not. He's here. I swear he is.

VICTOR: Well, what of it?

AMANDA: I can't enjoy a honeymoon with you, with Elyot liable to bounce in at any moment.

VICTOR: Really, Mandy.

AMANDA: Can't you see how awful it is? It's the most embarrassing thing that ever happened to me in my whole life.

VICTOR: Did he see you?

AMANDA: No, he was running.

VICTOR: What was he running for?

AMANDA: How on earth do I know? Don't be so annoying.

VICTOR: Well, as long as he didn't see you it's all right, isn't it?

AMANDA: It isn't all right at all. We must leave immediately.

VICTOR: But why?

AMANDA: How can you be so appallingly obstinate?

VICTOR: I'm not afraid of him.

AMANDA: Neither am I. It isn't a question of being afraid. It's just a horribly awkward situation.

VICTOR: I'm damned if I can see why our whole honeymoon should be upset by Elyot.

AMANDA: My last one was.

VICTOR: I don't believe he's here at all.

AMANDA: He is, I tell you. I saw him.

VICTOR: It was probably an optical illusion. This half light is very deceptive.

AMANDA: It was no such thing.

VICTOR: I absolutely refuse to change all our plans at the last moment, just because you think you've seen Elyot. It's unreasonable and ridiculous of you to demand it. Even if he is here I can't see that it matters. He'll probably feel much more embarrassed than you, and a damned good job too; and if he annoys you in any way I'll knock him down.

AMANDA: That would be charming.

VICTOR: Now don't let's talk about it any more.

AMANDA: Do you mean to stand there seriously and imagine that the whole thing can be glossed over as easily as that?

VICTOR: I'm not going to leave, Mandy. If I start giving in to you as early as this, our lives will be unbearable.

AMANDA [*outraged*]: Victor!

VICTOR [*calmly*]: You've worked yourself up into a state over a situation which really only exists in your mind.

AMANDA [*controlling herself with an effort*]: Please, Victor, please, for this last time I implore you. Let's go to Paris now, to-night. I mean it with all my heart—please——

VICTOR [*with gentle firmness*]: No, Mandy!

AMANDA: I see quite clearly that I have been foolish enough to marry a fat old gentleman in a club armchair.

VICTOR: It's no use being cross.

AMANDA: You're a pompous ass.

VICTOR [*horrified*]: Mandy!

AMANDA [*enraged*]: Pompous ass, that's what I said, and that's what I meant. Blown out with your own importance.

VICTOR: Mandy, control yourself.

AMANDA: Get away from me. I can't bear to think I'm married to such rugged grandeur.

VICTOR [*with great dignity*]: I shall be in the bar. When you are ready to come down and dine, let me know.

AMANDA [*flinging herself into a chair*]: Go away, go away.

[*Victor stalks off, at the same moment that Elyot stamps on, on the other side, followed by Sibyl in tears.*]

ELYOT: If you don't stop screaming, I'll murder you.

SIBYL: I wish to heaven I'd never seen you in my life, let alone

married you. I don't wonder Amanda left you, if you behaved
to her as you've behaved to me. I'm going down to have dinner
by myself and you can just do what you like about it.

ELYOT: Do, and I hope it chokes you.

SIBYL: Oh Elli, Elli——

[*She goes wailing indoors. Elyot stamps down to the balustrade
and lights a cigarette, obviously trying to control his nerves. Amanda
sees him, and comes down too.*]

AMANDA: Give me one for God's sake.

ELYOT [*hands her his case laconically*]: Here.

AMANDA [*taking a cigarette*]: I'm in such a rage.

ELYOT [*lighting up*]: So am I.

AMANDA: What are we to do?

ELYOT: I don't know.

AMANDA: Whose yacht is that?

ELYOT: The Duke of Westminster's I expect. It always is.

AMANDA: I wish I were on it.

ELYOT: I wish you were too.

AMANDA: There's no need to be nasty.

ELYOT: Yes, there is every need. I've never in my life felt a
greater urge to be nasty.

AMANDA: And you've had some urges in your time, haven't
you?

ELYOT: If you start bickering with me, Amanda, I swear I'll
throw you over the edge.

AMANDA: Try it, that's all, just try it.

ELYOT: You've upset everything, as usual.

AMANDA: I've upset everything! What about you?

ELYOT: Ever since the first moment I was unlucky enough to
set eyes on you, my life has been insupportable.

AMANDA: Oh do shut up, there's no sense in going on like that.

ELYOT: Nothing's any use. There's no escape, ever.

AMANDA: Don't be melodramatic.

ELYOT: Do you want a cocktail? There are two here.

AMANDA: There are two over here as well.

ELYOT: We'll have my two first.

[*Amanda crosses over into Elyot's part of the terrace. He gives her one, and keeps one himself.*]

AMANDA: Shall we get roaring screaming drunk?

ELYOT: I don't think that would help, we did it once before and it was a dismal failure.

AMANDA: It was lovely at the beginning.

ELYOT: You have an immoral memory, Amanda. Here's to you.

[*They raise their glasses solemnly and drink.*]

AMANDA: I tried to get away the moment after I'd seen you, but he wouldn't budge.

ELYOT: What's his name?

AMANDA: Victor, Victor Prynne.

ELYOT [*toasting*]: Mr. and Mrs. Victor Prynne. [*He drinks.*] Mine wouldn't budge either.

AMANDA: What's her name?

ELYOT: Sibyl.

AMANDA [*toasting*]: Mr. and Mrs. Elyot Chase. [*She drinks.*] God pity the poor girl.

ELYOT: Are you in love with him?

AMANDA: Of course.

ELYOT: How funny.

AMANDA: I don't see anything particularly funny about it, you're in love with yours, aren't you?

ELYOT: Certainly.

AMANDA: There you are then.

ELYOT: There we both are then.

AMANDA: What's she like?

ELYOT: Fair, very pretty, plays the piano beautifully.

AMANDA: Very comforting.

ELYOT: How's yours?

AMANDA: I don't want to discuss him.

ELYOT: Well, it doesn't matter, he'll probably come popping out in a minute and I shall see for myself. Does he know I'm here?

AMANDA: Yes, I told him.

ELYOT [*with sarcasm*]: That's going to make things a whole lot easier.

AMANDA: You needn't be frightened, he won't hurt you.

ELYOT: If he comes near me I'll scream the place down.

AMANDA: Does Sibyl know I'm here?

ELYOT: No, I pretended I'd had a presentiment. I tried terribly hard to persuade her to leave for Paris.

AMANDA: I tried too, it's lucky we didn't both succeed, isn't it? Otherwise we should probably all have joined up in Rouen or somewhere.

ELYOT [*laughing*]: In some frowzy little hotel.

AMANDA [*laughing too*]: Oh dear, it would have been much, much worse.

ELYOT: I can see us all sailing down in the morning for an early start.

AMANDA [*weakly*]: Lovely, oh lovely.

ELYOT: Glorious! [*They both laugh helplessly.*]

AMANDA: What's happened to yours?

ELYOT: Didn't you hear her screaming? She's downstairs in the dining-room, I think.

AMANDA: Mine is being grand, in the bar.

ELYOT: It really is awfully difficult.

AMANDA: Have you known her long?

ELYOT: About four months, we met in a house party in Norfolk.

AMANDA: Very flat, Norfolk.

ELYOT: How old is dear Victor?

AMANDA: Thirty-four, or -five; and Sibyl?

ELYOT: I blush to tell you, only twenty-three.

AMANDA: You've gone a mucker all right.

ELYOT: I shall reserve my opinion of your choice until I've met dear Victor.

AMANDA: I wish you wouldn't go on calling him "Dear Victor." It's extremely irritating.

ELYOT: That's how I see him. Dumpy, and fair, and very considerate, with glasses. Dear Victor.

AMANDA: As I said before I would rather not discuss him. At least I have good taste enough to refrain from making cheap gibes at Sibyl.

ELYOT: You said Norfolk was flat.

AMANDA: That was no reflection on her, unless she made it flatter.

ELYOT: Your voice takes on an acid quality whenever you mention her name.

AMANDA: I'll never mention it again.

ELYOT: Good, and I'll keep off Victor.

AMANDA [*with dignity*]: Thank you.

[*There is silence for a moment. The orchestra starts playing the same tune that they were singing previously.*]

ELYOT: That orchestra has a remarkably small repertoire.

AMANDA: They don't seem to know anything but this, do they?

[*She sits down on the balustrade, and sings it, softly. Her eyes are looking out to sea, and her mind is far away. Elyot watches her while she sings. When she turns to him at the end, there are tears in her eyes. He looks away awkwardly and lights another cigarette.*]

ELYOT: You always had a sweet voice, Amanda.

AMANDA [*a little huskily*]: Thank you.

ELYOT: I'm awfully sorry about all this, really I am. I wouldn't have had it happen for the world.

AMANDA: I know. I'm sorry too. It's just rotten luck.

ELYOT: I'll go away to-morrow whatever happens, so don't you worry.

AMANDA: That's nice of you.

ELYOT: I hope everything turns out splendidly for you, and that you'll be very happy.

AMANDA: I hope the same for you, too.

[*The music, which has been playing continually through this little scene, returns persistently to the refrain. They both look at one another and laugh.*]

ELYOT: Nasty insistent little tune.

AMANDA: Extraordinary how potent cheap music is.

ELYOT: What exactly were you remembering at that moment?

AMANDA: The Palace Hotel Skating Rink in the morning, bright strong sunlight, and everybody whirling round in vivid colours, and you kneeling down to put on my skates for me.

ELYOT: You'd fallen on your fanny a few moments before.

AMANDA: It was beastly of you to laugh like that, I felt so humiliated.

ELYOT: Poor darling.

AMANDA: Do you remember waking up in the morning, and standing on the balcony, looking out across the valley?

ELYOT: Blue shadows on white snow, cleanness beyond belief, high above everything in the world. How beautiful it was.

AMANDA: It's nice to think we had a few marvellous moments.

ELYOT: A few? We had heaps really, only they slip away into the background, and one only remembers the bad ones.

AMANDA: Yes. What fools we were to ruin it all. What utter, utter fools.

ELYOT: You feel like that too, do you?

AMANDA [*wearily*]: Of course.

ELYOT: Why did we?

AMANDA: The whole business was too much for us.

ELYOT: We were so ridiculously over in love.

AMANDA: Funny, wasn't it?

ELYOT [*sadly*]: Horribly funny.

AMANDA: Selfishness, cruelty, hatred, possessiveness, petty jealousy. All those qualities came out in us just because we loved each other.

ELYOT: Perhaps they were there anyhow.

AMANDA: No, it's love that does it. To hell with love.

ELYOT: To hell with love.

AMANDA: And yet here we are starting afresh with two quite different people. In love all over again, aren't we? [*Elyot doesn't answer.*] Aren't we?

ELYOT: No.

AMANDA: Elyot.

ELYOT: We're not in love all over again, and you know it. Good-night, Amanda. [*He turns abruptly, and goes towards the French windows.*]

AMANDA: Elyot—don't be silly—come back.

ELYOT: I must go and find Sibyl.

AMANDA: I must go and find Victor.

ELYOT [*savagely*]: Well, why don't you?

AMANDA: I don't want to.

ELYOT: It's shameful, shameful of us.

AMANDA: Don't: I feel terrible. Don't leave me for a minute, I shall go mad if you do. We won't talk about ourselves any more, we'll talk about outside things, anything you like, only just don't leave me until I've pulled myself together.

ELYOT: Very well. [*There is a dead silence.*]

AMANDA: What have you been doing lately? During these last years?

ELYOT: Travelling about. I went round the world, you know, after——

AMANDA [*hurriedly*]: Yes, yes, I know. How was it?

ELYOT: The world?

AMANDA: Yes.

ELYOT: Oh, highly enjoyable.

AMANDA: China must be very interesting.

ELYOT: Very big, China.

AMANDA: And Japan——

ELYOT: Very small.

AMANDA: Did you eat sharks' fins, and take your shoes off, and use chopsticks and everything?

ELYOT: Practically everything.

AMANDA: And India, the burning Ghars, or Ghats, or whatever they are, and the Taj Mahal. How was the Taj Mahal?

ELYOT [*looking at her*]: Unbelievable, a sort of dream.

AMANDA: That was the moonlight, I expect, you must have seen it in the moonlight.

ELYOT [*never taking his eyes off her face*]: Yes, moonlight is cruelly deceptive.

AMANDA: And it didn't look like a biscuit box, did it? I've always felt that it might.

ELYOT [*quietly*]: Darling, darling, I love you so.

AMANDA: And I do hope you met a sacred Elephant. They're lint white I believe, and very, very sweet.

ELYOT: I've never loved anyone else for an instant.

AMANDA [*raising her hand feebly in protest*]: No, no, you mustn't —Elyot—stop.

ELYOT: You love me, too, don't you? There's no doubt about it anywhere, is there?

AMANDA: No, no doubt anywhere.

ELYOT: You're looking very lovely, you know, in this damned moonlight. Your skin is clear and cool, and your eyes are shining, and you're growing lovelier and lovelier every second as I look at you. You don't hold any mystery for me, darling, do you mind? There isn't a particle of you that I don't know, remember, and want.

AMANDA [*softly*]: I'm glad, my sweet.

ELYOT: More than any desire anywhere, deep down in my deepest heart I want you back again—please——

AMANDA [*putting her hand over his mouth*]: Don't say any more, you're making me cry so dreadfully.

[*He pulls her gently into his arms and they stand silently, completely oblivious of everything but the moment and each other. When finally they separate, they sit down, rather breathlessly, on the balustrade.*]

AMANDA: What now? Oh darling, what now?

ELYOT: I don't know, I'm lost, utterly.

AMANDA: We must think quickly, oh quickly——

ELYOT: Escape?

AMANDA: Together?

ELYOT: Yes, of course, now, now.

AMANDA: We can't, we can't, you know we can't.

ELYOT: We must.

AMANDA: It would break Victor's heart.

ELYOT: And Sibyl's too probably, but they're bound to suffer anyhow. Think of the hell we'd lead them into if we stayed. Infinitely worse than any cruelty in the world, pretending to love them, and loving each other so desperately.

AMANDA: We must tell them.

ELYOT: What?

AMANDA: Call them, and tell them.

ELYOT: Oh no, no, that's impossible.

AMANDA: It's honest.

ELYOT: I can't help how honest it is, it's too horrible to think of. How should we start? What should we say?

AMANDA: We should have to trust to the inspiration of the moment.

ELYOT: It would be a moment completely devoid of inspiration. The most appalling moment imaginable. No, no, we can't, you must see that, we simply can't.

AMANDA: What do you propose to do then? As it is they might appear at any moment.

ELYOT: We've got to decide instantly one way or another. Go away together now, or stay with them, and never see one another again, ever.

AMANDA: Don't be silly, what choice is there?

ELYOT: No choice at all, come—— [*He takes her hand.*]

AMANDA: No, wait. This is sheer raving madness, something's happened to us, we're not sane.

ELYOT: We never were.

AMANDA: Where can we go?

ELYOT: Paris first, my car's in the garage, all ready.

AMANDA: They'll follow us.

ELYOT: That doesn't matter, once the thing's done.

AMANDA: I've got a flat in Paris.

ELYOT: Good.

AMANDA: It's in the Avenue Montaigne. I let it to Freda Lawson, but she's in Biarritz, so it's empty.

ELYOT: Does Victor know?

AMANDA: No, he knows I have one but he hasn't the faintest idea where.

ELYOT: Better and better.

AMANDA: We're being so bad, so terribly bad, we'll suffer for this, I know we shall.

ELYOT: Can't be helped.

AMANDA: Starting all those awful rows all over again.

ELYOT: No, no, we're older and wiser now.

AMANDA: What difference does that make? The first moment either of us gets a bit nervy, off we'll go again.

ELYOT: Stop shilly-shallying, Amanda.

AMANDA: I'm trying to be sensible.

ELYOT: You're only succeeding in being completely idiotic.

AMANDA: Idiotic indeed! What about you?

ELYOT: Now look here, Amanda——

AMANDA [*stricken*]: Oh my God!

ELYOT [*rushing to her and kissing her*]: Darling, darling, I didn't mean it——

AMANDA: I won't move from here unless we have a compact, a sacred, sacred compact never to quarrel again.

ELYOT: Easy to make but difficult to keep.

AMANDA: No, no, it's the bickering that always starts it. The moment we notice we're bickering, either of us, we must promise on our honour to stop dead. We'll invent some phrase or catchword, which when either of us says it, automatically cuts off all conversation for at least five minutes.

ELYOT: Two minutes, dear, with an option of renewal.

AMANDA: Very well, what shall it be?

ELYOT [*hurriedly*]: Solomon Isaacs.

AMANDA: All right, that'll do.

ELYOT: Come on, come on.

AMANDA: What shall we do if we meet either of them on the way downstairs?

ELYOT: Run like stags.

AMANDA: What about clothes?

ELYOT: I've got a couple of bags I haven't **unpacked** yet.

AMANDA: I've got a small trunk.

ELYOT: Send the porter up for it.

AMANDA: Oh this is terrible—terrible——

ELYOT: Come on, come on, don't waste time.

AMANDA: Oughtn't we to leave notes or something?

ELYOT: No, no, no, we'll telegraph from somewhere on the road.

AMANDA: Darling, I daren't, it's too wicked of us, I simply daren't.

ELYOT [*seizing her in his arms and kissing her violently*]: Now will you behave?

AMANDA: Yes, but Elyot darling——

ELYOT: Solomon Isaacs!

[*They rush off together through Elyot's suite. After a moment or so, Victor steps out on to the terrace and looks round anxiously. Then he goes back indoors again, and can be heard calling "Mandy." Finally he again comes out on to the terrace and comes despondently down to the balustrade. He hears Sibyl's voice calling "Elli" and looks round as she comes out of the French windows. She jumps slightly upon seeing him.*]

VICTOR: Good evening.

SIBYL [*rather flustered*]: Good evening—I was—er—looking for my husband.

VICTOR: Really, that's funny. I was looking for my wife.

SIBYL: Quite a coincidence. [*She laughs nervously.*]

VICTOR [*after a pause*]: It's very nice here, isn't it?

SIBYL: Lovely.

VICTOR: Have you been here long?

SIBYL: No, we only arrived to-day.

VICTOR: Another coincidence. So did we.

SIBYL: How awfully funny.

VICTOR: Would you care for a cocktail?

SIBYL: Oh no thank you—really——

VICTOR: There are two here on the table.

[*Sibyl glances at the two empty glasses on the balustrade, and tosses her head defiantly.*]

SIBYL: Thanks very much, I'd love one.

VICTOR: Good, here you are.

[*Sibyl comes over to Victor's side of the terrace. He hands her one and takes one himself.*]

SIBYL: Thank you.

VICTOR [*with rather forced gaiety*]: To absent friends. [*He raises his glass.*]

SIBYL [*raising hers*]: To absent friends. [*They both laugh rather mirthlessly and then sit down on the balustrade, pensively sipping their cocktails and looking at the view.*] It's awfully pretty, isn't it? The moonlight, and the lights of that yacht reflected in the water——

VICTOR: I wonder who it belongs to.

THE CURTAIN SLOWLY FALLS

ACT TWO

THE SCENE *is Amanda's flat in Paris. A few days have elapsed since Act One. The flat is charmingly furnished, its principal features being a Steinway Grand on the Left, facing slightly up stage. Down stage centre, a very large comfortable sofa, behind which is a small table. There is also another sofa somewhere about, and one or two small tables, and a gramophone. The rest can be left to the discretion and taste of the decorator.*

When the Curtain Rises it is about ten o'clock in the evening. The windows are wide open, and the various street sounds of Paris can be heard but not very loudly as the apartment is high up.

Amanda and Elyot are seated opposite one another at the table. They have finished dinner and are dallying over coffee and liqueurs. Amanda is wearing pajamas and Elyot a comfortable dressing-gown.

AMANDA: I'm glad we let Louise go. I am afraid she is going to have a cold.

ELYOT: Going to have a cold; she's been grunting and snorting all the evening like a whole herd of Bison.

AMANDA [*thoughtfully*]: Bison never sounds right to me somehow. I have a feeling it ought to be Bisons, a flock of Bisons.

ELYOT: You might say a covey of Bisons, or even a school of Bisons.

AMANDA: Yes, lovely. The Royal London School of Bisons. Do you think Louise is happy at home?

ELYOT: No, profoundly miserable.

AMANDA: Family beastly to her?

ELYOT [*with conviction*]: Absolutely vile. Knock her about dreadfully, I expect, make her eat the most disgusting food, and pull her fringe.

AMANDA [*laughing*]: Oh, poor Louise.

ELYOT: Well, you know what the French are.

AMANDA: Oh yes, indeed. I know what the Hungarians are too.

ELYOT: What are they?

AMANDA: Very wistful. It's all those pretzels I shouldn't wonder.

ELYOT: And the Poostza; I always felt the Poostza was far too big, Danube or no Danube.

AMANDA: Have you ever crossed the Sahara on a camel?

ELYOT: Frequently. When I was a boy we used to do it all the time. My grandmother had a lovely seat on a camel.

AMANDA: There's no doubt about it, foreign travel's the thing.

ELYOT: Would you like some brandy?

AMANDA: Just a little.

[*He pours some into her glass and some into his own.*]

ELYOT: I'm glad we didn't go out to-night.

AMANDA: Or last night.

ELYOT: Or the night before.

AMANDA: There's no reason to, really, when we're cosy here.

ELYOT: Exactly.

AMANDA: It's nice, isn't it?

ELYOT: Strangely peaceful. It's an awfully bad reflection on our characters. We ought to be absolutely tortured with conscience.

AMANDA: We are, every now and then.

ELYOT: Not nearly enough.

AMANDA: We sent Victor and Sibyl a nice note from wherever it was, what more can they want?

ELYOT: You're even more ruthless than I am.

AMANDA: I don't believe in crying over my bridge before I've eaten it.

ELYOT: Very sensible.

AMANDA: Personally I feel grateful for a miraculous escape. I know now that I should never have been happy with Victor. I was a fool ever to consider it.

ELYOT: You did a little more than consider it.

AMANDA: Well, you can't talk.

ELYOT: I wonder whether they met each other, or whether they've been suffering alone.

AMANDA: Oh dear, don't let's go on about it, it really does make one feel rather awful.

ELYOT: I suppose one or other or both of them will turn up here eventually.

AMANDA: Bound to; it won't be very nice, will it?

ELYOT [*cheerfully*]: Perfectly horrible.

AMANDA: Do you realise that we're living in sin?

ELYOT: Not according to the Catholics. Catholics don't recognise divorce. We're married as much as ever we were.

AMANDA: Yes, dear, but we're not Catholics.

ELYOT: Never mind, it's nice to think they'd sort of back us up. We were married in the eyes of Heaven, and we still are.

AMANDA: We may be all right in the eyes of Heaven, but we look like being in the hell of a mess socially.

ELYOT: Who cares?

AMANDA: Are we going to marry again, after Victor and Sibyl divorce us?

ELYOT: I suppose so. What do you think?

AMANDA: I feel rather scared of marriage really.

ELYOT: It is a frowzy business.

AMANDA: I believe it was just the fact of our being married, and clamped together publicly, that wrecked us before.

ELYOT: That, and not knowing how to manage each other.

AMANDA: Do you think we know how to manage each other now?

ELYOT: This week's been very successful. We've hardly used Solomon Isaacs at all.

AMANDA: Solomon Isaacs is so long, let's shorten it to Sollocks.

ELYOT: All right.

AMANDA: Darling, you do look awfully sweet in your little dressing-gown.

ELYOT: Yes, it's pretty ravishing, isn't it?

AMANDA: Do you mind if I come round and kiss you?

ELYOT: A pleasure, Lady Agatha.

[*Amanda comes round the table, kisses him, picks up the coffee pot, and returns to her chair.*]

AMANDA: What fools we were to subject ourselves to five years' unnecessary suffering.

ELYOT: Perhaps it wasn't unnecessary, perhaps it mellowed and perfected us like beautiful ripe fruit.

AMANDA: When we were together, did you really think I was unfaithful to you?

ELYOT: Yes, practically every day.

AMANDA: I thought you were too; often I used to torture myself with visions of your bouncing about on divans with awful widows.

ELYOT: Why widows?

AMANDA: I was thinking of Claire Lavenham really.

ELYOT: Oh Claire.

AMANDA [*sharply*]: What did you say "Oh Claire" like that for? It sounded far too careless to me.

ELYOT [*wistfully*]: What a lovely creature she was.

AMANDA: Lovely, lovely, lovely!

ELYOT [*blowing her a kiss*]: Darling!

AMANDA: Did you ever have an affair with her? Afterwards I mean?

ELYOT: Why do you want to know?

AMANDA: Curiosity, I suppose.

ELYOT: Dangerous.

AMANDA: Oh not now, not dangerous now. I wouldn't expect you to have been celibate during those five years, any more than I was.

ELYOT [*jumping*]: What?

AMANDA: After all, Claire was undeniably attractive. A trifle over vivacious I always thought, but that was probably because she was fundamentally stupid.

ELYOT: What do you mean about not being celibate during those five years?

AMANDA: What do you think I mean?

ELYOT: Oh God! [*He looks down miserably.*]

AMANDA: What's the matter?

ELYOT: You know perfectly well what's the matter.

AMANDA [*gently*]: You mustn't be unreasonable, I was only trying to stamp out the memory of you. I expect your affairs well outnumbered mine anyhow.

ELYOT: That is a little different. I'm a man.

AMANDA: Excuse me a moment while I get a caraway biscuit and change my crinoline.

ELYOT: It doesn't suit women to be promiscuous.

AMANDA: It doesn't suit men for women to be promiscuous.

ELYOT [*with sarcasm*]: Very modern dear; really your advanced views quite startle me.

AMANDA: Don't be cross, Elyot, I haven't been so dreadfully

loose actually. Five years is a long time, and even if I did nip off with someone every now and again, they were none of them very serious.

ELYOT [*rising from the table and walking away*]: Oh, do stop it please——

AMANDA: Well, what about you?

ELYOT: Do you want me to tell you?

AMANDA: No, no, I don't—I take everything back—I don't.

ELYOT [*viciously*]: I was madly in love with a woman in South Africa.

AMANDA: Did she have a ring through her nose?

ELYOT: Don't be revolting.

AMANDA: We're tormenting one another. Sit down, sweet, I'm scared.

ELYOT [*slowly*]: Very well. [*He sits down thoughtfully.*]

AMANDA: We should have said Sollocks ages ago.

ELYOT: We're in love all right.

AMANDA: Don't say it so bitterly. Let's try to get the best out of it this time, instead of the worst.

ELYOT [*stretching his hand across the table*]: Hand, please.

AMANDA [*clasping it*]: Here.

ELYOT: More comfortable?

AMANDA: Much more.

ELYOT [*after a slight pause*]: Are you engaged for this dance?

AMANDA: Funnily enough I was, but my partner was suddenly taken ill.

ELYOT [*rising and going to the gramophone*]: It's this damned smallpox epidemic.

AMANDA: No, as a matter of fact it was kidney trouble.

ELYOT: You'll dance it with me, I hope?

AMANDA [*rising*]: I shall be charmed.

ELYOT [*as they dance*]: Quite a good floor, isn't it?

AMANDA: Yes, I think it needs a little Borax.

ELYOT: I love Borax.

AMANDA: Is that the Grand Duchess Olga lying under the piano?

ELYOT: Yes, her husband died a few weeks ago, you know, on his way back from Pulborough. So sad.

AMANDA: What on earth was he doing in Pulborough?

ELYOT: Nobody knows exactly, but there have been the usual stories.

AMANDA: I see.

ELYOT: Delightful parties Lady Bundle always gives, doesn't she?

AMANDA: Entrancing. Such a dear old lady.

ELYOT: And so gay. Did you notice her at supper blowing all those shrimps through her ear trumpet?

[*The tune comes to an end. Amanda sits on the edge of the sofa, pensively.*]

ELYOT: What are you thinking about?

AMANDA: Nothing in particular.

ELYOT: Come on, I know that face.

AMANDA: Poor Sibyl.

ELYOT: Sibyl?

AMANDA: Yes, I suppose she loves you terribly.

ELYOT: Not as much as all that, she didn't have a chance to get really under way.

AMANDA: I expect she's dreadfully unhappy.

ELYOT: Oh, do shut up, Amanda, we've had all that out before.

AMANDA: We've certainly been pretty busy trying to justify ourselves.

ELYOT: It isn't a question of justifying ourselves, it's the true values of the situation that are really important. The moment we saw one another again we knew it was no use going on. We knew it instantly really, although we tried to pretend to ourselves that we didn't. What we've got to be thankful for is that we made the break straight away, and not later.

AMANDA: You think we should have done it anyhow?

ELYOT: Of course, and things would have been in a worse mess than they are now.

AMANDA: And what if we'd never happened to meet again? Would you have been quite happy with Sibyl?

ELYOT: I expect so.

AMANDA: Oh, Elyot!

ELYOT: You needn't look so stricken. It would have been the same with you and Victor. Life would have been smooth, and amicable, and quite charming, wouldn't it?

AMANDA: Poor dear Victor. He certainly did love me.

ELYOT: Splendid.

AMANDA: When I met him I was so lonely and depressed, I felt that I was getting old, and crumbling away unwanted.

ELYOT: It certainly is horrid when one begins to crumble.

AMANDA [wistfully]: He used to look at me hopelessly like a lovely spaniel, and I sort of melted like snow in the sunlight.

ELYOT: That must have been an edifying spectacle.

AMANDA: Victor really had a great charm.

ELYOT: You must tell me all about it.

AMANDA: He had a positive mania for looking after me, and protecting me.

ELYOT: That would have died down in time, dear.

AMANDA: You mustn't be rude, there's no necessity to be rude.

ELYOT: I wasn't in the least rude, I merely made a perfectly rational statement.

AMANDA: Your voice was decidedly bitter.

ELYOT: Victor had glorious legs, hadn't he? And fascinating ears.

AMANDA: Don't be silly.

ELYOT: He probably looked radiant in the morning, all flushed and tumbled on the pillow.

AMANDA: I never saw him on a pillow.

ELYOT: I'm surprised to hear it.

AMANDA [*angrily*]: Elyot!

ELYOT: There's no need to be cross.

AMANDA: What did you mean by that?

ELYOT: I'm sick of listening to you yap, yap, yap, yap, yap, yapping about Victor.

AMANDA: Now listen, Elyot, once and for all——

ELYOT: Oh my dear, Sollocks! Sollocks!—two minutes—Sollocks.

AMANDA: But——

ELYOT [*firmly*]: Sollocks!

[*They sit in dead silence, looking at each other. Amanda makes a sign that she wants a cigarette. Elyot gets up, hands her the box, and lights one for her and himself. Amanda rises and walks over to the window, and stands there, looking out for a moment. Presently Elyot joins her. She slips her arm through his, and they kiss lightly. They draw the curtains and then come down and sit side by side on the sofa. Elyot looks at his watch. Amanda raises her eyebrows at him and he nods, then they both sigh, audibly.*]
That was a near thing.

AMANDA: It was my fault. I'm terribly sorry, darling.

ELYOT: I was very irritating, I know I was. I'm sure Victor was awfully nice, and you're perfectly right to be sweet about him.

AMANDA: That's downright handsome of you. Sweetheart! [*She kisses him.*]

ELYOT [*leaning back with her on the sofa*]: I think I love you more than ever before. Isn't it ridiculous? Put your feet up.

[*She puts her legs across his, and they snuggle back together in the corner of the sofa, his head resting on her shoulder.*]

AMANDA: Comfortable?

ELYOT: Almost, wait a minute. [*He struggles a bit and then settles down with a sigh.*]

AMANDA: How long, Oh Lord, how long?

ELYOT [*drowsily*]: What do you mean, "how long, Oh Lord, how long?"

AMANDA: This is far too perfect to last.

ELYOT: You have no faith, that's what's wrong with you.

AMANDA: Absolutely none.

ELYOT: Don't you believe in——? [*He nods upwards.*]

AMANDA: No, do you?

ELYOT [*shaking his head*]: No. What about——? [*He points downwards.*]

AMANDA: Oh, dear no.

ELYOT: Don't you believe in anything?

AMANDA: Oh yes, I believe in being kind to everyone, and giving money to old beggar women, and being as gay as possible.

ELYOT: What about after we're dead?

AMANDA: I think a rather gloomy merging into everything, don't you?

ELYOT: I hope not, I'm a bad merger.

AMANDA: You won't know a thing about it.

ELYOT: I hope for a glorious oblivion, like being under gas.

AMANDA: I always dream the most peculiar things under gas.

ELYOT: Would you be young always? If you could choose?

AMANDA: No, I don't think so, not if it meant having awful bull's glands popped into me.

ELYOT: Cows for you dear. Bulls for me.

AMANDA: We certainly live in a marvellous age.

ELYOT: Too marvellous. It's all right if you happen to be a

specialist at something, then you're too concentrated to pay attention to all the other things going on. But, for the ordinary observer, it's too much.

AMANDA [*snuggling closer*]: Far, far too much.

ELYOT: Take the radio for instance.

AMANDA: Oh darling, don't let's take the radio.

ELYOT: Well, aeroplanes then, and Cosmic Atoms, and Television, and those gland injections we were talking about just now.

AMANDA: It must be so nasty for the poor animals, being experimented on.

ELYOT: Not when the experiments are successful. Why in Vienna I believe you can see whole lines of decrepit old rats carrying on like Tiller Girls.

AMANDA [*laughing*]: Oh, how very, very sweet.

ELYOT [*burying his face in her shoulder*]: I do love you so.

AMANDA: Don't blow, dear heart, it gives me the shivers.

ELYOT [*trying to kiss her*]: Swivel your face round a bit more.

AMANDA [*obliging*]: That better?

ELYOT [*kissing her lingeringly*]: Very nice, thank you kindly.

AMANDA [*twining her arms round his neck*]: Darling, you're so terribly, terribly dear, and sweet, and attractive. [*She pulls his head down to her again and they kiss lovingly.*]

ELYOT [*softly*]: We were raving mad, ever to part, even for an instant.

AMANDA: Utter imbeciles.

ELYOT: I realised it almost immediately, didn't you?

AMANDA: Long before we got our decree.

ELYOT: My heart broke on that damned trip round the world. I saw such beautiful things, darling. Moonlight shining on old temples, strange barbaric dances in jungle villages, scarlet flamingoes flying over deep, deep blue water. Breathlessly lovely, and completely unexciting because you weren't there to see them with me.

AMANDA [*kissing him again*]: Take me, please, take me at once, let's make up for lost time.

ELYOT: Next week?

AMANDA: To-morrow.

ELYOT: Done.

AMANDA: I must see those dear flamingoes. [*There is a pause.*] Eight years, all told, we've loved each other. Three married and five divorced.

ELYOT: Angel. Angel. Angel. [*He kisses her passionately.*]

AMANDA [*struggling slightly*]: No, Elyot, stop now, stop——

ELYOT: Why should I stop? You know you adore being made love to.

AMANDA [*through his kisses*]: It's so soon after dinner.

ELYOT [*jumping up rather angrily*]: You really do say most awful things.

AMANDA [*tidying her hair*]: I don't see anything particularly awful about that.

ELYOT: No sense of glamour, no sense of glamour at all.

AMANDA: It's difficult to feel really glamorous with a crick in the neck.

ELYOT: Why didn't you say you had a crick in your neck?

AMANDA [*sweetly*]: It's gone now.

ELYOT: How convenient. [*He lights a cigarette.*]

AMANDA [*holding out her hand*]: I want one, please.

ELYOT [*throwing her one*]: Here.

AMANDA: Match?

ELYOT [*impatiently*]: Wait a minute, can't you?

AMANDA: Chivalrous little love.

ELYOT [*throwing the matches at her*]: Here.

AMANDA [*coldly*]: Thank you very much indeed. [*There is a silence for a moment.*]

ELYOT: You really can be more irritating than anyone in the world.

AMANDA: I fail to see what I've done that's so terribly irritating.

ELYOT: You have no tact.

AMANDA: Tact. You have no consideration.

ELYOT [*walking up and down*]: Too soon after dinner indeed.

AMANDA: Yes, much too soon.

ELYOT: That sort of remark shows rather a common sort of mind, I'm afraid.

AMANDA: Oh it does, does it?

ELYOT: Very unpleasant, makes me shudder.

AMANDA: Making all this fuss just because your silly vanity is a little upset.

ELYOT: Vanity? What do you mean, vanity?

AMANDA: You can't bear the thought that there are certain moments when our chemical, what d'you call 'ems, don't fuse properly.

ELYOT [*derisively*]: Chemical what d'you call 'ems? Please try to be more explicit.

AMANDA: You know perfectly well what I mean, and don't try to patronize me.

ELYOT [*loudly*]: Now look here, Amanda——

AMANDA [*suddenly*]: Darling Sollocks! Oh, for God's sake, Sollocks!

ELYOT: But listen——

AMANDA: Sollocks, Sollocks. Oh dear—triple Sollocks!

[*They stand looking at one another in silence for a moment, then Amanda flings herself down on the sofa and buries her face in the cushions. Elyot looks at her, then goes over to the piano. He sits down and begins to play idly. Amanda raises her head, screws herself round on the sofa, and lies there listening. Elyot blows a kiss to her and goes on playing. He starts to sing softly to her, never taking his eyes off her. When he has finished the little refrain, whatever it was, he still continues to play it looking at her.*]

AMANDA: Big romantic stuff, darling.

ELYOT [*smiling*]: Yes, big romantic stuff.

[*He wanders off into another tune. Amanda sits up cross-legged on the sofa, and begins to sing it, then, still singing, she comes over and perches on the piano. They sing several old refrains from dead and gone musical comedies, finishing with the song that brought them together again in the first Act. Finally Amanda comes down and sits next to him on the piano stool, they both therefore have their backs half turned to the audience. She rests her head on his shoulder, until finally his fingers drop off the keys, and they melt into one another's arms.*]

ELYOT [*after a moment*]: You're the most thrilling, exciting woman that was ever born.

AMANDA [*standing up, and brushing her hand lightly over his mouth*]: Dearest, dearest heart——

[*He catches at her hand and kisses it, and then her arm, until he is standing up, embracing her ardently. She struggles a little, half laughing, and breaks away, but he catches her, and they finish up on the sofa again, clasped in each other's arms, both completely given up to the passion of the moment, until the telephone bell rings violently, and they both spring apart.*]

ELYOT: Good God!

AMANDA: Do you think it's them?

ELYOT: I wonder.

AMANDA: Nobody knows we're here except Freda, and she wouldn't ring up.

ELYOT: It must be them then.

AMANDA: What are we to do?

ELYOT [*suddenly*]: We're all right, darling, aren't we—whatever happens?

AMANDA: Now and always, Sweet.

ELYOT: I don't care then. [*He gets up and goes defiantly over to the telephone, which has been ringing incessantly during the little preceding scene.*]

AMANDA: It was bound to come sooner or later.

ELYOT [*at telephone*]: Hallo—hallo—what—comment? Madame, qui? 'allo—'allo—oui c'est ça. Oh, Madame Duvallon —Oui, oui, oui. [*He puts his hand over the mouthpiece.*] It's only somebody wanting to talk to the dear Madame Duvallon.

AMANDA: Who's she?

ELYOT: I haven't the faintest idea. [*At telephone*]: Je regrette beaucoup monsieur, mais Madame Duvallon viens de partir— cette après midi, pour Madagascar. [*He hangs up the telephone.*] Whew; that gave me a fright.

AMANDA: It sent shivers up my spine.

ELYOT: What shall we do if they suddenly walk in on us?

AMANDA: Behave exquisitely.

ELYOT: With the most perfect poise?

AMANDA: Certainly. I shall probably do a Court Curtsey.

ELYOT [*sitting on the edge of the sofa*]: Things that ought to matter dreadfully, don't matter at all when one's happy, do they?

AMANDA: What is so horrible is that one can't stay happy.

ELYOT: Darling, don't say that.

AMANDA: It's true. The whole business is a very poor joke.

ELYOT: Meaning that sacred and beautiful thing, Love?

AMANDA: Yes, meaning just that.

ELYOT [*striding up and down the room dramatically*]: What does it all mean, that's what I ask myself in my ceaseless quest for ultimate truth. Dear God, what does it all mean?

AMANDA: Don't laugh at me, I'm serious.

ELYOT [*seriously*]: You mustn't be serious, my dear one, it's just what they want.

AMANDA: Who's they?

ELYOT: All the futile moralists who try to make life unbearable. Laugh at them. Be flippant. Laugh at everything, all their sacred shibboleths. Flippancy brings out the acid in their damned sweetness and light.

AMANDA: If I laugh at everything, I must laugh at us too.

ELYOT: Certainly you must. We're figures of fun all right.

AMANDA: How long will it last, this ludicrous, overbearing love of ours?

ELYOT: Who knows?

AMANDA: Shall we always want to bicker and fight?

ELYOT: No, that desire will fade, along with our passion.

AMANDA: Oh dear, shall we like that?

ELYOT: It all depends on how well we've played.

AMANDA: What happens if one of us dies? Does the one that's left still laugh?

ELYOT: Yes, yes, with all his might.

AMANDA [*wistfully clutching his hand*]: That's serious enough, isn't it?

ELYOT: No, no, it isn't. Death's very laughable, such a cunning little mystery. All done with mirrors.

AMANDA: Darling, I believe you're talking nonsense.

ELYOT: So is everyone else in the long run. Let's be superficial and pity the poor philosophers. Let's blow trumpets and squeakers, and enjoy the party as much as we can, like very small, quite idiotic school-children. Let's savour the delight of the moment. Come and kiss me, darling, before your body rots, and worms pop in and out of your eye sockets.

AMANDA: Elyot, worms don't pop.

ELYOT [*kissing her*]: I don't mind what you do, see? You can paint yourself bright green all over, and dance naked in the Place Vendôme, and rush off madly with all the men in the world, and I shan't say a word, as long as you love me best.

AMANDA: Thank you, dear. The same applies to you, except that if I catch you so much as looking at another woman, I'll kill you.

ELYOT: Do you remember that awful scene we had in Venice?

AMANDA: Which particular one?

ELYOT: The one when you bought that little painted wooden snake on the Piazza, and put it on my bed.

AMANDA: Oh, Charles. That was his name, Charles. He did wriggle so beautifully.

ELYOT: Horrible thing, I hated it.

AMANDA: Yes, I know you did. You threw it out of the window into the Grand Canal. I don't think I'll ever forgive you for that.

ELYOT: How long did the row last?

AMANDA: It went on intermittently for days.

ELYOT: The worst one was in Cannes when your curling irons burnt a hole in my new dressing-gown. [*He laughs.*]

AMANDA: It burnt my comb too, and all the towels in the bathroom.

ELYOT: That was a rouser, wasn't it?

AMANDA: That was the first time you ever hit me.

ELYOT: I didn't hit you very hard.

AMANDA: The manager came in and found us rolling on the floor, biting and scratching like panthers. Oh dear, oh dear—— [*She laughs helplessly.*]

ELYOT: I shall never forget his face. [*They both collapse with laughter.*]

AMANDA: How ridiculous, how utterly, utterly ridiculous.

ELYOT: We were very much younger then.

AMANDA: And very much sillier.

ELYOT: As a matter of fact the real cause of that row was Peter Burden.

AMANDA: You knew there was nothing in that.

ELYOT: I didn't know anything of the sort, you took presents from him.

AMANDA: Presents: only a trivial little brooch.

ELYOT: I remember it well, bristling with diamonds. In the worst possible taste.

AMANDA: Not at all, it was very pretty. I still have it, and I wear it often.

ELYOT: You went out of your way to torture me over Peter Burden.

AMANDA: No, I didn't, you worked the whole thing up in your jealous imagination.

ELYOT: You must admit that he was in love with you, wasn't he?

AMANDA: Just a little perhaps. Nothing serious.

ELYOT: You let him kiss you. You said you did.

AMANDA: Well, what of it?

ELYOT: What of it!

AMANDA: It gave him a lot of pleasure, and it didn't hurt me.

ELYOT: What about me?

AMANDA: If you hadn't been so suspicious and nosy you'd never have known a thing about it.

ELYOT: That's a nice point of view, I must say.

AMANDA: Oh dear, I'm bored with this conversation.

ELYOT: So am I, bored stiff. [*He goes over to the table.*] Want some brandy?

AMANDA: No thanks.

ELYOT: I'll have a little, I think.

AMANDA: I don't see why you want it, you've already had two glasses.

ELYOT: No particular reason, anyhow they were very small ones.

AMANDA: It seems so silly to go on, and on, and on with a thing.

ELYOT [*pouring himself out a glassful*]: You can hardly call three liqueur glasses in a whole evening going on, and on, and on.

AMANDA: It's become a habit with you.

ELYOT: You needn't be so grand, just because you don't happen to want any yourself at the moment.

AMANDA: Don't be so stupid.

ELYOT [*irritably*]: Really, Amanda——

AMANDA: What?

ELYOT: Nothing.

[*Amanda sits down on the sofa, and, taking a small mirror from her bag, gazes at her face critically, and then uses some lipstick and powder. A trifle nastily.*]

Going out somewhere, dear?

AMANDA: No, just making myself fascinating for you.

ELYOT: That reply has broken my heart.

AMANDA: The woman's job is to allure the man. Watch me a minute, will you?

ELYOT: As a matter of fact that's perfectly true.

AMANDA: Oh, no, it isn't.

ELYOT: Yes it is.

AMANDA [*snappily*]: Oh be quiet.

ELYOT: It's a pity you didn't have any more brandy; it might have made you a little less disagreeable.

AMANDA: It doesn't seem to have worked such wonders with you.

ELYOT: Snap, snap, snap; like a little adder.

AMANDA: Adders don't snap, they sting.

ELYOT: Nonsense, they have a little bag of venom behind their fangs and they snap.

AMANDA: They sting.

ELYOT: They snap.

AMANDA [*with exasperation*]: I don't care, do you understand? I don't care. I don't mind if they bark, and roll about like hoops.

ELYOT [*after a slight pause*]: Did you see much of Peter Burden after our divorce?

AMANDA: Yes, I did, quite a lot.

ELYOT: I suppose you let him kiss you a good deal more then.

AMANDA: Mind your own business.

ELYOT: You must have had a riotous time. [*Amanda doesn't answer, so he stalks about the room.*] No restraint at all—very enjoyable—you never had much anyhow.

AMANDA: You're quite insufferable; I expect it's because you're drunk.

ELYOT: I'm not in the least drunk.

AMANDA: You always had a weak head.

ELYOT: I think I mentioned once before that I have only had three minute liqueur glasses of brandy the whole evening long. A child of two couldn't get drunk on that.

AMANDA: On the contrary, a child of two could get violently drunk on only one glass of brandy.

ELYOT: Very interesting. How about a child of four, and a child of six, and a child of nine?

AMANDA [*turning her head away*]: Oh do shut up.

ELYOT [*witheringly*]: We might get up a splendid little debate about that, you know, Intemperate Tots.

AMANDA: Not very funny, dear; you'd better have some more brandy.

ELYOT: Very good idea, I will. [*He pours out another glass and gulps it down defiantly.*]

AMANDA: Ridiculous ass.

ELYOT: I beg your pardon?

AMANDA: I said ridiculous ass!

ELYOT [*with great dignity*]: Thank you.

[*There is a silence. Amanda gets up, and turns the gramophone on.*]

You'd better turn that off, I think.

AMANDA: [*coldly*]: Why?

ELYOT: It's very late and it will annoy the people upstairs.

AMANDA: There aren't any people upstairs. It's a photographer's studio.

ELYOT: There are people downstairs, I suppose?

AMANDA: They're away in Tunis.

ELYOT: This is no time of the year for Tunis. [*He turns the gramophone off.*]

AMANDA [*icily*]: Turn it on again, please.

ELYOT: I'll do no such thing.

AMANDA: Very well, if you insist on being boorish and idiotic. [*She gets up and turns it on again.*]

ELYOT: Turn it off. It's driving me mad.

AMANDA: You're far too temperamental. Try to control yourself.

ELYOT: Turn it off.

AMANDA: I won't.

[*Elyot rushes at the gramophone. Amanda tries to ward him off. They struggle silently for a moment then the needle screeches across the record.*]

There now, you've ruined the record. [*She takes it off and scrutinises it.*]

ELYOT: Good job, too.

AMANDA: Disagreeable pig.

ELYOT [*suddenly stricken with remorse*]: Amanda darling—Sollocks.

AMANDA [*furiously*]: Sollocks yourself. [*She breaks the record over his head.*]

ELYOT [*staggering*]: You spiteful little beast. [*He slaps her face. She screams loudly and hurls herself sobbing with rage on to the sofa, with her face buried in the cushions.*]

AMANDA [*wailing*]: Oh, oh, oh——

ELYOT: I'm sorry, I didn't mean it—I'm sorry, darling, I swear I didn't mean it.

AMANDA: Go away, go away, I hate you.

[*Elyot kneels on the sofa and tries to pull her round to look at him.*]

ELYOT: Amanda—listen—listen——

AMANDA [*turning suddenly, and fetching him a welt across the face*]: Listen indeed; I'm sick and tired of listening to you, you damned sadistic bully.

ELYOT [*with great grandeur*]: Thank you. [*He stalks towards the door, in stately silence. Amanda throws a cushion at him, which misses him and knocks down a lamp and a vase on the side table.*] [*Elyot laughs falsely.*] A pretty display, I must say.

AMANDA [*wildly*]: Stop laughing like that.

ELYOT [*continuing*]: Very amusing indeed.

AMANDA [*losing control*]: Stop—stop—stop— [*She rushes at him, he grabs her hands and they sway about the room, until he manages to twist her round by the arms so that she faces him, closely, quivering with fury.*] I hate you—do you hear? You're conceited, and overbearing, and utterly impossible!

ELYOT [*shouting her down*]: You're a vile-tempered, loose-living wicked little beast, and I never want to see you again so long as I live.

[*He flings her away from him, she staggers and falls against a chair. They stand gaping at one another in silence for a moment.*]

AMANDA [*very quietly*]: This is the end, do you understand? The end, finally and forever.

[*She goes to the door, which opens on to the landing, and wrenches it open. He rushes after her and clutches her wrist.*]

ELYOT: You're not going like this.

AMANDA: Oh yes I am.

ELYOT: You're not.

AMANDA: I am; let go of me—— [*He pulls her away from the door, and once more they struggle. This time a standard lamp crashes to the ground. Amanda, breathlessly, as they fight*]: You're a cruel fiend, and I hate and loathe you; thank God I've realized in time what you're really like; marry you again, never, never, never. . . . I'd rather die in torment——

ELYOT [*at the same time*]: Shut up; shut up. I wouldn't marry you again if you came crawling to me on your bended knees, you're a mean, evil-minded little vampire—I hope to God I never set eyes on you again as long as I live——

[*At this point in the proceedings they trip over a piece of carpet, and fall on to the floor, rolling over and over in paroxysms of rage. Victor and Sibyl enter quietly, through the open door, and stand staring at them in horror. Finally Amanda breaks free and half gets up, Elyot grabs her leg, and she falls against a table, knocking it completely over.*]

AMANDA [*screaming*]: Beast; brute; swine; cad; beast; beast; brute; devil——

[*She rushes back at Elyot who is just rising to his feet, and gives him a stinging blow, which knocks him over again. She rushes blindly off Left, and slams the door, at the same moment that he jumps up and rushes off Right, also slamming the door. Victor and Sibyl advance apprehensively into the room, and sink on to the sofa.*]

THE CURTAIN FALLS

ACT THREE

THE SCENE *is the same as Act Two. It is the next morning. The time is about eight-thirty. Victor and Sibyl have drawn the two sofas across the doors Right, and Left, and are stretched on them, asleep. Victor is in front of Amanda's door, and Sibyl in front of Elyot's. The room is in chaos, as it was left the night before. As the curtain rises, there is the rattling of a key in the lock of the front door, and Louise enters. She is rather a frowzy looking girl, and carries a string bag with various bundles of eatables crammed into it, notably a long roll of bread, and a lettuce. She closes the door after her, and in the half light trips over the standard lamp lying on the floor. She puts her string bag down, and gropes her way over to the window. She draws the curtains, letting sunlight stream into the room. When she looks round, she gives a little cry of horror. Then she sees Victor and Sibyl sleeping peacefully, and comes over and scrutinises each of them with care, then she shakes Sibyl by the shoulder.*

SIBYL [*waking*]: Oh dear.

LOUISE: Bonjour, madame.

SIBYL [*bewildered*]: What?—Oh—bonjour.

LOUISE: Qu'est-ce que vous faites ici, madame?

SIBYL: What—what?—Wait a moment, attendez un instant—oh dear——

VICTOR [*sleepily*]: What's happening? [*Jumping up.*] Of course, I remember now. [*He sees Louise.*] Oh!

LOUISE [*firmly*]: Bonjour, monsieur.

VICTOR: Er—bonjour. What time is it?

LOUISE [*rather dully*]: Eh, monsieur?

SIBYL [*sitting up on the sofa*]: Quelle heure est-il s'il vous plaît?

LOUISE: C'est neuf heures moins dix, madame.

VICTOR: What did she say?

SIBYL: I think she said nearly ten o'clock.

VICTOR [*taking situation in hand*]: Er—voulez—er—wake—reveillez Monsieur et Madame—er—toute suite?

LOUISE [*shaking her head*]: Non, monsieur. Il m'est absolument défendu de les appeler jusqu'à ce qu'ils sonnent. [*She takes her bag and goes off into the kitchen.*]

[*Victor and Sibyl look at each other helplessly.*]

SIBYL: What are we to do?

VICTOR [*with determination*]: Wake them ourselves. [*He goes towards Amanda's door.*]

SIBYL: No, no, wait a minute.

VICTOR: What's the matter?

SIBYL [*plaintively*]: I couldn't face them yet, really, I couldn't; I feel dreadful.

VICTOR: So do I. [*He wanders gloomily over to the window.*] It's a lovely morning.

SIBYL: Lovely. [*She bursts into tears.*]

VICTOR [*coming to her*]: I say, don't cry.

SIBYL: I can't help it.

VICTOR: Please don't, please——

SIBYL: It's all so squalid, I wish we hadn't stayed; what's the use?

VICTOR: We've got to see them before we go back to England, we must get things straightened out.

SIBYL [*sinking down on to the sofa*]: Oh dear, oh dear, oh dear, I wish I were dead.

VICTOR: Hush, now, hush. Remember your promise. We've got to see this through together and get it settled one way or another.

SIBYL [*sniffling*]: I'll try to control myself, only I'm so . . . so tired, I haven't slept properly for ages.

VICTOR: Neither have I.

SIBYL: If we hadn't arrived when we did, they'd have killed one another.

VICTOR: They must have been drunk.

SIBYL: She hit him.

VICTOR: He'd probably hit her, too, earlier on.

SIBYL: I'd no idea anyone ever behaved like that; it's so disgusting, so degrading. Elli of all people—oh dear——[*She almost breaks down again, but controls herself.*]

VICTOR: What an escape you've had.

SIBYL: What an escape we've both had.

[*Amanda opens her door and looks out. She is wearing travelling clothes, and is carrying a small suitcase. She jumps, upon seeing Sibyl and Victor.*]

AMANDA: Oh!—good morning.

VICTOR [*with infinite reproach in his voice*]: Oh, Amanda.

AMANDA: Will you please move this sofa, I can't get out.

[*Victor moves the sofa, and she advances into the room and goes towards the door.*]

VICTOR: Where are you going?

AMANDA: Away.

VICTOR: You can't.

AMANDA: Why not?

VICTOR: I want to talk to you.

AMANDA [*wearily*]: What on earth is the use of that?

VICTOR: I must talk to you.

AMANDA: Well, all I can say is, it's very inconsiderate. [*She plumps the bag down by the door and comes down to Victor.*]

VICTOR: Mandy, I——

AMANDA [*gracefully determined to rise above the situation*]: I suppose you're Sibyl; how do you do?

[*Sibyl turns her back on her.*]

Well, if you're going to take up that attitude, I fail to see the point of your coming here at all.

SIBYL: I came to see Elyot.

AMANDA: I've no wish to prevent you, he's in there, probably wallowing in an alcoholic stupor.

VICTOR: This is all very unpleasant, Amanda.

AMANDA: I quite agree, that's why I want to go away.

VICTOR: That would be shirking; this must be discussed at length.

AMANDA: Very well, if you insist, but not just now, I don't feel up to it. Has Louise come yet?

VICTOR: If Louise is the maid, she's in the kitchen.

AMANDA: Thank you. You'd probably like some coffee, excuse me a moment. [*She goes off into the kitchen.*]

SIBYL: Well! How dare she?

VICTOR [*irritably*]: How dare she what?

SIBYL: Behave so calmly, as though nothing had happened.

VICTOR: I don't see what else she could have done.

SIBYL: Insufferable I call it.

[*Elyot opens his door and looks out.*]

ELYOT [*seeing them*]: Oh God. [*He shuts the door again quickly.*]

SIBYL: Elyot—Elyot—— [*She rushes over to the door and bangs on it.*] Elyot—Elyot—Elyot——

ELYOT [*inside*]: Go away.

SIBYL [*falling on to the sofa*]: Oh, oh, oh. [*She bursts into tears again.*]

VICTOR: Do pull yourself together, for heaven's sake.

SIBYL: I can't, I can't—oh, oh, oh——

[*Amanda re-enters.*]

AMANDA: I've ordered some coffee and rolls, they'll be here soon. I must apologise for the room being so untidy. [*She picks up a cushion, and pats it into place on the sofa. There is a silence except for Sibyl's sobs. Amanda looks at her, and then at Victor; then she goes off into her room again, and shuts the door.*]

VICTOR: It's no use crying like that, it doesn't do any good.

[*After a moment, during which Sibyl makes renewed efforts to control her tears, Elyot opens the door immediately behind her, pushes the sofa, with her on it, out of the way, and walks towards the front door. He is in travelling clothes, and carrying a small suitcase.*]

SIBYL [*rushing after him*]: Elyot, where are you going?

ELYOT: Canada.

SIBYL: You can't go like this, you can't.

ELYOT: I see no point in staying.

VICTOR: You owe it to Sibyl to stay.

ELYOT: How do you do, I don't think we've met before.

SIBYL: You must stay, you've got to stay.

ELYOT: Very well, if you insist. [*He plumps his bag down.*] I'm afraid the room is in rather a mess. Have you seen the maid Louise?

VICTOR: She's in the kitchen.

ELYOT: Good. I'll order some coffee. [*He makes a movement towards the kitchen.*]

VICTOR [*stopping him*]: No, your—er—my—er—Amanda has already ordered it.

ELYOT: Oh, I'm glad the old girl's up and about.

VICTOR: We've got to get things straightened out, you know.

ELYOT [*looking around the room*]: Yes, it's pretty awful. We'll get the concierge up from downstairs.

VICTOR: You're being purposely flippant, but it's no good.

ELYOT: Sorry. [*He lapses into silence.*]

VICTOR [*after a pause*]: What's to be done?

ELYOT: I don't know.

SIBYL [*with spirit*]: It's all perfectly horrible. I feel smirched and unclean as though slimy things had been crawling all over me.

ELYOT: Maybe they have, that's a very old sofa.

VICTOR: If you don't stop your damned flippancy, I'll knock your head off.

ELYOT [*raising his eyebrows*]: Has it ever struck you that flippancy might cover a very real embarrassment?

VICTOR: In a situation such as this, it's in extremely bad taste.

ELYOT: No worse than bluster, and invective. As a matter of fact, as far as I know, this situation is entirely without precedent. We have no prescribed etiquette to fall back upon. I shall continue to be flippant.

SIBYL: Oh Elyot, how can you—how can you?

ELYOT: I'm awfully sorry, Sibyl.

VICTOR: It's easy enough to be sorry.

ELYOT: On the contrary, I find it exceedingly difficult. I seldom regret anything. This is a very rare and notable exception, a sort of red-letter day. We must all make the most of it.

SIBYL: I'll never forgive you, never. I wouldn't have believed anyone could be so callous and cruel.

ELYOT: I absolutely see your point, and as I said before, I'm sorry.

[*There is silence for a moment. Then Amanda comes in again. She has obviously decided to carry everything off in a high-handed manner.*]

AMANDA [*in social tones*]: What! Breakfast not ready yet? Really, these French servants are too slow for words. [*She smiles gaily.*] What a glorious morning. [*She goes to the window.*] I do love Paris, it's so genuinely gay. Those lovely trees in the Champs Élysées, and the little roundabouts for the children to play on, and those shiny red taxis. You can see Sacré Cœur quite clearly to-day, sometimes it's a bit misty, particularly in August, all the heat rising up from the pavements, you know.

ELYOT [*drily*]: Yes, dear, we know.

AMANDA [*ignoring him*]: And it's heavenly being so high up. I found this flat three years ago, quite by merest chance. I happened to be staying at the Plaza Athenee, just down the road——

ELYOT [*enthusiastically*]: Such a nice hotel, with the most enchanting courtyard with a fountain that goes plopplopplop-plopplopplopplopplopplopplop——

VICTOR: This is ridiculous, Amanda.

ELYOT [*continuing*]: Plop plop plop plop plop plop plop plop plop plop——

AMANDA [*overriding him*]: Now, Victor, I refuse to discuss anything in the least important until after breakfast. I couldn't concentrate now, I know I couldn't.

ELYOT [*sarcastically*]: What manner. What poise. How I envy it. To be able to carry off the most embarrassing situation with such tact, and delicacy, and above all—such subtlety. Go on, Amanda, you're making everything so much easier. We shall all be playing Hunt the Slipper in a minute.

AMANDA: Please don't address me, I don't wish to speak to you.

ELYOT: Splendid.

AMANDA: And what's more, I never shall again as long as I live.

ELYOT: I shall endeavour to rise above it.

AMANDA: I've been brought up to believe that it's beyond the pale, for a man to strike a woman.

ELYOT: A very poor tradition. Certain women should be struck regularly, like gongs.

AMANDA: You're an unmitigated cad, and a bully.

ELYOT: And you're an ill-mannered, bad-tempered slattern.

AMANDA [*loudly*]: Slattern indeed.

ELYOT: Yes, slattern, slattern, slattern, and fishwife.

VICTOR: Keep your mouth shut, you swine.

ELYOT: Mind your own damned business.

[*They are about to fight, when Sibyl rushes between them.*]

SIBYL: Stop, stop, it's no use going on like this. Stop, please.
[*To Amanda*]: Help me, do, do, do, help me——

AMANDA: I'm not going to interfere. Let them fight if they want to, it will probably clear the air anyhow.

SIBYL: Yes, but——

AMANDA: Come into my room, perhaps you'd like to wash or something.

SIBYL: No, but——

AMANDA [*firmly*]: Come along.

SIBYL: Very well.

[*She tosses her head at Elyot, and Amanda drags her off.*]

VICTOR [*belligerently*]: Now then!

ELYOT: Now then what?

VICTOR: Are you going to take back those things you said to Amanda?

ELYOT: Certainly, I'll take back anything, if only you'll stop bellowing at me.

VICTOR [*contemptuously*]: You're a coward too.

ELYOT: They want us to fight, don't you see?

VICTOR: No, I don't, why should they?

ELYOT: Primitive feminine instincts—warring males—very enjoyable.

VICTOR: You think you're very clever, don't you?

ELYOT: I think I'm a bit cleverer than you, but apparently that's not saying much.

VICTOR [*violently*]: What?

ELYOT: Oh, do sit down.

VICTOR: I will not.

ELYOT: Well, if you'll excuse me, I will, I'm extremely tired. [*He sits down.*]

VICTOR: Oh, for God's sake, behave like a man.

ELYOT [*patiently*]: Listen a minute, all this belligerency is very right and proper and highly traditional, but if only you'll think for a moment, you'll see that it won't get us very far.

VICTOR: To hell with all that.

ELYOT: I should like to explain that if you hit me, I shall certainly hit you, probably equally hard, if not harder. I'm just as strong as you, I should imagine. Then you'd hit me again, and I'd hit you again, and we'd go on until one or the other was knocked out. Now if you'll explain to me satisfactorily how all that can possibly improve the situation, I'll tear off my coat, and we'll go at one another hammer and tongs, immediately.

VICTOR: It would ease my mind.

ELYOT: Only if you won.

VICTOR: I should win all right.

ELYOT: Want to try?

VICTOR: Yes.

ELYOT [*jumping up*]: Here goes then—— [*He tears off his coat.*]

VICTOR: Just a moment.

ELYOT: Well?

VICTOR: What did you mean about them wanting us to fight?

ELYOT: It would be balm to their vanity.

VICTOR: Do you love Amanda?

ELYOT: Is this a battle or a discussion? If it's the latter I shall put on my coat again, I don't want to catch a chill.

VICTOR: Answer my question, please.

ELYOT: Have a cigarette?

VICTOR [*stormily*]: Answer my question.

ELYOT: If you analyse it, it's rather a silly question.

VICTOR: Do you love Amanda?

ELYOT [*confidentially*]: Not very much this morning, to be perfectly frank, I'd like to wring her neck. Do you love her?

VICTOR: That's beside the point.

ELYOT: On the contrary, it's the crux of the whole affair. If you do love her still, you can forgive her, and live with her in peace and harmony until you're ninety-eight.

VICTOR: You're apparently even more of a cad than I thought you were.

ELYOT: You are completely in the right over the whole business, don't imagine I'm not perfectly conscious of that.

VICTOR: I'm glad.

ELYOT: It's all very unfortunate.

VICTOR: Unfortunate? My God!

ELYOT: It might have been worse.

VICTOR: I'm glad you think so.

ELYOT: I do wish you'd stop about being so glad about everything.

VICTOR: What do you intend to do? That's what I want to know. What do you intend to do?

ELYOT [*suddenly serious*]: I don't know, I don't care.

VICTOR: I suppose you realise that you've broken that poor little woman's heart?

ELYOT: Which poor little woman?

VICTOR: Sibyl, of course.

ELYOT: Oh, come now, not as bad as that. She'll get over it, and forget all about me.

VICTOR: I sincerely hope so . . . for her sake.

ELYOT: Amanda will forget all about me too. Everybody will

forget all about me. I might just as well lie down and die in fearful pain and suffering, nobody would care.

VICTOR: Don't talk such rot.

ELYOT: You must forgive me for taking rather a gloomy view of everything but the fact is, I suddenly feel slightly depressed.

VICTOR: I intend to divorce Amanda, naming you as co-respondent.

ELYOT: Very well.

VICTOR: And Sibyl will divorce you for Amanda. It would be foolish of either of you to attempt any defence.

ELYOT: Quite.

VICTOR: And the sooner you marry Amanda again, the better.

ELYOT: I'm not going to marry Amanda.

VICTOR: What?

ELYOT: She's a vile tempered wicked woman.

VICTOR: You should have thought of that before.

ELYOT: I did think of it before.

VICTOR [*firmly*]: You've got to marry her.

ELYOT: I'd rather marry a ravening leopard.

VICTOR [*angrily*]: Now look here. I'm sick of all this shilly-shallying. You're getting off a good deal more lightly than you deserve; you can consider yourself damned lucky I didn't shoot you.

ELYOT [*with sudden vehemence*]: Well, if you'd had a spark of manliness in you, you would have shot me. You're all fuss and fume, one of these cotton-wool Englishmen. I despise you.

VICTOR [*through clenched teeth*]: You despise me?

ELYOT: Yes, utterly. You're nothing but a rampaging gas bag! [*He goes off into his room and slams the door, leaving Victor speechless with fury.*]

[*Amanda and Sibyl re-enter.*]

AMANDA [*brightly*]: Well, what's happened?

VICTOR [*sullenly*]: Nothing's happened.

AMANDA: You ought to be ashamed to admit it.

SIBYL: Where's Elyot?

VICTOR: In there.

AMANDA: What's he doing?

VICTOR [*turning angrily away*]: How do I know what he's doing?

AMANDA: If you were half the man I thought you were, he'd be bandaging himself.

SIBYL [*with defiance*]: Elyot's just as strong as Victor.

AMANDA [*savagely*]: I should like it proved.

SIBYL: There's no need to be so vindictive.

AMANDA: You were abusing Elyot like a pickpocket to me a little while ago, now you are standing up for him.

SIBYL: I'm beginning to suspect that he wasn't quite so much to blame as I thought.

AMANDA: Oh really?

SIBYL: You certainly have a very unpleasant temper.

AMANDA: It's a little difficult to keep up with your rapid changes of front, but you're young and inexperienced, so I forgive you freely.

SIBYL [*heatedly*]: Seeing the depths of degradation to which age and experience have brought you, I'm glad I'm as I am!

AMANDA [*with great grandeur*]: That was exceedingly rude. I think you'd better go away somewhere. [*She waves her hand vaguely.*]

SIBYL: After all, Elyot is my husband.

AMANDA: Take him with you, by all means.

SIBYL: If you're not very careful, I will! [*She goes over to Elyot's door and bangs on it.*] Elyot—Elyot——

ELYOT [*inside*]: What is it?

SIBYL: Let me in. Please, please let me in; I want to speak to you!

AMANDA: Heaven preserve me from nice women!

SIBYL: Your own reputation ought to do that.

AMANDA [*irritably*]: Oh, go to hell!

[*Elyot opens the door, and Sibyl disappears inside. Amanda looks at Victor, who is standing with his back turned, staring out of the window, then she wanders about the room, making rather inadequate little attempts to tidy up. She glances at Victor again.*]

AMANDA: Victor.

VICTOR [*without turning*]: What?

AMANDA [*sadly*]: Nothing. [*She begins to wrestle with one of the sofas in an effort to get it in place.*]

[*Victor turns, sees her, and comes down and helps her, in silence.*]

VICTOR: Where does it go?

AMANDA: Over there. [*After they have placed it, Amanda sits on the edge of it and gasps a little.*] Thank you, Victor.

VICTOR: Don't mention it.

AMANDA [*after a pause*]: What did you say to Elyot?

VICTOR: I told him he was beneath contempt.

AMANDA: Good.

VICTOR: I think you must be mad, Amanda.

AMANDA: I've often thought that myself.

VICTOR: I feel completely lost, completely bewildered.

AMANDA: I don't blame you. I don't feel any too cosy.

VICTOR: Had you been drinking last night?

AMANDA: Certainly not!

VICTOR: Had Elyot been drinking?

AMANDA: Yes—gallons.

VICTOR: Used he to drink before? When you were married to him?

AMANDA: Yes, terribly. Night after night he'd come home roaring and hiccoughing.

VICTOR: Disgusting!

AMANDA: Yes, wasn't it?

VICTOR: Did he really strike you last night?

AMANDA: Repeatedly. I'm bruised beyond recognition.

VICTOR [*suspecting slight exaggeration*]: Amanda!

AMANDA [*putting her hand on his arm*]: Oh, Victor, I'm most awfully sorry to have given you so much trouble, really I am! I've behaved badly, I know, but something strange happened to me. I can't explain it, there's no excuse, but I am ashamed of having made you unhappy.

VICTOR: I can't understand it at all. I've tried to, but I can't. It all seems so unlike you.

AMANDA: It isn't really unlike me, that's the trouble. I ought never to have married you; I'm a bad lot.

VICTOR: Amanda!

AMANDA: Don't contradict me. I know I'm a bad lot.

VICTOR: I wasn't going to contradict you.

AMANDA: Victor!

VICTOR: You appal me—absolutely!

AMANDA: Go on, go on, I deserve it.

VICTOR: I didn't come here to accuse you; there's no sense in that!

AMANDA: Why did you come?

VICTOR: To find out what you want me to do.

AMANDA: Divorce me, I suppose, as soon as possible. I won't make any difficulties. I'll go away, far away, Morocco, or Tunis, or somewhere. I shall probably catch some dreadful disease, and die out there, all alone—oh dear!

VICTOR: It's no use pitying yourself.

AMANDA: I seem to be the only one who does. I might just as

well enjoy it. [*She sniffs.*] I'm thoroughly unprincipled; Sibyl was right!

VICTOR [*irritably*]: Sibyl's an ass.

AMANDA [*brightening slightly*]: Yes, she is rather, isn't she? I can't think why Elyot ever married her.

VICTOR: Do you love him?

AMANDA: She seems so insipid, somehow——

VICTOR: Do you love him?

AMANDA: Of course she's very pretty, I suppose, in rather a shallow way, but still——

VICTOR: Amanda!

AMANDA: Yes, Victor?

VICTOR: You haven't answered my question.

AMANDA: I've forgotten what it was.

VICTOR [*turning away*]: You're hopeless—hopeless.

AMANDA: Don't be angry, it's all much too serious to be angry about.

VICTOR: You're talking utter nonsense!

AMANDA: No, I'm not, I mean it. It's ridiculous for us all to stand round arguing with one another. You'd much better go back to England and let your lawyers deal with the whole thing.

VICTOR: But what about you?

AMANDA: I'll be all right.

VICTOR: I only want to know one thing, and you won't tell me.

AMANDA: What is it?

VICTOR: Do you love Elyot?

AMANDA: No, I hate him. When I saw him again suddenly at Deauville, it was an odd sort of shock. It swept me away completely. He attracted me; he always has attracted me, but only the worst part of me. I see that now.

VICTOR: I can't understand why? He's so terribly trivial and superficial.

AMANDA: That sort of attraction can't be explained, it's a sort of a chemical what d'you call 'em.

VICTOR: Yes; it must be!

AMANDA: I don't expect you to understand, and I'm not going to try to excuse myself in any way. Elyot was the first love affair of my life, and in spite of all the suffering he caused me before, there must have been a little spark left smouldering, which burst into flame when I came face to face with him again. I completely lost grip of myself and behaved like a fool, for which I shall pay all right, you needn't worry about that. But perhaps one day, when all this is dead and done with, you and I might meet and be friends. That's something to hope for, anyhow. Good-bye, Victor dear. [*She holds out her hand.*]

VICTOR [*shaking her hand mechanically*]: Do you want to marry him?

AMANDA: I'd rather marry a boa constrictor.

VICTOR: I can't go away and leave you with a man who drinks, and knocks you about.

AMANDA: You needn't worry about leaving me, as though I were a sort of parcel. I can look after myself.

VICTOR: You said just now you were going away to Tunis, to die.

AMANDA: I've changed my mind, it's the wrong time of the year for Tunis. I shall go somewhere quite different. I believe Brioni is very nice in the summer.

VICTOR: Why won't you be serious for just one moment?

AMANDA: I've told you, it's no use.

VICTOR: If it will make things any easier for you, I won't divorce you.

AMANDA: Victor!

VICTOR: We can live apart until Sibyl has got her decree against Elyot, then, some time after that, I'll let you divorce me.

AMANDA [*turning away*]: I see you're determined to make me serious, whether I like it or not.

VICTOR: I married you because I loved you.

AMANDA: Stop it, Victor! Stop it! I won't listen!

VICTOR: I expect I love you still; one doesn't change all in a minute. You never loved me. I see that now, of course, so perhaps everything has turned out for the best really.

AMANDA: I thought I loved you, honestly I did.

VICTOR: Yes, I know, that's all right.

AMANDA: What an escape you've had.

VICTOR: I've said that to myself often during the last few days.

AMANDA: There's no need to rub it in.

VICTOR: Do you agree about the divorce business?

AMANDA: Yes. It's very, very generous of you.

VICTOR: It will save you some of the mud-slinging. We might persuade Sibyl not to name you.

AMANDA [*ruefully*]: Yes, we might.

VICTOR: Perhaps she'll change her mind about divorcing him.

AMANDA: Perhaps. She certainly went into the bedroom with a predatory look in her eye.

VICTOR: Would you be pleased if that happened?

AMANDA: Delighted. [*She laughs suddenly.*]

[*Victor looks at her, curiously. Sibyl and Elyot come out of the bedroom. There is an awkward silence for a moment.*]

SIBYL [*looking at Amanda triumphantly*]: Elyot and I have come to a decision.

AMANDA: How very nice!

VICTOR: What is it?

AMANDA: Don't be silly, Victor. Look at their faces.

ELYOT: Feminine intuition, very difficult.

AMANDA [*looking at Sibyl*]: Feminine determination, very praiseworthy.

SIBYL: I am not going to divorce Elyot for a year.

AMANDA: I congratulate you.

ELYOT [*defiantly*]: Sibyl has behaved like an angel.

AMANDA: Well, it was certainly her big moment.

[*Louise comes staggering in with a large tray of coffee and rolls, etc., she stands peering over the edge of it, not knowing where to put it.*]

ELYOT: Il faut le mettre sur la petite table là-bas.

LOUISE: Oui, monsieur.

[*Elyot and Victor hurriedly clear the things off the side table, and Louise puts the tray down, and goes back into the kitchen. Amanda and Sibyl eye one another.*]

AMANDA: It all seems very amicable.

SIBYL: It is, thank you.

AMANDA: I don't wish to depress you, but Victor isn't going to divorce me either.

ELYOT [*looking up sharply*]: What!

AMANDA: I believe I asked you once before this morning, never to speak to me again.

ELYOT: I only said "What." It was a general exclamation denoting extreme satisfaction.

AMANDA [*politely to Sibyl*]: Do sit down, won't you?

SIBYL: I'm afraid I must be going now. I'm catching the Golden Arrow, it leaves at twelve.

ELYOT [*coaxingly*]: You have time for a little coffee surely?

SIBYL: No, I really must go!

ELYOT: I shan't be seeing you again for such a long time.

AMANDA [*brightly*]: Living apart? How wise!

ELYOT [*ignoring her*]: Please, Sibyl, do stay!

SIBYL [*looking at Amanda with a glint in her eye*]: Very well, just for a little.

AMANDA: Sit down, Victor darling.

[*They all sit down in silence. Amanda smiles sweetly at Sibyl and holds up the coffee pot and milk jug.*]
Half and half?

SIBYL: Yes, please.

AMANDA [*sociably*]: What would one do without one's morning coffee? That's what I often ask myself.

ELYOT: Is it?

AMANDA [*withering him with a look*]: Victor, sugar for Sibyl. [*To Sibyl*]: It would be absurd for me to call you anything but Sibyl, wouldn't it?

SIBYL [*not to be outdone*]: Of course, I shall call you Mandy.
[*Amanda represses a shudder.*]

ELYOT: Oh God! We're off again. What weather!
[*Amanda hands Sibyl her coffee.*]

SIBYL: Thank you.

VICTOR: What's the time?

ELYOT: If the clock's still going after last night, it's ten-fifteen.

AMANDA [*handing Victor cup of coffee*]: Here, Victor dear.

VICTOR: Thanks.

AMANDA: Sibyl, sugar for Victor.

ELYOT: I should like some coffee, please.
[*Amanda pours some out for him, and hands it to him in silence.*]

AMANDA [*to Victor*]: Brioche?

VICTOR [*jumping*]: What?

AMANDA: Would you like a brioche?

VICTOR: No, thank you.

ELYOT: I would. And some butter, and some jam. [*He helps himself.*]

AMANDA [*to Sibyl*]: Have you ever been to Brioni?

SIBYL: No. It's in the Adriatic, isn't it?

VICTOR: The Baltic, I think.

SIBYL: I made sure it was in the Adriatic.

AMANDA: I had an aunt who went there once.

ELYOT [*with his mouth full*]: I once had an aunt who went to Tasmania.

[*Amanda looks at him stonily. He winks at her, and she looks away hurriedly.*]

VICTOR: Funny how the South of France has become so fashionable in the summer, isn't it?

SIBYL: Yes, awfully funny.

ELYOT: I've been laughing about it for months.

AMANDA: Personally, I think it's a bit too hot, although of course one can lie in the water all day.

SIBYL: Yes, the bathing is really divine!

VICTOR: A friend of mine has a house right on the edge of Cape Ferrat.

SIBYL: Really?

VICTOR: Yes, right on the edge.

AMANDA: That must be marvellous!

VICTOR: Yes, he seems to like it very much.

[*The conversation languishes slightly.*]

AMANDA [*with great vivacity*]: Do you know, I really think I love travelling more than anything else in the world! It always gives me such a tremendous feeling of adventure. First of all, the excitement of packing, and getting your passport visa'd and everything, then the thrill of actually starting, and trundling along on trains and ships, and then the most thrilling thing of all, arriving at strange places, and seeing strange people, and eating strange foods——

ELYOT: And making strange noises afterwards.

[*Amanda chokes violently. Victor jumps up and tries to offer assistance, but she waves him away, and continues to choke.*]

VICTOR [*to Elyot*]: That was a damned fool thing to do.

ELYOT: How did I know she was going to choke?

VICTOR [*to Amanda*]: Here, drink some coffee.

AMANDA [*breathlessly gasping*]: Leave me alone. I'll be all right in a minute.

VICTOR [*to Elyot*]: You waste too much time trying to be funny.

SIBYL [*up in arms*]: It's no use talking to Elyot like that; it wasn't his fault.

VICTOR: Of course it was his fault entirely, making rotten stupid jokes——

SIBYL: I thought what Elyot said was funny.

VICTOR: Well, all I can say is, you must have a very warped sense of humour.

SIBYL: That's better than having none at all.

VICTOR: I fail to see what humour there is in incessant trivial flippancy.

SIBYL: You couldn't be flippant if you tried until you were blue in the face.

VICTOR: I shouldn't dream of trying.

SIBYL: It must be very sad not to be able to see any fun in anything.

[*Amanda stops choking, and looks at Elyot. He winks at her again, and she smiles.*]

VICTOR: Fun! I should like you to tell me what fun there is in——

SIBYL: I pity you, I really do. I've been pitying you ever since we left Deauville.

VICTOR: I'm sure it's very nice of you, but quite unnecessary.

SIBYL: And I pity you more than ever now.

VICTOR: *Why* now particularly?

SIBYL: If you don't see why, I'm certainly not going to tell you.

VICTOR: I see no reason for you to try to pick a quarrel with me. I've tried my best to be pleasant to you, and comfort you.

SIBYL: You weren't very comforting when I lost my trunk.

VICTOR: I have little patience with people who go about losing luggage.

SIBYL: I don't go about losing luggage. It's the first time I've lost anything in my life.

VICTOR: I find that hard to believe.

SIBYL: Anyhow, if you'd tipped the porter enough, everything would have been all right. Small economies never pay; it's absolutely no use——

VICTOR: Oh, for God's sake be quiet!

[*Amanda lifts her hand as though she were going to interfere, but Elyot grabs her wrist. They look at each other for a moment, she lets her hand rest in his.*]

SIBYL [*rising from the table*]: How dare you speak to me like that!

VICTOR [*also rising*]: Because you've been irritating me for days.

SIBYL [*outraged*]: Oh!

VICTOR [*coming down to her*]: You're one of the most completely idiotic women I've ever met.

SIBYL: And you're certainly the rudest man I've ever met!

VICTOR: Well then, we're quits, aren't we?

SIBYL [*shrilly*]: One thing, you'll get your deserts all right.

VICTOR: What do you mean by that?

SIBYL: You know perfectly well what I mean. And it'll serve you right for being weak-minded enough to allow that woman to get round you so easily.

VICTOR: What about you? Letting that unprincipled roué persuade you to take him back again!

[*Amanda and Elyot are laughing silently. Elyot blows her a lingering kiss across the table.*]

SIBYL; He's nothing of the sort, he's just been victimized, as you were victimized.

VICTOR: Victimized! What damned nonsense!

SIBYL [*furiously*]: It isn't damned nonsense! You're very fond of swearing and blustering and threatening, but when it comes to the point you're as weak as water. Why, a blind cat could see what you've let yourself in for.

VICTOR [*equally furious*]: Stop making those insinuations.

SIBYL: I'm not insinuating anything. When I think of all the things you said about her, it makes me laugh, it does really; to see how completely she's got you again.

VICTOR: You can obviously speak with great authority, having had the intelligence to marry a drunkard.

SIBYL: So that's what she's been telling you. I might have known it! I suppose she said he struck her too!

VICTOR: Yes, she did, and I'm quite sure it's perfectly true.

SIBYL: I expect she omitted to tell you that she drank fourteen glasses of brandy last night straight off; and that the reason their first marriage was broken up was that she used to come home at all hours of the night, screaming and hiccoughing.

VICTOR: If he told you that, he's a filthy liar.

SIBYL: He isn't—he isn't!

VICTOR: And if you believe it, you're a silly scatter-brained little fool.

SIBYL [*screaming*]: How dare you speak to me like that! How dare you! I've never been so insulted in my life! How dare you!

[*Amanda and Elyot rise quietly, and go, hand in hand, towards the front door.*]

VICTOR [*completely giving way*]: It's a tremendous relief to me to have an excuse to insult you. I've had to listen to your weeping and wailings for days. You've clacked at me, and snivelled at me until you've nearly driven me insane, and I controlled my nerves and continued to try to help you and look after you, because I was sorry for you. I always thought you were stupid from the first, but I must say I never realised that you were a malicious little vixen as well!

SIBYL [*shrieking*]: Stop it! Stop it! You insufferable great brute!

She slaps his face hard, and he takes her by the shoulders and shakes her like a rat, as Amanda and Elyot go smilingly out of the door, with their suitcases, and—

THE CURTAIN FALLS

BITTER
SWEET

CHARACTERS

THE MARCHIONESS OF SHAYNE

DOLLY CHAMBERLAIN

LORD HENRY JEKYLL

VINCENT HOWARD

SARAH MILLICK

CARL LINDEN

MRS. MILLICK

HUGH DEVON

VICTORIA

HARRIET

GLORIA

HONOR

JANE

EFFIE

LOTTE

FREDA

HANSI

GUSSI

MANON [LA CREVETTE]

CAPTAIN AUGUST LUTTE

HERR SCHLICK

~~~~~~
~~~~~~

ACT ONE: SCENE I

Characters: THE MARCHIONESS OF SHAYNE, DOLLY CHAMBER-
LAIN, LORD HENRY JEKYLL, VINCENT HOWARD, NITA, HELEN,
JACKIE, FRANK, PARKER, GUESTS, MUSICIANS, *etc. The scene
is Lady Shayne's house in Grosvenor Square. The Year is
1929.*

THE SCENE *is Lady Shayne's house in Grosvenor Square.*

*There is a small dance in progress. At the back of the stage in
the centre are large double doors leading into the supper room.
On the left-hand side is a small jazz band which is playing in front
of the open windows. On the right-hand side a smaller door opens
into the library.*

*When the curtain rises the stage is crowded with Dancers and the
conversation and laughter combined with the band music should give
an effect almost of pandemonium. The music comes to an end with
the usual flourish and there is a smattering of applause from the
Dancers. Parker throws open the double doors at the back and announces supper. Everyone goes in laughing and talking and can be
seen taking their places at small tables. The double doors are closed
and the members of the band retire on to the balcony for a little fresh
air, with the exception of Vincent Howard, who remains at the piano
improvising syncopations softly.*

Dolly Chamberlain and Henry Jekyll come in from the library.

Dolly is pretty and attractive, about twenty. Henry is a trifle older and inclined to be faintly pompous.

DOLLY: They've all gone in to supper—come on.

HENRY: It's damned hot.

DOLLY: You've been grumbling about one thing and another all the evening.

HENRY: Sorry, old darling.

DOLLY: Do you think you love me really?

HENRY: Of course. Don't be an ass.

DOLLY: Enough?

HENRY: Enough for what?

DOLLY: Oh, I don't know—enough to spend your life with me, I suppose.

HENRY: It's a little late to worry about that now—with the wedding next Monday.

[*Vincent strikes a chord with some viciousness. Dolly looks sharply over her shoulder at him.*]

DOLLY: You're right, it is hot.

HENRY: Where's Lady Shayne?

DOLLY [*pointing to supper room*]: In there, I expect.

HENRY: Strange old girl.

DOLLY: I hope I shall be like that when I'm seventy.

HENRY: She can't be as much as that.

DOLLY: She is—she was at school with my grandmother.

HENRY: Good God!

DOLLY: It must be funny to look back over so many years. I wonder if she minds.

HENRY: Minds what?

DOLLY: Being old, of course—to have led such a thrilling life and then suddenly to realise there's nothing left to look forward to.

HENRY: Well, she certainly is a gay old bird.

DOLLY: Henry! [*She looks at him almost shocked.*]

HENRY: What?

DOLLY: How silly that sounds—A gay old bird.

HENRY: Well, it's true, isn't it?—That's what she is, always travelling around and giving parties and staying up all night —it's almost indecent—I wouldn't like to see my grandmother going on like that.

DOLLY: Well, you needn't worry. [*She laughs.*]

HENRY: How do you mean?

DOLLY: All your relations are too pompous to enjoy anything.

HENRY: Dolly!

DOLLY: Well, they are—they've all got several feet in the grave, there's no life left in them, if ever there was any, which I doubt—you'll probably be like that too in a few years.

HENRY: You think Lady Shayne's life has been thrilling, do you? [*He smiles superciliously.*] That's funny.

DOLLY: Yes, I do—I do—and it isn't so funny either.

HENRY: Now look here, Dolly, if you knew some of the things about Lady Shayne that *I* know——

DOLLY: I know more than you know—I know that she justified her existence—she lived for something——

HENRY: She was thoroughly immoral in her youth—lovers and awful second-rate people round her all the time. It was lucky for her she met Shayne and got back.

DOLLY: Got back to what?

HENRY: Decent people—society.

DOLLY: Oh, dear. I can laugh now.

HENRY: Now Dolly, my girl—I——

DOLLY [*suddenly with vehemence*]: Shut up—shut up—go away from me—you're pompous and silly and I can't bear it——

HENRY: Dolly!

DOLLY [*wildly*]: Go away—go away!

HENRY: You're impossible. [*He stamps off into the supper room.*]

VINCENT: Can I stop playing now?

DOLLY [*in a stifled voice*]: No—go on.

VINCENT: I can't bear it much longer—darling.

DOLLY: Vincent—don't.

VINCENT: Please come over here and sit close to me.

DOLLY: I'd better not, I think.

VINCENT: Afraid?

DOLLY: Yes. [*She goes over and sits beside him—he goes on playing.*]

VINCENT: I love you so.

DOLLY: Oh, God! I'm so utterly, utterly miserable. [*She buries her head in her arms.*]

VINCENT: Don't cry—you're going to marry a rich man and have rich friends and a rich house and rich food, and some day if you're really rich enough you'll be able to engage me to come and play for you. [*He laughs bitterly.*]

DOLLY: How can you be so horrid!

VINCENT: You'll be safe anyhow.

DOLLY: I don't want to be safe.

VINCENT: Come away with me then—I've got no money— nothing to offer you—you'd look fine singing my songs in some cheap cabaret somewhere—and living in third-rate hotels and just—well, earning your living——

DOLLY: It sounds marvellous.

VINCENT: Don't be a damned fool!

DOLLY: Vincent——

VINCENT: It's hell—— [*He stops playing and goes towards the window.*]

DOLLY: Where are you going?

VINCENT: To call the boys—we've got to work some more.

DOLLY: I shan't see you again until—until—after I'm married.

VINCENT: Never mind—safety first.

DOLLY: What am I to do?——

VINCENT: Good-bye, you poor little kid——

[*He suddenly takes her in his arms and kisses her. She twines her arms round his neck and they stand there clasped tight. Lady Shayne enters from the supper room. She watches them silently for a moment. She is seventy years old, but her figure is still slim; her hair is snow-white, and her gown is exquisite.*]

LADY S.: Dolly!

[*Dolly and Vincent break away from one another.*]

I come on an errand of peace from your fiancé. If it is inopportune, I apologise.

DOLLY: Oh, Lady Shayne.

LADY S. [*to Vincent*]: You are the piano player in the band, aren't you?

VINCENT: I'm the leader of the band.

LADY S.: What a pity! It's not a very good band.

VINCENT: I'm sorry for what happened just now, your ladyship. It—it was an accident.

LADY S.: In what way—an accident?

VINCENT: I—er—we were saying good-bye.

LADY S.: Your drummer is too loud, and I can't bear the man who plays the saxophone.

DOLLY: Lady Shayne—I—let me explain.

LADY S.: When a man plays off key the only explanation is that he is a bad musician.

DOLLY: Lady Shayne—I love Vincent and—and he loves me.

LADY S.: And this is Vincent?

DOLLY: Yes, of course.

LADY S.: And Henry, your future husband, is in there—practically weeping into the cold asparagus.

VINCENT: You're laughing at us—your ladyship.

LADY S.: I laugh at almost everything now—it's only when one is very old indeed that one can see the joke all the way round.

DOLLY: What joke?

LADY S.: Life and death and happiness and despair and love. [*She laughs again.*]

VINCENT: Don't laugh like that, please—your ladyship.

LADY S.: So you're a musician—an amiable, sensitive-looking young man—and you've been making love to this child—or has she been making love to you?—everything seems to have changed round lately.

VINCENT: It just happened—we—at least that is—I don't know.

LADY S.: Are you a married man?

VINCENT: No—of course not.

LADY S.: Well, you needn't be so vehement. I merely thought you might have forgotten——

VINCENT: My intentions are quite honourable, if presumptuous.

DOLLY: Are you angry?

LADY S.: Not in the least, my dear. What do you intend to do?

DOLLY: I don't know.

LADY S.: Well, if I were you, I should make up my mind. [*She turns towards the supper room.*]

DOLLY: You *are* angry.

LADY S.: I detest indecision.

DOLLY: I don't understand——

[*Several people come out of the supper room, including Nita and Helen.*]

NITA: Dolly—what have you been doing to Henry—he's plunged in gloom.

HELEN: He's sending out thought waves of depression and I got the lot, being next to him.

[*Jackie rushes out of the supper room with Frank and several others.*]

JACKIE: What's happened to the band? Oh, Mr. Howard, play something—play something romantic—I want to dance.

LADY S. [*laughing*]: Yes—play something romantic.

VINCENT [*savagely*]: I'll play anything anybody wants—that's what I'm hired for——— [*He goes to the piano.*] Here's romance for you—how's this———

[*He plays a swift jazz tune. Everyone begins to dance and jig about. Nita Charlestons a few steps, while Helen and Jackie clap their hands and sing. Suddenly Lady Shayne stamps her foot sharply.*]

LADY S.: Stop—stop—it's hideous—you none of you know anything or want anything beyond noise and speed—your dreams of romance are nightmares. Your conception of life grotesque. Come with me a little—I'll show you—listen—listen———

FRANK [*softly*]: Oh, God, what's the old girl up to now?

DOLLY: Be quiet.

[*Lady Shayne begins to sing—everyone squats down on the floor, some of them giggling furtively. Vincent and Dolly stare at her as though transfixed.*]

"THE CALL OF LIFE"

LADY S.: Your romance could not live the length of a day,
  You hesitate and analyse,
  Betray your love with compromise,
 Till glamour fades away;
  And all too soon you realise
  That there is nothing left to say.

CHORUS: Hey, hey—hey, hey,
  How does she get that way;

She'd be more light-hearted
If she started—to Charleston;
She's never danced it,
She's never chanced it;
Perhaps her muscles are disinclined,
Perhaps she hasn't the strength of mind.

LADY S.: Love that's true can mean naught to you but a name,
A thing that isn't part of you;
Can never touch the heart of you;
It's nothing but a game,
A fire without a flame.

MEN: We find it difficult to grasp your meaning.

LADY S.: Maybe the past is intervening.

CHORUS: We very much regret that times have changed so,
Life is more speedily arranged so.

LADY S.: In your world of swiftly turning wheels
Life must be extremely grey.

CHORUS: We've no time to waste on Love Ideals,
That which to our senses most appeals
Is all we can obey.

LADY S.: No—no. Not so;
There must be something further on,
A vision you can count upon,
To help you to acquire
A memory when Youth is gone
Of what was once your heart's desire.

There is a call that echoes sweetly
When it is Spring and Love is in the air;
Whate'er befall, respond to it completely,
Tho' it may bring you sadness and despair;
Fling far behind you

The chains that bind you,
That love may find you
In joy or strife;
Tho' Fate may cheat you,
And defeat you,
Your Youth must answer to the Call of Life.

[*The lights slowly go out, and through the darkness her voice grows sweeter and younger, until presently the lights go up again and disclose a young girl of about seventeen standing demurely in a prim Victorian room with spring sunlight flooding through the windows behind her. Seated beside her at an Erard grand pianoforte is a young Music Master—he is playing the piano, but his eyes are gazing up at her face and he is smiling a trifle wistfully as she comes to the end of the song.*]

CURTAIN

ACT ONE: SCENE II

Characters: SARAH MILLICK, CARL LINDEN, MRS. MILLICK, HUGH DEVON. *The scene is the Millicks' house in Belgrave Square. The Year is* 1875.

WHEN SARAH *finishes singing, Carl allows his hands to drop from the keys, and still gazing into her eyes, he speaks:*

CARL: That was excellent, Miss Sarah—you are improving in a very marked manner.

SARAH [*demurely*]: Thank you.

CARL: I wrote that song for you when I was sixteen years old.

SARAH: But, Mr. Linden, that cannot be true—we have only known each other during the past year.

CARL: I mean that I wrote it for someone like you.

SARAH [*quickly*]: Oh!

CARL: Not a real person—just an ideal in my mind, someone young and charming—holding out her arms as you did just now—expectantly.

SARAH: Expectant of what, Mr. Linden?

CARL [*hopelessly turning away*]: I don't know.

SARAH: I think it is the loveliest song I ever heard.

CARL [*looking at her again*]: Do you?

SARAH [*meeting his eyes*]: Yes—of course.

CARL: You took the high note too much at the back of your throat.

SARAH: I'm sorry.

CARL: It doesn't matter.

SARAH: Oh, but, surely it does.

CARL: Nothing matters but just these few moments.

SARAH: Why do you say that, Mr. Linden?

CARL: Because it's spring, and I—I——

SARAH: Yes?

CARL: I fear I am talking nonsense.

SARAH [*smiling*]: Perhaps a little.

CARL: We have festivals in the spring in my country—and the young boys and girls dance and their clothes are brightly coloured, glinting in the sun, and the old people sit round under the trees, watching and tapping their sticks on the ground and reviving in their hearts memories of when they, too, were young and in love.

SARAH: In love.

CARL: Yes—as you are in love with your handsome Mr. Devon.

SARAH: Oh—Hugh—yes, of course. Tell me more about your country, Mr. Linden.

CARL: There is nothing to tell really—it seems so very far away—I've almost forgotten.

SARAH: You're homesick though, I can see you are.

CARL: Can you?

SARAH: Perhaps it's the climate here, it *is* depressing——

CARL: Yes, a little [*He sings*]:

Tho' there may be beauty in this land of yours,
　　Skies are very often dull and grey;
If I could but take that little hand of yours,
　　Just to lead you secretly away.
We would watch the Danube as it gently flows,
　　Like a silver ribbon winding free;
Even as I speak of it my longing grows,
　　Once again my own dear land to see.
　　If you could only come with me,
　　If you could only come with me.

SARAH: Oh, Mr. Linden.

CARL: Yes.

SARAH: How very strange everything is to-day.

CARL: Will you forgive me, Miss Sarah, when I tell you that I shall be unable to play at your wedding reception.

SARAH [*disappointed*]: Oh!

CARL: I must go away on that day—to Brussels.

SARAH: Brussels?

CARL [*hurriedly*]: Yes, a concert—I have to play at a concert—it is very important.

SARAH: I understand.

CARL: Do you?

SARAH: Yes—but it is very, very disappointing.

CARL: But I am deeply grateful for the honour you have done me in asking me.

SARAH [*lightly, but turning away*]: This is the last time we shall meet then for ever so long.

CARL: To-night—I am playing to-night for the dance.

SARAH: But that is different. There will be so many people——

CARL: This is indeed the last time we shall be alone together.

SARAH [*looking down*]: Yes.

CARL: You have been a charming pupil—I shall always look back on these months with happiness.

SARAH: Happiness?

CARL: And sadness too.

SARAH: Oh, dear.

CARL: There are tears in your eyes.

SARAH: In yours also.

CARL: I know—I am sorry to be so foolish.

SARAH: Dear Mr. Linden——

[*She gives him her hand, he kisses it fervently, then pulls himself together with a tremendous effort.*]

CARL: Once more now—your exercises—just once more through.

SARAH [*tearfully*]: Very well.

[*Carl strikes a chord—Sarah sings up and down, saying "Ah." Suddenly a barrel organ strikes up in the street outside a sugary sentimental melody. Sarah perseveres with her exercises, then Carl begins to sing to her, accompanied by the orchestra, with the barrel organ as a background*]:

"I'LL SEE YOU AGAIN"

CARL: Now Miss Sarah, if you please,
        Sing a scale for me.

SARAH: Ah—Ah—Ah——

CARL: Take a breath and then reprise
        In a different key.

SARAH: Ah—Ah—Ah——

CARL: All my life I shall remember knowing you,
All the pleasure I have found in showing you
 The different ways
 That one may phrase
The changing light, and changing shade;
 Happiness that must die,
 Melodies that must fly,
 Memories that must fade,
 Dusty and forgotten by and by.

SARAH: Learning scales will never seem so sweet again
Till our Destiny shall let us meet again.

CARL: The will of Fate
 May come too late.

SARAH: When I'm recalling these hours we've had
 Why will the foolish tears
 Tremble across the years,
Why shall I feel so sad,
Treasuring the memory of these days
Always?

CARL: I'll see you again,
Whenever Spring breaks through again;
 Time may lie heavy between,
 But what has been
  Is past forgetting.

SARAH: This sweet memory,
Across the years will come to me;
 Tho' my world may go awry,
 In my heart will ever lie,
 Just the echo of a sigh.
Good-bye.

[*Mrs. Millick enters with Hugh Devon. During the ensuing scene, until Carl's exit, the love theme should be continued in the orchestra very softly.*]

MRS. M: Darling child—your lesson should have been over a quarter of an hour ago. There is so much to be done—I declare I'm nearly frantic—Hugh has been telling me about his aunt— poor Lady Ettleworth, she developed acute gastritis yesterday evening, and it may mean postponing the wedding, and on the other hand it may not. I'm certain it was the peas she ate at lunch here. They were like bullets. Good afternoon, Mr. Linden.

CARL [*bowing*]: Good afternoon, Mrs. Millick.

HUGH: Good afternoon.

CARL [*bowing*]: Good afternoon.

HUGH: You look tired, Sarah.

SARH: I am a little—I—it is quite hot to-day.

MRS. M.: I fear I must hurry you away, Mr. Linden—Sarah has a dressmaker at four-thirty—and there is so much to be done.

CARL: I quite understand.

MRS. M.: Doubtless Sarah will resume her lessons with you when she is settled down in her new home.

SARAH: Mother—I——

MRS. M.: It will be an occupation—I always believe in young married women having an occupation.

CARL: I should have thought being married would be sufficient.

MRS. M. [*slightly scandalised*]: Mr. Linden——

CARL [*bitterly*]: Your daughter must learn from someone else when she is a young married woman, Mrs. Millick. I shall not be here.

MRS. M.: Well, I'm sure I'm very sorry, I——

CARL [*looking fixedly at Sarah*]: I shall be far away in my own country—but each year when spring comes round again, I shall remember you, Miss Sarah, and what a charming pupil you were,

and how, although you sometimes sang your top notes from the
back of your throat, and your middle notes through your nose,
you always sang your deep notes from your heart.

MRS. M.: My dear Mr. Linden!

CARL: This is good-bye, Miss Sarah, except for to-night, when
there will be so many people—too many people.

[*He bows abruptly and goes out. The music swells loudly in the
orchestra, the theme of "The Call of Life." Sarah begins to sing
it brokenly. Hugh advances towards her, but she pushes him away
and falls weeping into her mother's arms as the lights fade out.*]

CURTAIN

ACT ONE: SCENE III

Characters: SARAH MILLICK, CARL LINDEN, MRS. MILLICK,
HUGH DEVON, LADY DEVON, SIR ARTHUR FENCHURCH, VIC-
TORIA, HARRIET, GLORIA, HONOR, JANE, EFFIE, THE MARQUIS
OF STEERE, LORD EDGAR JAMES, LORD SORREL, MR. VALE, MR.
BETHEL, MR. PROUTIE, FOUR FOOTMEN, GUESTS, MUSICIANS,
etc. *The scene is the ballroom of the Millicks' house in Bel-
grave Square. The Year is* 1875.

IT IS *the ballroom of the Millicks' house in Belgrave Square.
There are three windows at the back opening on to a balcony over-
looking the Square. On the left at an angle are double doors opening
on to the landing and staircase. On the right is a small dais upon
which the orchestra is playing conducted by Carl Linden. Below
this double doors lead into the supper room and on the left below the
big doors is a small door leading into the drawing-room. There*

are coloured lights festooned over the balcony which look charming against the shadowy trees in the Square.

When the curtain rises, the ball is nearly over. A mazurka is in progress: the dresses of the guests are almost entirely pastel shades with the exception of a few chaperons in black and grey and purple, who are seated on small chairs and sofas below the orchestra. At the end of the mazurka most of the couples leave the floor; some go out on to the balcony, some into the supper room, and some into the drawing-room.

Lady Devon, an imposing dowager, meets Mrs. Millick as she billows in from the supper room.

LADY D.: Charming, Violet—quite delightful—I congratulate you.

MRS. M.: The young people seem very happy, I think.

LADY D.: I thought Sarah looked radiant but a trifle flushed when she was waltzing with Hugh a little while ago.

MRS. M.: She has been flushed all the evening. I hope she isn't feverish—I feel quite disturbed about her.

LADY D.: I feel sure you have no cause to be—she was positively hilarious in the supper room.

MRS. M.: Unnaturally so.

LADY D.: She is in love, my dear.

[*Hugh enters from the supper room.*]

HUGH [*in harassed tones*]: Oh, there you are.

LADY D. [*fondly*]: Happy boy.

HUGH: I am very worried.

MRS. M.: Why—what has happened?

HUGH: Sarah is behaving in a most peculiar manner—she upset a full glass of claret cup over Sir Arthur Fenchurch and laughed.

MRS. M.: Laughed!

LADY D.: Sir Arthur—Good heavens!

[*Sir Arthur enters, a pompous-looking old gentleman. He is obviously restraining a boiling fury with great effort. His shirt-front is claret-stained and his manner frigid.*]

SIR A. [*bowing to Mrs. Millick furiously but politely*]: A delightful evening, Mrs. Millick—thank you a thousand times.

MRS. M.: But, Sir Arthur—you mustn't think of going.

SIR A.: I couldn't think of staying—so many fresh young people enjoying themselves so very thoroughly—I feel out of place.

LADY D.: But, Sir Arthur——

SIR A. [*firmly*]: Good night, Lady Devon. Good night, Mrs. Millick. [*To Hugh*]: My boy—I sincerely *hope* your marriage will be a happy one.

MRS. M.: Well!

HUGH: There now.

LADY D.: How very, very unfortunate.

[*Sarah enters from the supper room; she looks lovely, but her manner is strained and almost defiant.*]

SARAH: Has he gone?

MRS. M.: Sarah—I'm ashamed of you.

SARAH: He patted my hand, mamma, then he patted my head. I detest being patted.

HUGH: He's one of the most influential men in London.

MRS. M.: And so kind.

SARAH: And so pompous.

LADY D.: Sarah!

MRS. M.: The first thing to-morrow morning you shall write him a letter of apology.

[*She moves away with Lady Devon.*]

SARAH: To-morrow is so far away. [*She laughs.*]

HUGH: I don't understand you to-night, Sarah.

SARAH: I don't think I quite understand myself.

HUGH: Why did you cry this afternoon in the music room?

SARAH: Are you glad you are going to marry me, Hugh?

HUGH: Why did you cry like that?

SARAH: And will you be kind to me—always?

HUGH: You haven't answered me.

SARAH: And do you love me?

HUGH [*irritably*]: Sarah!

SARAH: Do you?

HUGH: Of course I do—what is the matter with you?

[*Carl Linden stands up on the orchestra dais where the band have been regaling themselves with refreshments, and very softly plays on the violin "I'll See You Again." Sarah starts and then begins to laugh hysterically.*]

SARAH: Don't look so solemn, Hugh—I'm in love.

HUGH: My dear girl, that's all very well——

SARAH: Is it?

HUGH: But you really must restrain yourself.

SARAH [*almost rudely*]: What a stupid tune, Mr. Linden—so dismal——

HUGH: Sarah!

SARAH [*peremptorily*]: Play something gay, please—immediately.

HUGH [*softly*]: Sarah, you must not speak like that—have you taken leave of your senses?

SARAH [*vehemently*]: Let me alone—please go away—let me alone!

[*Hugh goes angrily on to the balcony. Carl strikes up a tremendously gay melody*]:

"WHAT IS LOVE?"

Play something gay for me,
Play for me, play for me;

Set me free,
I am in a trance to-night,
   Can't you see
How I want to dance to-night?
Madly my heart is beating,
   Some insane melody possessing me,
   In my brain thrilling and obsessing me;
How can I leave it to call in vain?
Is it joy or pain?
   Live your life, for Time is fleeting,
   Some insistent voice repeating;
   Hear me—hear me,
How can I leave it to call in vain?
Is it joy or pain?

Refrain

Tell me—tell me—tell me, what is love?
Is it some consuming flame;
   Part of the moon, part of the sun,
   Part of a dream barely begun?
When is the moment of breaking-waking?
Skies change, nothing is the same,
Some strange magic is to blame;
   Voices, that seem to echo round me and above,
   Tell me, what is love, love, love?

Play something gay for me,
Play for me—play for me;
   Tell me why
Spring has so enchanted me,
   Why this shy
Passion has so enchanted me,

Passion has been granted me;
Am I awake or dreaming?
    Far and near
Every lover follows you,
    Swift and clear,
Flying as the swallows do;
Leave me no longer to call in vain,
Are you joy or pain?
Leave me not by Love forsaken,
If I sleep, then let me waken;
    Hear me—hear me,
Leave me no longer to call in vain
Are you joy or pain?

Repeat Refrain

[*Sarah begins to waltz round the stage by herself, and as she passes the supper room, the library and the balcony, Guests join her in her dance, until the whole stage is encircled by a wheel of young people laughing and chattering. At the end of this, the band plays "God Save the Queen"; everyone naturally stands still, and then the party breaks up. Sarah takes her place at the door with her mother, in order to bid good-bye to the Guests. The Musicians are packing up their instruments, and finally all go out, including Carl. Hugh comes in from the balcony. Sarah leaves her mother talking to some Guests and runs up to him.*]

SARAH: I'm sorry, Hugh.

HUGH [*stiffly*]: It doesn't matter.

SARAH: Oh, but it does—I was unkind and silly.

HUGH: It doesn't matter.

SARAH: Will you please forgive me?

HUGH: There is nothing to forgive.

SARAH: I shall be bad again if you are so polite.

HUGH: My dear Sarah!

SARAH [*desperately*]: Are you always going to be like this—after we are married, I mean—cold and unbending?

HUGH: I can only hope you are not often going to behave as you have to-night.

SARAH: Oh, dear.

HUGH: I don't feel that you realise yet the dignity of the position you will hold as my wife.

SARAH: I am not your wife yet.

HUGH: I enjoy being high-spirited as much as anyone.

SARAH: Do you?

HUGH: But there is a time and place for everything.

SARAH: Then I can look forward to us being very high-spirited when we are alone—when no one is looking—you might wear a funny hat at breakfast.

HUGH: I am very fond of you, my dear, but you must remember I am older than you.

SARAH: Not so very much.

HUGH: And it is part of my profession to consider appearances.

SARAH: Diplomatically speaking.

HUGH: Are you laughing at me?

SARAH: No, but I'm looking at you—just as though I had never seen you before.

[*Lady Devon enters.*]

LADY D.: Hugh, *dear.*

HUGH: Yes, mother?

LADY D.: I have been waiting for you downstairs. The carriage is at the door. Good night, Sarah.

SARAH: Good night. I have been telling Hugh I was sorry to have behaved so badly.

LADY D. [*smiling*]: I am afraid you're marrying a tomboy, Hugh.

SARAH: No, no—I won't be one any more.

LADY D.: Dear child. [*She kisses her.*] Come, Hugh. [*She moves over to Mrs. Millick at the door.*]

HUGH: Good night, Sarah.

SARAH: Good night, Hugh.

HUGH: Will you drive with me to-morrow afternoon in Regent's Park?

SARAH: Thank you—that will be delightful.

HUGH: Until to-morrow—my dear. [*He looks round carefully and then kisses her chastely and departs with Lady Devon.*]

MRS. M.: Well, that's over. Where are the girls?

SARAH: Harriet and Gloria?

MRS. M.: Yes.

SARAH: Sitting out somewhere with Lord Edgar and Mr. Proutie.

MRS. M.: And Effie and Jane and Honor and Victoria?

SARAH: They're sitting out, too.

MRS. M.: Come with me—we must find them—really you modern young people have no sense of behaviour at all.

[*She goes with Sarah into the supper room while the music strikes up the introductory bars of a concerted number. Harriet and Lord Edgar peep round the library door and tiptoe out on to the stage. Gloria and Mr. Proutie do the same from the balcony—Effie, Jane, Honor, Victoria, Mr. Vale and Lord Sorrel, Lord Steere, Mr. Bethel all join them.*]

"THE LAST DANCE"

MEN: They've all gone now—have no fear—
GIRLS: Sarah's mother may be near,
       If she should hear
ALL: She might be rather cross with us,
       Elderly people make too much fuss.

MEN: Always insist on a chaperone,
            Never leave love alone.

GIRLS: We feel frightened, if you please
            Don't flirt or tease.

MEN: Gentle and sweet in your purity,
            We give our hearts as security.

GIRLS: We shall be scolded a lot for this.

MEN: You won't miss just one kiss.

[*They all kiss.*]

GIRLS: Think of the consequences, please, you haven't
           realised
          What an appalling thing for us to be so compromised,
          So dreadfully, dreadfully, dreadfully compromised.

MEN: Everything's ending,
         The moon is descending,
          Behind the tall trees in the park.

GIRLS: Silence falls,
         Slumber calls.

MEN: We men together
      Were wondering whether
         We might have a bit of a lark.

GIRLS: No jokes in the dark, please,
       What sort of a lark, please?

ALL: Just a slight dance,
         One more dream-of-delight dance;
       Just a sort of good-night dance
         Would be glorious fun.

MEN: Won't you let us, please let us, just stay for a while,
     Won't you, please won't you, be gay for a while?
     All we desire is to play for a while
       Now the party's done.

GIRLS: Just a fast waltz,
Till the world seems a vast waltz:
Very often the last waltz
Is the birth of Romance.

ALL: It's a June night,
There's a thrill in the moonlight;
Let's give way to the tender surrender
Of our last dance.

[At the end of the number all the men, with the exception of Mr. Proutie, creep out, leaving the Girls seated demurely on gilt chairs at some distance from one another all round the stage. Mr. Proutie, being very smitten with Gloria, hides behind the sofa. Mrs. Millick re-enters, looking rather agitated, followed by Sarah.]

MRS. M.: Girls—where have you been?

HARRIET: Nowhere, Aunt Violet.

MRS. M.: Where is Lord Edgar?

HONOR: He went hours ago, Mrs. Millick.

MRS. M.: And Lord Steere, Mr. Bethel, Mr. Vale and Lord Sorrel?

VICTORIA [*sighing*]: All gone.

MRS. M.: And Mr. Proutie?

GLORIA: He was so tired he left early.

MRS. M.: Come out from behind that sofa, Mr. Proutie.

[Mr. Proutie comes out, looking very sheepish. All the Girls giggle. Mr. Proutie is very young and cherubic.]

MR. P.: I—I—fell asleep—I apologise.

MRS. M.: I quite understand.

MR. P. [*appealingly to Gloria*]: Miss Gloria, I——

MRS. M.: Good night, Mr. Proutie.

MR. P.: Miss Gloria said that——

MRS. M. [*sternly*]: Good *night*, Mr. Proutie.

MR. P.: Er—er—— Good night—thank you for having me —er—good night. [*He goes out, covered with embarrassment.*]

MRS. M.: Gloria—what does this mean?

GLORIA: Nothing, Aunt Violet.

MRS. M.: If it were not that this was a festive occasion, I should punish you severely for your deceit.

HARRIET: Dear Aunt Violet—don't be cross.

MRS. M.: To bed with the lot of you.

EFFIE: Oh, not yet—just ten minutes more.

MRS. M.: Certainly not—it's nearly one o'clock—fine bridesmaids you'll make on Thursday, if you stay up so late.

HARRIET: Won't you let us stay up just a little longer?

HONOR: Oh, Mrs. Millick, do—please do.

MRS. M.: No—Sarah's tired——

SARAH: No, I'm not, mother—I know I couldn't sleep for ages.

GLORIA: Just a short while—please!

[*They all cluster round her and speak at once—finally she breaks away from them.*]

MRS. M.: Very well—ten minutes then and no more. Sarah, come into my room and say good night.

SARAH: Yes, mother.

MRS. M.: Remember now—in ten minutes' time I shall tell Parker to come and put out the lights—and don't make too much noise——

HARRIET: We won't, we promise.

GLORIA: Good night, Aunt Violet.

[*Mrs. Millick goes out amid a chorus of "Good nights." The moment the door has closed upon her the Girls fling aside their demure manner and dance about the stage. Harriet jumps on to the orchestra dais and begins to strum the piano. Effie, Honor, and Sarah sing gaily while Victoria and Jane dance.*]

HONOR: Oh, Sarah—I do envy you—being married and going to Paris and everything.

SARAH: Do you?

EFFIE: Aren't you dying of excitement?—I know I should be.

SARAH: No, not exactly—I feel strange somehow.

GLORIA: What sort of strange?

SARAH: I don't know—it's difficult to explain—perhaps I'm frightened.

JANE: Nobody could be frightened of Hugh.

VICTORIA: When I marry, it must be somebody just like Hugh.

HARRIET: I shall choose someone taller—more robust, you know.

EFFIE: How can you, Harriet—Hugh's just the right size.

GLORIA: I shall marry Mr. Proutie.

ALL: Gloria!—What do you mean?

GLORIA [calmly]: He adores me.

JANE: Has he asked you?

GLORIA: Of course.

HONOR: And you said yes?

GLORIA: I said no. But that doesn't matter—he'll ask me again.

EFFIE: Are you in love with him?

GLORIA: No—not a bit.

HONOR: How can you, Gloria?

GLORIA: I'd much rather marry someone I didn't love really.

ALL: "Gloria!" "Really!" "You're dreadful!" "Why?" etc.

GLORIA: Because I could manage him better.

HARRIET: I agree with Gloria.

VICTORIA: So do I.

SARAH: I don't—I want love.

EFFIE [giggling]: So do I—but you'll get it before I do——
[They all laugh.]

HONOR: I mean to have a lot of babies——

JANE: I want someone to protect me always—someone strong that I can look up to——

HARRIET: Fiddlesticks!

VICTORIA: Rubbish!

GLORIA: Old-fashioned nonsense!

JANE: Let's play a game.

SARAH: What game?

EFFIE: Yes, yes—any game.

HONOR: Postman's knock.

SARAH: No—no—that means one of us going out——

JANE: How, when and where.

EFFIE: So does that.

SARAH: Let's play an exciting game—a noisy game.

HARRIET: Aunt Violet will hear.

SARAH: No—she's two floors up.

GLORIA: Blind Man's Buff.

EFFIE: Yes—yes.

SARAH: That will do——

VICTORIA: Who'll be it——

JANE: Eeeny meeny miny mo—we must do eeny meeny miny mo——

FINALE

GLORIA:	Eeeny meeny miny mo
HARRIET:	Catch a nigger by his toe
VICTORIA:	If he hollers let him go
ALL:	O.U.T. spells out and so
GLORIA:	Out goes she. [*She points to Effie.*]
EFFIE:	Out goes me. [*Skipping about.*] This is the love-liest, loveliest part of the party.
GLORIA:	Eeny meeny miny mo
HARRIET:	Catch a nigger by his toe

VICTORIA: If he hollers let him go
ALL: O.U.T. spells out and so
GLORIA: Out goes she. [*She points to Harriet.*]
HARRIET: Out goes me.

[*She and Effie take hands and twirl around.*]

HARRIET: ⎫
EFFIE: ⎭   Now we're free who knows who'll be he!

GLORIA: Eeny meeny miny mo
VICTORIA: Catch a nigger by his toe
SARAH: If he hollers let him go
ALL: O.U.T. spells out and so
VICTORIA: Out goes she. [*She points to Gloria.*]
GLORIA: Out goes me. [*She joins Effie and Harriet.*]

HARRIET: ⎫
EFFIE: ⎬   This is the loveliest, loveliest part of the party.
GLORIA: ⎭

VICTORIA: Eeny meeny miny mo
SARAH: Catch a nigger by his toe
JANE: If he hollers let him go
   Out goes she. [*Points to Victoria.*]
VICTORIA: Out goes me. [*She joins Effie, Harriet and Gloria.*]
ALL: This is the loveliest, loveliest part of the party.
EFFIE: ⎫   Only three of them left now we're excited to
HARRIET: ⎭   see
GLORIA: ⎫   Who is going to be blind man, who's it going to
VICTORIA:⎭   be.
SARAH: I have a strange presentiment it's me.
JANE: Eeny meeny miny mo
   Out goes she. [*She points to Honor, who joins the others.*]
SARAH: Eeny meeny mo
   Out goes she. [*She points to Jane.*]

I'm He—it's me
It's me—I'm He.

GIRLS: Just get a handkerchief and bind it around her
eyes.

SARAH: Not too tight, not too tight.

[*They blindfold her.*]

GIRLS: She mustn't see a thing no matter how much she
tries.

SARAH: That's all right—that's all right.

GIRLS: She will cheat if she can,
That corner's raised a bit,
Turn her round till she's dazed a bit,
Are you ready now,
One, two, three!

SARAH: Since the party began,
Something's been taunting me,
Some presentiment haunting me,
What can it be?

GIRLS: Start now—start now,
She can see the ground,
She can see the ground.

SARAH: Somehow, somehow,
Some forgotten sound,
Some forgotten sound,
Echoes deep in my heart,
Strangely enthralling me,
Someone secretly calling me,
Like a melody far away.

GIRLS: Oh, for Heaven's sake start,
Here go along with you,
We can see nothing wrong with you,
We want to play.

[*They all dance about and dodge her. The door on the right opens quietly and Carl Linden comes into the room. He moves across to the piano and collects his music and is on his way out when Sarah clasps him round the neck. All the Girls laugh. Carl is staggered for a moment, drops his music, and then completely losing all restraint kisses her on the mouth. She snatches the bandage from her eyes and stares into his face. All the other Girls are watching aghast.*]

SARAH [*softly*]: It's you I love—now and always.

[*She kisses him, then draws back and they stand there staring at one another oblivious of everything. Effie giggles suddenly and then stops herself.*]

HARRIET: Sarah——

GLORIA: Sarah—don't be silly—Sarah——

[*Neither Carl nor Sarah turn their heads.*]

CARL: Come with me——

SARAH: Now?

CARL: Yes—now—to-night.

SARAH: I'll come with you—wherever you want me to.

CARL: I love you—do you hear—I've loved you for months —for years really—ever since I was a boy I've known you were waiting for me somewhere—I'll take care of you—live for you —die for you.

SARAH:　　Don't say that, my darling. [*Singing*]:

> Should happiness forsake me,
> And disillusion break me,
> Come what may,
> Lead the way,
> Take me, take me.
> Although I may discover,
> Love crucifies the lover,

Whate'er Fate has in store,
My heart is yours for evermore.

CARL [*singing*]:
Oh Lady, you are far above me,
And yet you whisper that you love me,
Can this be true or is it just some foolish dream?

SARAH [*speaking*]: You know it's true, look in my eyes—can't you see?

CARL [*speaking softly*]: Oh, my dear, dear love. [*Singing*]:

Now tho' your fears are sleeping,
Look well before the leaping.
Love of me
May be repaid
By weeping.
Life can be bitter learning,
When there is no returning,
Whate'er Fate has in store,
My heart is yours for evermore,
I love you—I love you—I love you.

GLORIA: You cannot realise the things you say.
            You quite forget yourself, please go away.

HARRIET: Now leave this all to me, my dear,
            It's really too absurd.

EFFIE: It's quite the most romantic thing that I have ever heard!

VICTORIA [*speaking*]: Effie, be quiet.

[*Sarah kisses him again full on the mouth. Harriet rushes up and drags them apart.*]

HARRIET: Sarah—are you mad?—Mr. Linden, please go at once.

CARL [*smiling*]: How can I go?

GLORIA: Harriet—leave this to me——

SARAH: Stop—don't say another word.

EFFIE [*rushing up hysterically*]: It's the most wonderfully thrilling thing that ever happened in the world.

HARRIET: Don't be an idiot, Effie.

SARAH [*quietly*]: Effie's right, Harriet.

HARRIET: I'm going straight upstairs to fetch Aunt Violet.

EFFIE [*struggling with her*]: You shan't! You shan't!—They love each other—look at them—Honor, Victoria, Jane, help me!

[*Honor, Victoria and Jane come to her assistance.*]

SARAH AND CARL [*singing*]:

> I'll see you again,
> Whenever Spring breaks through again,
> Always I'll be by your side,
> No time or tide
> Can part us ever——

VICTORIA: Shhh! Someone's coming—hide—quickly——

[*They all hide behind sofas and chairs.*]

[*Four Footmen enter pompously to music.*]

FOOTMEN QUARTETTE

Now the party's really ended,
And our betters have ascended,
All with throbbing heads,
To their welcome beds,
Pity us, who have to be up,
Sadly clearing the debris up,
Getting for our pains,
Most of the remains.
Though the Major-Domo is a trifle tight,
Though the mistress hiccoughed when she said good night,
We in our secluded garret,

Mean to finish up the claret-
Cup all right.
When we've doused the final candles,
We'll discuss the latest scandals
We have overheard,
Pleasure long deferred.
When the Duke of So and So stares
At his wife, we know below stairs,
While she smirks and struts,
That he hates her guts.
Though we all disguise our feelings pretty well,
What we mean by "Very good" is "Go to hell."
Though they're all so grand and pompous,
Most of them are now non compos,
Serve them right,
Good night.

[*They extinguish all the lights and close the windows and go out, closing the doors behind them. All the Girls come out, and lastly Carl and Sarah. Sarah goes up to Harriet. Gloria lights two candles.*]

SARAH: Harriet—whatever you do won't be the slightest use—
I love Carl—I'm going with him—I don't care where or how—
but this is my life, you understand—my whole life—so help
me—all you can—please—please——

HARRIET: Think of Hugh—you're mad.

SARAH: Perhaps I am mad, but I'm happy—can't you see!—
I'm really happy——

HARRIET: Mr. Linden, I appeal to you.

GLORIA: It's no use, Harriet.

HARRIET: I feel as if I were in a dream.

CARL: You are.

HARRIET: What are your prospects—have you any money?

CARL: None—no money—but I can earn enough.

SARAH: So can I—I'll sing——

VICTORIA: Sarah!

CARL: Yes—Sarah will sing and I will play and we will make a living—come, Sarah.

SARAH: Like this?

EFFIE: Quickly, Jane—your bedroom is nearest—your hat and cape.

[*Jane and Effie fly out of the room. "The Call of Life" theme plays softly. Sarah runs up to the windows and flings them open, singing. Carl joins her.*]

SARAH AND CARL [*singing*]:

Fling far behind you
The chains that bind you,
That Love may find you
In joy or strife;
Tho' Fate may cheat you,
And defeat you,
Your youth must answer to the Call of Life.

[*Effie and Jane return with a hat and cape. They dress her in them, and she and Carl go out together. As the orchestra crashes out the final chords, the others rush to the balcony to wave.*]

CURTAIN

ACT TWO: SCENE I

Characters: SARI LINDEN, CARL LINDEN, MANON [LA CRE-
VETTE], LOTTE, FREDA, HANSI, GUSSI, CAPTAIN AUGUST LUTTE,
HERR SCHLICK, WAITERS, CLEANERS, ORCHESTRA, etc. *The
scene is Herr Schlick's café in Vienna. The Year is* 1880.

THE SCENE *is the interior of Schlick's café in Vienna. It is about*
12 *o'clock noon, and Waiters in shirt sleeves are tidying up the
tables and polishing brasses. There are also some cleaners and char-
women swabbing the floor. Carl, in shirt sleeves, is rehearsing with
the orchestra on the orchestra platform ot the back. Lotte, Hansi,
and Freda, three ladies of the town, elaborately dressed, are seated
at a table down stage left.*

*The opening chorus is sung in snatches by the Waiters, Cleaners,
etc.*

WAITERS: Life in the morning isn't too bright,
        When you've had to hurry round and carry
           plates all night;
        And the evening isn't too gay,
        When you know you've got to rise and be at
           work all day.
        This café merely caters
        For a horde of drunken satyrs,
    Why, oh why, we're waiters nobody can say.

CLEANERS: Oh dear, it's clear to see that cleaners lead a worse
             life,
             Every day we curse life;
             More and more
          The muscles on our brawny arms like iron bands
             are
             Scrubbing till our hands are sore;
             We scour and polish till our fingers ache.

WAITERS [*humming*]: Hum—hum——!

CLEANERS: Each hour we feel as tho' our backs would break,

WAITERS: Hum—hum!

CLEANERS: We weep and keep our growing families as well,
             Why we're here at all nobody can tell.

WAITERS: Life in the morning isn't too bright,
             When you've had to hurry round and carry plates
             all night.

CLEANERS: Oh dear, it's clear to see that cleaners lead a worse
             life.

WAITERS: And the evening isn't too gay,
             When you know you've got to rise and be at
             work all day.

CLEANERS: You see the reason why each day we want to curse
             life.

WAITERS: For this café merely caters

CLEANERS: Weary

WAITERS: For a horde of drunken satyrs;

CLEANERS: Dreary

WAITERS: Why, oh why, we're waiters nobody can say.

CLEANERS: Every day.

WAITERS: Ah—Ah—Ah——

CLEANERS: Ah—Ah—Ah——

[*At the end of it, Carl rests his orchestra for a moment.*]

LOTTE: He left me at half-past ten, my dear, he kissed my hand, à la grand chevalier, which made me laugh, I *must* say.

FREDA: Is that all he left you with—a kiss?

LOTTE: Don't be vulgar, Freda, everything was arranged last night in his carriage—we drove round and round the Ringstrasse.

HANSI: I hope it didn't make you too giddy, dear.

LOTTE: You none of you understand, this is an "affaire de cœur," I'm sure of it.

[*Fritz, a waiter, brings Lotte a bill for the coffee and brioches they have been having.*]

LOTTE: It's not my turn—Hansi?

HANSI: I paid yesterday.

LOTTE: Come along, Freda—no fumbling.

FREDA: I wasn't fumbling—I was just trying to count up how many times I've paid during the last month.

HANSI: That oughtn't to take you long

FREDA [*rather crossly*]: Oh, here you are, then. [*She gives him some money.*]

[*He nods and goes off.*]

LOTTE: Where was I?

FREDA: Driving round the Ringstrasse, my dear, talking business.

LOTTE: You can all jeer if you like, but just you wait and see. Anyhow, I feel positively exhausted, having had to get up so early.

HANSI: I'm tired too.

[*Gussi enters, elaborately dressed and wearing a fur tippet and muff.*]

GUSSI: Hallo, girls.

FREDA: Oh, my God, look at Gussi.

HANSI [*fingering the tippet*]: Where did you get it?

GUSSI: Here, leave off, surely you've seen a bit of mink before?

HANSI: Not on you.

GUSSI: Well, have a good look now and enjoy it.

LOTTE: Who gave it to you?

GUSSI [*with great coyness*]: I hardly like to tell you, it was such a delightful surprise—I had been spending the night with my dear old grandmother——

HANSI: I hope she took her spurs off.

[*They all laugh. Gussi sits down at the table.*]

LOTTE: Do you want some coffee?

GUSSI: No thanks, it would spoil my lunch.

FREDA: I'm lunching at Sacher's—I can bring a friend—Hansi?

HANSI: No thank you, dear.

FREDA: Lotte?

LOTTE: Who are you lunching with, the old ostrich?

FREDA: No, he's gone to Warsaw. This is a banker—quite young, but common, no use for dinner—do you want to come?

LOTTE: I don't mind.

HANSI: I can't imagine, Freda, why you waste your time with small fry.

FREDA: I don't consider any free meal small fry.

[*Lotte, Freda and Hansi sing a trio*]:

"LADIES OF THE TOWN"

Though we're often accused of excessively plastic, drastic sins,
When we're asked to decide on the wrong or the right life,
Night life wins,
We know that destiny will never bring
A wedding ring about.
Our moral sense may really not be quite the thing
To fling about, sing about;
We'll achieve independence before it's too late, and
Wait and see.
What care, what care we?

Refrain

Ladies of the town,
Ladies of the town,
Though we've not a confessional air,
We have quite a professional flair,
Strolling up and down, strolling up and down,
We employ quite an amiable system
Of achieving renown,
Though the church and state abuses us,
For as long as it amuses us,
We'll remain, no matter how they frown,
Naughty, naughty, ladies of the town.

We can often behave in a very disarming, charming way,
Which can frequently add to the money we lay by,
Day by day.
If we are told of something on the Stock Exchange,
We pry a bit,
And if it's safe we get some kindly banker
To supply a bit, buy a bit,
And if later our helpers may wish to forget us,
Set us free,
What care, what care we?

Refrain

Ladies of the town, ladies of the town,
Though we're socially under a cloud,
Please forgive us for laughing aloud,
Strolling up and down, strolling up and down,
Disapproval may sometimes submerge us,
But we none of us drown,

We have known in great variety
Members of the best society,
And should we decide to settle down,
We'll be wealthy ladies of the town.

[*When Lotte, Freda and Hansi have gone off, Carl addresses his orchestra on the dais.*]

CARL: It is lacking in colour. Strings, when you take the theme in the first refrain, bring it out, let it live and breathe, and mean something. In the last four bars I've marked a rallentando—Now then——

[*He raises his baton and the orchestra begins La Crevette's Song —as the music swells Manon enters briskly. She is, naturally, in day clothes and a hat; she listens for a moment, and then stamps her foot. Carl stops the orchestra.*]

MANON: No, Carl—it must be quicker there.

CARL: When we were working yesterday that was the exact spot you wanted it slower.

MANON: Listen—it starts so—— [*She sings*]: "Lorsque j'étais petite fille en marchant parmi les prés"—swift, staccato like that, then "J'entendis la voix d'ma tante, qui murmura à côté"—just a leetle slower—not much, you understand——

CARL: Very well. [*He starts the music again.*]

[*Manon stops him.*]

MANON: No, no, no—you are so stubborn.

CARL: Stubborn?

MANON: Yes—you are a musician, yes, but you know nothing about singers, especially when they have no voice like me.

CARL [*coming down to her*]: You have a beautiful voice, Manon.

MANON [*laughing suddenly*]: Now you are being earnest and sincere, it is so many years since I saw that solemn look in your eyes——

CARL: You can't expect me to pay you compliments often, when you try to quarrel with me all the time.

MANON: I quarrel! Don't be a fool.

CARL [*turning away*]: It's you who are a fool——

MANON [*touching his arm, softly*]: No, Carl—I was once—but I'm not any more.

CARL: What do you mean?

MANON: Where is Sari—your little English Sarah?

CARL: She will be here soon.

MANON [*mockingly*]: How exciting!

CARL: You do hate her, don't you?

MANON [*gaily*]: Passionately—I should like to scratch her eyes out and pull her nose off and wring her neck——

CARL: Manon!

MANON: ——in a friendly way. [*She laughs again.*]

CARL: Don't laugh like that.

MANON: You used to love my laughter—it was so gay and charming, you said—I think you mentioned once that it reminded you of a bird chirruping, that was a very pretty thought, Carl——

CARL: Please go away now—I must continue my rehearsal.

MANON: Carl——

CARL: Yes.

MANON: I'm only teasing you and irritating you because I'm jealous——

CARL: But, Manon——

MANON [*holding up her hand*]: No, don't protest and say I have no right to be jealous! I know that well—ours was such a silly little affair really, and so long ago, but somehow it was very sweet and it left a small sting behind——

CARL: It was your fault that it ended.

MANON: I know that too—and I'm glad—I was very proud of

myself finishing it all suddenly like that—because it was for the best—I'm no good for you really—not faithful enough, and you should be free always, because you're an artist. [*She turns away.*] But now you'll never be free, so my beautiful little sacrifice was all in vain. [*She laughs.*] Go back to your work—I'll run through my words here——

CARL: Manon—I——

MANON: Please—play my music for me—I'm not sure of it yet—I'm not sure of anything.

[*Carl looks at her silently for a moment, and then goes thoughtfully back to the orchestra. Manon calls Fritz and orders herself a drink. He brings it immediately and she sings her song quietly*]:

"IF LOVE WERE ALL"

Life is very rough and tumble,
For a humble
  Diseuse,
One can betray one's troubles never,
Whatever
  Occurs,
Night after night,
Have to look bright,
Whether you're well or ill
People must laugh their fill.
You mustn't sleep
Till dawn comes creeping.
Though I never really grumble
Life's a jumble.
Indeed——
And in my efforts to succeed
I've had to formulate a creed—

Refrain

I believe in doing what I can,
In crying when I must,
In laughing when I choose.
Heigho, if love were all
I should be lonely.
I believe the more you love a man,
The more you give your trust,
The more you're bound to lose.
Although when shadows fall
I think if only——
Somebody splendid really needed me,
Someone affectionate and dear,
Cares would be ended if I knew that he
Wanted to have me near.
But I believe that since my life began
The most I've had is just
A talent to amuse.
Heigho, if love were all!
Tho' life buffets me obscenely,
It serenely
Goes on.
Although I question its conclusion,
Illusion
Is gone.
Frequently I
Put a bit by
Safe for a rainy day.
Nobody here can say
To what, indeed,
The years are leading.

Fate may often treat me meanly,
But I keenly
Pursue
A little mirage in the blue.
Determination helps me through.

Repeat Refrain

[*Manon goes off after song. Carl, at the end of Manon's song, dismisses the orchestra, who go off. He comes down from the dais, putting on his coat, when Gussi enters.*]

GUSSI: Hallo, Carl.

CARL [*absently*]: Hallo.

GUSSI: Like a drink?

CARL: No, thanks.

GUSSI: Are you lunching with anyone?

CARL: Yes, my wife.

GUSSI: I might have known it. [*She slips her arm through his.*] Let me know when you feel like being unfaithful to her, won't you?

CARL [*smiling*]: You're bad, Gussi, thoroughly bad—go along with you.

GUSSI: Here listen, you know that dark red coat of mine?

CARL: Yes.

GUSSI: Would your Sari like it? I've had this given to me. [*She waves her muff.*] I shan't need it any more.

CARL: It's very, very sweet of you, Gussi.

GUSSI: You both look so pinched—it depresses me to look at you—bring Sarah along to lunch at my flat——

CARL: Very well.

[*Captain August Lutte enters. Captain August is a debonair, imposing-looking man.*]

GUSSI: Just a moment, some good news has come in—come at 1.30, if I'm not back tell Liza to serve you.

CARL: But, Gussi——

GUSSI [*firmly*]: *Good* bye, *dear* Carl——

[*Carl goes off laughing. Gussi sidles up to Captain August.*]

GUSSI: Good morning.

CAPTAIN [*bowing stiffly*]: Good morning.

GUSSI: Can I do anything for you?

CAPTAIN: I wish to see Herr Schlick.

GUSSI [*grimacing*]: How nice.

CAPTAIN [*abruptly*]: You are very pretty.

GUSSI [*shrinking away*]: Oh, Captain—my salts—my salts.

CAPTAIN: Perhaps you will make a rendezvous with me for next week?

GUSSI: I may be dead next week, what's the matter with now?

CAPTAIN: I fear that I am otherwise engaged.

[*Herr Schlick enters, oily and ingratiating.*]

HERR S.: Captain—forgive me please—I—— [*Sees Gussi.*] What are you doing here?

GUSSI: Just feeding the swans—— Good-bye. [*She goes off.*]

CAPTAIN: Herr Schlick, I have a complaint to make.

HERR S.: It shall be rectified—before you say it, whatever is wrong is rectified.

CAPTAIN: Among your professional dancing partners you have been careless enough to engage an iceberg.

HERR S.: Good God!

CAPTAIN: A beautiful, alluring, unsociable iceberg—her name is Sari.

HERR S.: She is new, Captain; she has only been here a few weeks.

CAPTAIN: Even a few weeks is surely time enough to enable her to melt sufficiently to sup with me——

HERR S.: She is English, Captain, one must make allowances.

CAPTAIN: I do not come to a café of this sort to make allowances—I come to amuse myself and to pay for it.

[*Manon re-enters on the dais just above them. She is looking for Carl, but stops on hearing their voices.*]

HERR S. [*very flurried*]: Captain—I assure you—anything that you wish—I will arrange as soon as possible.

CAPTAIN: I wish for this Sari to sup with me—to-night.

HERR S.: She shall, Captain, she shall.

CAPTAIN: You will please have a special supper laid ready in a quiet room—No. 7 is the best, I think——

HERR S.: You are sure that you would not rather have Lotte or perhaps Hansi——

CAPTAIN: Quite sure.

HERR S.: You see this English girl is the wife of my orchestra leader—they are said to be in love—it will be a little difficult——

CAPTAIN [*rising*]: I hope I have made myself quite clear——

HERR S.: But, Captain——

CAPTAIN: You will please arrange things as I have suggested—to-night I wish no allowances to be made.

[*He bows as he is about to go out, and meets Sari coming in. She has grown more poised and mature during the years spent with Carl. She starts visibly on seeing Captain August—he clicks his heels and bows.*]
Good morning.

SARI: Good morning.

CAPTAIN: It is a beautiful morning.

SARI: Beautiful.

CAPTAIN: But chilly.

SARI: It is very warm out.

CAPTAIN: Would you honour me by lunching with me?

SARI: I'm so sorry, but I am already engaged.

CAPTAIN: Perhaps a drive a little later on; we might go up to Cobenzil——

SARI: Please forgive me, but to-day it is impossible.

CAPTAIN: I quite understand. [*He bows again.*] Until to-night, madame. [*He goes off.*]

HERR S. [*furiously*]: It may interest you to know that you are losing me one of my most valued clients—I'll deal with you later. Captain—a moment, please—Captain——

[*He rushes off. Sari looks after him pensively for a moment and then sighs. Manon comes down from the dais.*]

MANON: Sari.

SARI: Oh!

MANON: Don't look so startled——

SARI: I came to find Carl. Have you seen him?

MANON: Yes, I've just been rehearsing with him.

SARI: Oh!

MANON: He's about somewhere.

SARI: I'll find him. [*She turns to go.*]

MANON: I want to speak to you.

SARI [*coldly*]: Yes? What is it?

MANON: Oh, why do you always look at me like that?

SARI: Like what?

MANON: Aloof and superior.

SARI: I wasn't conscious of being either of those things.

MANON: Yes, you were—you know you were—you always are with me. But, listen, never mind about that now—I heard Schlick arranging for you to have supper in a private room with Captain August to-night.

SARI: What!

MANON: So be careful.

SARI [*incredulously*]: You heard Schlick arranging for *me*——

MANON: Yes—yes, yes—I thought you might like to know.

SARI: How horrible!

MANON: Not so horrible as all that; lots of the girls here would be glad of the chance, but as Carl is in love with you and you are apparently in love with him, I thought——

SARI [*rather stiffly*]: Thank you, Manon.

MANON: Not at all. [*She turns to go.*]

SARI: Manon——

MANON [*stopping*]: Yes?

SARI: I'm sorry.

MANON: What for?

SARI: If my manner is—well, unkind——

MANON [*patting her arm*]: All is well, my dear—I don't love him any more, really, at least I don't think I do, and anyhow you have no reason to be jealous, nothing to be afraid of. Look at me, and then look in the glass. [*She kisses her lightly, and goes off humming a reprise of her former song.*]

[*Carl enters from left.*]

SARI: Carl.

CARL: Darling! [*He kisses her fondly.*] How quick you've been dressing. I crept out without waking you.

SARI: Yes, I know; you must never do that again.

CARL: Why—what's the matter?

SARI: I dreamt—something dreadful. I awoke terrified—I came straight here without any coffee or anything—to see if you were safe.

CARL: I safe? Why, of course I'm safe—why shouldn't I be?

SARI: I don't know, I'm frightened. I hate this place—let's go away. I'd rather go back to singing in the streets again, at least we were independent then and together.

CARL: We're together now—always.

SARI [*wildly*]: No, no—not here we're not—we're separated

by hundreds of things and people—you're the chef d'orchestre and I'm a professional dance partner. I hate it, I tell you—I can't be gay and enjoy it like the other girls, because I love you— I can't feel happy when the cavalry officers put their arms round my waist and dance and flirt with me, because I love you, and because I'm scared.

CARL: Why are you scared?

SARI: Something horrible will happen if we stay here. I know it, I feel it——

CARL: Come along and have a little lunch, then you'll feel better. We're going to Gussi's flat—she's got a present for you —you know that red coat——

SARI: Oh, Carl, Carl, you won't understand!——

[*Carl takes her in his arms.*]

"EVERMORE AND A DAY"

CARL: Why are you weeping, dear?
  What shadows haunted you in sleeping, dear?
  Tho' portents and fears
  Your Courage may be plundering
  Your Faith in my Love
  Should leave no time for wondering.
  Even your Dreams are in my keeping, dear.

SARI: Ah! No! My sweet
  Fate knows our Happiness is too complete
  Tho' now in our Love's security
  We live awhile,
  A little of Hearts' content
  The Gods may give awhile,
  Time's on the wing, my love,
  And Time is fleet.

CARL: Peace enfold you,
Here in my arms I will hold you,
Fears receding
Further and further away.

Refrain

SARI: Tho' the world may divide us
And ill fortune betide us
Yet our Love is a token
That cannot be broken
Or stolen away.
There's a Passionate glory
In the heart of our story,
We have something to guide us
Evermore and a day.

CARL: Peace enfold you,
Here in my arms I will hold you,
Fears receding
Further and further away,
Why are you weeping, dear,
You know your heart is in my keeping, dear.

CARL: You must take hold of your courage, my sweet—we must both put up with things now in order to be secure later on—no more street singing—it broke my heart to see you hungry—that's all past—you've been so splendid and brave all through—just hold on for a few weeks more until we have enough to start that little café——

SARI [*hysterically*]: Laugh at me then—laugh everything away, stop me being solemn—we're both too young to be dreary and sentimental—make me forget the present in planning for the future—where will our café be? How shall we manage it? Shall I be able to sing your songs there?—one day I might make them famous—I love your music so very much—I want it to be known all over the world, and one day it will be, I'm sure of it —do you think I could help—do you?

CARL [*kissing her*]: Darling.

"LITTLE CAFÉ"

CARL: We share a mutual ambition
      Which naught can disarrange,
SARI: Based on the hopeful supposition
      That soon our luck will change.
CARL: Tho' we very often wonder whether
      Poverty will win the day,
SARI: Just as long as we remain together
      Troubles seem to fade away.
BOTH: However hard the bed one lies on
      The same old dreams begin,
    We're always scanning the horizon
      For when our ship comes in.

Refrain
CARL: We'll have a sweet little café
      In a neat little square,
SARI: We'll find our fortune
      And our happiness there.
CARL: We shall thrive on the vain and resplendent
SARI: And contrive to remain independent.
CARL: We'll have a meek reputation
      And a chic clientele.
SARI: Kings will fall under our spell.
BOTH: We'll be so zealous
      That the world will be jealous

Of our sweet little café in our square.
SARI: Can you imagine our sensations
    When we've security?
CARL: And all our dreary deprivations
    Are just a memory.
SARI: Tho' we're very often driven frantic,
    Peace is very hard to find.
CARL: All these dreadful days will seem romantic
    When we've left them far behind.
BOTH: Fate needn't be quite such a dragon,
    He knows how tired we are.
    We'll hitch our hopeful little wagon
    On to a lucky star.

Refrain

CARL: We'll have a sweet little café
    In a neat little square,
SARI: We'll find our fortune
    And our happiness there.
CARL: We shall thrive on the vain and resplendent
SARI: And contrive to remain independent.
CARL: We'll have a meek reputation
    And a chic clientele.
SARI: Kings will fall under our spell.
BOTH: We'll be so zealous
    That the world will be jealous
    Of our sweet little café in our square.

[*At the end of the last refrain Carl takes Sari in his arms and the curtain falls.*]

ACT TWO: SCENE II

Characters: SARI LINDEN, CARL LINDEN, MANON [LA CRE-VETTE], CAPTAIN AUGUST LUTTE, LIEUTENANT TRANISCH, HERR SCHLICK, LOTTE, FREDA, HANSI, GUSSI, SIX SPECIAL DANCERS, OFFICERS, GUESTS, WAITERS, MUSICIANS, etc. *The scene is the same as* ACT TWO, SCENE I.

THE SCENE *is the same, except that the atmosphere has changed from a frowsy daylight squalor to a tinselled gas-light gaiety.*

It is about 2 a.m.

When the curtain rises everyone is waltzing. Carl is conducting the orchestra on the dais. Some of the Girls have Male Partners and some are dancing with one another. The stage should look as hot and crowded as possible. At the end of the opening waltz Carl stops his orchestra and the theatre orchestra takes up the Officers' entrance music. About a dozen smart Officers come marching on in attractive undress uniform. They sing a concerted introductory number with the Girls.

"OFFICERS' CHORUS"

OFFICERS: We wish to order wine, please,
Expressly from the Rhine, please,
    The year we really don't much care.

LADIES: Oh dear,
Now that you're here
    Think of the wear and tear.

OFFICERS: We hope without insistence
To overcome resistance
    In all you little ladies fair.

LADIES: Oh well,
How can we tell
    Whether you'd really dare?

OFFICERS: We sincerely hope it's really not a thankless task
    Amusing us,
    Won't you please agree?

LADIES: Ah, me!

OFFICERS: You could quickly break our hearts by everything
        we ask
    Refusing us;
    Cruel that would be
    Ladies, can't you see!
    We're officers and gentlemen,
    Reliable and true,
    Considerate and chivalrous
    In everything we do.
    Though we're gay and drunk a trifle,
    All our laughter we should stifle,
    Were we summoned by a bugle call.
    We're amorous and passionate,
    But dignified and stern,
    Which if you play us false you'll quickly learn.
    Do not let our presence grieve you,
    When we've loved you we shall leave you,
    For we're officers and gentlemen, that's all!

[*After song, Captain August and Tranisch enter, and Captain August and the Officers sing "Tokay," of which everyone joins in the last Refrain*]:

"TOKAY"

OFFICERS: Tokay!

CAPTAIN A.: When we're thoroughly wined and dined,
    And the barracks are left behind,
    We come down to the town to find
    Some relief from the daily grind.

Love is kind,
Love is blind.
OFFICERS: Tokay!
CAPTAIN A.: When the thoughts of a man incline
To the grapes of a sunlit vine,
On the banks of the golden Rhine,
Slowly ripening pure and fine,
Sweet divine,
Lover's wine.
Lift your voices till the rafters ring,
Fill your glasses to the brim and sing:

Refrain

Tokay!
The golden sunshine of a summer day,
Tokay!
Will bear the burden of your cares away.
Here's to the love in you,
The hate in you,
Desire in you.
OFFICERS: Wine of the sun that will waft you along,
Lifting you high on the wings of a song.
CAPTAIN A.: Dreams in you,
The flame in you,
The fire in you,
Tokay—Tokay.
OFFICERS: So while forgetfulness we borrow,
Never minding what to-morrow has to say,
CAPTAIN A.:   Tokay!
ALL: The only call we all obey,
Tokay—Tokay—Tokay!

[*Some go off to the bar, others seat themselves at tables and order wine. Sari and Manon come in and sit at a table below the balcony to the right. Sari is simply dressed in white. Manon is very gay in scarlet sequins.*]

SARI: I'm so tired.

MANON: Well, for heaven's sake don't look as if you were.

SARI: I'm sick of pretending.

MANON: So am I, but it's no use worrying about that. The whole business is pretending. Life's pretending.

SARI: That hateful Captain August—he smiled at me in the bar—an odious smile.

MANON: I hope you smiled back.

SARI: I certainly did not.

MANON: Well, that was very foolish of you—there's nothing so alluring to that type of man as snowy chastity.

SARI: How can you, Manon. [*She smiles.*] I'm so miserable really, it's horrid of you to laugh at me.

MANON: That's better—you're smiling yourself, now.

[*Lieutenant Tranisch enters from the bar, comes to their table and bows to Manon.*]

TRANISCH: Mademoiselle la Crevette.

MANON: Yes?

TRANISCH: We have never spoken before, but I wish to say you are an admirable artiste—you sing like an angel.

MANON [*laughing very loudly*]: You Viennese are so gallant. I sing like a frog.

TRANISCH: Will you come to the bar and take a drink with me?

MANON: What is this now—what does this mean? Is it the birth of a romance? I feel so flattered.

TRANISCH [*slightly embarrassed*]: Mademoiselle—I——

MANON: Never mind, Lieutenant, I am not deceived—you think

I sing well, that is very kind—now tell me—cards on the table
—to which of the more attractive women here do you want me
to introduce you?

TRANISCH: Really—you misunderstand me—I——

MANON: Come now—tell me—I have no sensibilities.

TRANISCH: There is a small blonde lady like a kitten in yellow
—I will admit to you frankly—she enthrals me strangely.

MANON: That would be Gussi. [*She rises.*] Excuse me for a
moment, Sari.

SARI: Of course.

TRANISCH [*clicking his heels and bowing to Sari*]: Fräulein.

MANON: Come along—but let me warn you—Gussi is a collector.

TRANISCH: Collector?

MANON: Yes, of antiques—very enthusiastic—old jewellery
for preference. If your acquaintance ripens, let me advise you
when walking to keep to the more modern thoroughfares. [*She
looks at Sari smilingly.*] Heigho—if love were all!

[*She and Tranisch go off to the bar. Captain August enters and
comes to Sari's table, but as he does so Carl sees him and comes down
from the orchestra.*]

CAPTAIN A. [*bowing*]: Madame——

CARL: Sari, I want to talk to you. You remember the second
movement in the concerto I was scoring yesterday, I have had
the most magnificent idea—instead of using strings alone, I shall
strengthen it with the zimbale just towards the end where it
goes—tum tum tum tum—— [*He hums.*]

SARI: Yes, I know—*what* a good idea. [*She also hums.*] Tum
tum—tum tum tum——

[*They both hum together, and finally Captain August, finding
himself completely ignored, turns on his heel and marches back into
the bar.*]

[*Half laughing*]: Oh, Carl—that was wonderful of you.

CARL: I was watching—I'm always watching to see that no harm comes to you.

SARI: I hate him so—he won't leave me alone—he embarrasses me.

CARL: Cheer up, my dearest.

SARI: I'll try. [*She smiles.*] Oh, Carl, there's something so heavy weighing down on my heart—I felt it this morning, and it's there again now.

CARL [*looking at her*]: You're very strange to-night—you've been strange all day—eager and tense like a frightened child. Is there anything the matter really?

SARI: Yes—no—I don't know. I feel as though fate were too strong for us, as though our love for one another and our happiness together was making the gods angry. I feel suddenly insecure.

CARL: We'll go away, then, to-morrow.

SARI: Carl!

CARL: We have a little money saved anyhow. I hate Schlick and this place as much as you do really. To-night is the end of it. We'll go to Frankfort. Heinrich is there, he'll help us.

SARI: To-night is the end of it.

CARL: You remember Heinrich—with the long brown beard —you laughed at him.

SARI: Yes, he was funny, but I liked him.

CARL: Do you feel happier now?

SARI: Oh, yes, much, much happier.

CARL: So do I—we'll be free again—independent—I must get back. Au revoir, my dear love.

SARI: Au revoir.

[*She kisses her hand to him and goes off. Gussi and Lieutenant Tranisch come on, followed by Hansi and Freda, who are giggling.*]

GUSSI: Louis Quinze—of course it was only paste, but definitely Louis Quinze.

TRANISCH: How interesting.

GUSSI: I'll show it to you to-morrow—we can drive there after luncheon.

TRANISCH: We haven't had supper yet.

GUSSI: No, but we will—we'll sit here—I shall have to dance in a minute—Fritz—Hans——

[She sits down with Tranisch at a small table and calls the waiters. Freda and Hansi sit down also, but on the opposite side of the stage, at the same table at which Carl and Sari played the preceding scene.]

HANSI: I'll tell you one thing here and now, whatever Gussi is talking about is *not* paste.

FREDA: I doubt if it's even Louis Quinze.

[Sari comes in.]

HANSI: Here comes the snow queen.

FREDA: Hullo, Sari.

SARI: Hello.

HANSI: Any offers to-night?

FREDA: Don't tease her, Hansi—she's in love.

SARI *[smiling]*: No, no offers so far.

HANSI: Do you want a drink?

SARI: Yes—I'd love one.

HANSI: Fritz—— *[She calls the waiter and orders wine.]*

FREDA: That's pretty, that dress—is it new?

SARI: Yes. I made it myself from a pattern.

FREDA: It sags a little behind—here—look—give me a pin, Hansi.

HANSI: You can have this brooch for the time being, but give it back, it's not valuable, but lucky.

[She gives Sari a brooch. Sari stands up while Freda fixes the

brooch on to the dress. Captain August comes in and bows ironically to Sari.]

CAPTAIN A.: Will you honour me with this dance, please?

SARI [*jumping slightly*]: Oh—no, I'm sorry—I'm engaged.

CAPTAIN A.: I fear that is not strictly true.

FREDA: I'll dance with you, if you like.

CAPTAIN A.: Please do not think me impolite, but I have set my heart on dancing with Fräulein Sari.

SARI: Forgive me, Captain, but it's quite impossible.

CAPTAIN A.: We shall see. [*He bows abruptly and walks across the stage to where Schlick is standing talking to two other officers. He is obviously very angry. He speaks to Schlick swiftly and angrily.*]

SARI: I hate him—he's always tormenting me.

FREDA: You're unwise, my dear—it's best to humour them a little.

SARI: I've tried—I've danced with him, but he presses me too close and whispers horrible things to me.

HANSI: He's very rich and, I believe, generous.

SARI: Yes, but that doesn't interest me.

HANSI [*wistfully*]: There's no doubt about it—love is very bad for business.

[*Schlick comes to their table.*]

SCHLICK: Sari——

SARI: Yes, Herr Schlick.

SCHLICK: You are engaged and paid by me as a dancing partner for my clients, are you not?

SARI: Yes.

SCHLICK: I have received several complaints from Captain August Lutte—he says you persistently refuse to dance with him.

SARI: He takes advantage of my position.

SCHLICK: It would be better if you realised once and for all that you have no position—after to-night you may consider your engagement at an end.

SARI [*with spirit*]: It is an end anyhow—my husband and I are leaving Vienna to-morrow.

SCHLICK: Oho—I see. Well, I should like to remind you that you both have a week's salary owing to you, and unless you dance willingly and agreeably with Captain August or any other of the officers when they ask you to, neither you nor your husband will receive a penny of your salary—I run my café on business lines, you understand.

SARI: But, Herr Schlick, that is unfair—my behaviour has nothing to do with my husband.

SCHLICK: That is enough. I am sick to death of your stupid mincing airs and graces—unless you behave yourself to-night, you will both leave to-morrow without your money, and be damned to you!

[*He leaves Sari, who sinks miserably into her chair. Hansi and Freda try to comfort her and give her some wine. Schlick advances to the middle of the floor to announce the commencement of the entertainment.*]

Ladies and Gentlemen, I crave your kind attention for the most superb musical entertainment ever offered in Vienna.

[*Everyone applauds.*]

Thank you. Thank you. My first number will be my six magnificent dancing girls—trained exclusively in the finest ballet schools in the world. Lise, Trude, Fritz, Toni, Greta and Elsa.

[*Six Girls rise from their various tables and make a line in the middle of the floor. There is a lot of applause. Carl strikes up their music and they dance, after which they return to their tables amid cheers. Schlick again takes the floor.*]

Gentlemen—Ladies and Gentlemen—I beg attention for my

favourite, your favourite, the world's favourite star—Manon la
Crevette.

[*He steps aside and Manon comes running on. She is greeted with
vociferous applause. She sings a very saucy French song, "Bonne
Nuit, Merci!," interspersed with a good deal of back-chat and
ogling*]:

"BONNE NUIT, MERCI!"

MANON: Lorsque j'étais petite fille
En marchant parmi les prés
J'entendit la voix d'ma tante
Qui murmura à côté,
"N'oublie pas la politesse
Lorsque viendra un amant,
Car tout le bonheur réside là dedans."

Refrain

C'est pourquoi dans mes affaires,
Soit de cœur ou soit d'esprit,
C'est pourquoi je tâche de plaire
Toute la foule de mes amis,
Soit qu'ils m'offrent pied-à-terre
Ou me montrent une bonne affaire
J'leur réponds, "Vas-y. Bonne Nuit.
Merci!"

Lorsque je suis v'nue à Paris
J'étais sage de nature,
Mais que faire dans la vie
Etant jeune pour rester pure!
Quand ma politesse m'obligea
Lorsqu' je suivais par hasard
Une aventure dans les boîtes des boulevards.

Refrain

Et j'ai rencontré en ville
Un monsieur bien comme il faut,
Il m'a dit, "ma petite fille,
Veux-tu faire un p'tit do-do?"
Lorsqu' j'arrive chez lui tout de suite
I'me dit "Deshabilles-toi vite!"
J'me suis dis "Vas-y. Bonne Nuit.
      Merci!"

[*As encore she sings a waltz song in which everybody joins.*]

"WALTZ SONG"

'Tis time that we were parted,
    You and I,
However broken-hearted,
    'Tis good-bye!
Although our love has ended
And darkness has descended,
I call to you with one last cry:

Refrain

    Kiss me
Before you go away!
    Miss me
Through every night and day.
Though clouds are grey above you,
    You'll hear me say I love you!
    Kiss me
Before you go away!

Parmi les chansons tristes
De l'amour,
Joies et chagrins existent
Tour à tour,
Et presqu'avec contrainte
On risque la douce étreinte
Qui nous sépare enfin toujours.

Refrain

Je t'aime,
Tes baisers m'ont grisée
Même
A l'heure de t'en aller,
La volupté troublante
Brise mes lèvres brûlantes,
Je t'aime,
A l'heure de t'en aller.

[*At the end of this Carl strikes up another waltz and everybody begins to dance. Schlick comes over to Sari's table and stands behind it. After a moment Captain August approaches and bows.*]

CAPTAIN A: Fräulein Sari has perhaps by now forgotten her other engagement.

SARI [*rising agitatedly*]: I—please—I——

SCHLICK: You are quite right, Captain, she has forgotten.

SARI: Captain August—I am very tired—will you please forgive me just this once?

CAPTAIN A.: One dance, please.

SCHLICK: I think you would be well advised to grant Captain August's request.

SARI [*pulling herself together*]: Certainly, Captain, I shall be charmed.

[*She gives one despairing look at Carl on the dais—he is watching anxiously—then she surrenders herself to the Captain's arms and they begin to waltz. Carl watches all the time. As the dance progresses Captain August is obviously becoming more and more aggressively amorous. Carl, with obvious agitation, perceptibly quickens the tempo of the music. Finally the Captain waltzes Sari into the centre of the floor—stops dead, tightens his arms round her and kisses her on the mouth passionately, bending her right back as he does so. She gives one cry, Carl stops the music dead with a crash and leaps over the railing of the dais on to the middle of the floor. He drags Sari away from Captain August, then, springing at him, strikes him in the face. Immediately the buzz of excitement dies down into dead silence.*]

CARL [*wildly*]: Swine—filthy, ill-mannered drunken swine!

SARI [*in a whisper*]: Carl!

MANON [*rushing forward*]: Carl—don't be a fool.

[*Captain August gives an unpleasant laugh and draws his sword.*]

CAPTAIN A.: Tranisch—look after our foolhardy young friend here, will you?

TRANISCH: Not now—not now—wait.

CAPTAIN A.: I regret—I cannot wait.

[*Tranisch draws his sword and hands it to Carl—Manon clutches his arm.*]

CARL: Stand back, Manon—look after Sari—please.

[*The Captain attacks him and they fight a brief duel, the crowd making a large ring round them. Suddenly Captain August knocks Carl's sword from his hand and runs him through. There is a general scream and everyone crowds forward. Sari silently and madly fights through the crowd and sinks to the ground, taking Carl in her arms. Tranisch motions the crowd back. There is silence except for Manon, who is crying loudly and hopelessly.*]

SARI [*softly—she is dry-eyed*]: I'll love you always—always—do you hear?

CARL [*weakly*]: Sari—Sari—my sweet, sweet Sari——

[*His head falls back in her lap, and she kneels there staring before her dazed and hopeless as the curtain falls.*]

ACT THREE: SCENE I

Characters: MADAME SARI LINDEN, THE MARQUIS OF SHAYNE,
LADY JAMES [HARRIET], MRS. PROUTIE [GLORIA], MRS. BETHEL
[EFFIE], LADY SORREL [HONOR], MRS. VALE [JANE], THE
DUCHESS OF TENTERDEN [VICTORIA], LORD JAMES, MR.
PROUTIE, MR. BETHEL, LORD SORREL, MR. VALE, THE DUKE
OF TENTERDEN, THE HON. HUGH DEVON, MRS. DEVON, VERNON
CRAFT, CEDRIC BALLANTYNE, BERTRAM SELLICK, LORD HENRY
JADE, ACCOMPANIST [*to* MADAME LINDEN], BUTLER, GUESTS,
*etc. The scene is Lord Shayne's house in London. The Year
is* 1895.

IT IS *the drawing room of the Marquis of Shayne's house in London.
Fifteen years have passed since Act Two, and it is now* 1895. *When
the curtain rises, Lord Shayne, a distinguished old man, is standing
a little to the right receiving his guests, who are announced by the
Butler. Lady James [Harriet] and Mrs. Proutie [Gloria] are
announced with their husbands, likewise Mrs. Bethel [Effie], Lady
Sorrel [Honor], Mrs. Vale [Jane], and lastly the Duchess of Tenterden [Victoria]. They are all by now smart middle-aged society
matrons. Their entrance and Lord Shayne's reception of them is all
part of the opening chorus.*

OPENING CHORUS

ALL: Tarara boom-de-ay,
             Tarara boom-de-ay,

We are the most effectual,
   Intellectual
Movement of the day.
Our moral standards sway
   Like Mrs. Tanqueray,
And we are theoretically
   Most æsthetically
   Eager to display
   The fact that we're aggressively
   And excessively
   Anxious to destroy
   All the snobbery
   And hob-nobbery
   Of the hoi-polloi.
   Tarara boom-de-ay.
It's mental washing day,
   And come what may
We'll scrub until the nation's morals shrink away.
   Tarara boom-de-ay!
EXQUISITES: Though we are languid in appearance,
   We're in the vanguard.
   We feel we can guard
   The cause of Art.
We shall ignore all interference,
   For our complacence
With this renaissance
Is frightfully smart.
Please do not think us unrelenting,
   Our charming frolic
   With the symbolic
   Is meek and mild.
We merely spend our time preventing

Some earnest stripling
From liking Kipling
Instead of Wilde.
Now that we find the dreary nineteenth century
    is closing,
We mean to start the twentieth in ecstasies of
    posing.

ALL: Tarara boom-de-ay,
It's mental washing day.
And come what may
We'll scrub until the tiresome bourgeois shrink
    away.
Tarara boom-de-ay!

[*Which is concluded by a sextette by Harriet, Gloria, Honor,
Jane, Effie and Victoria. Everyone else retires into the supper
room, leaving them on the stage.*]

"ALAS, THE TIME IS PAST"

Alas, the time is past when we
   Could frolic with impunity.
   Secure in our virginity,
   We sometimes look aghast
   Adown the lanes of memory,
   Alas, the time is past.
Ah, then the world was at our feet,
When we were sweet-and-twenty,
We never guessed that what we'd got,
   Tho' not a lot—was plenty.
   We gaily sought some Abelard
   To cherish, guard and own us,
But all we know of storm and strife
   Our married life—has shown us.

Alas, the time is past when we
   Could frolic with impunity,
   Secure in our virginity,
   We sometimes look aghast
   Adown the lanes of memory.
   Alas, the time is past.
Alack-a-day me—alack-a-day me!
Ah, then the world was at our feet,
   Alas, the time is past.

HARRIET: What have you done to your hair, Effie—it strikes me as peculiar.

EFFIE: Nothing in particular.

GLORIA: I'm afraid you're becoming a little pernickety, Harriet; you must guard against it.

HONOR: Where's your late husband, Victoria?

VICTORIA: Later than ever, my dear—he's at Boodles, I expect.

JANE: Talking too much.

HARRIET: And drinking much too much.

VICTORIA: You can't upset me by saying that, Harriet dear. I find alcohol one of the greatest comforts of matrimony!

HONOR: Victoria!

VICTORIA: In a husband, I mean—it leaves one free for one's charities.

JANE: A little too free sometimes, my pet.

HARRIET: Who is this woman?

EFFIE: Which woman?

HARRIET: The one we've been invited to meet.

VICTORIA: Some strange Hungarian singer—probably very glittering and rather stout.

HONOR: Oh, I shouldn't think so—Lord Shayne has been pursuing her for ages from capital to capital.

HARRIET: Central Europe is far too musical, there can be no two opinions about that.

JANE: I hear she's very beautiful.

[*Lord Shayne has entered unobserved from the supper room.*]

LORD S.: She is——

VICTORIA: Good heavens, how you made me jump!

LORD S.: She is one of the few really beautiful people in the world.

HARRIET: How very disconcerting!

HONOR: Do you think we shall like that?

LORD S.: I shall be very interested to see the effect she has on you—you are all—if I may say so—so very representative.

VICTORIA: Of what, dear Lord Shayne?

LORD S.: Shall we say "fin de siècle"?

HARRIET: I was afraid somebody would say that before the evening was over.

[*The Butler announces the Hon. Hugh Devon and Mrs. Devon. Lord Shayne moves over to greet them. Hugh has developed along the exact lines that one would have expected; he has become a good deal more pompous with the years, and has a tremendously diplomatic manner. His wife is fat and vague.*]

VICTORIA: Margaret dear, how are you?

MRS. D.: Shattered, completely shattered! Our cabby was raving mad. He kept saying the oddest things to his horse, at least I hope they were to his horse. I pretended not to understand, one has to think of prestige——

LORD S.: I hear you're going to Vienna.

HUGH: Yes, next week, thank God! I believe Mullins has been making a fearful hash of everything.

MRS. D.: Isn't it exciting! I was so afraid we were going to be sent to Riga or Christiania or somewhere draughty like that.

HARRIET: Hugh generally gets what he wants.

MRS. D.: As it is, I don't know what I shall do with the children. I can't help feeling that Eva is the wrong age for Vienna.

LORD S.: No one is the wrong age for Vienna—it's a city of enchantment—magnificent.

HUGH: I'm told the plumbing is appalling.

VICTORIA: Lord Shayne has fallen in love again—haven't you, my dear?

LORD S.: I am always in love with beauty.

HUGH: Admirably put, Shayne. I quite agree with you.

JANE: We're all on tenterhooks to see Madame Linden—she's due at any moment.

MRS. D.: What are tenterhooks? I never know.

[*The Butler throws open the doors and announces Madame Sari Linden. Sarah enters, exquisitely gowned and radiantly beautiful, carrying herself with tremendous poise; her jewels are superb, and the years have invested her with a certain air of decision which is almost metallic as compared with the tremulous diffidence of her youth. Lord Shayne goes forward and kisses her hand.*]

LORD S.: My dear, how enchanting to see you again. [*He turns with a smile.*] I think you know everyone here.

HARRIET: Good heavens, Sarah!

VICTORIA [*astounded*]: Sarah!

EFFIE: It can't be—it can't be——

[*She rushes up and kisses her. There is a babel of surprised and excited conversation. Hugh stands a little apart, looking a trifle embarrassed.*]

HONOR: We heard that you had died, ages and ages ago.

SARI: I did die. Fifteen years ago to be exact. Things happened and I couldn't come back. I didn't want to come back, so I thought I'd better die, vaguely and obscurely. It was the only thing to do—it sort of rounded everything off so satisfactorily.

JANE: It's unbelievable, Sarah, dear Sarah.

SARI: Please don't be quite so pleased to see me. It makes me feel ashamed, particularly with Hugh standing there, looking so stern. How do you do, Hugh?

HUGH: I'm delighted to see you again. Margaret, I want you to meet Sarah—Sarah——? [*He looks questioningly at her.*]

SARI: Linden—don't say you've forgotten Carl Linden, the man I eloped with, practically under your nose, Hugh?

HUGH: I remember perfectly—how is he?

SARI: He's dead—I'm so glad to meet you, Mrs. Devon. I do hope Hugh is a charming husband and not too embittered—I treated him abominably, you know.

MRS. D. [*shaking hands with her*]: It's all so very surprising—very, very surprising—Hugh told me the whole story, when he heard of your death in Prague or somewhere. He was dreadfully upset, weren't you, Hugh?

HUGH: Yes, indeed, I was.

SARI [*smiling and tapping him lightly with her fan*]: Dear Hugh, never mind—everything always turns out for the best, doesn't it? At least, almost everything.

LORD S.: Won't you have a little supper—Sari?

HONOR: "Sari"—it does sound pretty, doesn't it—"Sari."

SARI: Only a very little if you want me to sing for you.

[*They all go into the supper room, chattering and laughing, while the Orchestra very softly and lightly plays a reprise of the "Blindman's Buff Finale" in Act One. When the supper-room doors close behind them, the other doors open and four over-exquisitely dressed young men enter. They all wear in their immaculate buttonholes green carnations. Vernon Craft, a poet, Cedric Ballantyne, a painter, Lord Henry Jade, a dilettante, and Bertram Sellick, a playwright.*]

BERTIE: It's entirely Vernon's fault that we are so entrancingly late.

VERNON: My silk socks were two poems this evening and they refused to scan.

HENRY: It's going to be inexpressibly dreary, I can feel it in my bones.

CEDRIC: Don't be absurd, Henry, your whole charm lies in the fact that you have no bones.

[*They sing a quartette, "We All Wore a Green Carnation"*]:

"WE ALL WORE A GREEN CARNATION"

> Blasé boys are we,
>   Exquisitely free
> From the dreary and quite absurd
> Moral views of the common herd.
>   We like porphyry bowls,
>   Chandeliers and stoles,
> We're most spirited,
>   Carefully filleted "souls."

Refrain

> Pretty boys, witty boys, too, too, too
>   Lazy to fight stagnation,
> Haughty boys, naughty boys, all we do
>   Is to pursue sensation.
>   The portals of society
>   Are always opened wide,
> The world our eccentricity condones,
>   A note of quaint variety
>   We're certain to provide.
> We dress in very decorative tones.
> Faded boys, jaded boys, womankind's
>   Gift to a bulldog nation,
> In order to distinguish us from less enlightened minds,
>   We all wear a green carnation.

We believe in Art,
Though we're poles apart
From the fools who are thrilled by Greuze.
We like Beardsley and Green Chartreuse.
Women say we're too
Bored to bill and coo,
We smile wearily,
It's so drearily true!

Refrain

Pretty boys, witty boys, you may sneer
At our disintegration,
Haughty boys, naughty boys, dear, dear, dear!
Swooning with affectation.
Our figures sleek and willowy,
Our lips incarnadine,
May worry the majority a bit,
But matrons rich and billowy,
Invite us out to dine,
And revel in our phosphorescent wit.
Faded boys, jaded boys, come what may,
Art is our inspiration,
And as we are the reason for the "Nineties" being gay,
We all wear a green carnation.

Refrain

Pretty boys, witty boys, yearning for
Permanent adulation,
Haughty boys, naughty boys, every pore
Bursting with self-inflation,

We feel we're rather Grecian,
As our manners indicate,
Our sense of moral values isn't strong.
For ultimate completion
We shall really have to wait
Until the Day of Judgment comes along.
Faded boys, jaded boys, each one craves
    Some sort of soul salvation,
But when we rise reluctantly but gracefully from our graves,
    We'll all wear a green carnation.

[*They go off. Lord Shayne and Sari come in from the supper room.*]

LORD S.: I want to talk to you.

SARI: I know.

LORD S.: You can guess what I am going to say?

SARI: Yes, I think so.

LORD S.: I love you.

SARI [*smiling*]: I was right.

LORD S.: Will you honour me by becoming my wife? You've now refused me in practically every capital in Europe—London is the last on the list.

SARI: Why should London prove the exception?

LORD S.: It's home.

SARI [*sighing*]: Yes—I suppose it is.

LORD S.: It has charm, London—a very peaceful charm, particularly for anyone who is tired like you. You can drive in the Park in the Spring and look at the crocuses.

SARI: Please don't talk of Spring.

LORD S.: Then there's the Autumn, when the leaves fall in the Square, and you can sit on a rickety iron chair and watch the children searching for horse chestnuts.

SARI [*wistfully*]: Whose children?

LORD S.: Just anybody's.

SARI: The fogs come in November.

LORD S.: Fogs can be delightful.

SARI: Can they? [*She smiles.*]

LORD S.: Particularly when you're warm and snug by a crackly fire drinking tea, while from the yellow gloom outside the trees look in at you like ghosts.

SARI: I don't like tea or ghosts.

LORD S.: You're very hard to please.

SARI: How do you know I'm tired?

LORD S.: By your voice, and your eyes.

SARI: I'm afraid I don't love you—actually! I think you're kind and understanding and gay and very dear, but you know I've only really loved one man all my life. I know it's tiresome to be so faithful, particularly to a mere memory, but there it is.

LORD S.: I think perhaps I could make you happy—anyhow happier.

SARI: May I think it over a little? I'll let you know a little later——

[*The supper-room doors open and everyone comes noisily into the room.*]

VICTORIA: Sarah—aren't you going to sing soon?

HONOR: Do you remember our singing lessons at Madame Claire's before you met Carl Linden—I mean—Oh, dear——

SARI [*smiling*]: I remember! I do hope my voice has improved since then.

LORD S.: Silence, please! Madame Sari Linden will sing us some of Carl Linden's enchanting songs, the songs she has made so famous.

[*All applaud and arrange themselves comfortably.*]

SARI: Where is my accompanist, is he here?

[*A foreign-looking Young Man detaches himself from the crowd.*]

YOUNG MAN: Here I am.

SARI: What shall we start with?

YOUNG MAN: "The River Song"?

SARI: No, that's too difficult to begin with.

YOUNG MAN: "Zigeuner"?

SARI: That will do. Ladies and Gentlemen, this song needs a slight preface. My husband wrote it when he was only sixteen. He visited Germany for the first time and sailed down the Rhine past forests and castles and gipsy encampments, and they fired his imagination so much that he wrote this song of a lovely flaxen-haired German Princess who fell in love with a Zigeuner-gipsy.

[*The Young Man starts the introduction and Sari takes her stand by the piano. Lord Shayne stands pensively near her, gazing at her. She sings "Zigeuner"*]:

"ZIGEUNER"

Once upon a time
Many years ago,
Lived a fair Princess,
Hating to confess
Loneliness was torturing her so.
Then a gipsy came.
Called to her by name.
Woo'd her with a song,
Sensuous and strong,
All the summer long;
Her passion seemed to tremble like a living flame.

[*Is taken up after the first verse by the Orchestra.*]

Bid my weeping cease,
Melody that brings
Merciful release,
Promises of peace;
Through the gentle throbbing of the strings.

Music of the plain,
Music of the wild,
Come to me again,
Hear me not in vain,
Soothe a heart in pain,
And let me to my happiness be reconciled.

Refrain
Play to me beneath the summer moon,
Zigeuner!—Zigeuner!—Zigeuner!
All I ask of life is just to listen
To the songs that you sing,
My spirit like a bird on the wing
Your melodies adoring—soaring,
Call to me with some barbaric tune,
    Zigeuner!—Zigeuner!—Zigeuner!
Now you hold me in your power,
Play to me for just an hour,
        Zigeuner!

[*At the end of it everyone applauds. She silences them by raising her hand.*]
This is a very simple, sentimental little song. I do hope you won't laugh at it—it means a very great deal to me. [*She unpins a bunch of white violets from her waist and throws them to Lord Shayne. Then she begins to sing the refrain of "I'll See You Again"*]:

Reprise

I'll see you again,
I live each moment through again.
Time has lain heavy between,
   But what has been
   Can leave me never;
   Your dear memory
Throughout my life has guided me.
Though my world has gone awry,
Though the years my tears may dry,
I shall love you till I die,
   Good-bye!

[*At the end the lights dim and the Orchestra crashes out the melody. When the lights go up again, it is the present day, the same as Act One, Scene I, and she is an old woman singing to a lot of young people sprawling on the floor. When she finishes singing, Dolly Chamberlain springs to her feet.*]

DOLLY: It is the most thrilling, divine, marvellous thing I've ever heard—Vincent, I'm mad about you—d'you hear—I love you.

[*She flings herself into his arms, he gently and rather absently disengages himself.*]

VINCENT: What a melody—my God, what a melody!

[*He goes to the piano and begins to play "I'll See You Again," softly as a fox-trot. The rest of the band join in and then the Orchestra. Everyone gets up "heyheying" and Charlestoning and finally, led by Dolly, they all go jazzing out through the double doors, followed by Vincent and the members of the dance band. Lady Shayne is left alone, standing quite still. Suddenly she begins to laugh, a strange, cracked, contemptuous laugh; she rises to her feet, and then, suddenly holding out her arms wide, she sings*]:

SARI: Though my world has gone awry,
Though the end is drawing nigh,
I shall love you till I die,
Good-bye!

THE CURTAIN FALLS

POST-
MORTEM

CHARACTERS

JOHN CAVAN

LADY CAVAN

SIR JAMES CAVAN

TILLEY

SHAW

BABE ROBINS

PERRY LOMAS

JENNER, A BATMAN

CORPORAL MACEY

MONICA CHELLERTON

BERTIE CHELLERTON

KITTY HARRIS

EGGIE BRACE

DRAKE, A BUTLER

ALFRED BORROW

MISS BEAVER

LADY STAGG-MORTIMER

THE BISHOP OF KETCHWORTH

SIR HENRY MERSTHAM

A BUTLER

ILLEY [aged 43]

SHAW [aged 39]

BABE ROBINS [aged 32]

The action of this play should be continuous, and the changes of scene managed as quickly as possible, during which the auditorium should remain in darkness.

SCENE I

THE SCENE *is a company headquarters in a quiet section of the Front Line in the spring of* 1917. *It is a roughly built shelter with a sloping corrugated tin roof. There is an entrance up Right Centre which leads round into the front trench and a doorway left. At the back there is a sand-bag wall reaching to within a few feet of the roof; through this opening can be seen the higher wall of the back trench topped with mud and grass and a few old tins; beyond this can be seen occasionally the flashes of guns far back. Every few moments during the whole scene there is the flare of a Very light.*

It is about 8:30 *in the evening.*

Tilley, Shaw, Babe Robins, and John Cavan have just finished dinner, and as the curtain rises Jenner, the batman, is serving them with mugs of coffee. Robert Tilley is a man of about thirty, pleasant looking, with certain authority, as befits a company commander. Shaw is younger, about twenty-six, fattish and good-humoured and inclined to be raucous in jollity. Babe Robins is nineteen, nice and clean looking. His face, which is ordinarily cheerful, is now set and strained. John Cavan is about twenty-seven or twenty-eight. He is tall, not remarkable looking in any way; his face is rather pale, and his eyes look tired. He has had command of the company for several months until a few weeks back, when Tilley returned from leave after being wounded and took over from him. Shaw is seated on a bunk, Left, with his legs stuck out in front of him, chuckling over a copy of the Daily Mercury. *Tilley is sitting at the back of the table,*

351

smoking. John is sprawled on the bunk, Right, and Babe Robins is at the end of the table, leaning against a post which supports the roof, and staring into space. Jenner, having given coffee to Tilley and John, offers some to Babe.

JENNER: Coffee, sir?

BABE [*focussing his attention*]: Er—er—no, thanks.

JENNER [*persuasively*]: Nice and 'ot to-night, sir.

BABE: No, thanks, Jenner. I don't want any.

[*Jenner goes across to Shaw.*]

JENNER: Coffee, sir?

SHAW [*taking a mug*]: Thanks. Put in a couple of spoonfuls for me.

JENNER [*doing so*]: Yes, sir. [*Jenner goes off Left.*]

SHAW [*laughing*]: God! This paper's rich, so full of plums it's downright indigestible.

TILLEY: What is it? The *Mercury?*

SHAW: Of course. I wouldn't read anything else, not while I'm out here, anyhow. A little honest English fun goes a long way out here. Have you read Lady Stagg-Mortimer's open letter to England? It's called "I gave my son."

TILLEY: And did she?

JOHN: Oh, yes. I was in the O.T.C. with him for three months. Whenever she came to visit the camp he used to lock himself in the latrine. They hated one another.

TILLEY [*to Robins*]: Want some port?

BABE: No, thanks, Tilley.

SHAW [*reading delightedly*]: "Every woman of England should be proud and glad to give and give and give, even the flesh of her flesh and the blood of her blood——"

TILLEY: And the tripe of her tripe. Sorry, John, I'd forgotten your father owns the bloody paper.

JOHN: Don't rub it in.

SHAW: One thing I will say about the *Mercury*, its moral tone is sound and high, and it's very right-minded about the war. It thinks war is evil all right, but necessary. And it's absolutely beastly about the Germans. It criticizes them most severely. Who is the *Mercury's* war correspondent, Cavan?

JOHN: Damned if I know.

SHAW: He seems to be a fine upstanding lad and observant. He's actually noticed the way we all go over the top cheering and shouting, "For God and Country."

JOHN: Oh, dry up! [*He laughs, and getting up, helps himself to port.*]

SHAW: You must have a nice talk to your father when you go home on leave. Tell him how we all kneel down and pray before an attack. You might take him a snapshot of it.

TILLEY: The light's not good enough.

SHAW: He could use a time exposure; surely you'd be willing to wait a few minutes for God and the *Mercury!*

BABE [*suddenly*]: Has any word come from battalion headquarters, Tilley?

TILLEY: No.

BABE: They'd let us know at once, wouldn't they, if——

TILLEY: Perry will be back soon, he went to the M.O. to have his hand seen to. He'll know how Armitage is.

BABE: Perhaps they've taken him down!

TILLEY: Perhaps. Don't worry.

BABE [*rising*]: I think I ll go and write a letter to his people, just to warn them. I don't go on duty till nine.

TILLEY: Right. Cheer up!

BABE: Thanks, Tilley. [*Babe goes out miserably.*]

JOHN: Do you think they've taken him down?

TILLEY [*shaking his head*]: No, he couldn't be moved. I doubt if he'll last more than a few hours.

SHAW: Bloody awful luck!

[*Corporal Macey enters and salutes.*]

TILLEY: Yes, Corporal Macey?

CORPORAL: Mr. Shaw, sir, please.

SHAW [*looking up*]: Yes?

CORPORAL: Carrying party just coming up with the R. E. material, sir.

SHAW [*rising and putting belt on*]: All right. Fall in the working party. I'll come straight up.

CORPORAL: Yes, sir. [*He salutes and exits.*]

TILLEY: Get things going as soon as you can, Shaw. I'll be round presently.

SHAW: Right. [*He picks up his electric torch from the bunk, puts on his gas mask and tin hat and goes towards the doorway.*]

[*Perry Lomas enters. He is thin and looks nervy. His hand is bandaged.*]

SHAW: Hallo! How's the hand?

PERRY: Nothing much, thanks.

SHAW: Cheero! [*Shaw goes out.*]

[*Perry takes off his helmet and mask and belt.*]

TILLEY: Well, what did he say?

PERRY: It'll be all right in a day or so. He told me to rest it as much as possible and gave me an anti-tetanus injection.

TILLEY: Good! You're on the new machine-gun emplacement, aren't you?

PERRY: Yes. I'm going up at nine.

TILLEY: On your way you might take a look and see how number 8 platoon's getting on with their bit of parapet.

PERRY: All right. [*Calling*]: Jenner—dinner, please!

JENNER [*off*]: Coming, sir.

[*Perry sits down at the table. Tilley continues to write in his notebook. Jenner brings in a plate of soup, puts it down in front of Perry, and exits.*]

PERRY [*starting his soup*]: Armitage is dead.

TILLEY [*looking up*]: When?

PERRY: Just before I left the Aid Post.

TILLEY: I thought as much. It looked pretty hopeless.

JOHN: Poor kid!

PERRY: He's well out of it.

TILLEY [*quietly*]: Shut up, Perry.

JOHN: Somebody's got to tell him.

TILLEY: Tell who—Robins?

PERRY: I think he knows.

JOHN: No. He's waiting for news, he's in his dugout. I'll tell him presently. [*There is a pause.*]

TILLEY [*rising*]: Well, if the adjutant calls up, give me a shout. I've got to go through these bloody returns with the company sergeant major.

JOHN: All right, Bob.

[*Tilley goes out.*]

[*Jenner reënters with a plate of meat and potatoes and exits with the empty soup plate. John goes on reading his magazine. Perry rises, takes Shaw's* Mercury *from his bunk, and props it up in front of him on the table. There is silence. Perry reads a little and then throws the paper on the floor.*]

PERRY [*angrily*]: Oh, Christ!

JOHN: What's up?

PERRY: That muck makes me sick!

JOHN [*wearily*]: What does it matter?

PERRY [*bitterly*]: "I gave my son." "Women of England!" "God and Country." Your father owns the blasted rag. Why don't you do something about it?

JOHN [*smiling*]: What could I do?

PERRY: Tell him the truth for a change!

JOHN: He knows—he's not a fool!

PERRY: You mean he's an ambitious hypocrite?

JOHN: Of course.

PERRY: Do you like him at all?

JOHN: No. I admire him rather.

PERRY: What for?

JOHN: For getting what he wants. He's a good climber.

PERRY: What does your mother think about him?

JOHN: I do wish you'd shut up, Perry. There's no sense in working yourself up into rages.

PERRY: I'm sorry. It gets in my mind and I can't get it out— all that mealy-mouthed cant being shoved down the people's throats!

JOHN: The demand creates the supply, I think. The civilian public must enjoy its war; and it also has to reconcile it with a strong sense of patriotism and a nice Christian God. It couldn't do that if it had the remotest suspicion of what really happens.

PERRY: Do you think it will ever know?

JOHN: I hope so, later on, much later, when it's all over.

PERRY [*violently*]: Never, never, never! They'll never know whichever way it goes, victory or defeat. They'll smarm it all over with memorials and Rolls of Honour and Angels of Mons, and it'll look so noble and glorious in retrospect that they'll all start itching for another war, egged on by dear old gentlemen in clubs who wish they were twenty years younger, and newspaper owners and oily financiers, and the splendid women of England happy and proud to give their sons and husbands and lovers, and even their photographs. You see, there'll be an outbreak of war literature in so many years. Everyone will write war books and war plays, and everyone will read them and see them and be vicariously thrilled by them, until one day someone will go too far and say something that's really true and be flung into prison for blasphemy, immorality, lese majesty, unnatural vice, contempt of court, and atheism, then there'll be a glorious religious revival, and we'll all be rushed across the Atlantic to conquer America, comfortably upheld by Jesus and the Right!

JOHN [*laughing*]: Wonderful, Perry—simply wonderful!

PERRY: Don't laugh, I mean it. Stop laughing!

JOHN [*continuing*]: I can't help it.

PERRY: You're not really laughing, anyhow—you're as sick as I am inside.

JOHN: Not quite. I don't think poor old England is as bad as all that.

PERRY: It isn't poor old England, particularly; it's poor old Human Nature. There isn't a hope for it anywhere; all this proves it.

JOHN: You're wrong. There are a few moments among these war years of higher value than any others, just a few every now and then.

PERRY [*sarcastically*]: Christian value, I suppose you mean? Christian forbearance, nobility of spirit, Lady Stagg-Mortimer.

JOHN: You know I don't mean that!

PERRY: What do you mean, then?

JOHN: You should see it quicker than I. You're a poet, aren't you?

PERRY: I was.

JOHN: Cheer up, Perry!

PERRY: I envy you, anyway. You've got a damned philosophic outlook, that's what you've got.

JOHN: Somebody must be learning something from all this.

PERRY: Nobody's learning anything. It's too big, too utterly futile.

JOHN: You can't be sure. Years and years and years ahead we may know.

PERRY: *We may know.*

JOHN: I didn't mean "we" personally. I'm taking a God's-eye view.

PERRY: Are you happy on your cloud, watching kids like Armitage torn to pieces, screaming in bloody pain—will it gratify your omnipotence as God to see his mother's face when she opens the telegram? He's an only son, I believe. He had his twenty-first birthday last week when we were out of the line— we had a grand evening—you remember, you were there——

JOHN: Yes, I was there.

PERRY: He wasn't even killed in an attack or a raid, no glory, just stupid chance.

JOHN [*quietly*]: Look here, Perry, I've been here longer than you, and I'm going to give you some advice, whether you like it or not. You're heading for a smash. Perhaps because you've got more temperament than I, or more imagination, or less control, but whatever it is, shut it off, keep it down, crush it! We can none of us afford a personal view out here, we're not strong enough—no one is strong enough. There's just a limited number of things we can bear to think about: sleep, warmth, food, drink, self preservation; no more—no more than that.

PERRY: Voluntary reversion to animalism.

JOHN: Not voluntary, compulsory.

PERRY: Aren't you touched by it any more? Not now, I don't mean now, when everything's comparatively quiet, but when we're in the thick of it, floundering through mud in an attack, treading on men's faces, some of them not dead, with the bloody din of the barrage in our ears, and thin human screams cutting through it—quite clearly like penny whistles in a thunder-storm——

JOHN: I'm all right then—too much to do, no time.

PERRY: What about when it's over and we fall back sometimes, back over that idiotic ground, having to go quickly, not hearing people groaning or crying for water—when we flop down in a dugout, safe, for the moment, time to think then, isn't there—can you help thinking then? [*He rises during this and stands over John's bunk.*]

JOHN: I believe something will come out of it—something must, when those who do get through go back home; they'll be strong enough to count somehow.

PERRY: Not they. They'll slip back into their smug illusions, England will make it hot for them if they don't. Remember, we're a Christian country.

JOHN: I'm waiting, treading water, waiting to see.

PERRY: You'll probably be blown to pieces if you wait long enough. Then you'll never see.

JOHN: I'm not so sure. I have a feeling that one might see the whole business just for a second before one dies. Like going under an anæsthetic, everything becomes blurred and enormous and then suddenly clears, just for the fraction of a fraction of a moment. Perhaps that infinitesimal moment is what we're all waiting for, really.

PERRY [*irritably*]: Well, in that case the war is highly to be commended: it's providing thousands of your infinitesimal moments per day per person. Very comforting!

JOHN: Just as comforting as anything else. Time is very interesting. Nobody has found out much about it; perhaps there isn't any; perhaps it's just a circle and Past and Future are the same. Funny if the current got switched and we all started remembering twenty years hence and looking forward to last Tuesday.

PERRY: God forbid that I should ever look forward to any of the last Tuesdays I've lived through.

JOHN: What's your particular devil?

PERRY: God, I think.

[*Babe Robins comes in. He looks at Perry anxiously.*]

BABE: Perry!

PERRY: Yes?

BABE: What's happened about Armitage? Have they taken him down yet?

PERRY [*after a slight pause*]: No, Babe—it wouldn't be any use—he's dead.

BABE: Oh, I see. [*There is a silence. Babe stands quite still.*]

PERRY [*awkwardly*]: Don't worry about him, kid, he didn't have much pain, he was unconscious. [*He shoots a bitter look at John and says more loudly*]: Unconscious! [*Perry goes out abruptly.*]

[*Babe sits down by the table.*]

BABE [*breaking the silence, dully*]: I'd just written to his mother saying he'd been pretty badly hit. She's—she's awfully nice; they live in Somerset.

JOHN [*rising*]: If I were you I'd have a spot of whisky. [*He goes to the table and pours some whisky into a mug and gives it to him.*]

BABE [*taking it*]: Thanks awfully. [*He gulps it down.*]

[*Jenner comes in and piles all the dinner things onto a tray.*]

JENNER [*to Babe*]: Shall I have a cup of tea ready for you, sir, when you come off duty?

[*Babe doesn't answer. John speaks quickly.*]

JOHN: Very good idea! I'd like a cup now. Can you hurry it along, Jenner?

JENNER: Yes, sir. [*He goes off with the tray.*]

[*John instinctively puts his arm round Babe's shoulders. Babe sits still for a moment, then gently disengages himself and walks over to the bunk, Left.*]

BABE [*unsteadily*]: Don't say anything to me, will you? I don't want to blub and make a fool of myself. You see we were at Sandhurst together and school, we've been together all along, for years really. I shall miss him—very much—— [*His voice breaks so he stops talking.*]

JOHN [*practically*]: Look here, old chap, you'd better stay here quietly for a little. I don't go on until midnight: we'll just swap duties. I'll take over your covering party now, and you can do my tour for me at twelve. That'll give you time to steady yourself a bit.

BABE: Thanks ever so much, it's awfully decent of you.

[*He fumbles in his pocket for a cigarette. John hastily hands him a tin from the table. Babe lights one and puffs at it. John puts on his belt and gas mask and hat.*]

JOHN: Lend me your torch, will you? I think Shaw's pinched mine.

BABE [*giving it to him with a slight smile*]: Here.

JOHN: Thanks. Cheero. [*As he is about to go out he meets Tilley coming in. He speaks quietly*]: Look here, Bob—[*he points to Babe*]—he's a bit knocked out over Armitage; if you've no objection I'll do his covering party. He'll go on for me later.

TILLEY: That's all right.

JOHN: Thanks.

[*Tilley sits at the table, and bringing a pile of loose papers out of his pocket, proceeds to check them through with a pencil. He glances over at Babe once or twice.*]

TILLEY: There's some port left in the bottle, Babe, d'you want a drop?

BABE: No thanks, Tilley.

[*Perry reënters and begins to put on his belt, gas mask, etc. He looks at his watch.*]

PERRY: I make it five to nine—is that right?

TILLEY [*looking at him*]: Yes. Try and get that emplacement done to-night. I want to avoid any work on it in the daylight.

PERRY: If it only stays quiet the way it has the last three nights, and that machine-gun from the sunken road doesn't start popping at us—we'll get through it in a few hours.

TILLEY: Right. I'll be along later.

[*There is a sudden outbreak of machine-gun fire, several bullets whistle over the top of the shelter.*]

[*Jumping to his feet*]: Blast! They've spotted the wiring party.

[*There is another burst of fire—Tilley and Perry stand listening.*]

PERRY: They must have got them in that flare.

TILLEY: I'll go and have a look.

[*They both move towards the entrance. Corporal Macey dashes in.*]

CORPORAL: Mr. Cavan been 'it, sir; got him just as 'e was getting out of the trench.

TILLEY: Anyone else hit?

CORPORAL: No, sir.

TILLEY: Bring Mr. Cavan in here, quick!

CORPORAL: Yes, sir. [*He goes off.*]

[*Jenner enters with a cup of tea.*]

TILLEY: Jenner!

JENNER: Yes, sir?

TILLEY: Get the stretcher bearers!

JENNER: Yes, sir. [*He puts the cup of tea on the table and rushes off.*]

[*Perry flings several papers and magazines off the bunk down-stage and makes a pillow from a pack that is lying near by. Two*

Men carry in John and lay him on the bunk. Babe jumps to his feet.]

BABE [*shrilly*]: What's happened? What's happened?

TILLEY: Quiet—get some water—quickly! [*He stands looking at John carefully.*]

[*Babe hurries over with a mug of water. Tilley takes it from him, and kneeling down, hoists John's head up a little and forces some water between his lips. Perry stands a little way off watching; his hands are twitching nervously.*]

BABE [*bursting into sobs*]: It's my fault! It's my fault! He was doing my duty for me, it ought to have been me. Oh, Christ! It ought to have been me! [*He crumples up against the table.*]

TILLEY: Shut up—for God's sake, be quiet!

JOHN [*opens his eyes and smiles, speaking painfully*]: I'll know now, Perry—I'm right, I bet you I'm right—I'll know—I'll know——

[*Two Stretcher Bearers come in as the light fades out, and there is complete darkness and silence except for the distant rumbling of guns.*]

CURTAIN

SCENE II

SIR JAMES CAVAN'S *house in Kent. It is a spring evening, about nine o'clock in the year* 1930. *The scene is Lady Cavan's bedroom. It is a comfortable and charmingly furnished room, and the view from the window is magnificent. First, low wooded hills, then the Romney Marshes, and beyond them, the sea.*

Lady Cavan is seated by the window at a bridge table playing

Canfield Patience. She is a graceful-looking old lady. The twilight is fading rapidly, and every now and then she pauses in her game to look out at the distant lights coming to life along the coast. When the curtain has been up for a few moments John walks quietly into the room. He is in uniform and looks exactly as he did in the preceding scene. As he comes in, there seems to be a distant rumble of guns a long way off, and the suggestion of a Very flare shining briefly and dying away. He stands by the table opposite to Lady Cavan. She sees him and puts down the pack of cards slowly.

LADY C. [*in a whisper*]: Johnnie!

JOHN: Hullo, Mother!

LADY C.: I daren't speak loudly or move, you might disappear.

JOHN: I won't disappear. I've only just come.

[*Lady Cavan holds out her arms. John comes round the table and kneels on the floor by her chair. She holds him tightly and very still.*]

LADY C.: It can't be a dream, I'm wide awake.

JOHN: I don't believe I've quite got away yet, really. I can still hear the guns. [*He suddenly bends and clutches his stomach.*] Oh, God!

LADY C. [*whispering*]: Does it hurt terribly, my darling?

JOHN: Just a bit—it'll pass off.

LADY C.: Keep very still for a minute.

JOHN: Darling Mum!

LADY C.: Will it matter if I turn on the reading lamp? It's so dark, and I do want to see you.

[*John makes a movement.*]

Don't move. I can do it with my left hand. [*She switches on a small lamp on the table.*] There! That's better!

JOHN [*smiling*]: Much better. [*He fidgets a little.*]

LADY C.: Are you uncomfortable?

JOHN: A little bit.

LADY C.: I'll leave go of you if you promise not to go away again without warning me.

JOHN: I promise. [*He kisses her, gets up and sits opposite to her at the table.*] Good old Canfield! [*He puts his hand across the table and takes hers.*]

LADY C.: I got it out yesterday.

JOHN: Without cheating?

LADY C. [*shaking her head*]: No.

JOHN [*looking out of the window*]: How lovely and quiet it is!

LADY C. [*in a strained voice*]: Oh, darling! You weren't in very great pain, were you, when——

JOHN: No—hardly any at all.

LADY C.: They said you couldn't have been because it was all over so quickly, but I wasn't sure.

JOHN: Don't let's think about that.

LADY C.: A little, of course, like just now, that can't be helped. [*She suddenly crumples onto the table with her head in her arms.*]

JOHN [*stroking her hair*]: Mum—don't—please, don't!

LADY C. [*brokenly*]: I'm a silly old fool, wasting precious time——

JOHN: It doesn't matter about time, really it doesn't—don't cry!

LADY C.: I'm not crying, it's something inside twisting horribly like it did years ago when—when—I couldn't cry then, I tried to because I thought it would be a relief, but it was no use, I couldn't, not for ages, and then only over stupid, trivial things. [*She raises her head and sits back in her chair.*] Oh, Johnnie—how dreadfully tired you look!

JOHN: We all look tired, I'm afraid.

LADY C.: Why didn't you come sooner?

JOHN [*surprised*]: Sooner? I wasn't hit until a few minutes ago.

LADY C.: Thirteen years ago.

JOHN [*wondering*]: Oh!

LADY C.: Didn't you know?

JOHN: I thought you looked a little older, I wondered why.

LADY C.: I nearly died last year. I'm glad I didn't now, although I was sorry then. I should have missed you.

JOHN [*stricken*]: Oh, Mum, that would have been unbearable. [*He clutches her hand again.*]

LADY C.: We'd have found each other, somehow.

JOHN: Thirteen years—then—it's—it's——

LADY C.: 1930.

JOHN: How funny that sounds! I wonder where I've been!

LADY C.: Can't you remember?

JOHN: No—not a thing—I just swapped duties with Babe because he was so upset over Armitage. I hopped over the parapet with the covering party. It was all pretty quiet, then there was a flare, and a lot of row suddenly, and I fell down and couldn't get up—I remember Perry looking at me, though, just for a second, that was later, I was in the shelter again—he's there now—I can see him now—Perry——

LADY C. [*gripping both his hands*]: No, no, darling—not yet—stay a little longer—not yet—please, please, please—— [*Her voice breaks.*]

JOHN [*quite naturally*]: All right, darling—don't fuss.

LADY C.: I won't ask any questions—don't try to remember anything—ask me things and I'll answer, ordinary things; there have been tremendous changes everywhere, London looks quite different—you should see Regent Street, and Park Lane—and you can telephone to America quite easily, your father does it from his office every day—just as though he were speaking to the next room——

JOHN: Father—where is he?

LADY C.: In London. He comes down for week-ends.

JOHN: Still the *Mercury?*

LADY C.: Yes.

JOHN: Oh, God!

LADY C.: A million copies a day, I believe.

JOHN: Is he just the same?

LADY C.: He's fatter.

JOHN: And is he still—I mean—still going on like he used to?

LADY C.: Yes. It's Viola Blake at the moment.

JOHN: Who's she?

LADY C.: A film actress, very pretty and quite civil; she pronounces it Viola.

JOHN: Sounds like a shaving stick!

LADY C.: They all came down here one day, a huge party of them with cameras and things, and she acted all over the garden with a bright yellow face.

[*They both laugh a little.*]

JOHN: Did you mind?

LADY C.: No, I rather enjoyed it. [*There is a pause for a moment.*]

JOHN [*quietly*]: What's happened to Monica?

LADY C. [*swiftly*]: Monica's married. Harriet's married, too, quite a nice little man called Stokes: he's a writer. Of course, he's completely under her thumb; she was always domineering, even when you were children, wasn't she?

JOHN [*thoughtfully*]: Yes.

LADY C.: And she's become a Christian Scientist, it's made her a trifle hard, I think, but she seems very pleased with it. They have a child, poor little thing!

JOHN: How old is Harriet?

LADY C.: Forty-two.

JOHN: Then I must be forty?

LADY C.: No, darling, no, you're not. Don't think about that.

JOHN [*patting her hand*]: Don't be frightened—go on talking! You said Monica was married.

LADY C.: Yes, she married very well.

JOHN: Who?

LADY C.: Bertie Chellerton.

JOHN: Oh! [*There is a pause.*] Is she happy?

LADY C.: I believe so. I haven't seen her for years, except in the illustrated papers.

JOHN [*putting his head down*]: I hope she's happy!

LADY C.: Please don't worry your head about her, darling. She seems to lead a lovely life, full of excitements and fun.

JOHN: I can't help worrying a bit. You see I'm still in love with her, I haven't had time not to be.

LADY C. [*sadly*]: I see.

JOHN: You never cared for her much, did you?

LADY C.: I tried to like her, Johnnie, for your sake.

JOHN: Yes, I knew that.

LADY C.: I never thought she was worthy of you.

JOHN: All mothers think that, don't they?

LADY C.: Perhaps they do.

JOHN: It's inevitable, I expect. A sort of jealousy without meaning to be.

LADY C.: I expect it is.

JOHN: So she married Bertie Chellerton. I don't think I've ever seen him. Is he nice?

LADY C.: He looks quite pleasant.

JOHN: Was she upset when—thirteen years ago?

LADY C.: She wrote me a very sweet letter.

JOHN: I'm glad. When did she marry?

LADY C.: 1920.

JOHN: Ten years ago?

LADY C.: Yes.

JOHN: It's nice to think she waited a bit. I want to see her awfully.

LADY C.: Oh, no—no.

JOHN: Yes, Mum, I must really, sometime. Are they in love still?

LADY C.: I suppose so. They go to the opera together, in the *Tatler*. [*She turns away.*]

JOHN [*impulsively*]: I'm sorry, dearest. We won't talk about her any more.

LADY C.: You're right. I am jealous, really. You see, you're all I've got, all I've ever had. Harriet never counted as much as you did, and now, in this strange moment between life and death, I want you all to myself. If I can't have you quite all, don't let me know, there's a dear boy! [*She tries to smile but doesn't succeed very well.*]

JOHN: I didn't mean to hurt you.

LADY C.: Don't be silly. Of course you didn't.

JOHN: I love you with all that's best in me—always. [*He gets up and wanders about the room. Lady Cavan watches him. He stops in front of a picture.*] I remembered that picture the other day, quite suddenly, just before an attack, wasn't it funny? I saw it as clearly as though someone had held it in front of my nose.

LADY C.: You always liked it, even when you were tiny.

JOHN: It isn't very good really, is it?

LADY C.: Your Aunt Lilian painted it when she was a girl. I was brought up to think it very beautiful indeed. I suppose it is dreadfully amateurish.

JOHN: The sheep look a bit lopsided. Apart from that, it's all right.

LADY C.: Sheep are very difficult.

[*John picks up a book from the table by the bed.*]

JOHN [*looking at it wonderingly*]: *Post-Mortem*, by Perry Lomas—Perry Lomas!

LADY C. [*rising*]: Put it down, darling—don't open it—please put it down. [*She comes over and takes it from him.*]

JOHN: Is it new?

LADY C.: Yes—it's only just published.

JOHN: Perry! So he came through all right.

LADY C.: He sent it to me; he said he thought you would have liked him to. I've got the letter somewhere. It's a bitter book and terribly sad.

JOHN: War?

LADY C.: Mostly. It's caused a great sensation. There's a rumour that it's going to be burnt publicly or something——

JOHN: Good God, why?

LADY C.: They say because it's blasphemous and seditious and immoral and lots of other things.

JOHN: They?

LADY C.: The Press.

JOHN: The *Mercury?*

LADY C.: Yes. I'm afraid the *Mercury* started all the trouble. Alfred Borrow wrote a violent attack on the front page. He's city editor now, and very important.

JOHN: That slimy little man who used to be Father's secretary?

LADY C.: Yes.

JOHN: What did you think of it, Mother?

LADY C.: I could hardly bear it, but I think that was because of you. There are hundreds of war books now, they're the fashion. Perhaps it's a good thing for those who forget too easily.

JOHN: But they can't burn Perry's book just because a rag like the *Mercury* makes a stunt of attacking it!

LADY C.: The *Mercury's* very powerful.

JOHN: So he's done it. He said somebody would. Give it to me, Mother. I want to read it.

LADY C.: No, no, don't! What's the use?

JOHN: I must see Father.

LADY C.: That wouldn't do any good. He doesn't care whether it's good or bad. It's just a scoop for the paper——

JOHN: Please give it to me.

LADY C.: Very well.

[*John takes it and opens it at random.*]

JOHN: I think I know it, somehow. Where is Perry—in London?

LADY C.: Yes. [*She smiles wistfully.*] You're going to see him, too, I suppose?

JOHN: I must. I must see them all. I've got to know what's happening.

LADY C. [*pleading*]: I can tell you everything that's happening if you'll only stay here quietly with me. I can tell you better than they can——

JOHN: That's why I came back—to find out something.

LADY C.: There's nothing, nothing worth finding out——

JOHN: I must see for myself.

LADY C. [*holding him imploringly*]: Listen to me, John; Johnnie, my darling, look at me! There's only one thing in the world worth finding, worth catching hold of, if only for a moment, and that's here in this room between you and me. Don't you understand? I don't want you to be hurt any more. Stay, ask me anything, I'll be able to answer, I know now. I'll tear the truth out of infinity for you, even if I break my heart in doing it. Only stay, don't leave me!

JOHN: You don't understand. There's a fraction of a fraction of a second when you have a chance of seeing everything for yourself if only you're strong enough. I must be strong enough.

That's why it all happened; that's why I'm here. I must try, even if I fail, I must try. Let me go, darling, please!

LADY C.: No, no, no!

JOHN: I won't go back finally without seeing you again. I promise, I swear it.

LADY C.: It isn't that. Go back now finally, say good-bye, my own dearest, and go, but don't open your eyes——

JOHN [*looking at her strangely*]: How much have you lost?

LADY C.: Everything but you.

JOHN: Everything—everything you've ever believed?

LADY C.: Yes. I'm too old to find new creeds, and the old ones are all gone, swept away!

JOHN: God?

LADY C.: Whose God? There are so many, and they're all so foolish.

JOHN: Life Force, Force for Good, something?

LADY C.: Death Force, Force for Evil, Nothing, equal in futility!

JOHN: You're denying what you said just now. What of this that is here, between us?

LADY C.: A poor little spark, flickering for an instant in Eternity. What can that matter?

JOHN: It does matter, it does, it must——

LADY C.: Then stay, stay! There's such a little time left, and I'm so lonely.

JOHN: I'll come back, but I must go now——

LADY C. [*brokenly*]: Please, please!

JOHN [*taking her in his arms and holding her close; her face is hidden in his coat—he speaks very gently*]: Listen, Mum, you understand really. It's just because you're tired that you're finding it hard to be brave. I felt like that often enough in the Line: the effort to be made seems too big for one's strength, immense and frightening, but it isn't too big actually once you start. You must steel your heart, darling, and let me go. I know about war—a bitter and cruel knowledge, horror upon horror, stretched far beyond breaking point, the few moments of gallant beauty there are not enough measured against the hideous ages of suffering! Now, I must know about Peace, I must know whether by losing so much we have gained anything at all, or whether it was just blind futility like Perry said it was, I must know whether the ones who came home have slipped back into the old illusions and are rotting there, smug in false security, blotting out memory with the flimsy mysticism of their threadbare Christian legend, or whether they've had the courage to remember clearly and strike out for something new—something different! I must know for myself; it's the urge inside me that's carved this brief moment out of Time. You do understand, don't you?

LADY C.: Yes, dear. I understand. Come back once more, you promised!

JOHN: I'll come back. I swear it.

[*They cling together, and for a moment it seems as though they are illumined by the vivid unnatural light of a Very flare. There is a faint rumbling of guns in the distance. As the flare fades away Lady Cavan speaks.*]

LADY C.: Take care of yourself, my dearest dear!

In the gathering darkness, John's figure moves away from her and disappears into the shadows. There is complete darkness for a moment, then twilight returns to the garden and then the room. Lady Cavan is seated at the table by the window. She holds a pack of cards in her hand and thoughtfully places one of those lying on the table as the lights fade and—

THE CURTAIN FALLS

SCENE III

THE CHELLERTONS' *house in Mount Street. The scene is Monica's sitting room. It is furnished in quite good ultra-modern taste, although tending slightly to exaggeration.*

When the curtain rises Monica is lying on the sofa attired in rather bizarre pajamas, which, in her epoch, have taken the place of tea gowns and negligees. She is reading Vogue, *smoking, and listening to a panatrope: one of the new kind which has been set with twelve records and seems to show no signs of flagging. Monica is not exactly handsome, nor pretty, but somehow brilliant looking. She has the reputation of being witty and her parties are always successful. John is standing at the head of the sofa just behind her, she hasn't seen him yet and goes on reading. He comes slowly down to the foot of the sofa.*

JOHN: Hallo, Monica!

MONICA [*looking up*]: My God!

JOHN: Don't be frightened, please!

MONICA [*wide-eyed, staring at him*]: John?

JOHN: Yes, I've come back for a little.

MONICA [*opening and shutting her eyes rapidly*]: I'm stark staring mad!

JOHN [*wonderingly*]: You have changed—tremendously!

MONICA: I suppose this is a dream?

JOHN: Not exactly, at least, I don't know, perhaps for you it is!

MONICA: What else could it be?

JOHN: Some sort of magic.

MONICA [*rallying*]: I don't know what to say quite.

JOHN: Are you pleased to see me?

MONICA: I don't know, it's such a shock [*her voice softens*]. Yes, of course I'm pleased to see you—dear John.

[*She puts out her hand with a slight effort. John takes it and she jerks it away again instinctively.*]

JOHN: I wish you wouldn't be frightened!

MONICA: I'm not. Not exactly frightened, but you must admit it's a little shattering for me.

JOHN: I suppose it must be.

MONICA: I expect it's the effect of all those damned war books, getting on my nerves; I'll take some aspirin when I wake up. I wish I could remember when I went to sleep—it is after dinner, isn't it?

JOHN: Yes. [*He looks at his watch.*] It's just nine.

MONICA: Have you dined?

JOHN: Yes, a little while ago.

MONICA: You look awfully tired. Would you like a drink or something? [*She laughs.*] Oh—it seems funny, offering a ghost a drink!

JOHN: I'm not quite a ghost yet, and I should like some brandy.

[*She rises and moves over to the bell, never taking her eyes off him.*]

MONICA [*pressing the bell*]: Do sit down, John dear—you can sit down, can't you?

JOHN: Could we stop the gramophone first?

MONICA: I'd forgotten it was going. [*She stops it.*]

JOHN: Does it go on playing forever?

MONICA: Practically!

[*He comes over to it.*]

You see that sinister little arm keeps on slapping them on and snatching them off all by itself. Horrid, isn't it?

JOHN: Good idea, really; saves all that business of winding.

MONICA: It's certainly convenient, but rather scare making,

don't you think? Everything's absolutely terrifying nowadays. I'm seriously thinking of going into a monastery.

[*She had said this at dinner a few nights ago and everybody had laughed. John smiles, rather absently*.]

JOHN: Oh, Monica! [*He sits down*.]

MONICA [*sensing disapproval*]: What's the matter?

JOHN: Nothing.

MONICA: Cigarette? [*She offers him a box*.]

JOHN [*looking at her as he takes one*]: Yes—thanks.

[*She lights it for him as Drake, the butler, enters*.]

DRAKE: You rang, my lady?

MONICA: Yes, bring some brandy, please. [*To John*]: Would you like some coffee?

JOHN: No, thank you.

MONICA [*to Drake*]: Just brandy, then.

DRAKE: Very good, my lady. [*He goes out*.]

MONICA [*conversationally*]: He's called Drake. Isn't he sweet?

JOHN [*smiling*]: Frightfully sweet.

MONICA: Once when we were dining out we saw him in a very grand car in Eaton Square, and Eggie said, "Drake is going West, lad." You'll like Eggie, he's terribly funny.

JOHN: Who's Eggie?

MONICA: Eggie Brace. He's Lord Verilow's son, you know, our old friend impoverished nobility, very enjoyable. Eggie's one of your father's toadies, he writes snappy gossip for the *Mercury*. You must have seen him, he's always with your father.

JOHN: I haven't seen Father yet.

MONICA: Darling Jumbo! We all worship him, particularly when he comes over Napoleonic—he's too lovely.

JOHN: I remember now. Maisie Lorrimer used to call Father "Jumbo."

MONICA [*surprised*]: Maisie Lorrimer! Why she's been dead for years. She fell out of something or other.

JOHN: Lots of things happen in thirteen years!

MONICA [*hurriedly*]: You'll see Eggie soon. He and Kitty Harris are coming to fetch me. We're going to a gloomy party at the Friedlanders'. [*She pauses.*] Will Kitty and Eggie be able to see you as well—I mean, if they come before I wake up?

JOHN: Yes, I expect so. Drake saw me all right, didn't he?

MONICA: You can never tell with Drake. He has such perfect manners. If he came in and found John the Baptist playing the gramophone without his head, he wouldn't flicker an eyelash! We'll see how many glasses he brings.

[*John laughs. Drake reënters with a tray on which there are two big glasses and a decanter. He pours some brandy into one and hands it to Monica. Then he pours some into the other glass and hands it to John.*]

JOHN: Thank you.

[*Drake goes out.*]

MONICA: There, now! He probably thinks you're going to a fancy-dress ball or something.

JOHN: Monica!

MONICA: Yes, John?

JOHN: Come off it.

MONICA: What do you mean?

JOHN: There's so much to say—we haven't said anything yet.

MONICA [*turning away*]: I don't understand.

JOHN: Yes, you do. You must, inside. You can't have changed as much as all that.

MONICA: You're not approving of me, are you? [*She laughs.*]

JOHN: I haven't seen you yet.

MONICA: You mustn't be pompous, dear.

JOHN: Isn't it any use?

MONICA [*irritably*]: Isn't what any use?

JOHN: How old are you?

MONICA: Thirty-three, and doing nicely, thank you.

JOHN: I keep on seeing you as you were and then trying to fit it in with you as you are.

MONICA: This isn't a very comfortable dream!

JOHN: Don't shut me out, it's awfully important. I've only got a little while.

MONICA: I'm not shutting you out. I'm delighted to see you again. I've just told you.

JOHN: Have you any children?

MONICA: No.

JOHN: What a shame!

MONICA: Why? Do you think I ought to have?

JOHN: Not if you don't want to.

MONICA: I'm not very good at children, you know. Not that I don't like them, I do really, when they're funny and nice.

JOHN [*smiling*]: And other people's?

MONICA: Exactly. Violet Furleigh's children, for instance. They adore me, and I play with them for hours. They always look forward to the week-ends that I'm going to be down there. But I'm afraid I can only be maternal in small doses.

JOHN: I see.

MONICA: You don't. You've got a Victorian look in your eye.

JOHN: Should we have had children if we'd married, I wonder?

MONICA [*in a softer voice*]: You were terribly in love with me, weren't you?

JOHN: Yes.

MONICA: Poor old John!

JOHN: Weren't you, with me?

MONICA: Of course. You knew I was, but it's a long time ago, isn't it? [*Her voice rises slightly.*] Isn't it?

JOHN: For you.

MONICA: You mean—you're still—still there?

JOHN: I'm afraid so.

MONICA: I see. [*There is silence for a moment.*]

JOHN: I was a fool to come.

MONICA: I feel awfully stupid, as if I were going to cry. [*She rises abruptly and goes to the window.*]

JOHN: Nothing to cry about.

MONICA: I'm not so sure.

JOHN: Monica! [*She doesn't answer.*] Monica!

MONICA [*turning*]: Don't speak, please. I want to wake up, I want to wake up!

JOHN: I'll go. [*He gets up.*] I don't want to upset you.

MONICA: John—don't go—please!

[*The door opens and Kitty Harris and Eggie Brace enter. Kitty is young and pretty and consistently silly. Eggie is moon-faced and has a slight stammer which never interferes with his good remarks and enhances some of his bad ones.*]

KITTY: Darling, you're not dressed or anything! [*She sees John.*] Oh!

MONICA [*mechanically*]: Kitty, this is John Cavan—Lady Catherine Harris, Lord Brace——

KITTY [*shaking hands vaguely*]: How do you do——

EGGIE: How do you do! [*Then to Monica*]: Jumbo's in great form to-night. He's gone trumpeting off to one of his conferences surrounded by bishops and deans. We've got the Home Secretary to stop all sales of this Lomas book. That's what they're all up to to-night. They want to get it publicly burnt like J-J-Joan of Arc. The *Mercury* Printing Presses are fairly bouncing up and down like V-v-virgin B-brides, waiting to be ravished by the story. Poor Lomas is for it all right. I haven't read the damned thing myself, but it's full of bits, from all accounts——

KITTY: I've read it, it's marvellous! I found a copy tucked away in Hatchard's just before the fuss started—it's probably worth millions now!

EGGIE: Can't we have a drink or something?

MONICA: Of course.

[*She goes towards the bell, but Drake has anticipated her and enters with a large tray of drinks which he places on a side table and exits.*]

[*Kitty switches on the panatrope, so the ensuing conversation is naturally pitched rather more loudly.*]

EGGIE [*waving a whisky bottle at John*]: Drink?

JOHN: No, thanks.

EGGIE: Kitty?

KITTY [*using her lipstick*]: Yes, please. Small one!

EGGIE: You'll have to hurry, Monica. You know what Millie is over her musical parties.

KITTY: Poor Millie! Her house is much too small——

EGGIE: Even for ch-ch-chamber music.

[*Everybody laughs except John.*]

[*To Monica*]: Drink?

MONICA: No, I've got some brandy somewhere.

EGGIE [*continuing the conversation*]: And her head's much too big.

MONICA: I'm not coming to the Friedlanders'!

KITTY: Monica!

MONICA: I want to talk to John.

KITTY: Bring him too.

EGGIE [*to John*]: Yes, it wouldn't take you long to change, would it?

JOHN: These are the only clothes I have.

KITTY: Do come, it's sure to be agony.

JOHN: No, thanks, really—I think I'd feel out of it.

KITTY: How absurd! You could talk about the war. Nobody who can talk about the war's out of it now, are they, Eggie?

EGGIE: I think the war's a bore, a b-b-bore war.

KITTY: Not very funny, my sweet. That will do for your column.

MONICA: I quite agree. It is a great bore, but John and I are not going to talk about the war, are we, John?

JOHN: I think I must be getting along, Monica. I've got to see Perry.

MONICA: Who on earth's Perry?

JOHN: Just an old friend of mine, nobody you know.

EGGIE [to Monica]: What's happened to Freddy?

MONICA: He's in Paris with Laura.

EGGIE: Somebody told me that, but I couldn't b-b-bring myself to believe it—you're beautifully composed about it.

MONICA: I don't see any reason to be anything else.

KITTY: Monica's always composed, aren't you, dear?

EGGIE: Hard as nails, utterly ruthless, when l-l-love is o-o-over how little lovers thingummy bob——

MONICA [sharply]: Shut up, Eggie!

KITTY: Freddy's a fool, anyhow! I always thought so.

MONICA: You didn't always show it!

KITTY: And Laura's a half-wit, they're admirably suited.

EGGIE: Go carefully, Kitty. There may be t-t-tendrils of affection still twining round Monica's stony heart! I shall write a dear little bit about Freddy and Laura being in Paris. Where are they—at the Ritz?

MONICA: You're too late, it's already in the *Standard*.

EGGIE: Did Burford ring you up?

MONICA: Don't be ridiculous, Eggie! As if I'd talk about my private affairs to the Press.

EGGIE: The Press seems to have a pretty good rough idea of them!

KITTY: Don't quarrel, you two!

EGGIE [*injured*]: Nobody ever gives me any news, I always have to scavenge round for it. It's a great mistake, writing about people you know.

MONICA [*sharply*]: If it was really *writing* it wouldn't matter so much!

KITTY [*taking Eggie's arm*]: Give up, Eggie, Monica's remarkably snappy to-night.

[*They both move away slightly towards the panatrope.*]

JOHN [*quietly to Monica*]: Good-bye!

MONICA [*with sudden intensity, unheard by the others*]: Please stay—you owe it to me—you haven't given me a chance yet!

JOHN: Get rid of them—for God's sake!

KITTY [*coming down*]: Darling—do hurry!

MONICA: I told you, I'm not coming.

KITTY: Just for a few minutes?

MONICA: No—[*almost wildly*] no!

KITTY: Well, you needn't snap my head off just because you've got a bit of private nonsense on. [*She looks at John and laughs.*] I do hope he'll be a comfort, darling, he looks a bit gloomy to me. Eggie!

EGGIE: What?

KITTY: Put on the "Blue Danube," dear, and come away!

EGGIE: What for? [*He stops the panatrope.*]

KITTY: Monica wants us to go!

EGGIE: How inhospitable! Is this true, Monica?

MONICA: Yes. I may join you later, I don't know, I'll see.

KITTY [*catching Eggie's arm*]: Come on!

EGGIE [*gulping down his drink*]: All right!—"Impoverished Peer Asked to Leave Lady Chellerton's House in Mount Street.

Full story on Page 8." [*He waves genially to John.*] See you later!

KITTY [*to Monica*]: Good-bye, darling—have fun! [*To John*]: Good-bye!

JOHN: Good-bye!

MONICA: Good-bye!

[*Eggie and Kitty go out.*]

MONICA: I'm sorry, John.

JOHN: What for?

MONICA: All that.

JOHN: Why—it's part of your life, isn't it?

MONICA: They don't matter a bit.

JOHN: Don't apologize for them, that makes it worse.

MONICA: I hate them, particularly Eggie: he's got a mind like a third-rate housemaid.

JOHN: You said he was a darling a little while ago, and terribly funny!

MONICA: He can be sometimes, but he wasn't to-night.

JOHN: That was my fault. I was the wrong note.

MONICA: Yes, that's probably true. [*She flings herself down on the sofa.*] Anyhow, you've managed to make me utterly miserable, if that's any comfort to you.

JOHN: I'm sorry!

MONICA: Why did you come? You might have known it would be a failure.

JOHN: How could I know? I've been too far away to know anything but the more concrete horrors.

MONICA: You're not going to begin about the war, are you? I couldn't bear it.

JOHN: Why couldn't you bear it?

MONICA: Because it's over and done with and boring to the last degree.

JOHN: It isn't over and done with for me!

MONICA: You're dead. Don't be silly, you're dead!

JOHN: I couldn't die until I was free.

MONICA: What do you mean?

JOHN: You've made it just a little easier for me. Only a few more minutes left. I must go——

[*He goes towards the door. Monica rises swiftly and intercepts him.*]

MONICA: No, no, forgive me, I didn't mean it. I wouldn't have talked like that if I hadn't been puzzled and bewildered and scared! Give me a chance to explain. I can't change back all in a minute, but I'll try. I swear I will, if you want me to enough!

JOHN [*gently*]: It doesn't matter, Monica. It's only my personal view! You go your own way and don't be upset. You've got a life to live, I haven't. Don't worry about me!

MONICA: I loved you! I swear I did. [*She is crying now.*]

JOHN [*leading her down to the sofa*]: There, there! That's all right—I know you did——

MONICA [*suddenly clinging to him*]: I could love you again, if you wanted me——

JOHN [*drawing away*]: No, Monica, don't say that!

MONICA [*wildly*]: It's true.

JOHN [*remotely*]: Our love wouldn't meet now, there's a gap of too many years!

MONICA [*whispering*]: John, don't be so dreadfully stern and sure. Kiss me, just once, won't you? Even if it's only to say good-bye—won't you, please?

JOHN: Of course.

[*He kisses her, she twines her arms round his neck and relaxes in his embrace. Bertie Chellerton enters. He is amiable-looking, about forty, a trifle puffy from good living, but possessing a certain charm. He is obviously embarrassed, but covers it more or less successfully after the first start. Monica and John break away.*]

BERTIE: I'm so sorry to come bursting in like that. I'd no idea you were at home!

MONICA [*with an effort*]: It doesn't matter, dear. John, this is my husband—John Cavan!

BERTIE [*shaking hands*]: Of course. Monica's often spoken of you. How are you?

JOHN [*suddenly*]: I'd like to apologize—you see Monica and I .were engaged once, years ago, and—and—we hadn't seen each other since. That's why——

BERTIE: I know—I know—don't say any more, please. It was my fault for blundering in. Monica and I understand one another perfectly. We've been married too long to be anything but just good friends. You were killed in 1916, weren't you?

JOHN: 1917.

BERTIE: Yes, of course. There was a great pal of mine in your show—Teddy Filson. Do you remember him?

JOHN: Yes. Quite well.

BERTIE: I must be getting along now. I'm supposed to be at the Pavilion with Mary and Jack. They've got a box or something. I was bringing this telegram to put on your desk, Monica, it's from the Burdons, asking us down on the twentieth. D'you want to go?

MONICA: I'll think about it and let you know later.

BERTIE: Right. [*He smiles at John.*] Cheero! [*Then under his breath to Monica*]: For God's sake, lock the door next time. That was damned awkward! [*He goes out.*]

[*There is a silence for a moment. John starts laughing—a strained laugh.*]

MONICA: Don't, John, please!

JOHN: I can't help it. It's funny.

MONICA: You'll never forgive me now, will you?

JOHN: Forgive you?

MONICA: You know what I mean.

JOHN: There's nothing to forgive, honestly there isn't. It hasn't anything to do with it.

MONICA: I'm sorry I've let you down.

JOHN: I don't matter. It's you that matters.

MONICA [*smiling*]: Mattered—past tense, please—mattered once, a long while ago, not any more, not now.

JOHN [*suddenly sitting down and burying his face in his hands*]: Oh, God! It's all so silly!

MONICA: Don't be miserable, please—if you'd come back all right years ago, and we'd married as we'd planned, it might all have been different.

JOHN [*looking up*]: I wonder!

MONICA: This won't last, will it—this feeling that I've got now? It'll pass away when I wake up, won't it?

JOHN: I expect so.

MONICA: I couldn't bear it if it didn't. I just couldn't bear it. I wish you wouldn't look at me like that.

JOHN: Good-bye, Monica dear. I'm really going this time, and I won't worry you again ever, even in dreams, I promise! Never think I regret having loved you, I'm grateful to you for a lot of happiness. It was jolly planning a future, it passed the time.

MONICA: Yes, it passed the time all right—and that's all I've done ever since, though I don't know what right you have to accuse me. Oh, I know you didn't actually in so many words, but your eyes did. You died young. Who are you to judge? You hadn't yet found out about everything being a bore.

[*John quietly goes away, but she goes on talking without seeing him—the lights begin to fade.*]

I don't see why I shouldn't try to justify myself really. I'm quite nice and kind to people. I don't cheat or lie, or steal, I like being popular and having people in love with me; why shouldn't I?

There's no harm in that, really; all the fuss that's made about having affairs, it's silly! I might have had an affair with you just now if Bertie hadn't come in. Funny having an affair with a ghost —funny having an affair with a ghost—— [*She speaks the last few lines in the pitch dark; the panatrope blares out, but the lights don't go up.*]

CURTAIN

SCENE IV

THE SCENE *is Perry Lomas's sitting room. It is poorly furnished; there is a bed on one side of the stage, and a few books about. One or two cane armchairs and a table in the Centre.*

When the curtain rises, Perry is seated at the table writing. There is a tray of half-eaten food which he has pushed on one side. Lying on the table just beyond the paper upon which he is writing is a revolver. Perry is still thin and nervy looking. His hair is scantier than in Scene I, and gray. John appears in the pool of light shed over the table from a hanging lamp.

JOHN: Perry?
PERRY [*not looking up*]: Yes?
JOHN: It's me—John!
PERRY [*peering at him*]: Oh, sit down.
JOHN: Don't you recognize me?
PERRY: Wait a minute till I've finished this.
JOHN: But, Perry!
PERRY: Wait, wait a minute, please!
[*John sits down. Perry goes on writing. He finally reads through*

the letter he has finished, and putting it into an envelope, seals it down. He sits back and looks at John; then he smiles.]
I thought you'd have vanished by the time I looked up again.

JOHN: I'm awfully glad to see you, Perry.

PERRY: Well, you're only just in time.

JOHN: What do you mean?

PERRY [*taking up the revolver*]: Good-bye!

[*He is about to place it to his head when John leans over and grabs his arm.*]

JOHN: Stop—no—not yet—Perry.

PERRY: So you're tangible. That's surprising!

JOHN: Give me that gun.

PERRY: If this is my brain beginning to snap I'm damned if I'm going to wait and watch it happen. [*He tries to lift his arm again.*] I'm going to anticipate it!

JOHN [*struggling with him*]: Not yet, please not yet, Perry.

PERRY: Let me go, damn you!

JOHN: Don't be a fool!

PERRY: That's not being a fool. There are thousands of ways of being a fool in life, but not in death. You must know all about that.

JOHN: I don't, I don't know anything, but I'm beginning to. It isn't as swift as you think.

PERRY: Don't put me off, there's a good chap. It's all I've got to look forward to.

JOHN: Just a few minutes can't make any difference.

PERRY: Why should I listen to you? My mind's made up. I'm all ready.

JOHN: I want to know why you're doing it.

PERRY: That's easy.

JOHN: Tell me. Put that revolver down and tell me.

PERRY: Heart to heart talk with spook, very difficult.

JOHN: Please!

PERRY: You always got your own way when you were alive, it's clever of you to keep it up when you're dead. [*He puts the revolver down.*] There! Would you like a drink? I believe there's still some left.

JOHN: No, thanks.

PERRY [*looking at him curiously*]: I remember you so clearly, in those last few moments lying on the bunk. I hated it, seeing you brought in like that. It came so unexpectedly. After all, there hadn't been any heavy shelling, everything was quiet, and you were so very very alive always, even when you were tired. What have you been up to all this time?

JOHN: I don't know; waiting, I suppose.

PERRY: Where?

JOHN: I don't know that either.

PERRY: Haven't you met any spirits yet, socially?

JOHN: Not one.

PERRY: Haven't you even been in touch with Sir Oliver Lodge?

JOHN: No.

PERRY: Well, you ought to be ashamed of yourself, a fine up-standing ghost of your age, shilly-shallying about and getting nowhere. I don't know what the spirit world's coming to, and that's a fact!

JOHN: It's what I was talking to you about, the infinitesimal moment, don't you remember? You see it's "now" for me and "then" for you.

PERRY [*flippantly*]: And "two for tea and tea for two!"

JOHN: Don't evade me by being flippant, Perry, it's not kind.

PERRY: You're so earnest, so very earnest.

JOHN: You can't talk, you're earnest enough to commit suicide.

PERRY: True—true!

JOHN: And you won't even tell me why!

PERRY: It's difficult to tabulate it in words.

JOHN: Try. I do want to know.

PERRY: Curiouser nor a cat!

JOHN: Why, Perry, why?

PERRY: A sort of hopelessness which isn't quite despair, not localized enough for that. A formless, deserted boredom, everything eliminated, whittled right down to essentials, essentials which aren't there.

JOHN: Are you sure?

PERRY: Yes, quite sure, for me, anyway.

JOHN: Personal view again.

PERRY: There's nothing else, that's all there is for any of us.

JOHN: No, you're wrong. There must be something more.

PERRY: Still floundering about after ultimate truths? Really, Master John, you're dead enough to know better.

JOHN: I'm beginning to wish I were.

PERRY: Why?

JOHN: I'm getting scared. I wasn't when I started.

PERRY: What's upset you?

JOHN: Change and decay. [*He laughs suddenly.*]

PERRY: Oh, good! Splendid! You're coming along nicely.

JOHN: I thought that would please you.

PERRY: It doesn't please me exactly, but it's interesting.

JOHN: I suppose it is.

PERRY: Where did you start?

JOHN: Mother!

PERRY: How did that go? How did you find her?

JOHN: Strong and clear as always.

PERRY: That's the only form of sex that really holds.

JOHN [*with sudden fury*]: Go to hell! You'll never find peace, not in a million deaths.

PERRY: Don't get rattled!

JOHN: Your bitterness is too bitter, deep down in your heart, nullifying any chance you might have.

PERRY: You mustn't be superior just because you've got a mother. I haven't. Never have had since I was two. No compromise for me.

JOHN [*looking down*]: I'm sorry.

PERRY: So you bloody well ought to be. Coming it over me with your mother love and Christmas decorations and frosted robins!

JOHN: Shut up—do shut up! [*He buries his face in his hands.*]

PERRY: Well, who else? Who else have you seen?

JOHN: Why should I tell you? You won't understand. I don't like you enough, really!

PERRY: You used to.

JOHN: That was different.

PERRY: And you've remembered to come and see me in your brief moment.

JOHN: I had to come.

PERRY: Why? It couldn't have been admiration of my point of view, reverence for my brain. You always thought me unbalanced.

JOHN: I felt sort of sorry for you.

PERRY: Very kind, I'm sure. Lady Bountiful bringing me a basket of goodies from the grave.

JOHN: Don't misunderstand me. Not that sort of sorry.

PERRY: You're gibbering, old dear, just gibbering. Not being honest trying to fit half truths together, but they're too jagged and unmanageable. Better stop trying and come off your perch.

JOHN: What do you mean?

PERRY: I know why you're here, even if you don't.

JOHN: Tell me then!

PERRY: A gesture to memory, rather a gallant gesture, particularly from you, a farewell salute to things that have lain unsaid between us.

JOHN [*embarrassed*]: Oh, Perry! Don't be such an ass.

PERRY: It's true! Nothing to be ashamed of. Look at me, through the me that's here, back to the me that you knew, and remember a little and be nice, because—because I'm feeling pretty low really. [*He looks fixedly at John, smiling, but his eyes are filled with tears.*]

JOHN [*wonderingly*]: Vulnerable, over me?

PERRY: I never said I wasn't vulnerable.

JOHN: So that's why I came.

PERRY: I think so.

JOHN: Youth is a long way away, isn't it?

PERRY: Yes, it doesn't matter any more

JOHN: Oh, God! What a muddle!

PERRY [*gently*]: You haven't answered my question. Who else have you seen?

JOHN: Nobody.

PERRY [*smiling*]: Liar!

JOHN: Nobody I expected to see anyhow.

PERRY: Monica Chellerton, I suppose!

JOHN: Do you know her?

PERRY: No, I know of her. I remembered that you were engaged to her when I saw of her marriage years ago—I've watched her progress since then. Did she let you down very hard?

JOHN: I don't think, perhaps, it was altogether her fault.

PERRY: What did you expect?

JOHN: I don't know.

PERRY: Why wasn't it her fault?

JOHN: Circumstances, environment, money, all those silly people hemming her in.

PERRY: She could get out if she wanted to.

JOHN: Not as easily as all that.

PERRY: Why are you making excuses for her? It isn't her that you love. You'd stored up a pretty little sentimental memory, separated from reality by war; then you came back and took her by surprise before she had time to play up. Damned unfair, I call it!

JOHN: Do you mean she was always playing up, even before?

PERRY: I expect so, it's her job.

JOHN: She loved me once.

PERRY: I'm sure she did, as much as she could. Don't worry about her, there are deeper sorrows than that. Hang around a bit longer and you'll see.

JOHN: I know about your book.

PERRY: Do you?

JOHN: Is it true that they're going to burn it?

PERRY: I expect so.

JOHN: Damn their eyes!

PERRY: They haven't got any to damn! They can't see, they can only grope with their instincts, and the principal one, as usual, is fear. They're afraid my book might start something, that if they let it get by, it might encourage someone else to write a better one, clearer, more concise, in simpler phrases. I tried to be as simple as possible, but I didn't succeed, that's what's wrong with the book. You have to talk to dogs in bone language, and it's difficult, particularly if you don't care for dogs.

JOHN: Is it because of the book that you're going to—to——

PERRY: Kill myself?

JOHN: Yes. Have they got you down? Is that why?

PERRY: Lord, no! I'm not killing myself because of the book: that's trivial compared with the rest. It was true, you see, as true as I could make it, and that's that. I've got it out of me. It was received as I expected it to be received—outraged squeaks and yells. But none of that matters, even to me, now.

JOHN: What is it, then?

PERRY: Deeper than that, far, far deeper. One little ego in the universe, mine, humiliated and shamed into the dust by being alive. You're all right, you're safe. You're naturally idealistic. I never was. You're young. I never was. You're mercifully dead. This coming back to see is all very well, a good trick but no more. It's really as futile as everything else, because as usual there's been a blunder. You're not the right sort to come back, you'll never see, your eyes are too kind. You can try, that's all, but you won't get far.

JOHN: It's nerves, this hatred in you. Nerves—you're ill! You've been working yourself to death over writing this book, and now it's done you're suffering from a reaction. You should go away quietly into the country somewhere and rest.

PERRY: Oh, John, good old John, how typical of you! Do you remember that night when somebody or other died, and I was a bit upset, and you told me to control my mind? You gave me a list of things to think about, a jolly little list: sleep, warmth, drink, food, self-preservation. You gave me that list without a trace of irony, do you remember?

JOHN: I was right. This is the smash I was warning you about, but it's come later than I thought.

PERRY: You said that you believed something would come out of the war, that there was a reason for all that ignorant carnage, all that vitality and youth dying as bravely as it could, not knowing why. Years and years hence, you said, we shall see, something will rise out of the ashes; didn't you, didn't you?

JOHN: I still believe that.

PERRY: Hurry, then, don't waste time with me.

JOHN: It may be that I've come back too soon.

PERRY [*rising irritably*]: Come back again, then. If your curiosity is tenacious enough, it can hold you indefinitely suspended
between the grave and the stars; you can keep on coming back,
but don't stay now, you've picked a bad moment.

JOHN: Why so bad? What is it? What's happening?

PERRY: Nothing's happening, really. There are strides being
made forward in science and equal sized strides being made backwards in hypocrisy. People are just the same: individually pleasant
and collectively idiotic. Machinery is growing magnificently,
people paint pictures of it and compose ballets about it, the artists
are cottoning on to that very quickly because they're scared that
soon there won't be any other sort of beauty left, and they'll be
stranded with nothing to paint and nothing to write. Religion is
doing very well. The Catholic Church still tops the bill as far
as finance and general efficiency go. The Church of England is
still staggering along without much conviction. The Evangelists
are screeching as usual and sending out missionaries. All the other
sects are flourishing about equally. Christian Science is coming
up smiling, a slightly superior smile, but always a smile. God is
Love, there is no pain. Pain is error. Everything that isn't Love
is error; like hell it is. Politically all is confusion, but that's
nothing new. There's still poverty, unemployment, pain, greed,
cruelty, passion, and crime. There's still meanness, jealousy,
money, and disease. The competitive sporting spirit is being
admirably fostered, particularly as regards the Olympic games.
A superb preparation for the next war, fully realized by everyone
but the public that will be involved. The newspapers still lie
over anything of importance, and the majority still believes them
implicitly. The only real difference in post-war conditions is that
there are so many men maimed for life and still existing, and so
many women whose heartache will never heal. The rest is the
same, only faster and more meretricious. The war is fashionable

now, like a pleasantly harrowing film. Even men who fought in it, some of them see in it a sort of vague glamour; they've slipped back, as I knew they would. Come and see if you must, John. You can stand up under a few blows in the guts, you're strong in courage and true as far as you know, but what are you doing it for? Why not be content with the suffering you've had already out there? All the rest is unnecessary and doesn't help. Go back to your mother for the time that's left, say good-bye to her, be sweet to her as you're sweet to everybody and just a little sweeter: that may be worth something, although it passes in a flash. A kid like you isn't going to do any good in all this muck. Hold close to your own love wherever it lies; don't leave it lonely while you wander about aimlessly in chaos searching for some half-formulated ideal. An ideal of what? Fundamental good in human nature! Bunk! Spiritual understanding? Bunk! God in some compassionate dream waiting to open your eyes to truth? Bunk! Bunk! Bunk! It's all a joke with nobody to laugh at it. Go back to your mother while you can.

JOHN: Cheer up, Perry.

PERRY: You'll see, I'm right. You'll see.

JOHN: You've given yourself away a bit.

PERRY: How do you mean?

JOHN: You laugh at me for being an idealist, but you're a greater one than I, far greater——

PERRY: Magnificent sophistry: you'll be saying everything's God's Will in a minute.

JOHN: I'm only idealistic about individuals, really; that's why I came back. I can only see causes and effects through a few people, the people I love. But you're different, capable of deeper depths and further heights, because your ideals catch at life itself, away beyond me, Perry, far beyond. You've been clutching at a star beyond my vision, looking to a future that's too dim for me even to imagine. It must be heartbreaking to be a poet!

PERRY: Cheering my last moments, that's what you're doing, aren't you? [*He smiles rather wearily.*]

JOHN [*picking up the revolver and handing it to him*]: Here!

PERRY [*taking it*]: Thanks. What's a little death among friends?

JOHN: Better than life among enemies. Poor old Perry! I see that much.

PERRY: An epigram, and from you—oh, John, how glorious!

JOHN [*rising*]: Good-bye, Perry!

PERRY [*rising also and standing above the table*]: Thanks for coming. You've made a strange difference. I'm deeply, deeply grateful!

[*John suddenly puts his arms round Perry tightly, then turns away and disappears into the shadows.*]

JOHN [*as he goes*]: Good-bye, old dear!

PERRY [*huskily*]: Cheero!

[*As the lights fade, Perry lifts the revolver to his head. He is smiling. The shot rings out in the dark.*]

CURTAIN

[*In the pitch darkness the voices of Babe Robins, Tilley, Shaw, and Perry are heard.*]

TILLEY: He's still breathing.

BABE [*hysterically*]: Will he die—will he die?

SHAW: Shut up, Babe.

PERRY: He's not quite unconscious, look at his eyes. I believe he opened his eyes.

SCENE V

SCENE: *The private office of Sir James Cavan in the* Daily Mercury *Building, London. The room is large and luxuriously furnished. The three windows look out over roof tops, and, as it is evening, electric light signs can be seen flashing in the distance. The big table in the Centre is placed in readiness for a conference. Note-books and pencils at each place and chairs drawn up. On the sideboard there is an elaborate cold supper laid out. There is a sofa downstage Left, and Sir James's desk downstage Right. There are two or three telephones on it, and neat piles of letters and papers. Far away, down below somewhere can be heard the faint rumble of printing presses.*

When the curtain rises, Sir James and Alfred Borrow are seated on the sofa; Miss Beaver is standing primly just above it with her note-book. Sir James is fattish and pink and shrewd. Alfred Borrow is also shrewd but in a different way. He is a measly-looking man. They are both in dinner jackets. Miss Beaver is watery and pale but obviously efficient; otherwise she would not be there. John comes quietly in from the door downstage Left. Sir James stops talking abruptly and rises to his feet.

SIR JAMES: John! My son, my son! [*He very beautifully takes John in his arms.*]

JOHN [*wriggling away*]: Hallo, Father!

SIR JAMES: I can't speak in this great, great moment. I can't speak, my heart is too full!

JOHN: Is it?

SIR JAMES [*with one eye on Borrow and Miss Beaver*]: You have passed from life into death, and back again from death into life to see your old father——

[*Borrow whispers something to Miss Beaver, and she makes a few shorthand notes.*]

Borrow, this is my son John, you remember him? John, you remember Borrow, don't you?

JOHN: Yes.

SIR JAMES: Borrow is now the live wire of the *Mercury*.

BORROW: This is very moving. I can only say welcome!

JOHN: How do you do! Thank you so much. How do you do!

BORROW [*shaking hands*]: We need you. Men like you—England needs you, you must tell England everything.

SIR JAMES: Your mother will be so happy. So, so happy! We must telephone her. Miss Beaver, get through immediately to her ladyship. How happy she will be!

JOHN: I've seen Mother.

SIR JAMES: Good, splendid! How happy it must have made her.

BORROW: Return of Sir James Cavan's only son after thirteen years! His mother, a white-haired patrician lady, smiled at our special representative with shining eyes. "My son," she said simply. Just that, but in those two words the meed of mother love was welling over.

JOHN [*impersonally*]: Worm, stinking little worm!

BORROW: A full page, nothing less than a full page! Have you any photographs of yourself aged two, then aged eight, then aged thirteen? Hurray for schooldays! Then seventeen, just enlisted, clear-eyed and clean-limbed, answering your country's call. "We're out to win," said Sir James Cavan's son smilingly. Just that, but in those simple words what a wealth of feeling, what brave, brimming enthusiasm.

JOHN [*dreamily*]: Filth—scavenging little rat!

BORROW: Death of Sir James Cavan's only son. "Thank God!" said Sir James Cavan huskily to our special representative, "he died fighting." Lady Cavan, when interviewed, was reserved and dry eyed, her mother grief was too deep for tears. "He was my only son," she said clearly. "Now he is gone, but he would

like to think we are carrying on, so we will, we will carry on!"
Just those few words, so simple, but, oh, what a wealth of heroic
suffering lay behind them!

JOHN: I can't touch you with words or blows, the nightmare
is too strong.

BORROW: What do you think of the modern girl? What do you
think of the longer skirts? Do you think bicycling women make
the best wives? Do you think the talkies will kill the theatre?
What do you think of the dear little Princess Elizabeth? Do you
think this vogue of war literature will last?

[*He walks up and down, followed closely and in step by Miss
Beaver, taking notes mechanically.*]

We will take off our hat to Sir Lawrence Weevil for saying,
"Thank God, we've got a navy." We take off our hat to Lady
Millicent Beauchamp for giving birth to a baby daughter. We
take off our hat to Cedric Bowleigh for making coloured paper
toys and being photographed in the nude. We take off our hat
to the Duchess of Lyme for appearing at the "Down with Cancer"
matinée as the infant Samuel. We take off our hat to Lieutenant
John Cavan for returning from death; returning from the grave;
returning from the other side; returning from the spirit world;
returning from the hinterland; returning from the beyond. [*He
turns to Sir James.*] What do you think best?

SIR JAMES: Hinterland.

BORROW: Miss Beaver.

MISS BEAVER: Beyond.

BORROW: Returning from beyond the hinterland.

SIR JAMES: Sunday. Save it all for Sunday.

[*The telephone rings. Miss Beaver goes to it.*]

MISS BEAVER [*at phone*]: Yes. Just a moment. [*To Sir James*]:
It's that painted strumpet, Viola Blake, Sir James.

SIR JAMES: Thank you, Miss Beaver. [*He goes to telephone.*]

MISS BEAVER [*relinquishing telephone*]: I think she's drunk again.

SIR JAMES [*at phone*]: Hallo! Yes, Viola; no, Viola; yes, Viola; no, Viola; yes, a conference. Very busy. Yes, darling; no, darling, later, darling. Good-bye, darling. [*Sir James hangs up the receiver and comes over to John.*] Long exciting legs, my boy, but no brain.

BORROW: Miss Viola Blake in a private interview admitted that she only used plain cold cream and a loofah. "Exercise," she said, "is absolutely essential. Every morning I ride and skip and play tennis and hunt in season. In the evenings I read and write and listen to good music. If I marry it must be a strong, good man who will understand me. I'm really very old-fashioned, in spite of the parts I play. I never use hot or cold water, or soap or cosmetics or massage. Just plain cold cream and a loofah— cold cream and a loofah—away with blackheads—cold cream and a loofah!"

MISS BEAVER: Silly drunken harlot! Any more notes, Sir James?

SIR JAMES: Not at the moment, Miss Beaver, but I'd like you to wait. Have a glass of champagne? We'll all have a glass of wine. The others will be here in a moment.

MISS BEAVER: No champagne for me, thank you. Just plain cold cream and a loofah! [*She laughs wildly and sits down in a corner.*]

[*Borrow pours out three glasses of champagne and hands one to John, one to Sir James, and keeps the other himself.*]

SIR JAMES [*lifting his glass*]: A toast to the war, and the heroic part played in it by my son!

BORROW [*lifting his glass*]: To the war!

JOHN: To the war! [*He drains his glass.*] More, please!

[*Borrow takes John's glass and refills it.*]

SIR JAMES: John, my boy, this is a great moment.

JOHN [*lifting his glass*]: Here's to you, Father. Liar, hypocrite,

conscientious money grubber, political cheat, licentious sentimentalist—my father. [*John drinks.*]

SIR JAMES [*jovially*]: Thank you, my boy, thank you—a great
moment.

BORROW: Lieutenant John Cavan drinks to his father. "Father
and I have always been good pals," he said to our representative.
"Even when I was so high, he was my ideal of what a man should
be." Then this serious war-scarred young soldier gave one of
his rare smiles. "I see no reason to change that early impression,"
he said. Such a simple unemotional sentence and yet what a wealth
of pride and adoration lay behind it.

SIR JAMES: The Bishop should be here. Why is he so late?

MISS BEAVER: It will be lovely to see a bishop close to—what
a lucky, lucky girl I am!

BORROW: I can't think what's detaining the old fool!

SIR JAMES: And Lady Stagg-Mortimer!

MISS BEAVER: And Sir Henry!

JOHN: Lady Stagg-Mortimer. I remember her name—she gave
her son!

SIR JAMES: A truly remarkable woman, deeply religious and a
wonderful mother!

JOHN: We were talking about her a minute ago, reading that
tripe. I'm glad she's coming. I want to see her.

SIR JAMES: The best type of womanhood in the world.

MISS BEAVER: Faded.

BORROW: Embittered.

SIR JAMES: Sexually repressed.

MISS BEAVER: Snobbish.

BORROW: Plain.

SIR JAMES: A truly remarkable woman!

[*The Butler enters.*]

BUTLER: Lady Stagg-Mortimer!

[*Lady Stagg-Mortimer comes slyly into the room. She is tall and thin, like a scraggy Burne-Jones. Her manner is alternatively ingratiating and authoritative. She is in a russet evening gown— her voice is shrill and high. She shakes hands with Sir James.*]

LADY S.-M.: How do you do? I should like a tongue sandwich, but no sherry. Sherry is the beginning of the end. [*To Borrow*]: How do you do? [*She shakes hands. To John*]: How do you do? [*She shakes hands.*]

SIR JAMES: My son—from beyond the hinterland!

LADY S.-M.: How interesting! If you're going to stay I'm afraid we must erase your name from the Roll of Honour. [*She looks at Miss Beaver.*] That woman is showing too much neck!

BORROW: Too much neck, Miss Beaver—make a note.

LADY S.-M.: It's indecent! Merely intended to arouse the beast in men, that's all she does it for. I know that kind: sly and quiet and utterly unreliable. Where's the Bishop?

SIR JAMES: Where's the Bishop, Borrow?

BORROW: Miss Beaver, where's the Bishop?

MISS BEAVER [*going to telephone*]: I'll find out.

LADY S.-M.: All that efficiency is all very well, but it's false. Look at the way she moves her hips when she walks!

MISS BEAVER [*at telephone*]: Where's the Bishop? Very well. [*She hangs up.*] He's downstairs washing his hands.

LADY S.-M.: Pert, too. They're all alike; look at her hair.

JOHN: I want to go back now. This is no use! I want to go back.

SIR JAMES: You can't. You must stay and help us, you're one of our most valuable allies, you shall speak at the conference— you're fresh from the Great War——

BORROW: The Great War for Civilization!

MISS BEAVER: The Great War for Freedom!

LADY S.-M.: The Great War for God!

SIR JAMES: You will be able to prove that this book by Perry Lomas is a living lie to be stamped out—defaming the memory of the Great War for humanity.

JOHN: What do you know of war? How did you see it, sitting at home here? Could any of the truth of it possibly have filtered through to your minds? How? By what channels? The newspapers, perhaps, the edited drama of cautious war correspondents, photographs of devastated areas, casualty lists, the things you were told by men on leave, men who spared you out of courtesy to your ignorance, who parried your idiotic questions because they were tired and wanted to rest a little. They said it was "All right, not so bad," that it would soon be over, and that you weren't to worry. And they went back, some of them almost gladly, because they loved you and were relieved to find how little you knew; others, less sentimental, were glad for different reasons. There's a quality in war that doesn't quite fit in with your gaudy labels, "God and Country!" "Martyred Belgium!" "The Great Sacrifice!" And all the rest of the cant you manufactured. There's a quality that you could never know, never remotely imagine, beyond your easy patriotism and your prayers. Beyond even what love you have, something intangible and desolately beautiful because it's based upon the deepest tragedy of all, disillusion beyond hope. Strangely enough, your whole religion is founded on that same tragedy, though in comparison with the war, the crucifixion becomes microscopic in importance. Christ was one man, the war was millions.

LADY S.-M.: You're a very interesting young man. You must come to lunch. Can you manage next Tuesday? or if not you might dine on the 25th. Quite a small party. Don't forget.

JOHN: You're nothing but a silly hypocrite, so confused you don't even know yourself. You did well in the war, didn't you? You ran a hospital, and organized gratifying charity matinées, and screeched out patriotic speeches at the top of your lungs. You even sang to the wounded. God help them! You achieved notable glory by writing an open letter to the Women of England when your son was killed. "I Gave My Son," it was called. In that very heading you stole from him his voluntary heroism, you used his memory to exalt yourself in the eyes of sheep. You implored other mothers to "give" their sons as you did, proudly and gladly. You'd better pray quickly to your tin-pot God, pray that your son never knows; he'll hate you even more than he did when he died.

LADY S.-M.: [*affably*]: It always comforts me to think that there is a little bit of England out there in France that is me! Part of *me!*

JOHN: I knew him, d'you hear me? I knew your son.

LADY S.-M.: No one will ever know how we women of England suffered, suffered, suffered! We gave our loved ones, but proudly! We'd give them again—again——

JOHN: He hated you, your loved one.

LADY S.-M. [*looking at Miss Beaver*]: Is it necessary for that woman to be present during the conference, Sir James?

SIR JAMES: I'm afraid so, she must take notes.

LADY S.-M.: Tell her to remain in the corner, then, and not to look at the Bishop. At all costs, she mustn't look at the Bishop.

[*The Butler enters.*]

BUTLER [*announcing*]: The Bishop of Ketchworth, Sir Henry Merstham.

[*The Bishop enters, followed by Sir Henry. The Bishop is genial and smiling. Sir Henry is tall and austere. He wears a monocle and carries his head a trifle on one side.*]

BISHOP: Forgive me, Sir James, I was detained. How do you do! Ah, Lady Stagg-Mortimer, what a pleasure to be sure. [*He shakes hands with Sir James and Lady Stagg-Mortimer.*]

SIR HENRY [*sepulchrally*]: I was also detained, in the House, a very stormy meeting. [*He shakes hands.*] Ah, Lady Stagg-Mortimer.

LADY S.-M.: Don't forget you're lunching with me on Tuesday and dining on the twenty-fifth. Quite a small party.

SIR JAMES: You both know my Right Hand, don't you, Mr. Borrow?

BISHOP: Certainly. How do you do! [*He shakes hands with Borrow.*]

SIR HENRY [*doing the same*]: How do you do!

SIR JAMES: This is my son from the Spirit World.

BISHOP [*shaking hands with John*]: Very interesting. How do you do!

SIR JAMES [*to Sir Henry*]: My son, from Out There.

SIR HENRY: Out where?

BISHOP: The war, my dear Henry, the war.

SIR HENRY: Oh, the war. [*He shakes hands absently with John.*] I was in Paris quite a lot during the war, very depressing, but still I took up a philosophical attitude over the whole thing. It was a time when we all had to pull our weight in the boat. No use grumbling, no use grumbling at all.

BISHOP: Let us get on with the Conference. I must get to bed early. I have a confirmation to-morrow at Egham. Very tedious.

SIR JAMES: A glass of champagne?

BISHOP: No, thank you, I never take it except at weddings, as a special gesture.

SIR JAMES: Sir Henry?

SIR HENRY: Afterwards, I should like some afterwards.

SIR JAMES: Very well. Lady Stagg-Mortimer!

[*He motions her to a seat at the table. He also indicates chairs for the Bishop and Sir Henry. Borrow sits on his left, with Miss Beaver behind his chair.*]

My son on my right.

[*John sits down.*]

LADY S.-M. [*confidentially to Sir Henry*]: Such a nice-looking boy. He knew Alan, you know, my Alan. They were the closest friends. We used to have such happy times when they were home on leave, just the three of us. They treated me just as though I were one of them, not an old woman at all. Oh, dear—— [*She sniffles and fumbles for her handkerchief.*]

SIR HENRY: Dear Lady Stagg-Mortimer, memory is a cruel thing, is it not? There—there—— [*He pats her hand.*]

SIR JAMES [*rising to his feet at the head of the table*]: We have met together to-night in order to discuss a very serious matter, to wit, the rising tide of Sedition, Blasphemy and Immoral Thought which, under the guise of "War Literature," is threatening to undermine the youth of our generation.

SIR HENRY: Hear, hear!

LADY S.-M.: Excellently put.

BISHOP: Delightful, quite delightful!

SIR JAMES: In order to decide upon a course of action which will uproot this—this—er—canker in our midst once and for all, I have called together in secret conclave three of the most brilliant and most powerful people of our time. My old friend the Bishop of Ketchworth, whose finger is ever upon the religious pulse of the nation——

LADY S.-M. [*skittishly blowing him a kiss*]: Dear Bishop!

SIR JAMES [*continuing*]: Sir Henry Merstham, whose sane and uncompromising decisions in his capacity as adviser on the committee of censorship have gone so far towards ridding our theatres and libraries of much that is base and unwholesome——

LADY S.-M.: All the same, Sir Henry, you should never have allowed them to produce that play about the Monk and the Chilean Ambassadress.

SIR JAMES: I never read the play, I was having a few weeks' holiday in Taormina.

LADY S.-M.: Very reprehensible!

BISHOP [*brightening up*]: Taormina—what an enchanting spot. Dear, dear, how time flies!

SIR JAMES [*continuing*]: Lady Stagg-Mortimer, whose indefatigable zeal in charity organizations, whose unswerving loyalty to her country, and whose passionate upholding of English-women's rights have made her name a byword, and her opinion a force to be reckoned with——

LADY S.-M.: Don't listen to him, Bishop, he's flattering me.

SIR JAMES: And last, but by no means least—my son! My own flesh and blood, returned by a miracle from the valley of the shadow, to give us the value of his personal war experience, the benefit of that splendid spirit of patriotism which caused him to lay down his life for God and Country. And, if necessary, the strength of his youthful right arm, in defense of those heroes who died for us, and whose memory is being defamed daily by these writers of so-called war books, who treat England's victory as ignoble, and the glory of her sacrifices as futile.

JOHN [*quietly*]: Death in war is above being defamed, even by you.

BORROW [*dictating to Miss Beaver*]: At the termination of Sir James Cavan's emphatic speech, John Cavan, his only son——

MISS BEAVER: Returned from B. the H.?

BORROW: Yes, returned from B. the H.—looked up at his father with a proud smile. "Dad's right," he said. Just two simple words, but, somehow, somehow, one understood.

BISHOP: We're here to discuss a book, I understand, a very unpleasant book. Let's get on with it. [*He smiles, and shuts his eyes.*]

SIR JAMES: You have all read this outrage?

BISHOP: Outrage? Another outrage! Some poor little girl, I

suppose, set upon in a country lane by some great hairy man! What happened—what happened?

[*He is quite excited, so Sir Henry calms him.*]

SIR JAMES: I was referring to this book, *Post-Mortem*, by a man called Perry Lomas.

JOHN: A poet.

LADY S.-M.: I've read it. I felt humiliated and ashamed.

JOHN: Good for you.

SIR HENRY: The book is a disgrace.

SIR JAMES: Bishop, I want your opinion on this book.

BISHOP: Which book?

SIR JAMES: *Post-Mortem*, by Perry Lomas. I sent it to you.

BISHOP: Very kind of you, I'm sure. I appreciate it very much.

SIR JAMES: Have you read it?

BISHOP: Alas, no. You see I have been so very occupied, what with one thing and another, and now there's this confirmation at Egham to-morrow——

SIR JAMES: Borrow. The Bishop of Ketchworth's opinion of *Post-Mortem*.

BORROW: Miss Beaver. The Bishop of Ketchworth's opinion of *Post-Mortem*.

MISS BEAVER [*producing a typewritten paper*]: Here it is.

SIR JAMES [*taking it and handing it to the Bishop*]: Will you sign here, please?

BISHOP: Where are my glasses?

SIR HENRY [*picking them up from the table*]: Here.

BISHOP: Thank you.

[*He puts them on and signs the paper, breathing rather heavily. When he has done so he sits back with a sigh and closes his eyes again. Sir Henry removes the glasses from his nose and replaces them on the table. Sir James takes the paper and coughs, preparatory to reading it aloud.*]

SIR JAMES [*reading*]: "Letter from the Bishop of Ketchworth to the editor of the *Daily Mercury*. Sir, with regard to the sentiments expressed in your editorial of May 14th concerning the book, *Post-Mortem*, I should like to say that I am in complete agreement with you on every point. Writing such as this, I will not dignity it by the name of Literature——"

[*Borrow smiles and exchanges a glance with Sir James.*]

"——should not only be forbidden publication in a Christian country, but ignominiously burnt."

SIR JAMES [*continuing*]: "It is a vile book and an ungodly book. Its content is blasphemous in the extreme——"

JOHN: "Etc., etc., etc., etc., etc., etc., etc.—signed The Bishop of Katchbush."

SIR JAMES [*smiling*]: My son! [*He pats his head.*]

JOHN [*jerking away*]: Don't touch me.

SIR HENRY: Have you written to the Home Office?

SIR JAMES: That is what I want you to do. I also want you to write a detailed letter to me for my next Sunday Edition.

SIR HENRY: I gather that pressure has already been brought to bear upon the publisher to suspend the book pending a decision from the Home Office?

SIR JAMES: Certainly, certainly.

BORROW: I myself have bought twenty copies, first editions, you understand. Possibly very valuable one day. [*He smiles.*]

BISHOP [*waking up*]: I have a first edition of *Alice in Wonderland*.

LADY S.-M. [*rising*]: Let me speak, I must speak now.

SIR JAMES: Borrow. Lady Stagg-Mortimer's speech.

BORROW: Miss Beaver. Lady Stagg-Mortimer's speech.

MISS BEAVER [*producing another typewritten sheet*]: Here it is.

[*Borrow reads the speech, while Lady Stagg-Mortimer gesticulates and opens and shuts her mouth silently.*]

BORROW [*reading*]: "Open letter to the Women of England. Women of England. Mothers, sweethearts and wives——"

JOHN: Sisters, and cousins, and aunts, and prostitutes, and murderesses.

SIR JAMES [*fondly patting, his head*]: My son! Proceed, Lady Stagg-Mortimer.

BORROW [*continuing*]: "——I have a message for you from my heart, the heart of a mother, who, like many of you, made the great sacrifice of her own flesh and blood in the great War for Humanity. Twelve years have passed since Britain's glorious victory was consummated in the signing of the Armistice. During those twelve years we have gone our ways, working and living, gallantly crushing down our sorrows, and, as a tribute to our glorious dead—carrying on!"

JOHN: What else could you have done?

BORROW [*continuing*]: "——Now, at a critical period in the progress of our nation towards world supremacy, we are faced with a contingency so sinister in its potential evil, so imminently and insidiously perilous, that the very contemplation of it appals me. I refer to——" [*Stops abruptly*]. Miss Beaver, what's that?

MISS BEAVER [*scrutinizing the paper*]: I can't think, I must have left some lines out. I apologize.

SIR JAMES: Let me see.

[*Borrow hands him the paper, he stares at it.*]
Can't make head or tail of it. [*He hands it back.*] Be more careful in future, please, Miss Beaver.

MISS BEAVER [*bursting into tears*]: It's the first time I've ever made a mistake. Oh dear, oh dear——

LADY S.-M. [*frantically*]: Never mind, never mind, go on with the speech—I must continue my speech.

BORROW [*continuing*]: —Etc., etc.—"the Union Jack."

LADY S.-M.: Go on from there, quickly, quickly!

BORROW [*continuing*]: "These puling men who write war books, blackening the name of our heroes, putting blasphemous words into the mouths of our soldiers, picturing them as drinking whisky and rum in the trenches, and making obscene jokes, and behaving like brutes. These men. These slandering scoundrels should be taken out and shot!"

JOHN [*losing control*]: Shut up, shut up! Stop!

[*He hammers the table with his fist. The Bishop wakes up with a start.*]

BISHOP: An air raid, an air raid, quickly, the coal cellar!

JOHN: The nightmare is wearing thin. I can't stay much longer.

SIR JAMES: Have some champagne.

JOHN: I see you clearly, even though a web of time separates us. You are representative. You are powerful. You always were, and you always will be. This is delirium, the delirium of dying, but the truth is here, mixed up with my dream, infinitely horrible. The war was glorious, do you hear me? Supremely glorious, because it set men free. Not the ones who lived, poor devils, but the ones who died. It released them from the sad obligation of life in a Christian world which has not even proved itself worthy of death.

LADY S.-M.: Charming, quite charming.

JOHN: War is no evil compared with this sort of living. War at least provides more opportunities for actions, decent instinctive clear actions, without time for thought or wariness, beyond the betrayal of fear and common sense, and all those other traitors to humanity which have been exalted into virtues. It is considered eminently wise to look before you leap. But that is thin and overprotective wisdom. Your only chance of seeing at all is after you have leapt. War makes you leap, and leap again into bloody chaos, but there are redeeming moments of vision which might, in smug content, be obscured forever.

SIR JAMES: England is proud of you, my son.

JOHN: England doesn't know me, or any like me. England now can only recognize false glory. Real England died in defeat without pretending it was Victory. [*There is the faint sound of guns far away.*] Listen—listen—can't you hear the guns?

SIR JAMES: He sacrificed his life for God and Country.

BORROW: God and Country.

[*They all chant "God and Country" in a monotone, quite softly, an accompaniment to John's voice as it rises. The guns sound nearer.*]

JOHN: Listen—listen—you can hear them more clearly now —blasting your Christianity to pieces. You didn't know, did you? You didn't realize that all the sons you gave, and the husbands you gave, and the lovers you gave in your silly pride were being set free. Free from your hates and loves and small pitiful prayers, for Eternity. You wouldn't have let them go so easily if you'd known that, would you? They've escaped—escaped. You'll never find them again either in your pantomime hell or your tinsel heaven. Long live War. Long live Death, and Destruction and Despair! Through all that there may be a hope, a million-to-one chance for us somewhere, a promise of something clearer and sweeter than anything your bloody gods have ever offered. Long live War——Long live War——

[*John is laughing hysterically. Sir James and the others continue to chant "God and Country." The guns grow louder and louder as the lights fade.*]

[*In the pitch dark there is suddenly dead silence. Then Perry's voice is heard, speaking quietly.*]

PERRY'S VOICE: I think he opened his eyes.

[*There is a far-off splutter of machine-gun fire.*]

CURTAIN

SCENE VI

SCENE: *Tilley, Shaw, Babe Robins, and John are seated around a dinner table. Dinner is over, and they are drinking coffee and brandy. There is no light anywhere but immediately over the table, beyond its radius is blackness. Tilley is forty-three, iron gray, and wearing pince-nez. Shaw, at thirty-nine, is extremely corpulent and pink. Babe Robins, aged thirty-two, has the appearance of any average young man in the motor business. All three of them look fairly prosperous. They are wearing dinner jackets, and smoking cigars, and there is somehow less life in them than there was when they were together in war. John is the same as he has been all through the play.*

JOHN [*raising his glass*]: I give you a toast. To Contentment.

TILLEY: Contentment?

JOHN: Yes, and Peace and Plenty.

SHAW: This really is the damnedest dream I've ever had.

BABE: Good old John. Contentment, Peace and Plenty. [*He drinks.*]

TILLEY: Why not? [*He drinks.*]

SHAW: Excellent brandy. [*He drinks.*]

BABE: Pity old Perry isn't here.

TILLEY: I think it's just as well.

JOHN: Why?

TILLEY: He wouldn't fit.

SHAW: He is a bit impossible, I'm afraid. I saw him the other day, changed beyond recognition, and now all this business about his book.

JOHN: You never liked him, did you, Tilley?

TILLEY: Oh, he was all right then. He had to conform more or less, we all had to.

BABE [*laughing loudly*]: You bet we did!

JOHN: You were always a stickler for discipline, Tilley.

TILLEY: Certainly. Sheer common sense.

JOHN: Are you still?

TILLEY: How do you mean?

JOHN: In civil life, do you still insist on immortal souls forming fours?

SHAW [*laughing and reaching for some more brandy*]: Immortal souls! I say——!

JOHN: Only a phrase—meaning nothing—I apologize.

TILLEY: I must be getting home soon.

JOHN: Where is home?

TILLEY: Hampstead.

JOHN: It's nice, Hampstead.

TILLEY: The air's good, anyhow.

JOHN: Wife and children?

TILLEY: Yes.

JOHN: How many?

TILLEY: Two. Both boys.

JOHN: You're married too, aren't you, Shaw?

SHAW: Yes.

JOHN: Children?

SHAW [*suddenly resentful*]: Mind your own business.

JOHN: Sorry.

SHAW: What is all this, anyhow?

JOHN [*raising his glass*]: Family life. Home Notes. Christians Awake!

TILLEY: Irony seems out of place in you, John, alive or dead.

JOHN: Do you remember Armitage, Babe?

BABE: What?

JOHN: I said, do you remember Armitage?

BABE: Of course I do. Why?

JOHN: How has his memory stayed with you? Is he still clear in your mind? Important?

BABE [*sullenly*]: I don't know what you mean.

JOHN: You loved him then.

BABE [*jumping to his feet*]: Look here, don't you talk such bloody rot.

JOHN: Don't misunderstand me. There is no slur in that. It was one of the nicest things about you, wholehearted and tremendously decent. It must be a weak moral code that makes you wish to repudiate it. Love among men in war is gallant and worth remembering. Don't let the safe years stifle that remembrance.

TILLEY: Sentimentalist.

JOHN: You're my last chance, you three. Don't resent me. There is so much I want to know. This is only a dream to you, so you can be honest. It's easier to be honest in a dream. I know barriers are necessary in waking life, barriers, and smoke screens, and camouflage. But here, in unreality, we're together again for a little. Let me see where you are and what you're doing. Is there no contact possible between you and me just because I'm dead? Is it as final as all that? Are you happy with your wives, and children, and prosperity, and peace? Or is it makeshift?

SHAW: I wish I knew what you were getting at.

JOHN: I'm trying to find a reason for survival.

TILLEY: Life is reason enough, isn't it?

JOHN: No, I don't believe it is.

TILLEY: Nonsense. Morbid nonsense.

JOHN: Have you completely forgotten that strange feeling we had in the war? Have you found anything in your lives since to equal it in strength? A sort of splendid carelessness it was, holding us together. Cut off from everything we were used to, but somehow not lonely, except when we were on leave, or when letters came. Depending only upon the immediate moment. No past, no future, and no conviction of God. God died early in the war, for most of us. Can you remember our small delights? How exciting they were? Sleep, warmth, food, drink, unexpected comforts snatched out of turmoil, so simple in enjoyment, and so incredibly satisfying.

TILLEY [*bitterly*]: What about the chaps one knew being blown to pieces? Lying out in the mud for hours, dying in slow agony. What about being maimed, and gassed, and blinded? Blinded for life.

JOHN: There was something there worth even that. Not to the individual, perhaps, but to the whole. Beyond life and beyond death. Just a moment or two.

TILLEY: To hell with your blasted moment or two. I'm going home.

JOHN: To Hampstead?

BABE: What's the matter with Hampstead? That's what I want to know. What's the matter with Hampstead?

JOHN: The air's good, anyhow.

SHAW: You make me sick, trying to be so damned clever.

JOHN: When your boys grow up, Tilley, and there's another war, will you be proud when they enlist?

BABE: There won't be another war.

JOHN: There'll always be another war. Will you let them go? Will you?

TILLEY: I don't flatter myself that it would be in my power to stop them.

JOHN: You could shoot them.

SHAW [*belligerently*]: If I had sons, and there were a war, I'd shoot them if they didn't go.

JOHN: Excellent sentiments, but why? From what motives?

SHAW: Because I don't believe in shirking one's responsibilities.

JOHN: To what would your sons be responsible?

SHAW: To the decent standards I'd taught them. To the things I'd brought them up to believe.

JOHN: What would you bring them up to believe?

SHAW: I'll tell you, and you can sneer as much as you like. I'd bring them up to believe in God, and the necessity of standing by their country in time of need, and to play the game according to the rules.

JOHN: And if they made their own rules, and didn't accept God, and didn't consider their country important enough— you'd shoot them?

SHAW: Yes, I would. And that's that.

JOHN: Well, you'd better pray for another war for your sons that are not yet born, because it will all be just as you want. They'll grow up and go off to fight gallantly for their God and country according to the rules, and you'll be proud, quite rightly proud, because they'll be nice, decent boys. I'm quite sure of that. What happens to them out there will be entirely beyond your comprehension, *then*. Even now, after only thirteen years, you've forgotten the essential quality. Then, you'll be more forgetful still, because you'll be old. You say truculently that you'd shoot them if they didn't go. Try with all your might to be brave enough to shoot them when they come back.

BABE [*hysterically*]: Stop talking like that! Leave us alone! Let us wake up!

JOHN: Hard luck, Babe. You might have died instead of me. Do you remember?

BABE: I didn't ask you to take over the covering party, you offered to, it was your own fault——

JOHN [*gently*]: Don't worry about that.

BABE: Let me go. Let me wake up.

JOHN: It will be over very soon now.

BABE: Oh, God! Oh, God! [*He buries his head in his arms and sobs.*]

[*From out of the shadows comes Babe as he was in Scene I, in uniform, aged nineteen. He stands still behind the chair. Guns sound faintly, far away.*]

JOHN: You see? Life hasn't compensated him enough for not dying.

SHAW [*to Babe*]: Shut up. Pull yourself together, for God's sake!

JOHN: Interesting that. "For God's sake."

SHAW: Go away. Damn your eyes! Get out—get out!

JOHN: Your mind is solemn now, and you're scared. You never used to be scared.

SHAW: Get out! Go away!

JOHN [*calling sharply*]: Shaw—Shaw—come here a minute. Make us laugh. You were always clowning. Come out, you lazy old bastard.

[*Shaw comes out of the shadows and stands behind his older self. He winks at John and grins broadly. The sound of guns accompanies him.*]

JOHN: That's better. More comfortable. Tilley?

TILLEY [*quietly*]: I hate you. You won't get me.

JOHN: Why do you hate me?

TILLEY: Stirring up trouble. Bloody ghost!

JOHN: You were always more intelligent than the others; is that why you're so set against remembering?

TILLEY: You're not as I remember you, anyhow. You're a complete stranger. Whatever you've learnt in death hasn't improved you. I intend to forget this dream even before my eyes open.

JOHN: Why—why?

TILLEY: I prefer to remember you as a damn good soldier,

a nice uncomplicated boy without overtones. Tuck yourself up on your abstract plane, your fourteenth dimension, wherever you are, and keep your inquisitive hands off my soul. I'm all right. I accept life and peace as I accepted death and war. They're equal as jobs, and I'm a worker.

JOHN: To what end?

TILLEY: I don't know, any more than you, and I care less. I'm passing the time, do you see? Just passing the time. [*He points contemptuously to Shaw and Babe.*] They're malleable, those two, and there are millions like them, easily swayed through their sentimental emotions. You were clever enough to get them on their weaknesses. "Hard luck, Babe, you might have died instead of me." Excellent psychology. You got him on the raw. Hero-worship. "Greater love hath no man, etc., etc." Heart interest. Sex confusion. He'll be like that until he dies. Then Shaw, with his public-school belligerence, shooting his mythical sons in a fine fury of right-minded patriotism. Look how you got him. "Come here a minute, make us laugh, come out, you lazy old bastard!" Chaps! Good old camaraderie! "Damn good times we had together." Of course he'd respond to that treatment. Look at him, fashioned for conviviality, round and pink and jolly, and sentimental as a housemaid. You can't catch me out so easily.

JOHN: All the same, you were sorrier than any of them when they carried me in—dying.

TILLEY: You were a very good second in command. I always hated losing reliable men.

JOHN: Was that all?

TILLEY: Absolutely.

JOHN: I don't believe it.

TILLEY: Funny, personal vanity hanging on so long.

JOHN: It wasn't all. It wasn't all. There was more warmth than that, I felt it.

TILLEY: You were delirious. What you felt doesn't count.

JOHN [*wildly*]: I'm not dead yet. There are still a few more seconds——

TILLEY: Get on with it and don't waste my time.

[*The lights begin to fade, and the guns sound louder.*]

JOHN: I can't yet. I've got to see Mother—I promised——

TILLEY: Hurry, hurry, I'm tired—don't keep us all hanging about.

[*The lights go out. In the dark Tilley's voice is heard speaking authoritatively. He says: "Hoist him up a little higher—gently—give me the water." Babe's voice says: "Is he—done for?"*]

CURTAIN

SCENE VII

SCENE: *The lights come up slowly on the Left-hand side of the stage. Lady Cavan is playing Patience by the window. John is standing by the table.*

JOHN [*urgently*]: Mother.

LADY C. [*rising*]: So soon?

JOHN: Yes.

LADY C.: It's all right. I won't cry or make a fuss.

JOHN [*holding her in his arms*]: Dearest.

LADY C.: It's forever, isn't it—this time?

JOHN [*whispering*]: Yes.

LADY C.: Tell me something. Could you—could you stay if things had been worth it?

JOHN: Perhaps. I don't know. I think so.

LADY C.: You're going—willingly?

JOHN: Yes.

LADY C.: What of me—what of me? [*Brokenly*]: Wouldn't I be enough?

JOHN: Only for a little, then you'd die and leave me—terribly alone. I never wanted to be born.

LADY C.: I see.

JOHN: Only a few more years, Mum, be brave.

LADY C.: Do you think there's any chance anywhere in that great void for us to be together again?

JOHN: Maybe. One in a million.

LADY C.: I'm still alive enough to mind. I know it's foolish.

JOHN: I'm on the border line and should be near to knowing; perhaps in eternity the mists will clear, but I doubt it.

LADY C. [*very quietly*]: I love you, my darling—with all the love that has ever been. It doesn't matter about eternity, wherever you are, in however deep oblivion your spirit rests, this love will be with you. I know it so very strongly—far beyond the limits of my understanding. I love you, my dear, dear one—I love you.

JOHN: Dearest Mum—good-bye.

LADY C. [*kissing him very tenderly*]: Good-bye, Johnnie. [*The lights fade and go out.*]

CURTAIN

SCENE VIII

THE LIGHTS *come up slowly revealing the dugout, exactly as it was at the close of Scene I, except that the Stretcher Bearers have advanced as far as the bunk upon which John is lying. They make a*

*movement preparatory to lifting him onto the stretcher. John moves
and opens his eyes.*

JOHN: You were right, Perry—a poor joke!
[*He falls back. Tilley motions the Stretcher Bearers away, and
then with infinite tenderness lifts John onto the stretcher as the curtain falls.*]

CURTAIN

THE
VORTEX

CHARACTERS

PRESTON

HELEN SAVILLE

PAUNCEFORT QUENTIN

CLARA HIBBERT

FLORENCE LANCASTER

TOM VERYAN

NICKY LANCASTER

DAVID LANCASTER

BUNTY MAINWARING

BRUCE FAIRLIGHT

ACT ONE

THE SCENE *is the drawing-room of Mrs. Lancaster's flat in London. The colors and decoration are on the verge of being original. The furniture is simple but distinctly expensive.*

Persons shown are Helen Saville and Pauncefort Quentin. Helen Saville and Pauncefort Quentin are shown in by Preston. Helen is a smartly dressed woman of about thirty. "Pawnie" is an elderly maiden gentleman.

PRESTON: I'm expecting Mrs. Lancaster in at any moment now, ma'am.

HELEN: Thank you, Preston, we'll wait a little.

PRESTON: Shall I get you some tea?

HELEN: No, thanks, we've already had some—give me a cigarette, Pawnie; they're in that box on the table.

[*Pawnie hands her cigarette box. Preston goes out.*]

PAWNIE: It may be tiresome of me, but I think all this coloring is oppressive.

HELEN: You make such a "fetish" of house decoration, Pawnie.

PAWNIE [*wandering round the room*]: Not at all, but I do like things to be good and right.

HELEN: Well, I don't consider the new frieze in your bathroom either good or right.

PAWNIE: How can you, Helen! It's too marvelous for words. Parelli designed it specially for me.

427

HELEN: Personally, it would make me self-conscious to sit in a bath surrounded by frisky gods and goddesses all with such better figures than mine.

PAWNIE: I find it encouraging. This whole room is so typical of Florence.

HELEN: In what way?

PAWNIE: Every way. Look at the furniture.

HELEN: A little artificial perhaps, but quite harmless.

PAWNIE: Dear Helen, you're such a loyal friend.

HELEN: I'm very fond of Florence.

PAWNIE: We all are. Oh, my God, look at that lampshade!

HELEN: I gave it to her last Christmas.

PAWNIE: Wasn't that a little naughty of you?

HELEN: I don't see why; it's extremely pretty.

PAWNIE: Too unrestrained. Such a bad example for the *servants*. [*He takes up frame from desk*.] Who's this boy?

HELEN: Tom Veryan. You must have seen him.

PAWNIE: Florence's past, present, or future?

HELEN: Present.

PAWNIE: He has that innocent look that never fails to attract elderly women.

HELEN: Don't be a cat.

PAWNIE: I wasn't meaning Florence; she's too divine to be in any marked category.

HELEN: I wonder.

PAWNIE: Oh, yes, Helen, deathless sort of magnetism, you know.

HELEN: I often wonder what will happen to Florence eventually.

PAWNIE: My dear, I'm far too occupied in wondering what's going to happen to me to worry about other people.

HELEN: I've always thought your course was quite clear, Pawnie.

PAWNIE: However offensive that remark was intended to be, Helen, I shall take it in the most complimentary spirit.

HELEN: I'm sure you will.

PAWNIE: I expect Florence will just go on and on, then suddenly become quite beautifully old, and go on and on still more.

HELEN: It's too late now for her to become beautifully old, I'm afraid. She'll have to be young indefinitely.

PAWNIE: I don't suppose she'll mind that, but it's trying for David.

HELEN: And fiendish for Nicky.

PAWNIE: Oh, no, my dear; you're quite wrong there. I'm sure Nicky doesn't care a damn.

HELEN: It's difficult to tell with Nicky.

PAWNIE: He's divinely selfish; all amusing people are.

HELEN: Did you hear him play in Paris?

PAWNIE: Yes.

HELEN: Well?

PAWNIE: Erratic—one or two things perfect, but he's slovenly.

HELEN: He only takes things seriously in spurts, but still he's very young.

PAWNIE: Do you really think that's a good excuse?

HELEN: No, I'm afraid not, especially when so much depends on it.

PAWNIE: What does depend on it?

HELEN: Everything—his life's happiness.

PAWNIE: Don't be so terribly intense, dear.

HELEN: It's true.

PAWNIE: I'm quite sure Nicky will be perfectly happy as long as he goes on attracting people; he loves being attractive.

HELEN: Naturally, he's Florence's son.

PAWNIE: Such an exciting thing to be.

HELEN: You don't believe Nicky's got anything in him at all, do you?

PAWNIE [*lightly*]: I don't think it matters, anyway.

HELEN: I do.

PAWNIE: But you've got a loving nature, Helen. I always knew it.

HELEN: Nicky hasn't had a chance.

PAWNIE: Nonsense—he's had everything he wanted ever since the day he was born, and he'll go on wasting his opportunities until he dies.

HELEN: Quite possibly.

PAWNIE: Well, there you are then.

HELEN: He may have had everything he wanted, but he's had none of the things he really needs.

PAWNIE: Are you talking socially or spiritually?

HELEN: You're quite right, Pawnie, you wouldn't be so beautifully preserved if you'd wasted any of your valuable time or sincerity.

PAWNIE: I forgive you for that, Helen, freely.

HELEN: Thank you so much.

PAWNIE: You must realize one thing, everyone is sacrificed to Florence—it's as it should be—of course, she's a couple of hundred years too late—she ought to have been a flaunting, intriguing King's mistress, with black page boys and jade baths and things too divine——

[*Enter Preston.*]

PRESTON [*announcing*]: Miss Hibbert.

[*Enter Clara Hibbert—she is affected, but quite well dressed. Preston goes out.*]

CLARA: My *dears*. Isn't Florence back *yet?*

HELEN: No, we're waiting for her.

PAWNIE: You look harassed, Clara.

CLARA: I am harassed.

HELEN: Why?

CLARA: I'm singing to-night for Laura Tennant—she's giving a dreadful reception at her dreadful house for some dreadful Ambassador——

PAWNIE: How dreadful!

CLARA: No one will listen to me, of course—they'll all be far too busy avoiding the Cup and searching for the Champagne.

HELEN: What are you singing?

CLARA: One Gabriel Faure, two Reynaldo Hahn's and an Aria.

PAWNIE: Which Aria?

CLARA: I can't think, but my accompanist will know—I've got a frightful headache.

HELEN: Why don't you take off your hat?

CLARA: My dear, I daren't—I've just had my hair done—I suppose you haven't got a "Cachet Faivre," either of you?

HELEN: No, but Florence has, I expect—Preston will know where they are—ring the bell, Pawnie.

PAWNIE [ringing bell]: My poor Clara—I do hope your singing to-night will justify the fuss you're making this afternoon.

CLARA: Don't be so brutal, Pawnie.

HELEN: Is Gregory going with you?

CLARA: Of course—I never sing unless he's there—he gives me such marvelous moral support.

PAWNIE: "Moral" is hardly the word I should have chosen, dear.

[Enter Preston.]

HELEN: Do you know if Mrs. Lancaster has any "Cachet Faivre" anywhere?

PRESTON: Yes, ma'am—I think so.

CLARA: Do get me one, Preston, I'm suffering tortures.

PRESTON: Very well, miss. [She goes out.]

PAWNIE: Preston has such wonderful poise, hasn't she?

HELEN: She needs it in this house.

CLARA: I do wish Florence would hurry up. I want to borrow her green fan. I've got a new Patou frock that positively *demands* it.

HELEN: She can't be long now.

CLARA: I suppose I daren't ask Preston for the fan and creep away with it?

HELEN: I shouldn't, if I were you—Florence is very touchy over that sort of thing.

CLARA: She promised it to me ages ago.

PAWNIE: Surely there isn't such a desperate hurry? You won't be singing until about half-past eleven.

CLARA: [*petulantly*]: My *dear*. I've got to *rehearse*—I don't know a *word*——

[*Re-enter Preston with a "Cachet Faivre" and a glass of water.*]

CLARA: You're a *saint*, Preston—thank you a *thousand times*——

PAWNIE: Soak it a little first, dear, or you'll choke, and I should *detest* that.

[*Clara soaks "Cachet" and then swallows it. Preston goes out.*]

CLARA: Now I must lie down *flat*—get out of the way, Helen.

PAWNIE: Perhaps you'd like us *both* to go *right* out of the room and sit in the *hall?*

CLARA: No, Pawnie, I should never expect the least consideration from you.

[*She lies down flat on the divan; Helen arranges cushions for her.*]

CLARA: Thank you, Helen darling—I shall always come to you whenever I'm ill.

HELEN: That *will* be nice.

[*Enter Florence Lancaster followed by Tom Veryan. Florence is brilliantly dressed almost to the point of being "outreé." Her face still retains the remnants of great beauty. Tom is athletic and good-looking. One feels he is good at games and extremely bad at everything else.*]

FLORENCE: Helen—Pawnie, have you been here long?

PAWNIE: No, only a few hours.

FLORENCE: My dear. I'm so frightfully sorry—we've been held up for ages in the traffic. Davis is a congenital idiot. Always manages to get to a turning just as the policeman puts out his hand. No initiative whatever. What's happened to Clara? Has she been run over?

CLARA: No, dear, I've got a frightful head.

FLORENCE: Pawnie, you know Tom, don't you?—Tom Veryan, Mr. Quentin, I'm sure you'll adore each other.

TOM [*shaking hands*]: How are you?

PAWNIE: Very well, thank you—how sweet of you to ask me.

FLORENCE: Is there anything I can do, Clara?

CLARA: Yes, dear, lend me your green fan for to-night.

FLORENCE: All right—but you *won't* get too carried away with it, will you, dear? I should hate the feathers to come out. Does anyone want any tea?

HELEN: No thanks, dear.

FLORENCE: Cocktails, then?

PAWNIE: It's too early.

FLORENCE [*ringing bell*]: It's never too early for a cocktail.

CLARA: I should like to go quite quietly into a convent and never see anybody again ever——

PAWNIE: Gregory would be bored stiff in a convent.

FLORENCE: We've just been to a most frightful Charity *matinée*. Nothing but inaudible speeches from dreary old actors, and leading ladies nudging one another all over the stage.

[*Preston enters.*]

Cocktails, Preston, and ask Barker to wrap up my green fan for Miss Hibbert to take away with her.

PRESTON: Very good, ma'am. [*She goes out.*]

CLARA: You're an angel, Florence—I think I'll sit up now.

FLORENCE: Do, dear, then Tom will be able to sit down.

CLARA [*sitting up*]: I really do feel most peculiar.

PAWNIE: You look far from normal, dear.

CLARA: If Pawnie's rude to me any more I shall burst into tears.

FLORENCE: Tom, give me a cigarette.

PAWNIE: Here are some.

FLORENCE: No, Tom has a special rather hearty kind that I adore.

CLARA: Lend me your lipstick, Helen; mine has sunk down into itself.

HELEN: Here you are.

CLARA: What a lovely color! I look far prettier than I feel.

FLORENCE [*to Tom*]: Thank you, angel.

CLARA: I shan't be able to get down to the house until Saturday evening, Florence—I'm seeing Gregory off to Newcastle.

PAWNIE: Why Newcastle?

CLARA: His home's just near there—isn't it too awful for him?

FLORENCE: Well, wire me the time of your train, won't you?

CLARA: Of course, dear.

HELEN: You're smelling divinely, Florence. What is it?

FLORENCE [*flicking her handkerchief*]: It is good, isn't it?

PAWNIE: "Narcisse Noir" of Caron. I use it.

FLORENCE: Yes, you would, Pawnie.

[*Re-enter Preston with parcel.*]

PRESTON: Here is the fan, miss.

CLARA [*taking it*]: Thank you *so* much—you are sweet, Florence. A fan gives me such a feeling of *security* when I'm singing modern stuff.

[*Preston goes out.*]

I must rush now——

FLORENCE: Don't you want a cocktail before you go?

CLARA: No, darling—I should only hiccup all the evening. Good-bye, you've been *such* a comfort—good-bye, Helen— Pawnie, you will be nicer to me over the week-end, won't you? I shall be *so* depressed, what with Gregory going away and everything.—Good-bye, Tom—I shall dine in bed and give way at every pore—— [*She goes out.*]

PAWNIE: Poor Clara—she eternally labors under the delusion that she really matters.

HELEN: We all do that a little.

FLORENCE [*laughing*]: You're awfully cruel to her, Pawnie.

PAWNIE: She upsets my vibrations.

FLORENCE [*before glass*]: I've taken a sudden hatred to this hat. [*She takes it off.*] That's better—are you going to the "New Elaine" to-night, either of you?

HELEN: I'm not—but Pawnie is, of course.

PAWNIE: It's going to be *amazing*—what a cast, my dear! Marvelous Selwyn Steele, Nora Dean, and that perfect woman, Lily Burfield——

HELEN: I can't stand her, she always over-acts.

PAWNIE [*incensed*]: How *can* you, Helen! Did you see her in "Simple Faith"?

HELEN: Yes, unfortunately.

PAWNIE: Oh, you're really too tiresome for words!

HELEN: Her technique creaks like machinery.

PAWNIE: It's sacrilege—she's too, too marvelous.

[*Enter Preston with a tray of cocktails. All help themselves.*]

FLORENCE: What do you think about it, Tom?

TOM: I've never seen her.

FLORENCE: Yes, you have. About three months ago, at the Comedy.

TOM: Oh. . . . I don't remember.

PAWNIE: Don't remember! An artist like that! Good God, it's agony!

HELEN: You'll look awfully tired at dinner-time, Pawnie, if you don't calm down a little.

FLORENCE: This is special—my own invention.

HELEN: Absolutely delicious.

TOM: A bit too sweet.

FLORENCE: Tom, *darling*, don't be so taciturn—he's always taciturn after a *matinée*.

PAWNIE: When's Nicky coming back?

FLORENCE: To-morrow. Isn't it too divine? He's been away for a whole year, but I saw him for a moment on my way through Paris last month.

PAWNIE: Has he been working hard?

FLORENCE: I suppose so, but you know what Nicky is—bless his heart!

PAWNIE: I heard him play at Yvonne Mirabeau's.

FLORENCE: She's a loathsome woman, isn't she?

HELEN: Not as bad as that.

PAWNIE: She's a half-wit. I can't bear half-wits.

FLORENCE: She goes on so dreadfully about things—devastating.

PAWNIE: Funny Nicky liking her so much.

FLORENCE: Only because she keeps on saying how wonderful he is—that always appeals to Nicky.

PAWNIE: How old is he now?

FLORENCE: Twenty-four. Isn't it absurd to think I have such a grown-up son—old General Fenwick said last Thursday that—— [*The telephone rings; she goes to it.*] Hallo—hallo! Yes, my dear. How are you? . . . Yes, so am I, simply worn out. . . . No. When? How perfectly marvelous! . . . No, dear, it's a prescription; but I can let you have a little in a jar. . . . Quite easy. All you do is just rub it on at night. . . . Don't be so silly. . . . Not in the least; if you send the car round that will be all right. . . . Very well. . . . Good-bye, darling. [*She hangs up receiver.*] I give Clara Hibbert ten for stupidity. Don't you, Helen?

HELEN: A hundred and ten.

PAWNIE: Ten's the limit.

TOM: I say, Florence—I think I'd better be getting along if I've got to be dressed and back here by half-past seven——

FLORENCE: You've got half an hour.

TOM: That's not very much.

FLORENCE: The car's outside . . . take it and send it straight back.

PAWNIE: Can it drop me, Florence dear? I always feel so much richer in your car than anyone else's.

FLORENCE: Of course, Pawnie.

[*The telephone rings again.*]

FLORENCE [*at telephone*]: Hallo! . . . Yes . . . speaking. . . . How do you do——?

PAWNIE: Good-bye, Helen. It's been divine——

HELEN: Ring me up at tea-time to-morrow.

FLORENCE: How perfectly sweet of you! . . . Now, now, really. . . . Well, naturally, if you persist in saying such charming things . . . [*laughing gayly*] . . . What nonsense! . . .

PAWNIE: Good-bye, Florence——

FLORENCE [*she puts her hand over mouthpiece*]: It's that awful General Fenwick. . . . Good-bye, Pawnie dear. You're coming down to the house on Friday?

PAWNIE: Yes; too lovely——

FLORENCE: Helen's coming by the five-o'clock—you'd better travel together.

PAWNIE: Perfect. [*To Tom*]: Are you ready?

TOM: Quite.

PAWNIE [*as they go out*]: You *can* drop me first, can't you? I'm not as young as I was——

FLORENCE [*at telephone*]: Please forgive me. People rushing in and out, this house grows more like a railway station every day. . . . Now, General, that was a deliberate compliment. [*She laughs.*] Ridiculous man. . . . Very well. . . . Good-bye. [*She hangs up receiver.*] My God! ten for dreariness!

HELEN: He's not a bad old thing.

FLORENCE: No, but he tries to be, and that's what's so frightful. [*Arranging her hair before glass*]: I look like Death. . . . Isn't Tom a darling?

HELEN: Yes, dear, without being aggressively brilliant.

FLORENCE: I'm afraid, Helen, you're getting rather bitter.

HELEN: Nonsense.

FLORENCE: It's silly to be sarcastic about Tom.

HELEN: It's better than being maudlin about him.

FLORENCE: I don't know what you mean, dear. I'm not in the least maudlin, and never have been about anybody. I sometimes wish I could be—I'm too hard.

HELEN [*taking a cigarette*]: Tom will let you down.

FLORENCE: Let me down? Why . . . how . . . I don't understand——

HELEN: You're more in love with him than he is with you.

FLORENCE: Don't be so *absurd*, Helen.

HELEN: It's true.

FLORENCE [*complacently*]: He adores me—worships me—he's never seen anyone like me before in his life. I'm something strange . . . exotic——

HELEN: You're more in love with him than he is with you.

FLORENCE: You're getting on my nerves to-day, Helen.

HELEN: You do see that I'm right, don't you?

FLORENCE: If you knew some of the things he's said to me.

HELEN: I can guess them.

FLORENCE: That boy was utterly unawakened until he met me.

HELEN: He's very young.

FLORENCE: I've taught him—everything.

HELEN: Or nothing.

FLORENCE: Helen, I believe you're jealous.

HELEN: Don't be a fool.

FLORENCE: I wish I hadn't this fatal knack of seeing through people.

HELEN: How's David?

FLORENCE: I don't know. He ought to be home soon.

HELEN: Doesn't he ever suspect anything?

FLORENCE: Of course not—he adores me.

HELEN: It seems so strange not to see——

FLORENCE: I'm devoted to David—I'd do anything for him, anything in the world—but he's grown old and I've kept young; it does muddle things up so. I can't help having a temperament, can I?

HELEN: Temperament. . . . No.

FLORENCE: David's always loved me and never understood me —you see, I'm such an extraordinary *mixture*. I have so many *sides* to my character. I adore being at home and running the house and looking after David and Nicky——

HELEN: You don't exactly overdo it.

FLORENCE: Well, Nicky's been away for such ages. Also, one must be in London for the season. You can't expect me to bury myself in the country indefinitely. I shall be there practically all through the spring and summer.

HELEN: Lovely tennis parties and cricket weeks and things——

FLORENCE: Certainly.

HELEN [*kissing her*]: You're a divine creature, Florence.

FLORENCE [*basking*]: Am I? [*The telephone rings.*] Hallo! . . . Yes—speaking. [*To Helen in a whisper*]: It's Inez Zulieta. I never went to her recital. . . . Inez *darling*, I never recognized your voice. . . . Didn't you get my note? . . . It was absolutely true, I was in agony. . . . Inez, don't be angry. If you only knew how I longed for the sound of your wonderful, wonderful voice. . . . Darling. . . . Inez, don't be so cruel. . . . To-morrow, then. [*She hangs up receiver.*] I do wish Inez wasn't so persistent.

HELEN: You never stop encouraging her.

FLORENCE: Oh, Helen, I'm so tired of everyone.

HELEN: Except Tom?

FLORENCE: Yes, except Tom; he's such a darling.

HELEN: How do you think he and Nicky will get on?

FLORENCE: Marvelously—Tom loves music.

HELEN: He says he does.

FLORENCE: My dear, I took him to that Russian thing the other day and he sat entranced from beginning to end.

HELEN: Poor Nicky!

FLORENCE: Why do you say that?

HELEN: Because I sometimes feel it.

FLORENCE [*suddenly furious*]: Oh, I wonder why we're such friends—we're so opposite—you don't understand me a bit. I used to think you did, but you've been different lately—unsympathetic.

HELEN: No, I haven't.

FLORENCE: Yes, you have—over Tom—I believe you're in love with him yourself.

HELEN [*smiling*]: No—it isn't that.

FLORENCE: Anyhow, you can't bear him being in love with me.

HELEN: I don't think he is—really. I quite realize that he *was* very violently infatuated, but that is wearing off a bit now. I'm beginning to see him as he is. . . .

FLORENCE: No, no, it's not true—you don't understand——

HELEN: We *are* friends, Florence, though we're so "opposite." Do you really know the truth—inside you? Or is all this shrill vanity real?

FLORENCE: What's the matter with you?

HELEN: You're ten years older than I am, but when I'm your age I shall be twenty years older than you.

FLORENCE: *Darling,* how deliciously involved—what *can* you mean by that?

HELEN: I mean, I think it's silly not to grow old when the time comes. [*She rises and goes towards door.*]

FLORENCE [*outraged*]: Helen!

[*There is suddenly heard a violent knocking at the front door.*] What on earth is that?

[*There is a noise outside, then the door bursts open and Nicky enters. He is extremely well dressed in traveling clothes. He is tall and pale, with thin, nervous hands.*]

FLORENCE: Nicky!

NICKY: Mother! [*He embraces her.*]

FLORENCE: But I'd no idea—I thought you were coming to-morrow.

NICKY: No, to-day—I wrote to you.

FLORENCE: I'm terribly, terribly excited.

NICKY: Helen, dear, how are you? [*He kisses her.*]

HELEN: Splendid, Nicky.

FLORENCE: I can't get over you arriving like this. . . . I never realized——

NICKY: Silly . . . you're looking awfully well.

FLORENCE: Am I?

NICKY: Wonderful, as usual.

FLORENCE: I was talking to George Morrison only last Thursday——

NICKY: The man who wrote that fearful book?

FLORENCE: It isn't a fearful book, it's brilliant—anyhow, he absolutely refused to believe that I had a grown-up son.

HELEN: My dears, I must fly.

NICKY: Don't go yet.

HELEN: I must—I'm hours late as it is.

NICKY: Be a little later, then.

FLORENCE: Remember, five o'clock train on Friday.

NICKY: Oh, is she coming down to the house? Divine!

HELEN: Yes, if Florence is still speaking to me. Good-bye. [*She goes out.*]

NICKY: Have you been having a scene?

FLORENCE: No, dear.

NICKY: She's a darling—Helen——

FLORENCE: Extremely stupid and tactless sometimes.

NICKY: It doesn't feel as though I'd been away at all.

FLORENCE: I've missed you appallingly—we had such a short time together in Paris. Did you enjoy all my letters?

NICKY: I adored them—so did John Bagot. I used to read most of them aloud to him. He's mad on you—saw your picture in the *Tatler*, or something, and fell in love with it.

FLORENCE: Is he nice?

NICKY: He's grand.

FLORENCE: We must all dine at the Embassy. When is he coming to England?

NICKY: Not until after Christmas.

FLORENCE: You must see my new photographs; they're wonderful. [*She takes large packet from desk.*]

NICKY: It's heavenly—being back.

FLORENCE: Look.

NICKY: I don't like that one.

FLORENCE: How can you, Nicky! Tom likes that one best of all.

NICKY: Who's Tom?

FLORENCE: Tom Veryan—he's a dear; you'll like him fright-fully—you know—the very nicest type of Englishman.

NICKY: I hate the very nicest type of Englishman.

FLORENCE: Don't be tiresome, Nicky; he's only twenty-four, and they all think *so* well of him——

NICKY: All who?

FLORENCE: All his officers and people; he's in the Brigade.

NICKY [*holding photograph away from him and scrutinizing it through half-closed eyes*]: Now that one really is *enchanting*—they've got your hair *beautifully*. Oh, yes, my dear, it's perfect——

FLORENCE [*complacently*]: It *is* good. She's sweet—Madame Henderson, she simply won't hear of my paying for these—she says it's quite sufficient to be allowed to exhibit them in the window.

NICKY: Is anyone dining this evening?

FLORENCE: No. Oh, dear! I'd forgotten—I'm dining out with Tom.

NICKY: Oh—I see.

FLORENCE: Your first night home, too—how perfectly fiendish. What a fool I am to have muddled it up.

NICKY: It doesn't matter, darling.

FLORENCE: Oh, but it *does*. I wonder if we could get another seat——

NICKY: Seat? What for?

FLORENCE: We're going to the first night of "The New Elaine." It's going to be marvelous.

NICKY: Who's in it?

FLORENCE: Nora Dean and Selwyn Steele——

NICKY: Oh, God!

FLORENCE: It's silly of you *always* to jeer at Selwyn Steele. He's a brilliant actor, if only he could get away from his wife. . . .

NICKY: I couldn't bear him to-night, anyway; I'm tired. Is father home yet?

FLORENCE: No, I don't think so. Oh, I do feel such a beast——

NICKY: Don't be silly—honestly, I don't mind a bit.

FLORENCE: I know—you have a nice quiet dinner here and join us at the Embassy afterwards.

NICKY: Is it a late night??

FLORENCE: Yes, they play the most heavenly tune there now —Tom always makes them do it over and over again—I'll put it on—— [*She goes to the gramophone.*]

NICKY: How's Iris?

FLORENCE: My dear, don't speak of her.

NICKY: Why—what's she done?

FLORENCE: She's been absolutely foul.

NICKY: In what way?

FLORENCE: Every way—I never trusted her, luckily.—Thank God I've got instincts about people—listen, isn't this marvelous? —She said the most filthy things to Gloria Craig about me— I always knew she was insanely jealous, but there are limits. I loathe being at people's beck and call. . . . Come and dance.

NICKY [*as they dance*]: I'm sorry you've rowed—I rather liked her——

FLORENCE: Only because she kept on saying how wonderful you were. . . . She doesn't know a thing about music really.

NICKY: Oh yes, she does.

FLORENCE: It's merely bluff—all that appreciation. *Darling,* how oddly you're dancing.

NICKY: It's probably because we haven't danced together for so long. . . .

FLORENCE: Anyhow, now she's gone off to Monte Carlo with Violet Fenchurch—silly fool——

[*Enter David Lancaster. He is an elderly gray-haired pleasant man.*]

DAVID [*delighted*]: Nicky—my boy——

NICKY [*kissing him*]: Hallo, father——

DAVID: I thought—Florence said—to-morrow——

NICKY: Mother muddled it up.

DAVID: You look rather tired.

NICKY: I'm splendid. How's everything?

DAVID: The same as usual. I've made lots of improvements down at the house.

FLORENCE: David thinks and talks of nothing but the farm——

DAVID: It's beginning to pay a bit—Peterson's an awfully good man.

NICKY: We'll make a grand tour of it on Sunday.

DAVID: Have you enjoyed yourself in Paris?

NICKY: Oh yes, rather—it's a splendid place to work.

DAVID: It never struck me that way, quite, but still——

FLORENCE: Sophie de Molignac said Nicky's playing had improved wonderfully.

DAVID: I'm so glad, Nicky.

NICKY: I've been doing some Spanish stuff lately.

DAVID: I wish I knew more about it.

NICKY: Never mind, father.

DAVID: Come to my room and talk. I can't bear that thing——

FLORENCE: Father's such a beast; he never will dance with me.

DAVID: Is the *Evening News* anywhere about?

NICKY: Yes, here. [*He gives it to him.*]

DAVID: I'm so glad you're home again, Nicky—don't forget —come and talk. . . . [*He goes out.*]

FLORENCE: David's so much happier in the country.

NICKY: Why on earth doesn't he retire and live at the house for good?

FLORENCE: Work has become such a habit with him—he's always hated giving up habits.

NICKY: Mother—I've got something rather important to tell you.

FLORENCE: Darling, how thrilling! What is it?

NICKY: I am engaged to be married.

FLORENCE: What!

NICKY: Practically—as much as one can be these days.

FLORENCE: Nicky!

NICKY: Don't look so stricken.

FLORENCE: But, Nicky—I never sort of visualized you being engaged, or married, or anything.

NICKY: Why not?

FLORENCE: You're not old enough.

NICKY: I'm twenty-four.

FLORENCE: You don't look it. . . . Thank God!

NICKY: What do you really feel about it, mother?

FLORENCE: *Darling*—I hardly know what to say—you've sprung it on me so suddenly. Who is she?

NICKY: A girl called Bunty Mainwaring.

FLORENCE: What a silly name!

NICKY: It isn't at all—it's very attractive.

FLORENCE: Is she an actress, or a student, or what?

NICKY: Neither—she is what is technically termed a "lady."

FLORENCE: Do you think she'll like me?

NICKY: She went mad over your photograph.

FLORENCE: Which one?

NICKY: The "looking out of the window" one.

FLORENCE: That really is one of the best I've ever had done.

NICKY: She said you had the face of an heroic little boy.

FLORENCE: What a *divine* thing to say! [*She glances at herself in the glass.*]

NICKY: She does say divine things—she's supremely intelligent.

FLORENCE: Is she in Paris?

NICKY: No, she came over with me to-day.

FLORENCE: Where does she live?

NICKY: Just round the corner in Carbury Square.

FLORENCE: Near the Churchingtons.

NICKY: It's her mother's house, but her mother's away just now, so I asked her to change quickly and come on here.

FLORENCE: Nicky!

NICKY: Why not? I wanted you to see her as soon as possible.

FLORENCE [*realizing parental responsibility*]: it's an awful shock, you know.

NICKY: Nonsense, mother—you're quite excited about it, really.

FLORENCE [*with determination*]: I shall be charming to her.

NICKY: Then she'll adore you at once—probably too much, and I shall be jealous.

FLORENCE: You'd better both dine here together and come on to the Embassy. How old is she?

NICKY: Twenty-three.

FLORENCE: What does she do?

NICKY: Nothing much—she writes things occasionally.

FLORENCE: Where did you meet her?

NICKY: First of all at a party at Olive Lloyd-Kennedy's.

FLORENCE: I can't bear Olive Lloyd-Kennedy—she's a cat.

NICKY: Then I met her again at Marion Fawcett's—a frightful sort of reception affair—she was staying with her.

FLORENCE: She seems to move exclusively with my worst enemies. Is she pretty?

NICKY: I don't know—I haven't really noticed.

FLORENCE [*with a touch of real feeling*]: Nicky darling, I do feel so extraordinary about it.

NICKY: Why extraordinary?

FLORENCE: It's a milestone, isn't it—you being engaged? A definite milestone? [*She catches sight of herself.*] Look at my nose. [*She powders it.*] I do hope she'll like me—I must go and dress now; Tom is fetching me at half-past seven. Bring her to my room when she comes.

NICKY: Don't go for a minute.

FLORENCE: I must, really—Tom will be furious.

NICKY: Oh, damn Tom!

FLORENCE: Oh, Nicky, *don't* go and take one of your tiresome prejudices against him.

NICKY [*smiling*]: All right, I'll try not to.

FLORENCE: He's frightfully good-looking.

NICKY: Oh!

FLORENCE: And he adores music.

NICKY: Now, then, mother——

FLORENCE: He does, honestly.

NICKY: Good.

FLORENCE: And he dances beautifully.

NICKY: I shall never stop dancing with him.

FLORENCE: And he's so good at games.

NICKY: He sounds adorable.

FLORENCE: Of course, he needs knowing.

NICKY: So do I.

FLORENCE: You will make an effort, though, darling, won't you? For my sake!

NICKY: Yes, mother.

FLORENCE: And we'll all have a divine time together, Tom and me and you and what's her name——

NICKY: Bunty.

FLORENCE: Oh yes, of course, Bunty.

[*Front door bell rings.*]

NICKY: This is her, I expect.

FLORENCE: Do you feel wonderful about her?

NICKY: Yes.

FLORENCE: It is thrilling, isn't it—being in love?

NICKY [*frowning a little*]: Yes.

FLORENCE: Your father was right—you look awfully tired, Nicky.

NICKY: What nonsense! I feel grand.

[*Enter Preston.*]

PRESTON [*announcing*]: Miss Mainwaring.

[*Bunty comes in, very self-assured and well-dressed. She is more attractive than pretty in a boyish sort of way.*]

[*Preston goes out.*]

NICKY: Bunty. You have been quick.

BUNTY: I've simply flown.

NICKY: Bunty . . . here is mother. . . .

BUNTY: Oh!

FLORENCE [*taking both her hands*]: This is frightfully exciting, isn't it? [*She kisses her.*]

NICKY: I've told her.

BUNTY: Are you furious?

FLORENCE: Of course not. Why should I be? 'Specially now.

BUNTY: It's absolutely incredible, you being Nicky's mother.

FLORENCE: Am I anything like you thought I'd be?

BUNTY: Yes, exactly—but I couldn't believe it until I saw you.

FLORENCE: Take off that perfectly divine cloak and have a cigarette. I've got to rush and dress now, because I'm *terribly* late, but you're dining here with Nicky and joining Tom Veryan and me at the Embassy afterwards.

BUNTY: Tom Veryan? . . .

FLORENCE: Yes. Do you know him?

BUNTY: I did when I was a child—if it's the same one. [*She takes off her cloak.*]

FLORENCE [*effusively*]: Nicky—I don't feel extraordinary about it any more—I'm *delighted*.

NICKY: Angel.

FLORENCE: Perhaps Bunty would like to come down to the house on Friday for the week-end?

NICKY: Oh yes! Marvelous.

BUNTY: It's awfully sweet of you, Mrs. Lancaster.

FLORENCE: You must call me Florence; I can't bear "Mrs. Lancaster." I must fly; Tom will be here at any moment—that's him on the desk.

BUNTY [*going over to photograph*]: Yes—it is the same one.

FLORENCE: How too divine! . . .

　[*Telephone rings.*]

Hallo! . . . Yes, speaking! . . . Elsa darling, how are you? . . . What? . . . To-night? . . . How perfectly heavenly! Of course, I'd adore it. . . . Listen. Nicky's just back from Paris. Can he come, too, with Bunty Mainwaring? . . . Yes, he's here. . . . See you to-night, dear . . . Here, Nicky, talk to Elsa. . . . [*She snatches up her hand-bag and fur coat and kisses Bunty effusively.*] I'm so glad about you and Nicky—It's too wonderful. [*She rushes out.*]

NICKY [*at telephone*]: Hallo, Elsa. . . . I'd no idea you were in London. I'm terribly thrilled. My dear, you haven't. . . . All those lovely tunes you played to me in Paris? . . . *How amazing!* I am glad. . . . Have you done anything with that Tango? . . . You must play it tonight; I want Bunty to hear it. . . . It is perfect, isn't it? . . . Good-bye, dear. [*He hangs up the receiver.*] Bunty.

BUNTY: What?

NICKY: I'm terribly happy.

BUNTY: So am I.

NICKY: Do you remember how we planned all this—coming home together—and breaking it to mother—and everything?

BUNTY: Rather.

NICKY: Do you really like her?

BUNTY: I adore her—she's a perfect angel.

NICKY: I told her your "heroic little boy" line; she loved it.

BUNTY: It's true, you know—rather defiant too—laughing at Fate.

NICKY: Doesn't Paris seem ages away now?

BUNTY: A different life altogether.

NICKY: That nasty little bit of Channel is such an enormous gulf, really. Did you put that dress on on purpose?

BUNTY [smiling]: Perhaps.

NICKY: You are a devil.

BUNTY: It's such fun being reminded of things.

NICKY: And such agony, too.

BUNTY: Nicky darling—why agony?

NICKY: It's always agony being in love, and I started loving you in that dress.

BUNTY: Did you?

NICKY: Don't pretend you didn't know.

BUNTY: I suppose one always knows—really.

NICKY: From the very first moment.

BUNTY: Yes.

NICKY: A sort of spark.

BUNTY: Your playing helped a lot.

NICKY: I meant it to.

BUNTY: Calculating pig.

NICKY: Have a cigarette?

BUNTY: All right. [He hands her box, and she takes one.]

NICKY [lighting her cigarette]: I wish we weren't so free.

BUNTY: Why? What do you mean?

NICKY: I feel I should like to elope, or something violently romantic like that.

BUNTY [*laughing*]: There wouldn't be much point in it now, would there?

NICKY: Perhaps not. How much do you love me?

BUNTY: I don't know.

NICKY: It's fun analyzing one's emotions.

BUNTY: Marvelous fun.

NICKY: And a comfort, too, when things go wrong—but it kills sentiment stone dead.

BUNTY: A good job, too.

NICKY: You're frightfully hard, Bunty.

BUNTY: Am I?

NICKY: Much harder than me—really.

BUNTY: You've got so much hysteria.

NICKY: I can't help it.

BUNTY: Of course not; it's your temperament. You burst out suddenly.

NICKY: Not so badly as I used to.

BUNTY: You're growing older.

NICKY: God, yes! Isn't it foul?

BUNTY: Hell, my dear.

NICKY: It's funny how mother's generation always longed to be old when they were young, and we strain every nerve to keep young.

BUNTY: That's because we see what's coming so much more clearly.

NICKY: Wouldn't it be terrible to know *exactly?*—I feel frightened sometimes.

BUNTY: Why?

NICKY: We're all so hectic and nervy. . . .

BUNTY: It doesn't matter—it probably only means we shan't live so long. . . .

NICKY [*suddenly*]: Shut up—shut up. . . .

[*Enter Preston.*]

PRESTON [*announcing*]: Mr. Veryan.

[*Enter Tom. Nicky greets him and shakes hands. Exit Preston.*]

NICKY: How are you? I'm Nicky—I came over to-day instead of to-morrow. . . .

TOM: Oh!

NICKY: Do you know Bunty Mainwaring?

TOM: Bunty—I say—I am glad.

[*They shake hands warmly.*]

NICKY: We'd better have some cocktails. [*He goes to the door and shouts*]: Preston . . . bring us some cocktails. . . .

TOM: This *is* jolly. I didn't know what had become of you.

BUNTY: I've been living in Paris a good deal.

TOM: How many years ago is it since we . . .

BUNTY: During the War. The last time I saw you you were at Sandhurst.

NICKY: Such a pretty place.

TOM: You've hardly altered a bit—more grown up, of course.

NICKY: All this is most affecting.

TOM: Bunty and I used to know each other awfully well.

NICKY: What fun!

BUNTY [*warningly*]: Nicky . . .

NICKY: But it is—it's thrilling—there's nothing so charming as a reunion.

BUNTY: Nicky and I have been traveling all day. . . . Boats and trains get on his nerves. . . .

NICKY: When the cocktails come, tell Preston to bring mine to me in father's room.

BUNTY: Nicky, don't be so silly.

NICKY: Surely it's not silly to want to talk to my aged father after a year's debauch in Paris? I fail to see why you should have the monopoly of reunions.

BUNTY: Well, don't be long.

TOM: Cheerio!

NICKY [*crossly*]: Oh, God! [*He goes out.*]

TOM: What's up?

BUNTY: These temperamental musicians.

TOM: Silly ass.

BUNTY: He isn't really—he's only jealous.

TOM: Why . . . is he . . .?

BUNTY: We're by way of being engaged.

TOM: What?

BUNTY: Why not?

TOM: Are you . . . are you in love with him?

BUNTY [*lightly*]: Yes—isn't it damnable?

TOM: Good Lord! [*He laughs.*]

BUNTY: What are you laughing at?

TOM: It seems so funny you being in love with that sort of chap.

BUNTY: What do you mean by "that sort of chap"?

TOM: Oh—I don't know, that type seems so unlike you.

BUNTY: Type?

TOM: Yes, you know—up in the air—effeminate.

BUNTY: You're more bucolic than you used to be, Tom.

TOM: Here, I say . . .

[*Enter Preston with cocktails.*]

BUNTY: Will you please take Mr. Nicky's in to him in his father's room?

PRESTON: Yes, miss.

TOM: Is Mrs. Lancaster nearly ready?

PRESTON: I think so, sir.

TOM: Ask her to hurry. We shall be late.

PRESTON: Yes, sir. [*He goes out.*]

BUNTY: I can laugh now. [*She does so.*]

TOM: Why?

BUNTY: I've just realized something.

TOM: What?

BUNTY: We shall meet again—over the week-end.

TOM: Are you coming down to the house?

BUNTY: Yes.

TOM: That's splendid. Come for a tramp Sunday morning and we'll talk.

BUNTY: What about?

TOM: Oh, lots of things—old times.

BUNTY [*lifting her cocktail*]: Old times, Tom.

TOM [*doing the same*]: Cheerio!

CURTAIN

~~~~~~

ACT TWO

THE SCENE *is the hall of Mrs. Lancaster's house, about forty miles from London.*

When the curtain rises it is just after dinner on the Sunday of the week-end party—the gramophone is going and there is a continual buzz of conversation. Clara Hibbert, an emaciated soprano, is dancing with Tom Veryan, Helen with Pawnie, and Nicky with Bunty. Florence is seated on the club fender, talking intellectually with Bruce Fairlight, an earnest dramatist, the squalor of whose plays is much appreciated by those who live in comparative luxury.

There must be a feeling of hectic amusement and noise, and the air black with cigarette smoke and superlatives. During the first part of the scene everyone must appear to be talking at once, but the actual lines spoken while dancing must be timed to reach the audience as the speakers pass near the footlights. This scene will probably be exceedingly difficult to produce, but is absolutely indispensable.

HELEN: It's much too fast, Nicky.

TOM: Do slow down a bit.

NICKY: It's the pace that's marked on the record.

PAWNIE: I've never danced well since the War, I don't know why.

FLORENCE: But your last act was so strong, when she came in half mad with fright and described everything minutely.

456

BRUCE: I try to write as *honestly* as possible.

CLARA: I gave her three for manners, but seven for charm, because I had to be a *little* nice!

TOM: I thought she was rather a decent sort.

BUNTY: No, but really, Nicky, his technique completely annihilated his inspiration.

NICKY: Not with Debussy and Ravel, with the older masters, yes; but he's probably tired of them.

BUNTY: That's so stupid, I think.

HELEN: My dear, it was the most "chic" thing you've ever seen, but unfortunately the wrong color.

PAWNIE: Marion Ferris had that Poiret model copied in the most frightful blue!

CLARA: I believe my shoe's coming off.

TOM: Shall we stop?

CLARA: No, it's all right.

FLORENCE: I wonder if you could gouge this cigarette-end out of the holder for me?

BRUCE: I'll try. [*He does so.*] I always smoke a pipe when I'm working.

FLORENCE: How soothing!

BUNTY: I suppose one can never really judge properly from a recital.

NICKY: Not with him, because he's not dramatic enough.

BUNTY: Dramatic pianists make me uncomfortable.

HELEN: Pawnie, your tongue grows more venomous every day.

PAWNIE [*giggling*]: Well, I had to say something—anyhow, it was true.

HELEN: Especially about her ankles.

PAWNIE: My dear, yes!

[*They both laugh. The record comes to an end, and Nicky begins to change it. Everyone talks and laughs.*]

CLARA: You must come next Sunday week.

TOM: Thanks awfully, I'd love to.

CLARA: I'm only singing ballads, but you know what Sunday concerts are.

TOM: Oh yes, rather.

CLARA [*to Nicky*]: What's on the other side?

NICKY: "You've got the cutest ears and eyes and nose."

PAWNIE: Do put on "Spoony Moon in Upper Carolina."

HELEN: No, don't put it on, Nicky; play it yourself; you always make the gramophone go too quickly.

BUNTY: Yes, go on, Nicky.

FLORENCE [*refusing Bruce's offer of a cigarette*]: No, thanks, not another—I'm dancing with Tom.

BUNTY: [*gayly*]: Missing one, Tom.

TOM: Righto!

[*Nicky commences to play a fox-trot.*]

BUNTY [*dragging Bruce to his feet*]: Come on, Mr. Fairlight, don't overdo the serious dramatist stunt!

BRUCE: I warn you I'm no good.

[*He dances with her, and confirms the truth of his warning. Clara Hibbert squashes down on the piano-seat next to Nicky and endeavors with one finger in the treble to follow the tune he is playing. Helen and Pawnie stand right down close to the footlights, smoking and talking; their backs are half turned to the audience, but their remarks must be perfectly audible.*]

HELEN: Tom Veryan doesn't dance as well as he thinks he does.

PAWNIE: With that figure he ought to be marvelous.

HELEN: He's too athletic.

PAWNIE: Anyhow, I'm sure he's a success at the Bath Club.

HELEN: Doesn't Florence look astounding?

PAWNIE: Absolutely. She knows exactly what suits her.

HELEN: Where's David?

PAWNIE: He went off to his study to smoke.

HELEN: I do wish Florence wouldn't be irritable with him in front of everybody. I felt acutely uncomfortable at dinner.

PAWNIE: It makes Nicky furious as a rule, but to-night he was too occupied with that stupid little fool Bunty Mainwaring to take any notice.

HELEN: She's an excellent type.

PAWNIE: Very average; I only hope nothing will come of Nicky's mania for her.

HELEN: I don't think we need worry.

PAWNIE: Why?

HELEN: Wait and see, my dear.

CLARA [*leaving Nicky at the piano and advancing on Pawnie*]: Come and dance, Pawnie, and tell me how divinely I sang on Tuesday.

PAWNIE [*agreeably*]: You didn't.

CLARA: Ten for cruelty.

[*They start to dance. Helen moves over to the mantelpiece for a cigarette.*]

HELEN: Have you a match, Nicky?

NICKY: Isn't this a marvelous tune?

HELEN: Fascinating! [*She goes over and sits next to him. Gently slipping her hand into his coat pocket*]: Darling, I *do* want a match. [*She brings out a little box.*] What a divine little box!

[*Nicky stops playing and jumps up.*]

NICKY [*violently*]: Helen, give that to me!——

[*Everyone stops dancing.*]

CLARA: Nicky dear, *don't* be tiresome.

NICKY [*recovering himself*]: I'm sick of playing. Let's have the gramophone again. [*To Helen*]: Here's a light, dearie.

[*He takes match-box out of another pocket and lights Helen's cigarette. She looks at him queerly for a moment, then he restarts*]

*the gramophone and everyone begins to dance again except Helen
and Bruce Fairlight. Helen goes over to the fireplace and takes a
coffee-cup from the mantelpiece.*]

HELEN: Whose coffee is this? Some one drank mine, and I'd
hardly touched it.

BRUCE: If it has no sugar in it, it's mine.

HELEN [*draining it*]: It had no sugar in it.

FLORENCE: You're dancing abominably, Tom.

TOM: Oh, am I?

FLORENCE: What's the matter with you?

TOM: I don't know. I suppose I'm tired.

FLORENCE: You're not usually tired when you're dancing with
me.

TOM: Oh, Florence, don't nag!

FLORENCE: How dare you speak to me like that? [*She stops
dancing and goes over to the fireplace.*]

TOM [*following her*]: I say, Florence—I'm sorry——

PAWNIE: Let's stop the music for a moment and think of something really marvelous to do.

BUNTY: No, let's go on dancing.

CLARA: I'm exhausted.

PAWNIE [*stopping the gramophone*]: What was that divine game
we played coming back from Paris, Helen?

HELEN: Just ordinary "Clumps," wasn't it?

BUNTY: I loathe "Clumps."

NICKY: What about the History game?

BRUCE: What's that?

BUNTY: Oh no, Nicky; it's too intellectual.

FLORENCE: There's a Mah-Jong set in the drawing-room.

PAWNIE: How divine! Let's make up a table immediately.

CLARA: I won't be happy until some one gives me a set made
entirely of jade.

NICKY: Come on, Bunty.

BUNTY [*looking at Tom*]: I can't play it.

NICKY: You can; you used to play in Paris with Yvonne.

BUNTY: I've forgotten it.

NICKY: You'll soon remember again. [*He drags her off.*]

PAWNIE: Come along, Clara.

CLARA: I insist on Mr. Fairlight learning.

BRUCE: I'm afraid I'm no good at that sort of thing.

CLARA: You'll be able to put it in one of your plays.

PAWNIE: Come and watch; it's too thrilling for words.

[*Clara, Bruce and Pawnie go off.*]

HELEN: Have you only one set, Florence?

FLORENCE: Yes. Isn't it maddening? Clara promised to bring hers down, but forgot.

HELEN: Does Bruce Fairlight play Bridge?

FLORENCE: No, I don't think so.

HELEN: Dramatists are such a comfort in a house party, aren't they? [*She goes off.*]

TOM: Are you coming, Florence?

FLORENCE: No.

TOM [*nonplussed*]: Oh!

FLORENCE: But please don't let me stop *you* going. I'm sure you're *dying* to be with the others.

TOM: I say, Florence, I wish you wouldn't go on like that.

FLORENCE: I don't know what's the matter with you; you've never behaved like this before.

TOM: I haven't behaved like anything.

FLORENCE: You've been exceedingly rude to me, both at dinner and afterwards.

TOM: I wasn't at dinner.

FLORENCE: Yes, you were; you snapped me up when I said I didn't like Elsie Saunders.

TOM: You know perfectly well she's a friend of mine.

FLORENCE: Well, she oughtn't to be, after the things she's said about me.

TOM: You will go on imagining.

FLORENCE: Nothing of the sort—I *know!* If you weren't so dense you'd see, too—the jealousy I have to put up with. I get so tired of it all, so desperately tired. [*She becomes a little pathetic.*]

TOM: Talk about being different, you're different too——

FLORENCE: I'm unhappy.

TOM: Why?

FLORENCE: Because I hate to see you being put against me.

TOM: Florence!

FLORENCE: You'll understand one day. They're all very subtle, but I can see.

TOM: Nobody's said a word to me about you; they'd better not try.

FLORENCE: Why, what would you do?

TOM: I'd—I'd be furious.

FLORENCE: Oh!

TOM: And I'd let them see it, too.

FLORENCE [*holding out her hands*]: Tom——

TOM: Yes?

FLORENCE: I forgive you.

TOM: I can't bear you being angry with me.

FLORENCE: Can't you, really?

TOM: It makes me feel beastly.

FLORENCE: Come and sit here.

TOM [*sitting next to her on the club fender*]: That's a lovely dress.

FLORENCE: It is sweet, isn't it?

TOM: You always wear wonderful clothes.

FLORENCE: Do I, Tom?

TOM: You know you do.

FLORENCE: Do you remember the very first time we met?

TOM: Rather.

FLORENCE: Oxford's so full of romance, isn't it?

TOM: It was when you came down.

FLORENCE: Thank you, Tom dear.

TOM: We did have fun.

FLORENCE: You used to come up to matinées, and I'd motor you back afterwards.

TOM: Ripping!

FLORENCE: That reminds me, I've got seats for "Rolling Stones" on Tuesday. Don't forget.

TOM: You never said you were going to get them.

FLORENCE: It doesn't matter. I thought I did. We'd better dine at Claridge's.

TOM: But, Florence, I—I can't come!

FLORENCE: Why not?

TOM: I promised to go out.

FLORENCE: Who with?

TOM: Mother.

FLORENCE: Can't you put her off? It will be such a good first night.

TOM: Well—you see, as a matter of fact—it's rather awkward. I put her off the other day—— [*There is a slight pause.*]

FLORENCE [*a trifle coldly*]: Oh, well, never mind, we'll go some other night.

[*Enter David.*]

DAVID: Hallo, Florence! I thought you were in the drawing-room.

FLORENCE: They're playing Mah-Jong, and there's only one set. I shall break in presently.

TOM: I'll just go and see how they're getting on.

[*This obvious excuse for getting out of the room is not lost upon Florence.*]

FLORENCE: Yes, do.

TOM: Come and play soon. [*He goes out quietly.*]

FLORENCE: Don't you think this is a divine frock?

DAVID: Very pretty.

FLORENCE: You and Helen seemed to be very thick at dinner. What were you talking about?

DAVID: Nothing much. I like Helen.

FLORENCE: Only because she flatters you and listens to everything you say.

DAVID: She doesn't flatter me.

FLORENCE: I suppose she was talking about the farm, and giving her opinions.

DAVID: We did discuss the farm a little.

FLORENCE: She doesn't know a thing about it, really.

DAVID: Perhaps not, but it passed the time. [*He goes out.*]

[*Florence sits still for a moment, then she wearily buries her face in her hands. Enter Nicky.*]

NICKY [*going to her*]: What's the matter, darling?

FLORENCE: Nothing. I've got a slight headache.

NICKY: Why don't you go Byes?

FLORENCE: I can't; it's much too early.

NICKY: I'm sick of Mah-Jong.

FLORENCE: Who's playing now?

NICKY: Pawnie and Helen and Clara are trying to teach Bruce Fairlight; he's an awful fool at it. [*He sits down at the piano and plays absently.*]

FLORENCE: You must get Bunty out of that habit of contradicting everything people say.

NICKY: I don't see why.

FLORENCE: It's bad breeding.

NICKY [*striking a note viciously*]: Who cares nowadays? We've all got a right to our opinions.

FLORENCE: She seems to forget that I'm much older than she is.

NICKY: That's no argument, mother; it's silly only to remember your age when some one says something you don't like.

FLORENCE: She's having a bad effect on you.

NICKY: Nonsense!

FLORENCE: You've changed since Paris.

NICKY: Naturally.

FLORENCE: You never used to be rude to me.

NICKY: Oh, damn, I'm not rude.

FLORENCE: Yes, you are.

NICKY: Well, don't start running down Bunty.

FLORENCE: Stop playing—stop playing!

NICKY [*getting up angrily*]: Oh, God!

[*He goes towards door and collides with Helen.*]

HELEN: What's happening?

FLORENCE: Nothing. Bunty's just putting Nicky against me. I knew she'd try to. [*She goes out.*]

HELEN: You must be having a delightful evening! You leave the drawing-room, having rowed with Bunty, and come here and row with Florence.

NICKY: Mother's impossible.

HELEN: She's no different from what she's always been.

NICKY: Well, I haven't realized it before.

HELEN [*taking a cigarette and lighting it*]: You haven't been engaged before.

NICKY: I'm hating this house party.

HELEN [*lightly*]: Don't say that, dear; it's not kind.

NICKY: You know I don't mean you.

HELEN: Are you very much in love?

NICKY: Yes.—No—I don't know.

HELEN: I wonder.

NICKY: It's utterly devastating, anyhow.

HELEN: When did you meet her?

NICKY: About five months ago.

HELEN: What was she doing in Paris?

NICKY: Oh, I don't know—fooling about.

HELEN: Splendid.

NICKY: She's been studying French literature.

HELEN: Why?

NICKY: She's going to write—herself—some day.

HELEN: Oh, I see!

NICKY: Helen, do you like her?

HELEN: I can't tell yet—yesterday was the first time I'd ever set eyes on her.

NICKY: She's wonderfully intelligent.

HELEN: Yes—I'm sure she is.

NICKY: You *don't* like her?

HELEN: I tell you—I'm not sure yet.

NICKY: It's generally the way—one's friends always hate one another.

HELEN [*smiling*]: It *is* difficult for you, isn't it?

NICKY: I should so like you to like her.

HELEN: Very well—I'll try.

NICKY: She's utterly opposite to me in every way.

HELEN: Yes, I see that.

NICKY: But that's as it ought to be, isn't it?

HELEN: It depends.

NICKY: I need a sort of restraining influence terribly.

HELEN: Yes, Nicky.

NICKY: She's awfully good for me.

HELEN: Is she?

NICKY: Yes—she curbs me when I get temperamental and silly.

HELEN: I always felt you needed encouraging more than curbing.

NICKY [*laughing*]: Oh, Helen—aren't you a darling!

HELEN: I mean it.

NICKY: You're wrong, though—I'm all over the place.

HELEN: Anyhow, I do hope you'll be very happy with her.

NICKY: I don't suppose I shall ever be that. I haven't got the knack.

HELEN: Do you work hard?

NICKY: Yes.

HELEN: Really hard?

NICKY: Frightfully.

HELEN: Liar!

NICKY: If you'd seen me in Paris—studying, studying—all night long until the gray dawn put the guttering candle to shame —and my nerveless hands dropped from the keys——

HELEN: Candles gutter awfully quickly when they're burned at both ends.

NICKY: Meaning that I look a debauched wreck of my former self?

HELEN: Exactly.

NICKY: If you go on encouraging me at this rate I shall commit suicide.

HELEN: You do resent anyone taking a real interest in you, don't you?

NICKY: I distrust it.

HELEN: Why?

NICKY: I don't know—I'm not worth it.

HELEN: You seem to be suffering from a slight inferiority complex.

NICKY: Not a bit of it—I'm gay and witty and handsome.

HELEN: Oh, Nicky, you're so maddening.

NICKY: Don't be cross, Helen.

HELEN: I'm one of the few people who know what you're really like, and you won't give me the credit for it.

NICKY: Do you think you do, honestly?

HELEN: Yes—and I'm exceedingly worried about you.

NICKY: You needn't be.

HELEN: You're sensitive and reserved and utterly foolish.

NICKY: Thank you—I'm beginning to feel beautifully picturesque.

HELEN: And you're scared.

NICKY: Why! What have I to be scared about?

HELEN: Would you like me to tell you?

NICKY: No.

HELEN: Why not?

NICKY: Because you're a sentimentalist, and you see things that aren't there at all.

HELEN: You're far more sentimental than I.

NICKY: Darling Helen—you've got such a lovely mind—like a Christmas card—with frosted robins and sheep wandering about in the snow—bleating.

HELEN: All the same, I should give up drugs if I were you.

NICKY: Helen!

HELEN: Well?

NICKY: I don't know what you mean.

HELEN: Do you think I can't see?

NICKY [forcing a laugh]: You're being terribly funny, aren't you?

HELEN: You fool! You unutterable little fool!

NICKY: Don't be dramatic, dear.

HELEN: I thought you had common sense; I credited you with more intelligence than that.

NICKY: If you persist in being absurd.

HELEN [*suddenly with intense feeling*]: Nicky, don't resist me, don't fight me; I'm your friend; I wouldn't have said a word if I weren't. You've got to stop it; you haven't gone very far yet; there's still time. For God's sake listen to reason.

NICKY: Shut up, shut up, don't speak so loudly.

HELEN: Nicky, throw it away.

NICKY: When did you find out?

HELEN: To-night, you know, when you were playing, but I've guessed for ages.

NICKY: You needn't be frightened, Helen; I only take just the tiniest little bit, once in a blue moon!

HELEN: If anything goes wrong, you'll take a lot. Throw it away.

NICKY: What could go wrong?

HELEN: Never mind, throw it away!

NICKY: I can't. Look out; somebody's coming.

[*Enter David.*]

DAVID: Hallo!

NICKY: Hallo, father!

DAVID: What's the matter?

NICKY: The matter—why?

DAVID: You look very worried.

NICKY: Helen and I have just had a grand heart-to-heart talk; we've undone our back hair, loosened our stays and wallowed in it.

DAVID: Oh, I see!

HELEN: We haven't seen one another for so long—it was inevitable.

DAVID: You never came and looked at the farm this morning. I waited for you.

NICKY: I'm awfully sorry, father—I just went on sleeping.

HELEN: I'll see you later, Nicky.

NICKY: All right.

[*Helen goes out.*]

DAVID: How do you think your mother's looking?

NICKY: Splendid—the same as ever.

DAVID: Would you like a cigar?

NICKY: No, thanks, father—I'm not very good at them.

DAVID: I was just on my way to bed—there are far too many people in the house.

NICKY [*smiling*]: You must be used to that by now.

DAVID: You ought to stay down here, you know—during the week, and get some fresh air.

NICKY: I've got such millions of things to do in London.

DAVID: Worth doing?

NICKY: Yes, of course.

DAVID: You look as though you needed a rest.

NICKY: You needn't worry about me—I feel splendid.

DAVID: She seems a nice girl.

NICKY: Who—Bunty?

DAVID: Yes. Quiet and untiresome.

NICKY: She's a darling!

DAVID: When do you propose to get married?

NICKY: I don't know. The engagement's only a sort of try-out, you know.

DAVID: Oh, I see. I didn't realize that. I'm so unversed in modern technicalities.

NICKY: It's her idea really—just to tread water for a bit.

DAVID: It sounds an excellent plan.

NICKY: I'm awfully glad you like her.

DAVID: Is she musical?

NICKY: Oh, yes—frightfully!

DAVID: Good!

NICKY: Father, I think I will come down here for a few days—and work quietly.

DAVID: If you do that I'll go up to London every other day. I see so little of you when you're at the flat.

NICKY: That's settled then. I wonder what mother will say!

DAVID: I'll talk to her.

NICKY: All right. She won't bother about us much.

DAVID: No—I don't suppose she will. I think I'll be getting along to bed now. Good night, my boy!

NICKY: Good night, father!

[*They shake hands, and David pats Nicky's shoulder rather tentatively. He goes upstairs and Nicky wanders to the piano. He plays absently, and Bunty enters.*]

BUNTY: I want to talk to you.

NICKY [*still playing*]: All right.

BUNTY: Perhaps you'd stop playing for a minute.

NICKY: Won't you let me woo you with a little Scriabine?

BUNTY: Please stop.

NICKY [*rising*]: I'm unappreciated—that's what it is. [*There is a slight pause—he goes over to her.*] I say, Bunty——

BUNTY: What?

NICKY: Before you say anything awful to me, I *am* sorry for being rude just now.

BUNTY: So you ought to be.

NICKY: Will you forgive me?

BUNTY: Yes, I forgive you.

NICKY: I've been irritable all the evening.

BUNTY: Give me a cigarette, Nicky.

NICKY: Here.

[*They both smoke.*]

BUNTY: Thanks.

NICKY: What did you want to talk to me about?

BUNTY: Lots of things—us!

NICKY [*hardening*]: Oh, I see!

BUNTY: Don't you think it's rather silly—being engaged?

NICKY: No, not at all.

BUNTY: I do.

NICKY: Just because we bickered a bit to-night?

BUNTY: No, not only because of that.

NICKY: Why then?

BUNTY: Can't you see?

NICKY: No.

BUNTY: Well, we're not very suited to each other, are we?

NICKY: Why do you suddenly say that?

BUNTY: Because I've only just realized it.

NICKY: I'm sorry.

BUNTY: It's not your fault particularly.

NICKY: I'm glad.

BUNTY: It's circumstances and surroundings.

NICKY: Oh, that can be altered quite easily. We'll change the shape of the house—we'll take all that wall away and turn that into a studio—you love studios, don't you?—then we'll transform the drawing-room into an enormous aviary.

BUNTY: It's practically that now!

NICKY: And then we'll——

BUNTY: Shut up, Nicky!

NICKY: I'm only trying to be amenable.

BUNTY: Are you, really?

NICKY: Yes, I'm putting up a sort of defense, Bunty. I have a feeling that you're going to be unpleasant, and I want to establish myself comfortably before you start.

BUNTY: I don't want to be unpleasant—only honest.

NICKY: You won't let the two run together, will you?

BUNTY [*with vehemence*]: You're hopeless, hopeless, hopeless!

NICKY: Yes—I think I am, rather.

BUNTY: In a way I'm glad—it makes it easier.

NICKY: Does it?

BUNTY: You're not in love with me, really—you couldn't be!

NICKY: Please don't say that.

BUNTY: Why don't you face things properly?

NICKY: One generally has to in the end. I like to put it off for as long as possible.

BUNTY: That's cowardly.

NICKY: Don't be pompous, darling.

BUNTY: You're a great help, I must say.

NICKY: Why should I help to destroy my own happiness?

BUNTY: That's self-pity and self-deception.

NICKY: Why are you going on like this?

BUNTY: Because I tell you—I've realized the truth.

NICKY: I suppose you've taken a hatred to mother!

BUNTY: No, not a hatred.

NICKY: You don't like her.

BUNTY: Not very much.

NICKY: Why not? She likes you.

BUNTY: She detests me.

NICKY: Nonsense! Why should she?

BUNTY: Because I'm young.

NICKY: What a filthy thing to say!

BUNTY: It's true.

NICKY: It's nothing of the sort.

BUNTY: You're so stupid sometimes.

NICKY: Thank you.

BUNTY: Don't let's start bickering again.

NICKY: We won't discuss mother any more then.

BUNTY: You started it.

NICKY: I wish I could make you understand her like I do. I mean she's awfully irritating, I know—but deep down she's marvelous in spite of everything.

BUNTY [*coldly*]: Everything?

NICKY [*vehemently*]: Yes, *everything!* Don't be a beast, Bunty; just try to see her point a little, even if you do dislike her. She is terribly silly about being "young," I know, but she's been used to so much admiration and flattery and everything always, she feels she sort of can't give it up—you do see that, don't you? And she hasn't really anything in the least comforting to fall back upon. She's not clever—real kind of brain cleverness—and father's no good, and I'm no good, and all the time she's wanting life to be as it was instead of as it is. There's no harm in her anywhere —she's just young inside. Can't you imagine the utter foulness of growing old? 'Specially if you've been lovely and attractive like she was. The beautiful Flo Lancaster! She used to be known as that. I can remember her when I was quite small, coming up to say good night to me, looking too perfectly radiant for words —and she used to come to the school, too, sometimes, and every one used to go mad over her, and I used to get frightfully proud and excited——

BUNTY: I've never heard you talk like this before.

NICKY: I don't think I ever have.

BUNTY: I like you better clear-cut, not blurred by sentiment.

[*Nicky looks at her for a moment in amazement.*]

NICKY: To describe you as hard would be inadequate—you're metallic!

BUNTY: I can see straight.

NICKY [*politely*]: Can you?

BUNTY: Yes. We could never be happy together.

NICKY: Perhaps not.

BUNTY: Shall we just—finish—then?

NICKY: Certainly, I'm sorry we were too modern to have an engagement ring; you'd have been able to give it back to me so beautifully.

BUNTY: Don't be ridiculous!

NICKY: Better than being blurred by sentiment.

[*Bunty lights another cigarette and, kicking off her shoes, perches on the club fender and proceeds to warm her feet at the fire.*]

[*Enter Clara Hibbert.*]

CLARA: My dear, I'm *shattered*—and I'm going straight to bed —probably for several weeks.

BUNTY: Why?

CLARA: Shshsh! He's coming.

BUNTY: Who's coming?

CLARA: Bruce Fairlight. I've been teaching him Mah-Jong. These master brains—agony, dear——

[*Enter Bruce Fairlight.*]

BRUCE: Very interesting, that game.

CLARA [*weakly*]: I thought you'd like it.

BRUCE: It's interesting *psychologically!* The concentration and suspense——

[*Enter Florence, Helen, Pawnie and Tom. Tom is grasping a whisky and soda—Pawnie is eating a biscuit.*]

PAWNIE: I'm quite exhausted; it must be the country air——

FLORENCE: —it was too lovely, because I started with two red dragons in my hand——

HELEN: I wondered who had them——

PAWNIE: One more tune, Nicky, before we go to bed——

FLORENCE: Yes, just one——

NICKY [*looking at Bunty*]: I'll play "I Love You"—such a romantic tune. [*He puts on the gramophone.*]

BUNTY: Do.

HELEN: What time's everyone going up in the morning?

FLORENCE: The ten-o'clock's the best—we'll have breakfast at nine downstairs.

PAWNIE [*confidentially*]: Do you know that in London I can never do more than nibble a piece of thin toast, and whenever I'm away I eat *enormously!*

NICKY: How very peculiar!

PAWNIE: Your tone revolts me, Nicky. You must never be irascible with your old friends.

NICKY: I haven't got any.

HELEN: Nicky!

NICKY: Sorry, Helen.

FLORENCE: I don't know what's the matter with Nicky. He's been in a vile temper all the evening—his first week-end home, too.

NICKY: Such a pity, when so much trouble has been taken to make me happy and cozy.

TOM: Come and dance, Bunty.

BUNTY: No, not now.

NICKY: Dance with him, Bunty. Chaps must have exercise.

FLORENCE: You dance with Bunty, Pawnie—I'll dance with Tom—come on.

[*She and Tom dance.*]

HELEN: The great thing in this world is not to be obvious, Nicky—over *anything!*

[*Florence and Tom dance, also Helen and Pawnie. Everyone talks at once, as in the beginning of the act.*]

PAWNIE: You are infuriating, Helen. It's a wonderful book.

HELEN: Thoroughly second-rate.

PAWNIE: What do you think about *Mischievous Passion*, Fairlight?

BRUCE: I never read novels on principle.

PAWNIE: Well, you must read this—it's colossal.

HELEN: Don't be led away by Pawnie, Mr. Fairlight, he has no discrimination.

PAWNIE: But I tell you it's brilliant! Absolutely *brilliant!*

HELEN: Nonsense.

PAWNIE: There are times, Helen, when I could willingly see you dead at my feet.

FLORENCE: A little slower, for Heaven's sake!

NICKY: How's that? [*He makes it far too slow.*]

FLORENCE: I think you'd better go to bed, Nicky.

HELEN: We're all going, anyhow.

NICKY: Not yet, please, mummy dear—I'm having such a lovely time! [*He slams off in a rage.*]

PAWNIE: I always knew the Continent was fatal for the young.

BUNTY: Nicky's upset—it's my fault—we're not engaged any more.

FLORENCE: Why—what's happened?

BUNTY: Nothing happened—it was never very serious, really.

HELEN: I had a feeling that it was.

BUNTY: You were wrong.

FLORENCE: Well, I must say it's all been rather abrupt.

BUNTY: It's better to finish things off at once—cleanly—if you're not quite sure, don't you think?

FLORENCE: Well, I'm sorry, Bunty. If you feel like that about it there's nothing more to be said.

BUNTY: I wouldn't have mentioned it at all—only you all seemed to be blaming him for being irritable——

HELEN: Poor Nicky!

CLARA: I really must go up to bed now. I'm so tired. Good night, Florence dear.

FLORENCE: Good night, Clara. Breakfast at nine. Have you got books and everything you want?

CLARA: Yes, thanks. Good night, everyone.

[*Everyone murmurs "Good night" politely.*]

FLORENCE: Tom, be an angel and fetch me a glass of milk. It's in the drawing-room.

TOM: All right. [*He goes off.*]

HELEN: Come on up, Florence. I'm dead.

FLORENCE: So am I. Will you turn out the lights when you come?

PAWNIE: With beautiful precision, dear.

FLORENCE [*as she and Helen go upstairs*]: Tell Tom to bring my milk up to me, somebody.

PAWNIE: All right.

FLORENCE: Good night, Mr. Fairlight.

BRUCE: Good night.

PAWNIE: Good night, Florence.

[*Florence and Helen go off.*]

BRUCE: I suppose we'd all better go up.

BUNTY: I don't feel I could sleep yet.

[*Re-enter Tom with glass of milk.*]

TOM: Hallo! Where's Florence?

BUNTY: Gone up to bed. Will you take her milk to her?

PAWNIE: What's become of Nicky?

TOM: In the smoking-room, I think.

BRUCE: Good night, Miss Mainwaring.

BUNTY: Good night.

[*They shake hands.*]

PAWNIE: I shall come, too—good night.

TOM: Good night.

PAWNIE [*to Bruce as they go upstairs*]: When you're writing, do your characters grow as you go along?

BRUCE: No, I think each one out minutely beforehand.

PAWNIE: How too intriguing.

[*They go off.*]

TOM: So you've broken it off already?

BUNTY: Yes.

TOM: I didn't know you were going to do it so soon.

BUNTY: It's better to get things over.

TOM: What did he say?

BUNTY: Nothing much.

TOM: Was he furious?

BUNTY: Oh, what does it matter? Don't let's go on about it.

TOM: It's all damned awkward.

BUNTY: What?

TOM: The whole thing.

BUNTY: You're rather scared, aren't you?

TOM: No, not exactly—now that I've got you to back me up.

BUNTY: I shall be glad when we're out of this house.

TOM: So shall I.

BUNTY: I hate the atmosphere.

TOM: I don't know how I've stood it for so long.

BUNTY: You didn't notice it until I came, any more than I noticed Nicky's atmosphere until you came.

TOM: It's queer, isn't it?

BUNTY: We're reverting to type, don't you see?

TOM: How d'you mean?

BUNTY: Never mind, it's true.

TOM: Do you think I'm being a cad to Florence?

BUNTY: Yes, I do rather.

TOM: But, Bunty! You said this morning——

BUNTY: That I didn't see how you could help yourself; neither I do. It's frightfully difficult, but it's not altogether your fault, any more than it would have been mine if I'd married Nicky.

One gets carried away by glamour, and personality, and magnetism—they're beastly treacherous things.

TOM: You are wonderful.

BUNTY: Don't be silly.

TOM: You're so cool and clear, and you see everything.

BUNTY: I'm sorry—for Nicky.

TOM: Oh, damn Nicky!

BUNTY [*laughing*]: Oh, Tom!

TOM: Why, what's up?

BUNTY: You're so dead set.

TOM: You're worth ten of him any day. What's the use of a chap like that? He *doesn't do* anything except play the piano —he can't play any games, he's always trying to be funny——

BUNTY: Shut up, Tom; you're being rather cheap. I haven't reverted to type so quickly that I can't see some of the things I'm missing.

TOM: I wish I knew what you were talking about.

BUNTY: Oh, God! I feel so miserable! [*She bursts into tears.*]

TOM [*flummoxed*]: I say—Bunty—for Heaven's sake—— [*He puts his arm round her.*]

BUNTY [*shaking him off*]: Don't, don't. Give me my shoes——

[*He picks up her shoes; she puts them on. She is half sobbing all the time.*]

TOM: I say, old girl, hadn't you better go to bed? You're all wrought up!

BUNTY: He said beastly things.

TOM: I'll wring his neck.

BUNTY [*with a fresh burst of tears*]: Shut up, Tom, shut up——

TOM: Bunty, stop crying—there's a dear; please, please stop crying——

[*He takes her in his arms and kisses her; she is groping for her handkerchief. Florence comes quietly downstairs.*]

BUNTY: I can't find my hanky!

TOM: Here's mine.

FLORENCE [*like a pistol shot*]: Tom!

[*Tom and Bunty break away.*]

TOM: Yes, Florence?

FLORENCE [*ominously*]: What does this mean?

TOM: I'm sorry, Florence—I——

FLORENCE: You utter cad!

BUNTY: Look here—I should like to say——

FLORENCE: Be quiet—mind your own business.

[*Nicky enters.*]

NICKY [*seeing tears on Bunty's face*]: What's the matter—is anybody hurt?

FLORENCE [*ominously*]: No, not hurt!

BUNTY: I banged my hand, that's all.

FLORENCE: Liar!

NICKY: Mother—don't be so stupid——

TOM: Florence—I——

FLORENCE: Don't *speak* to me——

NICKY [*quietly*]: Mother—not now—not now—it's all wrong. Control yourself! Bunty—Bunty—do go to bed—please. [*He goes to the piano and begins to play jazz.*]

BUNTY: All right—Tom——

[*Florence goes to the fireplace, trembling with rage. Nicky goes on playing. Tom and Bunty go towards the stairs.*]

FLORENCE: Stop—I want an explanation, please!

BUNTY: How dare you speak to me like that?

FLORENCE: Get out of my house! Get out of my house!

BUNTY: This is disgusting!

TOM: I say, Florence——

FLORENCE: Get out of my house!

BUNTY: I shall leave the first thing in the morning; it's much too late tonight. [*She goes off.*]

[*Nicky never stops playing for a moment.*]

FLORENCE: Tom.

[*He goes towards her, absolutely silent.*] You kissed her—you kissed her—I saw you!——

TOM: Yes.

FLORENCE: In this house!

TOM: Yes, Florence. I apologize.

FLORENCE: Apologize! You're beneath contempt. Never speak to me again, never touch me again—I hate you!

TOM: Look here, Florence—I'm desperately sorry. You see, I'm afraid I love her.

FLORENCE [*hysterically*]: You dare to stand there and say that to me? It's incredible—after all I've done for you—after all we've been to each other. Love! You don't know what it means. You've lied to me—all these months. It's contemptible—humiliating. Get out of my sight!

TOM [*turning and going upstairs*]: Very well.

FLORENCE [*suddenly realizing that he is gone*]: Tom—Tom—come back—come back!——[*She runs upstairs after him.*]

[*Nicky at last stops playing and lets his hands drop from the keys.*]

CURTAIN

ACT THREE

THE SCENE *is Florence's bedroom the same night. About two hours have elapsed. When the curtain rises Florence is lying face downwards on the bed; she is dressed in a very beautiful but slightly exotic négligé.*

Helen is standing by the window, fully dressed; she is holding the curtain aside, and a bar of moonlight comes in to mingle with the amber of the dressing-table lights. Florence is obviously extremely hysterical.

HELEN: Florence, what *is* the use of going on like that?

FLORENCE: I wish I were dead!

HELEN: It's so cowardly to give way utterly—as you're doing.

FLORENCE: I don't care—I don't care!

HELEN: If you don't face things in this world, they only hit you much harder in the end.

FLORENCE: He loved me—he adored me!

HELEN: Never! He hadn't got it in him.

FLORENCE: After all I've done for him, to go to—to Bunty!

HELEN [*leaving the window*]: If it hadn't been Bunty it would have been someone else—don't you see how inevitable it was?

FLORENCE: How dared they!—Here!—In this house!

HELEN: That's a little thing; it doesn't matter at all.

FLORENCE: It does—it does——

HELEN: Florence, sit up and pull yourself together.

FLORENCE [*sitting up slowly*]: I think I'm going mad.

HELEN: Not a bit of it; you're just thoroughly hysterical.

FLORENCE: Give me some water.

[*Helen goes to the bathroom and returns with a glass of water.*]

FLORENCE [*taking it*]: What time is it?

HELEN [*looking at her watch*]: Ten past one.

FLORENCE: Don't go to London by the early train, Helen; stay and come up with me in the car.

HELEN: Very well.

FLORENCE: Thank God, you were here!

HELEN: I wish I'd known what was happening; I might have done something.

FLORENCE: What can I do to get him back?

HELEN: Don't be silly.

FLORENCE: What can I do—what can I do?——

HELEN: Do you mean to say you'd *take* him back after to-night?

FLORENCE: No, never. Not if he crawled to me—never——

HELEN: Well, then, make up your mind definitely never to see him again whatever happens.

FLORENCE: Yes—I will.

HELEN: Why don't you go to bed now?

FLORENCE: I couldn't sleep.

HELEN: Put it all out of your mind—make an effort.

FLORENCE: I can't—I'm too unhappy.

HELEN: Think of Nicky.

FLORENCE: Nicky's young.

HELEN: That doesn't make it any better for him.

FLORENCE: He'll get over it in the long run.

HELEN: The long run never counts at the moment.

FLORENCE: He wasn't in love—really?

HELEN: As much as either you or he are capable of it.

FLORENCE: He's well rid of her. She'd never have appreciated him properly—she hasn't the intelligence.

HELEN: I don't agree with you there—she's got intelligence right enough.

FLORENCE: Treacherous little beast!

HELEN: Yes, but far-seeing.

FLORENCE: Are you standing up for her? Do you think it was *right* of her to get Tom away from me?

HELEN: Yes, quite right.

FLORENCE: Helen!

HELEN: To do her justice, she didn't deliberately set herself out to get him away from you at all. She discovered that in spite of the somewhat decadent years Tom was still her type, and likely to remain so. So with common sense she decided to shelve Nicky forthwith and go for him.

FLORENCE: Her type indeed!

HELEN: Yes, she'd have been quite a nice girl really if she'd been left alone and not allowed to go to Paris and get into the wrong set.

FLORENCE: You are extraordinary, Helen. Do you realize that you're making excuses for the girl who's betrayed your best friend?

HELEN: Don't be so utterly absurd. I'm not making excuses, and, anyhow, she hasn't betrayed you. She hardly knows you, in the first place, and she's just followed her instincts regardless of anyone else's feelings—as you've done thousands of times.

FLORENCE: Helen—you're being horrible to me!

HELEN: I'm not, I'm trying to make you see! You're battering your head against silly cast-iron delusions, and I want to dislodge them.

FLORENCE: Helen, I'm so unhappy—so desperately un-happy.

HELEN: Yes, but not because you've lost Tom; it's something far deeper than that.

FLORENCE: What then?

HELEN: You're on the wrong tack, and have been for years.

FLORENCE: I don't understand.

HELEN: You *won't* understand!

[*Florence gets off the bed and goes over to the dressing-table. She sits and stares at herself in the glass for a moment without speaking.*]

FLORENCE: My eyes are sore. [*She powders her face and sprays a little scent on her hair.*] It's so lovely, this—and so refreshing.

HELEN: I think I'll go to bed now.

FLORENCE: No, wait a little longer with me—please, Helen— just a few minutes.

HELEN: It's so hot in here.

FLORENCE: Open the window then.

HELEN: All right. [*She goes to the window and opens it.*]

[*Florence takes a cigarette out of a box and then shakes a scent-bottle and rubs the cigarette lightly with the stopper.*]

FLORENCE: Do you ever do this? It's divine.

HELEN: What a wonderfully clear night. You can see the hills right across the valley—the moon's quite strong.

[*Florence goes to the window and stands next to Helen, looking out—she is puffing her cigarette.*]

FLORENCE: I chose this room in the first place because the view was so lovely.

HELEN: Do you ever look at it?

FLORENCE [*listlessly*]: Of course I do, often!

HELEN: It's been raining. I wish you'd throw away that cigarette—it spoils the freshness.

FLORENCE [*turning away*]: It's soothing me—calming my nerves.

HELEN: I do wish I could help you—really!

FLORENCE: You are helping me, darling—you're being an angel.

HELEN [*suddenly angry*]: Don't talk so emptily, Florence; I'm worth more than that.

FLORENCE: I don't know what you mean.

HELEN: It sickens me to see you getting back so soon.

FLORENCE: Getting back?

HELEN: Yes, to your usual worthless attitude of mind.

FLORENCE: Helen!

HELEN: A little while ago you were really suffering for once, and in a way I was glad because it showed you were capable of a genuine emotion. Now you're glossing it over—swarming it down with your returning vanity; soon you won't be unhappy any more—just vindictive.

FLORENCE: Don't go on at me like that—I'm too wretched.

HELEN [*going to her*]: Florence dear, forgive me, but it's true— and I don't want it to be.

[*The door opens and Nicky enters. He is in dressing-gown and pyjamas. His face looks strained and white.*]

FLORENCE: Nicky!

NICKY: Helen, I want to talk to mother, please.

HELEN: All right, Nicky.

FLORENCE: What is it?

NICKY: I couldn't sleep.

HELEN: Florence dear—good night.

FLORENCE: No—no, Helen—don't go yet——

HELEN: I must.

FLORENCE: Helen—stay with me.

NICKY: Please go.

HELEN: I can't stay, Florence—it's quite impossible. [*She goes out.*]

FLORENCE: I don't know what you mean—by coming here and ordering Helen out of my room.

NICKY: I'm sorry, mother. I felt I had to talk to you alone.

FLORENCE: At this hour of the night? You're mad!

NICKY: No, I'm not; I think I'm probably more unhappy than I've ever been in my life.

FLORENCE: You're young—you'll get over it.

NICKY: I hope so.

FLORENCE: I knew the first moment I saw her—what sort of a girl she was.

NICKY: Oh, mother!

FLORENCE: It's true. I had an *instinct* about her.

NICKY: It's all been rather a shock, you know——

FLORENCE [*becoming motherly*]: Yes, dear—I know—I know—but you mustn't be miserable about her; she isn't worth it. [*She goes to kiss him.*]

NICKY [*gently pushing her away*]: Don't, mother!

FLORENCE: Listen, Nicky. Go back to bed now—there's a dear; my head's splitting.

NICKY: I can't yet.

FLORENCE: Take some aspirin; that'll calm your nerves.

NICKY: I'm afraid I'm a little beyond aspirin.

FLORENCE: I don't want you to think I don't sympathize with you, darling—my heart *aches* for you—I know so well what you're going through.

NICKY: Do you?

FLORENCE: It's agony—absolute agony—but, you see—it will wear off—it always does in time. [*Nicky doesn't answer.*] Nicky, please go now!

NICKY: I want to talk to you.

FLORENCE: To-morrow—we'll talk to-morrow.

NICKY: No, now—*now!*

FLORENCE: You're inconsiderate and cruel—I've told you my head's bursting.

NICKY: I want to sympathize with you, too—and try to understand everything—as well as I can——

FLORENCE: Understand everything?

NICKY: Yes, please.

FLORENCE: I don't know what you mean——

NICKY: Will you tell me things—as though I were somebody quite different?

FLORENCE: What kind of things?

NICKY: Things about you—your life.

FLORENCE: Really, Nicky—you're ridiculous—asking me to tell you stories at this hour!

NICKY [*with dead vehemence*]: Mother—sit down quietly. I'm not going out of this room until I've got everything straight in my mind.

FLORENCE [*sinking down—almost hypnotized*]: Nicky—please —I——

NICKY: Tom Veryan has been your lover, hasn't he?

FLORENCE [*almost shrieking*]: Nicky—how dare you!

NICKY: Keep calm—it's our only chance—keep calm.

FLORENCE [*bursting into tears*]: How dare you speak to me like that—suggest such a thing! I——

NICKY: It's true, isn't it?

FLORENCE: Go away—go away!

NICKY: It's true, isn't it?

FLORENCE: No—no!

NICKY: It's true, isn't it?

FLORENCE: No—I tell you—no—no—no!

NICKY: You're lying to me, mother. What's the use of that?

FLORENCE: You're mad—mad——

NICKY: Does father know?

FLORENCE: Go away!

NICKY: Does father know?

FLORENCE: Your father knows nothing—he doesn't understand me any more than you do.

NICKY: Then it's between us alone.

FLORENCE: I tell you I don't know what you're talking about.

NICKY: Mother—don't go on like that; it's useless. We've arrived at a crisis; wherever we go—whatever we do we can't escape from it. I know we're neither of us very strong-minded or capable, and we haven't much hope of coming through successfully—but let's try. It's no good pretending any more—our lives are built up of pretenses all the time. For years—ever since I began to think at all, I've been bolstering up my illusions about you. People have made remarks, not realizing that I was your son, and I've pretended that they were inspired by cattiness and jealousy. I've noticed things—trivial incriminating little incidents, and I've brushed them aside and not thought any more about them because you were my mother—clever and beautiful and successful—and naturally people *would* slander you *because* you were so beautiful—and now I *know*—they were right!

FLORENCE: Nicky—I implore you—go away now—leave me alone.

NICKY: No, I can't.

FLORENCE: You're cruel—cruel to torment me——

NICKY: I don't want to be cruel——

FLORENCE: Go to bed then, and we'll talk everything over quietly another time.

NICKY: It is true about Tom Veryan, isn't it?

FLORENCE: No. No——

NICKY: We're on awfully dangerous ground. I'm straining every nerve to keep myself under control. If you lie to me and try to evade me any more—I won't be answerable for what might happen.

FLORENCE [*dropping her voice—terrified*]: What do you mean?

NICKY: I don't know—I'm frightened.

FLORENCE: Nicky—darling Nicky—I—— [*She approaches him.*]

NICKY: Don't touch me, please.

FLORENCE: Have a little pity for me.

NICKY: Was Tom Veryan your lover?

FLORENCE [*in a whisper*]: Yes.

NICKY: I want to understand why——

FLORENCE: He loved me.

NICKY: But you—did you love him?

FLORENCE: Yes.

NICKY: It was something you couldn't help, wasn't it—something that's always been the same in you since you were quite, quite young?——

FLORENCE: Yes, Nicky—yes——

NICKY: And there have been others, too, haven't there?

FLORENCE [*with her face in her hands*]: I won't be cross-questioned any more—I won't—I won't——

NICKY: I wish you'd understand I'm not blaming you—I'm trying to help you—to help us both——

FLORENCE: What good can all this possibly do?

NICKY: Clear things up, of course. I can't go on any more half knowing——

FLORENCE: Why should that side of my life be any concern of yours?

NICKY: But, mother!

FLORENCE: I'm different from other women—completely different—and you expect me to be the same. Why can't you realize that with a temperament like mine it's impossible to live an ordinary humdrum life. You're not a boy any longer—you're a man—and——

NICKY: I'm nothing—I've grown up all wrong.

FLORENCE: It's not my fault.

NICKY: Of course it's your fault, mother—who else's fault *could* it be?

FLORENCE: Your friends—the people you mix with——

NICKY: It wouldn't matter *who* I mixed with if only I had a background.

FLORENCE: You've got as much money as you want—you've got your home——

NICKY [*bitterly*]: Home! That's almost funny—there's no peace anywhere—nothing but the ceaseless din of trying to be amused——

FLORENCE: David never complains.

NICKY: I don't suppose you've looked at father during the last few years—or you wouldn't say that.

FLORENCE: He's perfectly happy because he's sensible—he lives his own life and doesn't try to interfere with mine.

NICKY: It must be your vanity that makes you so dreadfully blind—and foolish.

FLORENCE: Understand once and for all, I *won't* be spoken to like this——

NICKY: You've had other lovers besides Tom Veryan—haven't you?

FLORENCE: Yes, I have—I have. Now then!

NICKY: Well, anyhow—that's the truth—at last—— [*He rises, turns his back on her and stands looking out of the window.*]

FLORENCE [*after a pause—going to him*]: Nicky—don't be angry—please don't be angry with me.

NICKY: I'm not angry a bit. I realize that I'm living in a world where things like this happen—and they've got to be faced and given the right value. If only I'd had the courage to realize everything before—it wouldn't be so bad now. It's the sudden shock that's thrown the whole thing out of focus for me—but I mean to get it right. Please help me!

FLORENCE [*dully*]: I don't know what to do.

NICKY: It's your life, and you've lived it as you've wanted to live it—that's fair——

FLORENCE: Yes—yes.

NICKY: You've wanted love always—passionate love, because you were made like that. It's not your fault—it's the fault of circumstances and civilization; civilization makes rottenness so much easier. We're utterly rotten—both of us——

FLORENCE: Nicky—don't—don't——

NICKY: How can we help ourselves? We swirl about in a vortex of beastliness. This is a chance—don't you see—to realize the truth—our only chance.

FLORENCE: Oh, Nicky, do stop—go away!

NICKY: Don't keep on telling me to stop when our only hope is to hammer it out.

FLORENCE: You're overwrought. It isn't as bad as you think.

NICKY: Isn't it?

FLORENCE: No, no. Of course it isn't. To-morrow morning you'll see things quite differently.

NICKY: You haven't understood.

FLORENCE: Yes, I have—I have.

NICKY: You haven't understood. Oh, my God, you haven't understood! You're building up silly defenses in your mind. I'm overwrought. To-morrow morning I shall see things quite differently. That's true—that's the tragedy of it, and you won't see. To-morrow morning I *shall* see things quite differently. All this will seem unreal—a nightmare—the machinery of our lives

will go on again and gloss over the truth as it always does—
and our chance will be gone forever.

FLORENCE: Chance—chance? What are you talking about—
what chance?

NICKY: I must make you see, somehow.

FLORENCE: You're driving me mad.

NICKY: Have patience with me—please—please——

FLORENCE [*wildly*]: How can I have patience with you? You
exaggerate everything.

NICKY: No, I don't—I wish I did.

FLORENCE: Listen—let me explain something to you.

NICKY: Very well—go on.

FLORENCE: You're setting yourself up in judgment on me—
your own mother.

NICKY: No, I'm not.

FLORENCE: You are—you are. Let me speak. You don't understand my temperament in the least—nobody does—I——

NICKY: You're deceiving yourself—your temperament's no
different from thousands of other women's, but you've been
weak and selfish and given way all along the line——

FLORENCE: Let me speak, I tell you!——

NICKY: What's the use? You're still pretending—you're building up barriers between us instead of helping me to break them
down.

FLORENCE: What are you accusing me of having done?

NICKY: Can't you see yet?

FLORENCE: No, I can't. If you're preaching morality, you've no
right to. That's my affair—I've never done any harm to anyone.

NICKY: Look at me.

FLORENCE: Why—what do you mean?

NICKY: You've given me *nothing* all my life—nothing that
counts.

FLORENCE: Now you're pitying yourself.

NICKY: Yes, with every reason.

FLORENCE: You're neurotic and ridiculous. Just because Bunty broke off your engagement you come and say wicked, cruel things to me——

NICKY: You forget what I've seen to-night, mother.

FLORENCE: I don't care what you've seen.

NICKY: I've seen you make a vulgar, disgusting scene in your own house, and on top of that humiliate yourself before a boy half your age. The misery of losing Bunty faded away when that happened—everything is comparative, after all.

FLORENCE: I didn't humiliate myself——

NICKY: You ran after him up the stairs because your vanity wouldn't let you lose him. It isn't that you love him—that would be easier—you never love anyone, you only love them loving you—all your so-called passion and temperament is false—your whole existence had degenerated into an endless empty craving for admiration and flattery—and then you say you've done no harm to anybody. Father used to be a clever man, with a strong will and a capacity for enjoying everything—I can remember him like that—and now he's nothing—a complete nonentity because his spirit's crushed. How could it be otherwise? You've let him down consistently for years—and God knows I'm nothing for him to look forward to—but I might have been if it hadn't been for you——

FLORENCE: Don't talk like that. Don't—don't. It can't be such a crime being loved—it can't be such a crime being happy——

NICKY: You're not happy—you're never happy—you're fighting—fighting all the time to keep your youth and your looks—because you can't bear the thought of living without them—as though they mattered in the end.

FLORENCE [*hysterically*]: What does anything matter—ever?

NICKY: That's what I'm trying to find out.

FLORENCE: I'm still young inside—I'm still beautiful. Why shouldn't I live my life as I choose?

NICKY: You're not young or beautiful; I'm seeing for the first time how old you are. It's horrible—your silly fair hair—and your face all plastered and painted——

FLORENCE: Nicky—Nicky—stop—stop—stop! [*She flings herself face downwards on the bed.*]

[*Nicky goes over to her.*]

NICKY: Mother!

FLORENCE: Go away—go away—I hate you—go away——

NICKY: Mother—sit up——

FLORENCE [*pulling herself together*]: Go out of my room——

NICKY: Mother——

FLORENCE: I don't ever want to see you again—you're insane —you've said wicked, wicked things to me—you've talked to me as though I were a woman off the streets. I can't bear any more—I can't bear any more!

NICKY: I have a slight confession to make——

FLORENCE: Confession?

NICKY: Yes.

FLORENCE: Go away—go away——

NICKY [*taking a small gold box from his pocket*]: Look——

FLORENCE: What do you mean—what is it——?

NICKY: Don't you know?

[*Nicky takes the box with trembling fingers and opens it. She stares at it for a moment. When she speaks again her voice is quite dead.*]

FLORENCE: Nicky, it isn't—you haven't——?

NICKY: Why do you look so shocked?

FLORENCE [*dully*]: Oh, my God!

NICKY: What does it matter?

[*Florence suddenly rises and hurls the box out of the window.*] That doesn't make it any better.

FLORENCE [*flinging herself on her knees beside him*]: Nicky, promise me, oh, promise you'll never do it again—never in your life—it's frightful—horrible——

NICKY: It's only just the beginning.

FLORENCE: What can I say to you—what can I say to you?

NICKY: Nothing—under the circumstances.

FLORENCE: What do you mean?

NICKY: It can't possibly matter—now.

FLORENCE: Matter—but it's the finish of everything—you're young, you're just starting on your life—you must stop—you must swear never to touch it again—swear to me on your oath, Nicky—I'll help you—I'll help you——

NICKY: You! [*He turns away.*]

FLORENCE [*burying her face in her hands and moaning*]: Oh—oh—oh!

NICKY: How could you possibly help me?

FLORENCE [*clutching him*]: Nicky!

NICKY [*almost losing control*]: Shut up—shut up—don't touch me——

FLORENCE [*trying to take him in her arms*]: Nicky—Nicky——

NICKY: I'm trying to control myself, but you won't let me— you're an awfully rotten woman, really.

FLORENCE: Nicky—stop—stop—stop—— [*She beats him with her fists.*]

NICKY: Leave go of me! [*He breaks away from her, and going up to the dressing-table he sweeps everything off on to the floor with his arm.*]

FLORENCE [*screaming*]: Oh—oh—Nicky——!

NICKY: Now then! Now then! You're not to have any more lovers; you're not going to be beautiful and successful ever again

—you're going to be my mother for once—it's about time I had one to help me, before I go over the edge altogether——

FLORENCE: Nicky—Nicky——

NICKY: Promise me to be different—you've got to promise me!

FLORENCE [*sinking on to the end of couch, facing audience*]: Yes—yes—I promise——[*The tears are running down her face.*]

NICKY: I love you, really—that's why it's so awful. [*He falls on his knees by her side and buries his face in her lap.*]

FLORENCE: No. No, not awful—don't say that—I love you, too.

NICKY [*sobbing hopelessly*]: Oh, mother——!

FLORENCE [*staring in front of her*]: I wish I were dead!

NICKY: It doesn't matter about death, but it matters terribly about life.

FLORENCE: I know——

NICKY [*desperately*]: Promise me you'll be different—promise me you'll be different——

FLORENCE: Yes, yes—I'll try——

NICKY: We'll both try.

FLORENCE: Yes, dear.—Oh, my dear——! [*She sits quite still, staring in front of her—the tears are rolling down her cheeks, and she is stroking Nicky's hair mechanically in an effort to calm him.*]

CURTAIN

HAY FEVER

CHARACTERS

JUDITH BLISS

DAVID BLISS

SOREL BLISS

SIMON BLISS

MYRA ARUNDEL

RICHARD GREATHAM

JACKIE CORYTON

SANDY TYRELL

CLARA

ACT ONE

Saturday afternoon

ACT TWO

Saturday evening

ACT THREE

Sunday morning

*The action of the play takes place in the hall of
the Blisses' house at Cookham, in June.*

~~~~~~
~~~~~~

ACT ONE

SCENE: *The hall of David Bliss's house is very comfortable and extremely untidy. There are several of Simon's cartoons scattered about the walls, masses of highly colored American and classical music strewn about the piano, and lots of flowers and comfortable furniture. A staircase ascends to a small balcony leading to the bedrooms, David's study and Simon's room. There is a door leading to the library down R. A service door above it under the stairs. There are French windows at back, and the front door on the L.*

When the curtain rises it is about three o'clock on a Saturday afternoon in June.

Simon, in an extremely dirty tennis shirt and baggy gray flannel trousers, is crouched in the middle of the floor, cutting out squares from cartridge paper.

Sorel, more neatly dressed, is stretched on the sofa, reading a very violently bound volume of poems which has been sent to her by an aspiring friend.

SOREL: Listen to this, Simon. [*She reads.*] "Love's a Trollop stained with wine—Clawing at the breasts of Adolescence— Nuzzling, tearing, shrieking, beating—God, why were we fashioned so!" [*She laughs.*]

SIMON: The poor girl's potty.

SOREL: I wish she hadn't sent me the beastly book. I must say something nice about it.

SIMON: The binding's very dashing.

SOREL: She used to be such fun before she married that gloomy little man.

SIMON: She was always a fierce *poseuse*. It's so silly of people to try and cultivate the artistic temperament. *Au fond* she's just a normal, bouncing Englishwoman.

SOREL: You didn't shave this morning.

SIMON: I know I didn't, but I'm going to in a minute, when I've finished this.

SOREL: I sometimes wish we were more normal and bouncing, Simon.

SIMON: Why?

SOREL: I should like to be a fresh, open-air girl with a passion for games.

SIMON: Thank God you're not.

SOREL: It would be so soothing.

SIMON: Not in this house.

SOREL: Where's mother?

SIMON: In the garden, practising.

SOREL: Practising?

SIMON: She's learning the names of the flowers by heart.

SOREL: What's she up to?

SIMON: I don't know.—Damn! that's crooked.

SOREL: I always distrust her when she becomes the Squire's lady.

SIMON: So do I.

SOREL: She's been at it hard all day—she tapped the barometer this morning.

SIMON: She's probably got a plan about impressing somebody.

SOREL [*taking a cigarette*]: I wonder who.

SIMON: Some dreary, infatuated young man will appear soon, I expect.

SOREL: Not to-day? You don't think she's asked anyone down to-day, do you?

SIMON: I don't know. Has father noticed anything?

SOREL: No; he's too immersed in work.

SIMON: Perhaps Clara will know.

SOREL: Yell for her.

SIMON [*calling*]: Clara! Clara! . . .

SOREL: Oh, Simon, I *do* hope she hasn't asked anyone down to-day.

SIMON: Why? Have you?

SOREL: Yes.

SIMON [*crossly*]: Why on earth didn't you tell me?

SOREL: I didn't think you'd care one way or another.

SIMON: Who is it?

SOREL: Richard Greatham.

SIMON: How exciting! I've never heard of him.

SOREL: I shouldn't flaunt your ignorance if I were you—it makes you look silly.

SIMON [*rising*]: Well, that's done. [*He rolls up the cartridge paper.*]

SOREL: Everybody's heard of Richard Greatham.

SIMON [*amiably*]: How lovely for them.

SOREL: He's a frightfully well-known diplomatist—I met him at the Mainwarings' dance.

SIMON: He'll need all his diplomacy here.

SOREL: I warned him not to expect good manners, but I hope you'll be as pleasant to him as you can.

SIMON [*gently*]: I've never met any diplomatists, Sorel, but as a class I'm extremely prejudiced against them. They're so suave and polished and debonair.

SOREL: You could be a little more polished without losing caste.

SIMON: Will he have the papers with him?

SOREL: What papers?

SIMON [*vaguely*]: Oh, any papers.

SOREL: I wish you'd confine your biting irony to your caricatures, Simon.

SIMON: And I wish you'd confine your girlish infatuations to London, and not force them on your defenseless family.

SOREL: I shall keep him out of your way as much as possible.

SIMON: Do, darling.

[*Enter Clara. She is a hot, round, untidy little woman.*]

SIMON: Clara, has mother asked anyone down this week-end?

CLARA: I don't know, dear. There isn't much food in the house, and Amy's got toothache.

SOREL: I've got some oil of cloves somewhere.

CLARA: She tried that, but it only burnt her tongue. The poor girl's been writhing about in the scullery like one o'clock.

SOREL: You haven't forgotten to put those flowers in the Japanese room?

SIMON: The Japanese room is essentially feminine, and entirely unsuited to the Pet of the Foreign Office.

SOREL: Shut up, Simon.

CLARA: The room looks lovely, dear—you needn't worry. Just like your mother's dressing-room on a first night.

SIMON: How restful!

CLARA [*to Sorel*]: Have you told her about your boy friend?

SOREL [*pained*]: Not boy friend, Clara.

CLARA [*going round, picking up things*]: Oh, well, whatever he is.

SIMON: I think Sorel's beginning to be ashamed of us all, Clara—I don't altogether blame her; we are very slapdash.

CLARA: Are you going to leave that picture in the guests' bathroom, dear? I don't know if it's quite the thing—lots of pink, naked women rolling about in a field.

SIMON [*severely*]: Nudity can be very beautiful, Clara.

CLARA: Oh, can it! Perhaps being a dresser for so long 'as spoilt me eye for it. [*She goes out.*]

SIMON: Clara's looking tired. We ought to have more servants and not depend on her so much.

SOREL: You know we can never keep them. You're right about us being slapdash, Simon. I wish we weren't.

SIMON: Does it matter?

SOREL: It must, I think—to other people.

SIMON: It's not our fault—it's the way we've been brought up.

SOREL: Well, if we're clever enough to realize that, we ought to be clever enough to change ourselves.

SIMON: I'm not sure that I want to.

SOREL: We're so awfully bad-mannered.

SIMON: Not to people we like.

SOREL: The people we like put up with it because they like us.

SIMON: What do you mean, exactly, by bad manners? Lack of social tricks and small-talk?

SOREL: We never attempt to look after people when they come here.

SIMON: Why should we? It's loathsome being looked after.

SOREL: Yes, but people like little attentions. We've never once asked anyone if they've slept well.

SIMON: I consider that an impertinence, anyhow.

SOREL: I'm going to try to improve.

SIMON: You're only going on like this because you've got a mania for a diplomatist. You'll soon return to normal.

SOREL [*earnestly*]: Abnormal, Simon—that's what we are. Abnormal. People stare in astonishment when we say what we consider perfectly ordinary things. I just remarked at Freda's lunch the other day how nice it would be if some one invented something to make all our faces go up like the Chinese, because

I was so bored with them going down—and they all thought I was mad!

SIMON: It's no use worrying, darling; we see things differently, I suppose, and if people don't like it they must lump it.

SOREL: Mother's been awfully restless lately.

SIMON: Yes, I know.

SOREL: Life must be terribly dull for her now, with nothing to do.

SIMON: She'll go back soon, I expect; people never retire from the stage for long.

SOREL: Father will be livid if she does.

SIMON: That won't matter.

[*Enter Judith from the garden. She is carrying an armful of flowers and wearing a teagown, a large garden hat, gauntlet gloves, and goloshes.*]

JUDITH: You look awfully dirty, Simon. What have you been doing?

SIMON [*nonchalantly*]: Not washing very much.

JUDITH: You should, darling, really. It's so bad for your skin to leave things about on it. [*She proceeds to take off her goloshes.*]

SOREL: Clara says Amy's got toothache.

JUDITH: Poor dear! There's some oil of cloves in my medicine cupboard. Who is Amy?

SOREL: The scullery maid, I think.

JUDITH: How extraordinary! She doesn't look Amy a bit, does she? Much more Flossie.—Give me a cigarette.

[*Sorel gives her a cigarette and lights it.*]
Delphiniums are those stubby red flowers, aren't they?

SIMON: No, darling, they're tall and blue.

JUDITH: Yes, of course. The red ones are somebody's name —asters, that's it. I knew it was something opulent. I do hope Clara has remembered about the Japanese room.

SOREL: Japanese room!

JUDITH: Yes; I told her to put some flowers in it and take Simon's flannels out of the wardrobe drawer.

SOREL: So did I.

JUDITH [*ominously*]: Why?

SOREL [*airily*]: I've asked Richard Greatham down for the week-end—I didn't think you'd mind.

JUDITH: Mind! How dared you do such a thing?

SOREL: He's a diplomatist.

JUDITH: That makes it much worse. We must wire and put him off at once.

SOREL: It's too late.

JUDITH: Well, we'll tell Clara to say we've been called away.

SOREL: That would be extremely rude, and, anyhow, I *want* to see him.

JUDITH: You mean to stand there in cold blood and tell me you've asked a complete stranger down for the week-end, and that you want to see him!

SOREL: I've often done it before.

JUDITH: I fail to see how that helps matters. Where's he going to sleep?

SOREL: The Japanese room.

JUDITH: Oh no, he isn't—Sandy Tyrell is sleeping in it.

SIMON: There now! What did I tell you?

SOREL: Sandy—what?

JUDITH: Tyrell, dear.

SIMON: Why didn't you tell us, mother?

JUDITH: I did. I've talked of nothing but Sandy Tyrell for days. I adore Sandy Tyrell.

SIMON: You've never mentioned him.

SOREL: Who is he, mother?

JUDITH: He's a perfect darling, and madly in love with me—at least, it isn't me really, it's my Celebrated Actress glamour—but it gives me a divinely cozy feeling. I met him at Nora Trent's.

SOREL: Mother, I wish you'd give up this sort of thing.

JUDITH: What exactly do you mean by "this sort of thing," Sorel?

SOREL: You know perfectly well what I mean.

JUDITH: Are you attempting to criticize me?

SOREL: I should have thought you'd be above encouraging silly, callow young men who are infatuated by your name.

JUDITH: That may be true, but I shall allow nobody but myself to say it. I hoped you'd grow up a good daughter to me, not a critical aunt.

SOREL: It's so terribly cheap.

JUDITH: Cheap! Nonsense! What about your diplomatist?

SOREL: Surely that's a little different, dear?

JUDITH: If you mean that because you happen to be a vigorous *ingénue* of nineteen you have the complete monopoly of any amorous adventure there may be about, I feel it my firm duty to disillusion you.

SOREL: But, mother——

JUDITH: Anyone would think I was eighty, the way you go on. It was a great mistake not sending you to boarding schools, and you coming back and me being your elder sister.

SIMON: It wouldn't have been any use. Everyone knows we're your son and daughter.

JUDITH: Only because I was stupid enough to dandle you about in front of cameras when you were little. I knew I should regret it.

SIMON: I don't see any point in trying to be younger than you are.

JUDITH: At your age, dear, it would be indecent if you did.

SOREL: But, mother darling, don't you see, it's awfully undignified for you to go flaunting about with young men?

JUDITH: I don't flaunt about—I never have. I've been morally an extremely nice woman all my life—more or less—and if dabbling gives me pleasure, I don't see why I shouldn't dabble.

SOREL: But it oughtn't to give you pleasure any more.

JUDITH: You know, Sorel, you grow more damnably feminine every day. I wish I'd brought you up differently.

SOREL: I'm proud of being feminine.

JUDITH [*kissing her*]: You're a darling, and I adore you; and you're very pretty, and I'm madly jealous of you.

SOREL [*with her arms round her*]: Are you really? How lovely.

JUDITH: You will be nice to Sandy, won't you?

SOREL [*breaking away*]: Can't he sleep in "Little Hell"?

JUDITH: My dear, he's frightfully athletic, and all those hot-water pipes will sap his vitality.

SOREL: They'll sap Richard's vitality too.

JUDITH: He won't notice them; he's probably used to scorching tropical embassies with punkahs waving and everything.

SIMON: He's sure to be deadly, anyhow.

SOREL: You're getting far too blasé and exclusive, Simon.

SIMON: Nothing of the sort. Only I loathe being hearty with your men friends.

SOREL: You've never been even civil to any of my friends, men or women.

JUDITH: Don't bicker.

SIMON: Anyhow, the Japanese room's a woman's room, and a woman ought to have it.

JUDITH: I promised it to Sandy—he loves anything Japanese.

SIMON: So does Myra.

JUDITH: Myra!

SIMON: Myra Arundel. I've asked her down.

JUDITH: You've—what?

SIMON: I've asked Myra down for the week-end—she's awfully amusing.

SOREL: Well, all I can say is, it's beastly of you. You might have warned me. What on earth will Richard say?

SIMON: Something exquisitely non-committal, I expect.

JUDITH: This is too much! Do you mean to tell me, Simon——

SIMON [*firmly*]: Yes, mother, I do. I've asked Myra down, and I have a perfect right to. You've always brought us up to be free about things.

JUDITH: Myra Arundel is straining freedom to its utmost limits.

SIMON: Don't you like her?

JUDITH: No, dear, I detest her. She's far too old for you, and she goes about using Sex as a sort of shrimping net.

SIMON: Really, mother——!

JUDITH: It's no use being cross. You know perfectly well I dislike her, and that's why you never told me she was coming until too late to stop her. It's intolerable of you.

SOREL [*grandly*]: Whether she's here or not is a matter of extreme indifference to me, but I'm afraid Richard won't like her very much.

SIMON: You're afraid he'll like her too much.

SOREL: That was an offensive remark, Simon, and rather silly.

JUDITH [*plaintively*]: Why on earth don't you fall in love with nice young girls, instead of self-conscious vampires?

SIMON: She's not a vampire, and I never said I was in love with her.

SOREL: He's crazy about her. She butters him up and admires his sketches.

SIMON: What about you picking up old gentlemen at dances?

SOREL [*furiously*]: He's *not* old!

JUDITH: You've both upset me thoroughly. I wanted a nice, restful week-end, with moments of Sandy's ingenuous affection to warm the cockles of my heart when I felt in the mood, and now the house is going to be full of discord—not enough food, everyone fighting for the bath—perfect agony! I wish I were dead!

SIMON: You needn't worry about Myra and me. We shall keep out of everyone's way.

SOREL: I shall take Richard on the river all day tomorrow.

JUDITH: In what?

SOREL: The punt.

JUDITH: I absolutely forbid you to go near the punt.

SIMON: It's sure to rain, anyhow.

JUDITH: What your father will say I tremble to think. He needs complete quiet to finish off *The Sinful Woman*.

SOREL: I see no reason for there to be any noise, unless Sandy What's-his-name is given to shouting.

JUDITH: If you're rude to Sandy I shall be extremely angry.

[*Together*]:

SOREL: Now, look here, mother——

SIMON: Why you should expect——

JUDITH: He's coming all the way down specially to be nice to me——

[*Enter David down stairs. He looks slightly irritable.*]

DAVID: Why are you all making such a noise?

JUDITH: I think I'm going mad.

DAVID: Why hasn't Clara brought me my tea?

JUDITH: I don't know.

DAVID: Where is Clara?

JUDITH: Do stop firing questions at me, David.

DAVID: Why are you all so irritable? What's happened?

[*Enter Clara, with a tray of tea for one.*]

CLARA: Here's your tea. I'm sorry I'm late with it. Amy forgot to put the kettle on—she's got terrible toothache.

DAVID: Poor girl! Give her some oil of cloves.

SOREL: If anyone else mentions oil of cloves, I shall do something desperate.

DAVID: It's wonderful stuff. Where's Zoe?

SIMON: She was in the garden this morning.

DAVID: I suppose no one thought of giving her any lunch?

CLARA: I put it down by the kitchen table as usual, but she never came in for it.

SOREL: She's probably mousing.

DAVID: She isn't old enough yet. She might have fallen into the river, for all you care. I think it's a shame!

CLARA: Don't you worry your head—Zoe won't come to any harm; she's too wily.

DAVID: I don't want to be disturbed. [*He takes his tray and goes upstairs; then he turns.*] Listen, Simon. There's a perfectly sweet flapper coming down by the four-thirty. Will you go and meet her and be nice to her? She's an abject fool, but a useful type, and I want to study her a little in domestic surroundings. She can sleep in the Japanese room. [*He goes off, leaving behind him a deathly silence.*]

JUDITH: I should like some one to play something very beautiful to me on the piano.

SIMON: Damn everything! Damn! Damn! Damn!

SOREL: Swearing doesn't help.

SIMON: It helps me a lot.

SOREL: What does father mean by going on like that?

JUDITH: In view of the imminent reception, you'd better go and shave, Simon.

SOREL [*bursting into tears of rage*]: It's perfectly beastly! Whenever I make any sort of plan about anything it's always done in by some one. I wish I were earning my own living somewhere—a free agent—able to do whatever I liked without being cluttered up and frustrated by the family——

JUDITH [*picturesquely*]: It grieves me to hear you say that, Sorel.

SOREL: Don't be infuriating, mother.

JUDITH [*sadly*]: A change has come over my children of late. I have tried to shut my eyes to it, but in vain. At my time of life one must face bitter facts!

SIMON: This is going to be the blackest Saturday till Monday we've ever spent.

JUDITH [*tenderly*]: Sorel, you mustn't cry.

SOREL: Don't sympathize with me; it's only temper.

JUDITH [*clasping her*]: Put your head on my shoulder, dear.

SIMON [*bitterly*]: Your head like the golden fleece . . .

SOREL: Richard'll have to have "Little Hell" and that horrible flapper the Japanese room.

JUDITH: Over my dead body!

SIMON: Mother, what *are* we to do?

JUDITH [*drawing him forcibly into her arms so that there is a charming little motherly picture*]: We must all be very, very kind to everyone!

SIMON: Now then, mother, none of that!

JUDITH [*aggrieved*]: I don't know what you mean, Simon.

SIMON: You were being beautiful and sad.

JUDITH: But I am beautiful and sad.

SIMON: You're not particularly beautiful, darling, and you never were.

JUDITH [*glancing at herself in the glass*]: Never mind; I made thousands think I was.

SIMON: And as for being sad——

JUDITH: Now, Simon, I will not be dictated to like this. If I say I'm sad, I *am* sad. You don't understand, because you're precocious and tiresome. . . . There comes a time in all women's lives——

SOREL: Oh dear!

JUDITH: What did you say, Sorel?

SOREL [*recovering*]: I said, "Oh dear!"

JUDITH: Well, please don't say it again, because it annoys me.

SOREL: You're such a lovely hypocrite.

JUDITH [*casting up her eyes*]: I'm sure I don't know what I've done to be cursed with such ungrateful children. It's very cruel at my time of life——

SIMON: There you go again!

JUDITH [*inconsequently*]: You're getting far too tall, Sorel.

SOREL: Sorry, mother.

JUDITH: Give me another of those disgusting cigarettes—I don't know where they came from.

SIMON [*giving her one*]: Here. [*He lights it for her.*]

JUDITH: I'm going to forget entirely about all these dreadful people arriving. My mind henceforward shall be a blank on the subject.

SOREL: It's all very fine, mother, but——

JUDITH: I made a great decision this morning.

SIMON: What kind of decision?

JUDITH: It's a secret.

SOREL: Aren't you going to tell us?

JUDITH: Of course. I meant it was a secret from your father.

SIMON: What is it?

JUDITH: I'm going back to the stage.

SIMON: I knew it!

JUDITH: I'm stagnating, you see. I won't stagnate as long as there's breath left in my body.

SOREL: Do you think it's wise? You retired so very finally last year. What excuse will you give for returning so soon?

JUDITH: My public, dear—letters from my public!

SIMON: Have you had any?

JUDITH: One or two. That's what decided me, really—I ought to have had hundreds.

SOREL: We'll write some lovely ones, and you can publish them in the papers.

JUDITH: Of course.

SOREL: You will be dignified about it all, won't you, darling?

JUDITH: I'm much more dignified on the stage than in the country—it's my *milieu*. I've tried terribly hard to be "landed gentry," but without any real success. I long for excitement and glamour. Think of the thrill of a first night; all those ardent playgoers willing one to succeed; the critics all leaning forward with glowing faces, receptive and exultant—emitting queer little inarticulate noises as some witty line tickles their fancy. The satisfied grunt of the *Daily Mail*, the abandoned gurgle of the *Sunday Times*, and the shrill, enthusiastic scream of the *Daily Express!* I can distinguish them all——

SIMON: Have you got a play?

JUDITH: I think I shall revive "Love's Whirlwind."

SOREL [*collapsing on to sofa*]: Oh, mother! [*She gurgles with laughter.*]

SIMON [*weakly*]: Father will be furious.

JUDITH: I can't help that.

SOREL: It's such a fearful play.

JUDITH: It's a marvelous part. You mustn't say too much against it, Sorel. I'm willing to laugh at it a little myself, but, after all, it *was* one of my greatest successes.

SIMON: Oh, it's appalling—but I love it. It makes me laugh.

JUDITH: The public love it too, and it doesn't make them laugh —much. [*She recites*]: "You are a fool, a blind, pitiable fool. You think because you have bought my body that you have bought my soul!" You must say that's dramatic.—"I've dreamed of love like this, but I never realized, I never knew how beautiful it could be in reality!" That line always brought a tear to my eye.

SIMON: The second act *is* the best, there's no doubt about that.

JUDITH: From the moment Victor comes in it's strong—tremendously strong. . . . Be Victor a minute, Sorel——

SOREL: Do you mean when he comes in at the end of the act?

JUDITH: Yes, you know—"Is this a game?"

SOREL [*with feeling*]: "Is this a game?"

JUDITH [*with spirit*]: "Yes—and a game that must be played to the finish."

SIMON: "Zara, what does this mean?"

JUDITH: "So many illusions shattered—so many dreams trodden in the dust!"

SOREL: I'm George now—"I don't understand! You and Victor —My God!"

JUDITH: "Sssh! Isn't that little Pam crying?"

SIMON [*savagely*]: "She'll cry more, poor mite, when she realizes her mother is a——"

JUDITH [*shrieking*]: "Don't say it—don't say it!"

SOREL: "Spare her that."

JUDITH: "I've given you all that makes life worth living—my youth, my womanhood, and now my child. Would you tear the very heart out of me? I tell you that it's infamous that men like you should be allowed to pollute society. You have ruined my life—I have nothing left—nothing. God in heaven, where am I to turn for help. . . ."

SOREL [*through clenched teeth*]: "Is this true? Answer me—is this true?"

JUDITH [*wailing*]: "Yes, yes!"

SOREL [*springing at Simon*]: "You cur!" [*The front door bell rings.*]

JUDITH: Damn! There's the bell.

SOREL [*rushing to the glass*]: I look hideous!

SIMON: Yes, dear.

[*Clara enters.*]

JUDITH: Clara—before you open the door—we shall be eight for dinner.

CLARA: My God!

SIMON: And for breakfast, lunch, tea, and dinner to-morrow.

JUDITH [*vaguely*]: Will you get various rooms ready?

CLARA: I shall have to—they can't sleep in the passage.

SOREL: How we've upset Clara.

JUDITH: It can't be helped—nothing can be helped. It's fate—everything that happens is fate. That's always a great comfort to me.

CLARA: More like arrant selfishness.

JUDITH: You mustn't be pert, Clara.

CLARA: Pert I may be, but I 'ave got some thought for others. Eight for dinner—Amy going home early. It's more nor less than an imposition.

[*The bell rings again.*]

SIMON: Hadn't you better let them all in?

[*Clara goes to the front door and admits Sandy Tyrell, who is a fresh-looking young man; he has an unspoiled, youthful sense of honor and rather big hands, owing to a misplaced enthusiasm for amateur boxing. Clara goes out.*]

SANDY [*to Judith*]: I say, it's perfectly ripping of you to let me come down.

JUDITH: Are you alone?

SANDY [*surprised*]: Yes.

JUDITH: I mean, you didn't meet anyone at the station?

SANDY: I motored down; my car's outside. Would you like me to meet anybody?

JUDITH: Oh no. I must introduce you. This is my daughter Sorel, and my son Simon.

SANDY [*shaking hands*]: How-do-you-do.

SOREL [*coldly*]: I'm extremely well, thank you, and I hope you are.

SIMON: So do I.

[*They both go upstairs rather grandly. Sandy looks shattered.*]

JUDITH: You must forgive me for having rather peculiar children. Have you got a bag or anything?

SANDY: Yes; it's in the car.

JUDITH: We'd better leave it there for the moment, as Clara has to get the tea. We'll find you a room afterwards.

SANDY: I've been looking forward to this most awfully.

JUDITH: It is nice, isn't it? You can see as far as Marlow on a clear day, they tell me.

SANDY: I meant I've been looking forward to seeing you.

JUDITH: How perfectly sweet of you. Would you like a drink?

SANDY: No, thanks. I'm in training.

JUDITH [*sitting on sofa and motioning him to sit beside her*]: How lovely. What for?

SANDY: I'm boxing again in a couple of weeks.

JUDITH: I must come to your first night.

SANDY: You look simply splendid.

JUDITH: I'm so glad. You know, you mustn't mind if Simon and Sorel insult you a little—they've been very bad-tempered lately.

SANDY: It's awfully funny you having a grown-up son and daughter at all. I can hardly believe it.

JUDITH [*quickly*]: I was married very young.

SANDY: I don't wonder. You know, it's frightfully queer the way I've been planning to know you for ages, and I never did until last week.

JUDITH: I liked you from the first, really, because you're such a nice shape.

SANDY [*slightly embarrassed*]: Oh, I see . . .

JUDITH: Small hips and lovely long legs—I wish Simon had smaller hips. Do you think you could teach him to box?

SANDY: Rather—if he likes.

JUDITH: That's just the trouble—I'm afraid he won't like. He's so dreadfully un—— that sort of thing. But never mind; you must use your influence subtly. I'm sure David would be pleased.

SANDY: Who's David?

JUDITH: My husband.

SANDY [*surprised*]: Oh!

JUDITH: Why do you say "Oh" like that? Didn't you know I had a husband?

SANDY: I thought he was dead.

JUDITH: No, he's not dead; he's upstairs.

SANDY: You're quite different from what you were the other day.

JUDITH: It's this garden hat—I'll take it off. [*She does so.*] There. I've been pruning the calceolarias.

SANDY [*puzzled*]: Oh?——

JUDITH: I love my garden, you know—it's so peaceful and quaint. I spend long days dreaming away in it—you know how one dreams.

SANDY: Oh yes.

JUDITH [*warming up*]: I always longed to leave the brittle glamour of cities and theaters and find rest in some Old World nook. That's why we came to Cookham.

SANDY: It's awfully nice—Cookham.

JUDITH: Have you ever seen me on the stage?

SANDY: Rather!

JUDITH: What in?

SANDY: That thing when you pretended to cheat at cards to save your husband's good name.

JUDITH: Oh, "The Bold Deceiver." That play was never quite right.

SANDY: You were absolutely wonderful. That was when I first fell in love with you.

JUDITH [*delighted*]: Was it, really?

SANDY: Yes; you were so frightfully pathetic and brave.

JUDITH [*basking*]: Was I?

SANDY: Rather! [*There is a pause.*]

JUDITH: Well, go on. . . .

SANDY: I feel such a fool, telling you what I think, as though it mattered.

JUDITH: Of course it matters—to me, anyhow.

SANDY: Does it—honestly?

JUDITH: Certainly.

SANDY: It seems too good to be true—sitting here and talking as though we were old friends.

JUDITH: We *are* old friends—we probably met in another life. Reincarnation, you know—fascinating!

SANDY: You do say ripping things.

JUDITH: Do I? Give me a cigarette and let's put our feet up.

SANDY: All right.

[*They settle themselves comfortably at opposite ends of the sofa, smoking.*]

JUDITH: Can you punt?

SANDY: Yes—a bit.

JUDITH: You must teach Simon—he always gets the pole stuck.

SANDY: I'd rather teach you.

JUDITH: You're so gallant and chivalrous—much more like an American than an Englishman.

SANDY: I should like to go on saying nice things to you forever.

JUDITH [*giving him her hand*]: Sandy! [*There comes a loud ring at the bell. Judith jumps.*] There now!

SANDY: Is anyone else coming to stay?

JUDITH: Anyone else! You don't know—you just don't know. Give me my hat.

SANDY [*giving it to her*]: You said it would be quite quiet, with nobody at all.

JUDITH: I was wrong. It's going to be very noisy, with herds of angry people stamping about.

[*Clara enters and opens the front door. Myra Arundel is posed outside, consciously well dressed, with several suitcases and a tennis racquet.*]

MYRA [*advancing*]: Judith—my—dear—this is divine!

JUDITH [*emptily*]: Too, too lovely.—Where are the others?

MYRA: What others? [*Clara goes out.*]

JUDITH: Did you come by the four-thirty?

MYRA: Yes.

JUDITH: Didn't you see anyone at the station?

MYRA: Yes; several people, but I didn't know they were coming here.

JUDITH: Well, they are.

MYRA: Sorel said it was going to be just ourselves this week-end.

JUDITH [*sharply*]: Sorel?

MYRA: Yes—didn't she tell you she'd asked me? Weren't you expecting me?

JUDITH: Simon muttered something about your coming, but Sorel didn't mention it. Wasn't that odd of her?

MYRA: You're a divinely mad family. [*To Sandy*]: How-do-you-do? It's useless to wait for introductions with the Blisses. My name's Myra Arundel.

JUDITH [*airily*]: Sandy Tyrell, Myra Arundel; Myra Arundel, Sandy Tyrell. There.

MYRA: Is that your car outside?

SANDY: Yes.

MYRA: Well, Judith, I *do* think you might have told me someone was motoring down. A nice car would have been so much more comfortable than that beastly train.

JUDITH: I never knew you were coming until a little while ago.

MYRA: It's heavenly here—after London. The heat was terrible when I left. You look awfully well, Judith. Rusticating obviously agrees with you.

JUDITH: I'm glad you think so. Personally, I feel that a nervous breakdown is imminent.

MYRA: My dear, how ghastly! What's the matter?

JUDITH: Nothing's the matter yet, Myra, but I have presentiments. Come upstairs, Sandy, and I'll show you your room. [*She begins to go upstairs, followed by Sandy. Then she turns.*] I'll send Simon down to you. He's shaving, I think, but you won't mind that, will you? [*She goes off.*]

[*Myra makes a slight grimace after her, then she helps herself to a cigarette and wanders about the hall—she might almost play the piano a little; anyhow, she is perfectly at home.*]

[*Simon comes downstairs very fast, putting on his coat. He has apparently finished his toilet.*]

SIMON: Myra, this is marvelous! [*He tries to kiss her.*]

MYRA [*pushing him away*]: No, Simon dear; it's too hot.

SIMON: You look beautifully cool.

MYRA: I'm more than cool really, but it's not climatic coolness. I've been mentally chilled to the marrow by Judith's attitude.

SIMON: Why, what did she say?

MYRA: Nothing very much. She was bouncing about on the sofa with a hearty young thing in flannels, and seemed to resent my appearance rather.

SIMON: You mustn't take any notice of mother.

MYRA: I'll try not to, but it's difficult.

SIMON: She adores you, really.

MYRA: I'm sure she does.

SIMON: She's annoyed to-day because father and Sorel have been asking people down without telling her.

MYRA: Poor dear! I quite see why.

SIMON: You look enchanting.

MYRA: Thank you, Simon.

SIMON: Are you pleased to see me?

MYRA: Of course. That's why I came.

SIMON: Darling!

MYRA: Sssh! Don't shout.

SIMON: I feel most colossally temperamental—I should like to kiss you and kiss you and kiss you and break everything in the house and then jump into the river.

MYRA: Dear Simon!

SIMON: You're everything I want you to be—absolutely everything. Marvelous clothes, marvelous looks, marvelous brain— Oh, God, it's terrible. . . .

MYRA: I dined with Charlie Templeton last night.

SIMON: Well, you're a devil. You only did it to annoy me. He's far too plump, and he can't do anything but dither about the Embassy in badly cut trousers. You loathe him, really; you know you do—you're too intelligent not to. You couldn't like him and me at the same time—it's impossible!

MYRA: Don't be so conceited.

SIMON: Darling—I adore you.

MYRA: That's right.

SIMON: But you're callous—that's what it is, callous! You don't care a damn. You don't love me a bit, do you?

MYRA: Love's a very big word, Simon.

SIMON: It isn't—it's tiny. What are we to do?

MYRA: What do you mean?

SIMON: We can't go on like this.

MYRA: I'm not going on like anything.

SIMON: Yes, you are; you're going on like Medusa, and there are awful snakes popping their heads out at me from under your hat—I shall be turned to stone in a minute, and then you'll be sorry.

MYRA [*laughing*]: You're very sweet, and I'm *very* fond of you.

SIMON: Tell me what you've been doing—everything.

MYRA: Nothing.

SIMON: What did you do after you'd dined with Charlie Templeton?

MYRA: Supped with Charlie Templeton.

SIMON: Well, I don't mind a bit. I hope you ate a lot and enjoyed yourself—there!

MYRA: Generous boy! Come and kiss me.

SIMON: You're only playing up to me now; you don't really want to a bit.

MYRA: I'm aching for it.

SIMON [*kissing her violently*]: I love you.

MYRA: This week-end's going to be strenuous.

SIMON: Hell upon earth—fifteen million people in the house. We'll get up at seven and rush away down the river.

MYRA: No, we won't.

SIMON: Don't let either of us agree to anything we say—we'll both be difficult. I love being difficult.

MYRA: You certainly do.

SIMON: But I'm in the most lovely mood now. Just seeing you makes me feel grand——

MYRA: Is your father here?

SIMON: Yes; he's working on a new novel.

MYRA: He writes brilliantly.

SIMON: Doesn't he? He drinks too much tea, though.

MYRA: It can't do him much harm, surely?

SIMON: It tans the stomach.

MYRA: Who is Sandy Tyrell?

SIMON: Never heard of him.

MYRA: He's here, with Judith.

SIMON: Oh, that poor thing with hot hands! We'll ignore him.

MYRA: I thought he looked rather nice.

SIMON: You must be mad. He looked disgusting.

MYRA [*laughing*]: Idiot!

SIMON [*flinging himself on the sofa*]: Smooth my hair with your soft white hands.

MYRA [*ruffling it*]: It's got glue on it.

SIMON [*catching her hand and kissing it*]: You smell heavenly. What is it?

MYRA: Borgia of Rosine.

SIMON: How appropriate. [*He pulls her down and kisses her.*]

MYRA [*breaking away*]: You're too demonstrative to-day, Simon.

[*The front door bell rings.*]

SIMON: Damn, damn! It's those drearies.

[*Myra powders her nose as Clara crosses to open door. Richard Greatham and Jackie Coryton come in. There is, by this time, a good deal of luggage on the step. Richard is iron-gray and tall; Jackie is small and shingled, with an ingenuous manner which will lose its charm as she grows older.*]

RICHARD: This is Mrs. Bliss's house.

CLARA [*offhand*]: Oh yes, this is it.

RICHARD: Is Miss Sorel Bliss in?

CLARA: I expect so. I'll see if I can find her. [*She goes upstairs, humming a tune.*]

SIMON: Hallo. Did you have a nice journey?

RICHARD: Yes, thank you, very nice. I met Miss Coryton at the station. We introduced ourselves while we were waiting for the only taxi to come back.

MYRA: Oh, *I* took the only taxi. How maddening of me.

RICHARD: Mrs. Arundel! How-do-you-do. I never recognized you.

[*They shake hands.*]

JACKIE: I did.

MYRA: Why? Have we met anywhere?

JACKIE: No; I mean I recognized you as the one who took the taxi.

RICHARD [*to Simon*]: You are Sorel's brother?

SIMON: Yes; she'll be down in a minute. Come out into the garden, Myra——

MYRA: But, Simon, we can't. . . .

SIMON [*grabbing her hand and dragging her off*]: Yes, we can. I shall go mad if I stay in the house a moment longer. [*Over his shoulder to Richard and Jackie*]: Tea will be here soon.

[*He and Myra go off.*]

JACKIE: Well!

RICHARD: A strange young man.

JACKIE: Very rude, I think.

RICHARD: Have you ever met him before?

JACKIE: No; I don't know any of them except Mr. Bliss—he's a wonderful person.

RICHARD: I wonder if he knows you're here.

JACKIE: Perhaps that funny woman who opened the door will tell him.

RICHARD: It was fortunate that we met at the station.

JACKIE: I'm frightfully glad. I should have been terrified arriving all by myself.

RICHARD: I do hope the weather will keep good over Sunday —the country round here is delightful.

JACKIE: Yes.

RICHARD: There's nowhere like England in the spring and summer.

JACKIE: No, there isn't, is there?

RICHARD: There's a sort of *quality* you find in no other countries.

JACKIE: Have you traveled a lot?

RICHARD [*modestly*]: A good deal.

JACKIE: How lovely. [*There is a pause.*]

RICHARD: Spain is very beautiful.

JACKIE: Yes, I've always heard Spain was awfully nice.

RICHARD: Except for the bull-fights. No one who ever really loved horses could enjoy a bull-fight.

JACKIE: Nor anyone who loved bulls, either.

RICHARD: Exactly.

JACKIE: Italy's awfully nice, isn't it?

RICHARD: Oh yes, charming.

JACKIE: I've always wanted to go to Italy.

RICHARD: Rome is a beautiful city.

JACKIE: Yes, I've always heard Rome was lovely.

RICHARD: And Naples and Capri—Capri's enchanting.

JACKIE: It must be.

RICHARD: Have you ever been abroad at all?

JACKIE: Oh yes: I went to Dieppe once—we had a house there for the summer.

RICHARD [*kindly*]: Dear little place—Dieppe.

JACKIE: Yes, it was lovely.

[*Judith comes downstairs, followed by Sandy, with his arms full of cushions. She motions him out into the garden, sits down and puts on her goloshes, and then follows him.*]

JACKIE: Well!

RICHARD: Russia used to be a wonderful country before the war.

JACKIE: It must have been. . . . Was that her?

RICHARD: Who?

JACKIE: Judith Bliss.

RICHARD: Yes, I expect it was.

JACKIE: I wish I'd never come.

RICHARD: You mustn't worry. They're a very Bohemian family, I believe.

JACKIE: I wonder if Mr. Bliss knows I'm here.

RICHARD: I wonder.

JACKIE: Couldn't we ring a bell, or anything?

RICHARD: Yes, perhaps we'd better. [*He finds bell and presses it.*]

JACKIE: I don't suppose it rings.

RICHARD: You mustn't be depressed.

JACKIE: I feel horrid.

RICHARD: It's always a little embarrassing coming to a strange house for the first time. You'll like Sorel—she's charming.

JACKIE [*desperately*]: I wonder where she is.

RICHARD [*consolingly*]: I expect tea will be here soon.

JACKIE: Do you think they *have* tea?

RICHARD [*alarmed*]: Oh yes—they must.

JACKIE: Oh, well, we'd better go on waiting, then. [*She sits down.*]

RICHARD: Do you mind if I smoke?

JACKIE: Not a bit.

RICHARD: Will you?

JACKIE: No, thank you.

RICHARD [*sitting down*]: I got this case in Japan. It's pretty, isn't it?

JACKIE: Awfully pretty.

[*They lapse into hopeless silence. Enter Sorel, down stairs.*]

SOREL: Oh, Richard, I'm dreadfully sorry. I didn't know you were here.

RICHARD: We've been here a good while.

SOREL: How awful! Please forgive me. I was upstairs.

RICHARD: This is Miss Coryton.

SOREL: Oh!

JACKIE: How-do-you-do.

SOREL: Have you come to see father?

JACKIE: Yes.

SOREL: He's in his study—you'd better go up.

JACKIE: I don't know the way.

SOREL [*irritably*]: Oh, well—I'll take you. Come on. Wait a minute, Richard. [*She takes her to the top of the stairs.*] It's along that passage, and the third door on the right.

JACKIE: Oh, thank you. [*She goes out despondently.*]

SOREL [*coming down again*]: The poor girl looks half-witted.

RICHARD: She's shy, I think.

SOREL: I hope father will find her a comfort.

RICHARD: Tell me one thing, Sorel, did your father and mother know I was coming?

SOREL: Oh yes; they were awfully pleased.

RICHARD: A rather nice-looking woman came down, in a big hat, and went into the garden with a young man, without saying a word.

SOREL: That was mother, I expect. We're an independent family—we entertain our friends sort of separately.

RICHARD: Oh, I see.

SOREL: It was sweet of you to come.

RICHARD: I wanted to come—I've thought about you a lot.

SOREL: Have you, really? That's thrilling.

RICHARD: I mean it. You're so alive and vital and different from other people.

SOREL: I'm so frightened that you'll be bored here.

RICHARD: Why should I be?

SOREL: Oh, I don't know. But you won't be, will you?—or if you are, tell me at once, and we'll do something quite different.

RICHARD: You're rather a dear, you know.

SOREL: I'm not—I'm devastating, entirely lacking in restraint. So's Simon. It's father's and mother's fault, really; you see, they're so vague—they've spent their lives cultivating their arts and not devoting any time to ordinary conventions and manners and things. I'm the only one who sees that, so I'm trying to be better. I'd love to be beautifully poised and carry off difficult situations with a lift of the eyebrows——

RICHARD: I'm sure you could carry off anything.

SOREL: There you are, you see, saying the right thing! You always say the right thing, and no one knows a bit what you're really thinking. That's what I adore.

RICHARD: I'm afraid to say anything now, in case you think I'm only being correct.

SOREL: But you are correct. I wish you'd teach Simon to be correct too.

RICHARD: It would be uphill work, I'm afraid.

SOREL: Why, don't you like him?

RICHARD: I've only met him for a moment.

SOREL: Would you like to see the garden?

RICHARD: Very much indeed.

SOREL: As a matter of fact, we'd better wait until after tea. Shall I sing you something?

RICHARD: Please—I should love it.

SOREL: I don't want to really a bit—only I'm trying to entertain you. It's as easy as pie to talk in some one else's house, like at the dance the other night, but here on my own ground I'm finding it difficult.

RICHARD [*puzzled*]: I'm sorry.

SOREL: Oh, it isn't your fault; honestly, it isn't—you're awfully kind and responsive. What shall we do?

RICHARD: I'm quite happy talking—to you.

SOREL: Can you play Mah Jong?

RICHARD: No, I'm afraid I can't.

SOREL: I'm *so* glad—I *do* hate it so.

[*Clara enters, with preparations for tea. Sorel sighs with relief.*] Here's tea.

CLARA: Where's your mother, dear?

SOREL: Out in the garden, I think.

CLARA: It's starting to rain.

SOREL: Oh, everyone will come dashing in, then. How awful!

RICHARD: Won't the luggage get rather wet, out there?

SOREL: What luggage?

CLARA: I'll bring it in when I've made the tea.

RICHARD [*rising*]: Oh, don't trouble; I'll do it now.

SOREL: We ought to have got William up from the village.

CLARA: It's Saturday.

SOREL: I know it is.

CLARA: He's playing cricket.

[*Richard opens the front door and proceeds to bring the luggage in. Sorel rushes to help him.*]

SOREL: Do sit down and smoke. I can easily manage it.

RICHARD: Certainly not.

SOREL: How typical of Myra to have so many bags. . . . Ooh! [*She staggers with a suitcase. Richard goes to her assistance, and they both drop it.*] There now!—we've probably broken something.

RICHARD: This is the last one. . . . [*He brings in a dressing-case, and wipes his hands on his handkerchief.*]

SOREL: Do you know where to wash if you want to?

RICHARD: No—but I'm all right.

[*Re-enter Clara, with tea and hot-water jug. Simon and Myra come in from the garden.*]

MYRA: Hullo, Sorel, how are you?

SOREL: I'm splendid. Do you know Mr. Greatham?

MYRA: Oh yes; we've met several times.

SIMON: Come and sit down, Myra.

[*David and Jackie come downstairs.*]

DAVID: Is tea ready?

SOREL: Yes; just.

DAVID: Simon, come and be nice to Miss Coryton.

SIMON: We've met already.

DAVID: That's no reason for you not to be nice to her.

MYRA [*firmly*]: How-do-you-do.

DAVID: How-do-you-do. Are you staying here?

MYRA: I hope so.

DAVID: You must forgive me for being rather frowsy, but I've been working hard.

SOREL: Father, this is Mr. Greatham.

DAVID: How are you? When did you arrive?

RICHARD: This afternoon.

DAVID: Good. Have some tea. [*He begins to pour it out.*] Everyone had better put their own sugar and milk in, or we shall get muddled. Where's your mother, Simon?

SIMON: She was last seen in the punt.

DAVID: How extraordinary! She can't punt.

SOREL: Sandy Tyrell's with her.

DAVID: Oh, well, she'll be all right then. Who is he?

SOREL: I don't know.

DAVID: Do sit down, everybody.

[*Enter Judith and Sandy from the garden.*]

JUDITH: There's going to be a thunderstorm. I felt sick this morning. This is Sandy Tyrell—everybody——

RICHARD [*shaking hands*]: How-do-you-do.

SOREL: Mother, I want you to meet Mr. Greatham.

JUDITH: Oh yes. You were here before, weren't you?

SIMON: Before *what*, darling?

JUDITH: Before I went out in the punt. There was somebody else here too—a fair girl—[*She sees Jackie.*] Oh, there you are. How-do-you-do. Sit down, Sandy, and eat anything you want. Give Sandy some bread-and-butter, Simon.

[*Everybody sits down.*]

SIMON [*ungraciously*]: Here you are.

SANDY: Thanks.

[*There is a long pause; then Myra and Richard speak together.*]

RICHARD: How far are you from Maidenhead exactly?

MYRA: What a pity it's raining—we might have had some tennis——

[*They both stop, to let the other go on. There is another terrible silence.*]

MYRA: I adore the shape of this hall—it's so——

RICHARD: The train was awfully crowded coming down——

[*They both stop again, and there is another dead silence, during which the curtain slowly falls.*]

ACT TWO

IT IS AFTER DINNER *on the Saturday evening. Everyone is talking and arguing. The following scene should be played with great speed.*

SIMON: Who'll go out?

SOREL: I don't mind.

SIMON: No; you always guess it too quickly.

JACKIE: What do we have to do?

JUDITH: Choose an adverb, and then——

SIMON: Some one goes out, you see, and comes in, and you've chosen a word among yourselves, and she or he or whoever it is asks you some sort of question and you have to——

SOREL: Not an ordinary question, Simon; they have to ask them to do something in the manner of the word, and then——

SIMON: Then, you see, you act whatever it is——

SOREL: The answer to the question, you see?

RICHARD [*apprehensively*]: What sort of thing is one expected to do?

JUDITH: Quite usual things, like reciting "If," or playing the piano——

RICHARD: I can't play the piano.

SIMON: Never mind; you can fake it, as long as it conveys an idea of the word.

JACKIE: The word we've all thought of?

534

SOREL [*impatient*]: Yes, the word we've chosen when whoever it is is out of the room.

JACKIE: I'm afraid I don't quite understand yet.

SIMON: Never mind; I'll explain. You see, some one goes out. . . .

SOREL: I'll go out the first time, just to show her.

JUDITH: It's quite simple—all you have to do is just act in the manner of the word.

SOREL: Look here, everybody, I'm going out.

SIMON: All right; go on.

MYRA: The History game's awfully good—when two people go out, and come back as Queen Elizabeth and Crippen or somebody.

SANDY [*despondently*]: I'm no earthly good at this sort of thing.

SOREL: I'll show you, Sandy. You see. . . .

JUDITH: There's always "How, When and Where?" We haven't played that for ages.

SIMON: We will afterwards. We'll do this one first.—Go on, Sorel.

SOREL: Don't be too long. [*She goes out.*]

SIMON: Now then.

JUDITH: "Bitterly."

SIMON: No, we did that last week; she'll know.

DAVID: "Intensely."

JUDITH: Too difficult.

RICHARD: There was an amusing game I played once at the Harringtons' house. Everyone was blindfolded except——

SIMON: This room's not big enough for that. What about "winsomely"?

JACKIE: I wish I knew what we had to do.

JUDITH: You'll see when we start playing.

MYRA: *If* we start playing.

SIMON: Mother's brilliant at this. Do you remember when we played it at the Mackenzies'?

JUDITH: Yes, and Blanche was so cross when I kissed Freddie's ear in the manner of the word.

RICHARD: What was the word?

JUDITH: I can't remember.

MYRA: Perhaps it's as well.

DAVID: What about "drearily"?

JUDITH: Not definite enough.

SIMON: "Winsomely" is the best.

JUDITH: She's sure to guess it straight off.

SIMON [*confidentially to Jackie*]: These games are much too brainy for me.

DAVID: Young Norman Robertson used to be marvelous— do you remember?

SIMON: Yes, wonderful sense of humor.

MYRA: He's lost it all since his marriage.

JUDITH: I didn't know you knew him.

MYRA: Well, considering he married my cousin——

RICHARD: We don't seem to be getting on with the game.

JUDITH: We haven't thought of a word yet.

MYRA: "Brightly."

SIMON: Too obvious.

MYRA: Very well—don't snap at me!

JUDITH: "Saucily." I've got a lovely idea for "saucily."

MYRA [*at Simon*]: I should think "rudely" would be the easiest.

SIMON: Don't be sour, Myra.

JUDITH: The great thing is to get an obscure word.

SIMON: What a pity Irene isn't here—she knows masses of obscure words.

MYRA: She's probably picked them up from her obscure friends.

SIMON: It's no use being catty about Irene; she's a perfect darling.

MYRA: I wasn't being catty at all.

SIMON: Yes, you were.

SOREL [*off*]: Hurry up!

JUDITH: Quickly, now! We must think——

JACKIE [*helpfully*]: "Appendicitis."

JUDITH [*witheringly*]: That's not an adverb.

SIMON: You're thinking of charades.

SANDY: Charades are damned good fun.

SIMON: Yes, but we don't happen to be doing them at the moment.

SANDY: Sorry.

JUDITH: "Saucily."

SIMON: No, "winsomely" is better.

JUDITH: All right. Call her in.

SIMON [*calling*]: Sorel—come on; we're ready.

[*Re-enter Sorel.*]

SANDY [*hoarsely to Simon*]: Which is it?—"saucily" or "winsomely"?

SIMON [*whispering*]: "Winsomely."

SOREL [*to Judith*]: Go and take a flower out of that vase and give it to Richard.

JUDITH: Very well. [*She trips lightly over to the vase, gurgling with coy laughter, selects a flower, then goes over to Richard; pursing her lips into a mock smile, she gives him the flower, with a little girlish gasp at her own daring, and wags her finger archly at him.*]

SIMON: Marvelous, mother!

SOREL [*laughing*]: Oh, lovely! . . . Now, Myra, get up and say good-bye to everyone in the manner of the word.

MYRA [*rises and starts with David*]: Good-bye. It really has been most delightful——

JUDITH: No, no, no!

MYRA: Why—what do you mean?

JUDITH: You haven't got the right intonation a bit.

SIMON: Oh, mother darling, do shut up!

MYRA [*acidly*]: Remember what an advantage you have over us poor amateurs, Judith, having been a professional for so long.

JUDITH: I don't like "so long" very much.

SOREL: Do you think we might go on now?

MYRA: Go to the next one; I'm not going to do any more.

SIMON: Oh, please do. You were simply splendid.

SOREL: It doesn't matter. [*To Richard*]: Light a cigarette in the manner of the word.

RICHARD: I've forgotten what it is.

JUDITH [*grimacing at him violently*]: You remember. . . .

RICHARD: Oh yes. [*He proceeds to light a cigarette with great abandon, winking his eye and chucking Sorel under the chin.*]

JUDITH: Oh, no, no, no!

MYRA: I can't think *what* that's meant to be.

RICHARD [*offended*]: I was doing my best.

JUDITH: It's so *frightfully* easy, and nobody can do it right.

SIMON: I believe you've muddled it up.

RICHARD: You'd better go on to the next one.

JUDITH: Which word were you doing? Whisper——

RICHARD [*whispering*]: "Saucily."

JUDITH: I knew it!—He was doing the wrong word. [*She whispers to him.*]

RICHARD: Oh, I see. I'm so sorry.

JUDITH: Give him another chance.

SIMON: No, it's Jackie's turn now; it will come round to him again, I'm afraid.

SOREL [*to Jackie*]: Do a dance in the manner of the word.

JACKIE [*giggling*]: I can't.

JUDITH: Nonsense! Of course you can.

JACKIE: I can't—honestly—I . . .

SIMON [*pulling her to her feet*]: Go on; have a shot at it.

JACKIE: No, I'd much rather not. Count me out.

JUDITH: Really, the ridiculous fuss everyone makes——

JACKIE: I'm awfully stupid at anything like this.

SOREL: It's only a game, after all.

DAVID: Come along—try.

JACKIE [*dragging back*]: I couldn't—please don't ask me to. I simply couldn't.

SIMON: Leave her alone if she doesn't want to.

SOREL [*irritably*]: What's the use of playing at all, if people won't do it properly?

JUDITH: It's *so* simple.

SANDY: It's awfully difficult if you haven't done it before.

SIMON: Go on to the next one.

SOREL [*firmly*]: Unless everyone's in it we won't play at all.

SIMON: Now don't lose your temper.

SOREL: Lose my temper! I like that! No one's given me the slightest indication of what the word is—you all argue and squabble——

DAVID: Talk, talk, talk! Everybody talks too much.

JUDITH: It's so surprising to me when people won't play up. After all——

JACKIE [*with spirit*]: It's a hateful game, anyhow, and I don't want to play it again ever.

SOREL: You haven't played it at all yet.

SIMON: Don't be rude, Sorel.

SOREL: Really, Simon, the way you go on is infuriating!

SIMON: It's always the way; whenever Sorel goes out she gets quarrelsome.

SOREL: Quarrelsome!

SIMON: Don't worry, Jackie; you needn't do anything you don't want to.

JUDITH: I think, for the future, we'd better confine our efforts to social conversation and not attempt anything in the least intelligent.

SIMON: How can you be so unkind, mother?

JUDITH [*sharply*]: Don't speak to me like that.

JACKIE: It's all my fault—I know I'm awfully silly, but it embarrasses me so terribly doing anything in front of people.

SOREL [*with acidity*]: I should think the word was "winsomely."

SIMON: You must have been listening outside the door, then.

SOREL: Not at all—Miss Coryton gave it away.

SIMON: Why "Miss Coryton" all of a sudden? You've been calling her Jackie all the evening. You're far too grand, Sorel.

SOREL: And you're absolutely maddening—I'll never play another game with you as long as I live.

SIMON: That won't break my heart.

JUDITH: Stop, stop, stop!

SIMON [*grabbing Jackie's hand*]: Come out in the garden. I'm sick of this.

SOREL: Don't let him take you on the river; he isn't very good at it.

SIMON [*over his shoulder*]: Ha, ha!—very funny. [*He drags Jackie off.*]

JUDITH: Sorel, you're behaving disgracefully.

SOREL: Simon ought to go into the army, or something.

DAVID: You both ought to be in reformatories.

SOREL: This always happens whenever we play a game. We're a beastly family, and I hate us.

JUDITH: Speak for yourself, dear.

SOREL: I can't, without speaking for everyone else too—we're all exactly the same, and I'm ashamed of us.—Come into the library, Sandy. [*She drags Sandy off.*]

MYRA: Charming! It's all perfectly charming.

DAVID: I think it would be better, Judith, if you exercised a little more influence over the children.

JUDITH: That's right—blame it all on me.

DAVID: After all, dear, you started it, by snapping everybody up.

JUDITH: You ought never to have married me, David; it was a great mistake.

DAVID: The atmosphere of this house is becoming more unbearable every day, and all because Simon and Sorel are allowed to do exactly what they like.

JUDITH: You sit upstairs all day, writing your novels.

DAVID: Novels which earn us our daily bread.

JUDITH: "Daily bread" nonsense! We've got enough money to keep us in comfort until we die.

DAVID: That will be very soon, if we can't get a little peace. [*To Myra*]: Come out into the garden——

JUDITH: I sincerely hope the night air will cool you.

DAVID: I don't know what's happened to you lately, Judith.

JUDITH: Nothing's happened to me—nothing ever does. You're far too smug to allow it.

DAVID: Smug! Thank you.

JUDITH: Yes, smug, smug, smug! And pompous!

DAVID: I hope you haven't been drinking, dear.

JUDITH: Drinking! Huh! that's very amusing!

DAVID: I think it's rather tragic, at your time of life. [*He goes out with Myra.*]

JUDITH: David's been a good husband to me, but he's wearing a bit thin now.

RICHARD: Would you like me to go? To leave you alone for a little?

JUDITH: Why? Are you afraid I shall become violent?

RICHARD [*smiling*]: No; I merely thought perhaps I was in the way.

JUDITH: I hope you're not embarrassed—I couldn't bear you to be embarrassed.

RICHARD: Not in the least.

JUDITH: Marriage is a hideous affair altogether, don't you think?

RICHARD: I'm really hardly qualified to judge, you see.

JUDITH: Do stop being non-committal, just for once; it's doubly annoying in the face of us all having lost control so lamentably.

RICHARD: I'm sorry.

JUDITH: There's nothing to be sorry for, really, because, after all, it's your particular "thing," isn't it?—observing everything and not giving yourself away an inch.

RICHARD: I suppose it is.

JUDITH: You'll get used to us in time, you know, and then you'll feel cozier. Why don't you sit down? [*She sits on sofa.*]

RICHARD: I'm enjoying myself very much.

JUDITH: It's very sweet of you to say so, but I don't see how you can be.

RICHARD [*laughing suddenly*]: But I am!

JUDITH: There now! that was quite a genuine laugh. We're getting on. Are you in love with Sorel?

RICHARD [*surprised and embarrassed*]: In love with Sorel?

JUDITH [*repentantly*]: Now I've killed it—I've murdered the little tender feeling of comfort that was stealing over you, by sheer tactlessness! Will you teach me to be tactful?

RICHARD: Did you really think I was in love with Sorel?

JUDITH: It's so difficult to tell, isn't it?—I mean, you might not know yourself. She's very attractive.

RICHARD: Yes, she is—very.

JUDITH: Have you heard her sing?

RICHARD: No, not yet.

JUDITH: She sings beautifully. Are you susceptible to music?

RICHARD: I'm afraid I don't know very much about it.

JUDITH: You probably are, then. I'll sing you something.

RICHARD: Please do.

JUDITH [*rising*]: It's awfully sad for a woman of my temperament to have a grown-up daughter, you know. I have to put my pride in my pocket and develop in her all the charming little feminine tricks which will eventually cut me out altogether.

RICHARD: That wouldn't be possible.

JUDITH: I do hope you meant that, because it was a sweet remark. [*She is at the piano, turning over music.*]

RICHARD [*following her*]: Of course I meant it.

JUDITH: Will you lean on the piano in an attentive attitude? It's such a help.

RICHARD: You're an extraordinary person.

JUDITH [*beginning to play*]: In what way extraordinary?

RICHARD: When I first met Sorel, I guessed what you'd be like.

JUDITH: Did you, now? And am I?

RICHARD [*smiling*]: Exactly.

JUDITH: Oh, well. . . . [*She plays and sings a little French song. There is a slight pause when it is finished.*]

RICHARD [*with feeling*]: Thank you.

JUDITH [*rising from the piano*]: It's pretty, isn't it?

RICHARD: Perfectly enchanting.

JUDITH: Shall we sit down again? [*She reseats herself on sofa.*]

RICHARD: Won't you sing any more?

JUDITH: No, no more—I want you to talk to me and tell me all about yourslef, and the things you've done.

RICHARD: I've done nothing.

JUDITH: What a shame! Why not?

RICHARD: I never realize how dead I am until I meet people like you. It's depressing, you know.

JUDITH: What nonsense! You're not a bit dead.

RICHARD: Do you always live here?

JUDITH: I'm going to, from now onwards. I intend to sink into a very beautiful old age. When the children marry, I shall wear a cap.

RICHARD [smiling]: How absurd!

JUDITH: I don't mean a funny cap.

RICHARD: You're far too full of vitality to sink into anything.

JUDITH: It's entirely spurious vitality. If you troubled to look below the surface, you'd find a very wistful and weary spirit. I've been battling with life for a long time.

RICHARD: Surely such successful battles as yours have been are not wearying?

JUDITH: Yes, they are—frightfully. I've reached an age now when I just want to sit back and let things go on around me— and they do.

RICHARD: I should like to know exactly what you're thinking about—really.

JUDITH: I was thinking of calling you Richard. It's such a nice uncompromising name.

RICHARD: I should be very flattered if you would.

JUDITH: I won't suggest you calling me Judith until you feel really comfortable about me.

RICHARD: But I do—Judith.

JUDITH: I'm awfully glad. Will you give me a cigarette?

RICHARD [producing case]: Certainly.

JUDITH [taking one]: That's a divine case.

RICHARD: It was given to me in Japan three years ago. All those little designs mean things.

JUDITH [*bending over it*]: What sort of things?

RICHARD: Charms for happiness, and luck, and—love.

JUDITH: Which is the charm for love?

RICHARD: That one.

JUDITH: What a dear!

RICHARD [*kissing her gently*]: Judith!

JUDITH [*jumping*]: Richard!

RICHARD: I'm afraid I couldn't help it.

JUDITH [*dramatically*]: What are we to do? What are we to do?

RICHARD: I don't know.

JUDITH: David must be told—everything!

RICHARD [*alarmed*]: Everything?

JUDITH [*enjoying herself*]: Yes, yes. There come moments in life when it is necessary to be honest—absolutely honest. I've trained myself always to shun the underhand methods other women so often employ—the truth must be faced fair and square——

RICHARD [*extremely alarmed*]: The truth? I don't quite understand.

JUDITH: Dear Richard, you want to spare me, I know—you're so chivalrous; but it's no use. After all, as I said before, David has been a good husband to me, according to his lights. This may, of course, break him up rather, but it can't be helped; he must be told. I wonder—oh, I wonder how he'll take it. They say suffering's good for writers, it strengthens their psychology. Oh my poor, poor David!—Never mind. You'd better go out into the garden and wait——

RICHARD [*flustered*]: Wait? What for?

JUDITH: For me, Richard, for me. I will come to you later. Wait in the summer-house. I had begun to think that Romance was dead, that I should never know it again. Before, of course, I had my work and my life in the theater, but now, nothing—

nothing! Everything is empty and hollow, like a broken shell.

RICHARD: Look here, Judith, I apologize for what I did just now. I——

JUDITH [*ignoring all interruption*]: But now you have come, and it's all changed—it's magic. I'm under a spell that I never thought to recapture again. Go along—— [*She pushes him towards the garden.*]

RICHARD [*protesting*]: But, Judith——

JUDITH [*pushing him firmly*]: Don't—don't make it any harder for me. I am quite resolved—it is my self-appointed Calvary, and it's the only possible way!

[*She pushes him into the garden and waves to him bravely with her handkerchief; then she comes back into the room and powders her nose before the glass and pats her hair into place. Then, assuming an expression of restrained tragedy, she opens the library door, from which she recoils genuinely shocked. After a moment or two Sorel and Sandy come out rather sheepishly.*]

SOREL: Look here, mother, I——

JUDITH: Sorel, what am I to say to you?

SOREL: I don't know, mother.

JUDITH: Neither do I.

SANDY: It was my fault, Mrs. Bliss—Judith——

JUDITH: What a fool I've been! What a blind fool!

SOREL: Mother, are you *really* upset?

JUDITH [*with feeling*]: I'm stunned.

SOREL: But, darling——

JUDITH [*gently*]: Don't speak for a moment, Sorel; we must all be very quiet and, think——

SOREL: It was nothing, really. For Heaven's sake——

JUDITH: Nothing! I open the library door, casually, and what do I see? I ask you, what do I see?

SANDY: I'm most awfully sorry. . . .

JUDITH: Ssshh! It has gone beyond superficial apologies.

SOREL: Mother, be natural for a minute.

JUDITH: I don't know what you mean, Sorel. I'm trying to realize a very bitter truth as calmly as I can.

SOREL: There's nothing so very bitter about it.

JUDITH: My poor child!

SOREL [*suddenly*]: Very well, then! I love Sandy, and he loves me!

JUDITH: That would be the only possible excuse for your behavior.

SOREL: Why shouldn't we love each other if we want to?

JUDITH: Sandy was in love with me this afternoon.

SOREL: Not real love—you know it wasn't.

JUDITH [*bitterly*]: I know now.

SANDY: I say—look here—I'm most awfully sorry.

JUDITH: There's nothing to be sorry for, really; it's my fault for having been so—so ridiculous.

SOREL: Mother!

JUDITH [*sadly*]: Yes, ridiculous. I'm getting old, old, and the sooner I face it the better.

SOREL [*hopelessly*]: But, darling . . .

JUDITH [*splendidly*]: Youth will be served. You're so pretty, Sorel, far prettier than I ever was—I'm very glad you're pretty.

SANDY: I feel a fearful cad.

JUDITH: Why should you? You've answered the only call that really counts—the call of Love, and Romance, and Spring. I forgive you, Sandy, completely. There.

SOREL: Well, that's all right, then.

JUDITH: I resent your tone, Sorel; you seem to be taking things too much for granted. Perhaps you don't realize that I am making a great sacrifice!

SOREL: Sorry, darling.

JUDITH: It's far from easy, at my time of life, to——

SOREL [*playing up*]: Mother—mother, say you understand and forgive!

JUDITH: Understand! You forget, dear, I am a woman.

SOREL: I know you are, mother. That's what makes it all so poignant.

JUDITH [*magnanimously, to Sandy*]: If you want Sorel, truly, I give her to you—unconditionally.

SANDY [*dazed*]: Thanks—awfully, Mrs. Bliss.

JUDITH: You can still call me Judith, can't you?—it's not much to ask.

SANDY: Judith.

JUDITH [*bravely*]: There, now. Away with melancholy. This is all tremendously exciting, and we must all be very happy.

SOREL: Don't tell father—yet.

JUDITH: We won't tell anybody; it shall be our little secret.

SOREL: You are splendid, mother.

JUDITH: Nonsense. I just believe in being honest with myself —it's awfully good for one, you know, so cleansing. I'm going upstairs now to have a little aspirin—— [*She goes upstairs, and turns.*] Ah, Youth, Youth, what a strange, mad muddle you make of things! [*She goes off.*]

[*Sorel heaves a slight sigh, and takes a cigarette.*]

SOREL: Well, that's that.

SANDY: Yes.

SOREL: It's all right. Don't look so gloomy—I know you don't love me really.

SANDY [*startled*]: I say, Sorel——

SOREL: Don't protest; you know you don't—any more than I love you.

SANDY: But you told Judith——

SOREL [*nonchalantly*]: I was only playing up—one always plays up to mother in this house; it's a sort of unwritten law.

SANDY: Didn't she mean all she said?

SOREL: No, not really; we none of us ever mean anything.

SANDY: She seemed awfully upset.

SOREL: It must have been a slight shock for her to discover us clasped tightly in each other's arms.

SANDY: I believe I do love you, Sorel.

SOREL: A month ago I should have let you go on believing that, but now I can't—I'm bent on improving myself.

SANDY: I don't understand.

SOREL: Never mind—it doesn't matter. You just fell a victim to the atmosphere, that's all. There we were alone in the library, with the windows wide open, and probably a nightingale some-where about——

SANDY: I only heard a cuckoo.

SOREL: Even a cuckoo has charm, in moderation. You kissed me because you were awfully nice and I was awfully nice and we both liked kissing very much. It was inevitable. Then mother found us and got dramatic—her sense of the theater is always fatal. She knows we shan't marry, the same as you and I do. You're under absolutely no obligation to me at all.

SANDY: I wish I understood you a bit better.

SOREL: Never mind about understanding me. Let's go back into the library.

SANDY: All right.

[*They go off. After a moment's pause, David and Myra enter from the garden.*]

DAVID: . . . And, you see, he comes in and finds her there waiting for him.

MYRA: She hadn't been away at all?

DAVID: No; and that's psychologically right, I'm sure. No woman, under those circumstances, *would*.

MYRA: It's brilliant of you to see that. I do think the whole thing sounds most excellent.

DAVID: I got badly stuck in the middle of the book, when the boy comes down from Oxford—but it worked out all right eventually.

MYRA [*sitting on sofa*]: When shall I be able to read it?

DAVID: I'll send you the proofs—you can help me correct them.

MYRA: How divine! I shall feel most important.

DAVID: Would you like a cigarette, or anything?

MYRA: No, thank you.

DAVID: I think I'll have a drink.

MYRA: Very well; give me some plain soda-water, then.

DAVID [*going to side table*]: There isn't any ice—d'you mind?

MYRA: Not a bit.

DAVID [*bringing her drink*]: Here you are.

MYRA: Thank you. [*She sips it.*] I wonder where everybody is.

DAVID: Not here, thank God.

MYRA: It must be dreadfully worrying for you, having a houseful of people.

DAVID [*having poured himself out a whisky-and-soda, sits down by her side*]: It depends on the people.

MYRA: I have a slight confession to make.

DAVID: Confession?

MYRA: Yes. Do you know why I came down here?

DAVID: Not in the least. I suppose one of us asked you, didn't they?

MYRA: Oh yes, they asked me, but——

DAVID: Well?

MYRA: I was invited once before—last September.

DAVID: I was in America then.

MYRA: Exactly.

DAVID: How do you mean "exactly"?

MYRA: I didn't come. I'm a very determined woman, you know, and I made up my mind to meet you ages ago.

DAVID: That was charming of you. I'm not much to meet really.

MYRA: You see, I'd read *Broken Reeds*.

DAVID: Did you like it?

MYRA: Like it! I think it's one of the finest novels I've ever read.

DAVID: There now!

MYRA: How do you manage to know so much about women?

DAVID: I'm afraid my knowledge of them is sadly superficial.

MYRA: Oh no; you can't call Evelyn's character superficial— it's amazing.

DAVID: Why are you being so nice to me? Have you got a plan about something?

MYRA [*laughing*]: How suspicious you are!

DAVID: I can't help it—you're very attractive, and I'm always suspicious of attractive people, on principle.

MYRA: Not a very good principle.

DAVID: I'll tell you something—strictly between ourselves.

MYRA: Do.

DAVID: You're wrong about me.

MYRA: Wrong? In what way?

DAVID: I write very bad novels.

MYRA: Don't be so ridiculous.

DAVID: And you *know* I do, because you're an intelligent person.

MYRA: I don't know anything of the sort.

DAVID: Tell me why you're being so nice to me?

MYRA: Because I want to be.

DAVID: Why?

MYRA: You're a very clever and amusing man.

DAVID: Splendid.

MYRA: And I think I've rather lost my heart to you.

DAVID: Shall we elope?

MYRA: David!

DAVID: There now, you've called me David!

MYRA: Do you mind?

DAVID: Not at all.

MYRA: I'm not sure that you're being very kind.

DAVID: What makes you think that?

MYRA: You're being rather the cynical author laughing up his sleeve at a gushing admirer.

DAVID: I think you're a very interesting woman, and extremely nice-looking.

MYRA: Do you?

DAVID: Yes. Would you like me to make love to you?

MYRA [*rising*]: Really—I wish you wouldn't say things like that.

DAVID: I've knocked you off your plate—I'll look away for a minute while you climb on to it again. [*He does so.*]

MYRA [*laughing affectedly*]: This is wonderful! [*She sits down again.*]

DAVID [*turning*]: That's right. Now then——

MYRA: Now then, what?

DAVID: You're   adorable—you're   magnificent—you're tawny——

MYRA: I'm not tawny.

DAVID: Don't argue.

MYRA: This is sheer affectation.

DAVID: Affectation's very nice.

MYRA: No, it isn't—it's odious.

DAVID: You mustn't get cross.

MYRA: I'm not in the least cross.

DAVID: Yes, you are—but you're very alluring.

MYRA [*perking up*]: Alluring?

DAVID: Terribly.

MYRA: I can hear your brain clicking—it's very funny.

DAVID: That was rather rude.

MYRA: You've been consistently rude to me for hours.

DAVID: Never mind.

MYRA: Why have you?

DAVID: I'm always rude to people I like.

MYRA: Do you like me?

DAVID: Enormously.

MYRA: How sweet of you!

DAVID: But I don't like your methods.

MYRA: Methods? What methods?

DAVID: You're far too pleasant to occupy yourself with the commonplace.

MYRA: And you spoil yourself by trying to be clever.

DAVID: Thank you.

MYRA: Anyhow, I don't know what you mean by commonplace.

DAVID: You mean you want me to explain?

MYRA: Not at all.

DAVID: Very well; I will.

MYRA: I shan't listen. [*She stops up her ears.*]

DAVID: You'll pretend not to, but you'll hear every word really.

MYRA [*sarcastically*]: You're so inscrutable and quizzical—just what a feminine psychologist should be.

DAVID: Yes, aren't I?

MYRA: You frighten me dreadfully.

DAVID: Darling!

MYRA: Don't call me darling.

DAVID: That's unreasonable. You've been trying to make me —all the evening.

MYRA: Your conceit is outrageous!

DAVID: It's not conceit at all. You've been firmly buttering me up because you want a nice little intrigue.

MYRA [*rising*]: How dare you!

DAVID [*pulling her down again*]: It's true, it's true. If it weren't, you wouldn't be so angry.

MYRA: I think you're insufferable!

DAVID [*taking her hand*]: Myra—dear Myra——

MYRA [*snatching it away*]: Don't touch me.

DAVID: Let's have that nice little intrigue. The only reason I've been so annoying is that I love to see things as they are first, and then pretend they're what they're not.

MYRA: Words! Masses and masses of words!

DAVID: They're great fun to play with.

MYRA: I'm glad you think so. Personally, they bore me stiff.

DAVID [*catching her hand again*]: Myra—don't be statuesque.

MYRA: Let go my hand!

DAVID: You're charming. [*He gets up and stands close to her.*]

MYRA [*furiously*]: Let go my hand.

DAVID: I won't.

MYRA: You will!

[*She slaps his face hard, and he seizes her in his arms and kisses her.*]

DAVID [*between kisses*]: You're—perfectly—sweet.

MYRA [*giving in*]: David!

DAVID: You must say it's an entrancing amusement.

[*He kisses her again. Judith appears at the top of the stairs and sees them. They break away.*]

JUDITH [*coming down*]: Forgive me for interrupting.

DAVID: Are there any chocolates in the house?

JUDITH: No, David.

DAVID: I should like a chocolate more than anything in the world, at the moment.

JUDITH: This is a very unpleasant situation, David.

DAVID [*agreeably*]: Horrible.

JUDITH: We'd better talk it all over.

MYRA [*making a movement*]: I shall do nothing of the sort.

JUDITH: Please—please don't be difficult.

DAVID: I apologize, Judith.

JUDITH: Don't apologize—I quite understand.

MYRA: Please let go of my hand, David; I should like to go to bed.

JUDITH: I should stay if I were you—it would be more dignified.

DAVID: There isn't any real necessity for a scene.

JUDITH: I don't want a scene. I just want to straighten things out.

DAVID: Very well—go ahead.

JUDITH: June has always been an unlucky month for me.

MYRA: Look here, Judith, I'd like to explain one thing——

JUDITH [*austerely*]: I don't wish to hear any explanations or excuses—they're so cheapening. This was bound to happen sooner or later—it always does, to everybody. The only thing is to keep calm.

DAVID: I am—perfectly.

JUDITH [*sharply*]: There is such a thing as being too calm.

DAVID: Sorry, dear.

JUDITH: Life has dealt me another blow, but I don't mind.

DAVID: What did you say?

JUDITH [*crossly*]: I said Life had dealt me another blow, but I didn't mind.

DAVID: Rubbish.

JUDITH [*gently*]: You're probably irritable, dear, because you're in the wrong. It's quite usual.

DAVID: Now, Judith——

JUDITH: Ssshhh! Let me speak—it is my right.

MYRA: I don't see why.

JUDITH [*surprised*]: I am the injured party, am I not?

MYRA: Injured?

JUDITH [*firmly*]: Yes, extremely injured.

DAVID [*contemptuously*]: Injured!

JUDITH: Your attitude, David, is nothing short of deplorable.

DAVID: It's all nonsense—sheer, unbridled nonsense.

JUDITH: No, David, you can't evade the real issues as calmly as that. I've known for a long time—I've realized subconsciously for years that you've stopped caring for me in "that way."

DAVID [*irritably*]: What do you mean—"that way"?

JUDITH [*with a wave of the hand*]: Just that way. . . . It's rather tragic, but quite inevitable. I'm growing old now—men don't grow old like women, as you'll find to your cost, Myra, in a year or two. David has retained his youth astonishingly, perhaps because he has had fewer responsibilities and cares than I——

MYRA: This is all ridiculous hysteria.

DAVID [*looking at her and not liking her very much*]: No, Myra—Judith is right. What are we to do?

MYRA [*furious*]: Do? Nothing!

JUDITH [*ignoring her*]: Do you love her truly, David?

DAVID: Madly.

MYRA [*astounded*]: David!

DAVID [*intensely*]: You thought just now that I was joking. Couldn't you see that all my flippancy was only a mask, hiding my real emotions—crushing them down desperately——?

MYRA [*scared*]: But, David, I——

JUDITH: I knew it! The time has come for the dividing of the ways.

MYRA: What on earth do you mean?

JUDITH: I mean that I am not the sort of woman to hold a man against his will.

MYRA: You're both making a mountain out of a molehill. David doesn't love me madly, and I don't love him. It's——

JUDITH: Ssshhh!—you *do* love him. I can see it in your eyes—

in your every gesture. David, I give you to her—freely and without rancor. We must all be good friends, always.

DAVID: Judith, do you mean this?

JUDITH [*with a melting look*]: You know I do.

DAVID: How can we ever repay you?

JUDITH: Just by being happy. I may leave this house later on—I have a feeling that its associations may become painful, specially in the autumn——

MYRA: Look here, Judith——

JUDITH [*shouting her down*]: October is such a mournful month in England. I think I shall probably go abroad—perhaps a *pension* somewhere in Italy, with cypresses in the garden. I've always loved cypresses.

DAVID: What about the children?

JUDITH: We must share them, dear.

DAVID: I'll pay you exactly half the royalties I receive from everything, Judith.

JUDITH [*bowing her head*]: That's very generous of you.

DAVID: You have behaved magnificently. This is a crisis in our lives, and thanks to you——

MYRA [*almost shrieking*]: Judith—I *will* speak—I——

DAVID: Ssshhh, Myra darling—we owe it to Judith to keep control of our emotions—a scene would be agonizing for her now. She has been brave and absolutely splendid throughout. Let's not make things harder for her than we can help. Come, we'll go out into the garden.

MYRA: I will *not* go out into the garden.

JUDITH [*twisting her handkerchief*]: Please go—I don't think I can bear any more just now.

DAVID: So this is the end, Judith?

JUDITH: Yes, my dear,—the end.

[*They shake hands sadly. Simon enters violently from the garden.*]

SIMON: Mother—mother, I've got something important to tell you.

JUDITH [*smiling bravely*]: Very well, dear.

SIMON: Where's Sorel.

JUDITH: In the library, I'm afraid.

SIMON [*opening library door*]: Sorel, come out—I've got something vital to tell you.

DAVID [*fatherly*]: You seem excited, my boy. What has happened?

SOREL [*entering with Sandy*]: What's the matter?

SIMON: I wish you wouldn't all look so depressed—it's good news!

DAVID: Good news! I thought perhaps Jackie had been drowned——

SIMON: No, Jackie hasn't been drowned—she's been something else.

JUDITH: Simon, what *do* you mean?

SIMON [*calling*]: Jackie—Jackie!

[*Jackie enters coyly from the garden.*]
She has become engaged—to me!

JUDITH [*in heartfelt tones*]: Simon!

SOREL: Good heavens!

JUDITH: Simon, my dear! Oh, this is too much! [*She cries a little.*]

SIMON: What on earth are you crying about, mother?

JUDITH [*picturesquely*]: All my chicks leaving the nest. Now I shall only have my memories left. Jackie, come and kiss me.

[*Jackie goes to her.*]
You must promise to make my son happy——

JACKIE [*worried*]: But, Mrs. Bliss——

JUDITH: Ssshhh! I understand. I have not been a mother for nothing.

JACKIE [*wildly*]: But it's not true—we don't——

JUDITH: You're trying to spare my feelings—I know——

MYRA [*furiously*]: Well, I'm not going to spare your feelings, or anyone else's. You're the most infuriating set of hypocrites I've ever seen. This house is a complete feather bed of false emotions—you're posing, self-centered egotists, and I'm sick to death of you.

SIMON: Myra!

MYRA: Don't speak to me. I've been working up for this, only every time I opened my mouth I've been mowed down by theatrical effects. You haven't got one sincere or genuine feeling among the lot of you—you're artificial to the point of lunacy. It's a great pity you ever left the stage, Judith—it's your rightful home. You can rant and roar there as much as ever you like——

JUDITH: Rant and roar! May God forgive you!

MYRA: And let me tell you this: You don't seem to grasp one thing that——

SIMON [*interrupting*]: I'm not going to allow you to say another word to mother——

[*Together*]:

SOREL: You ought to be ashamed of yourself——

MYRA: Let me speak—I will speak——

DAVID: Look here, Myra——

JUDITH: This is appalling—appalling!

SOREL: You must be stark, staring mad——

MYRA: Never again—never as long as I live——

SIMON: Why are you behaving like this, anyhow?

[*In the middle of the pandemonium of everyone talking at once, Richard comes in from the garden. He looks extremely apprehensive, imagining that the noise is the outcome of Judith's hysterical confession of their lukewarm passion. He goes to Judith's side, summon-*

ing all his diplomatic forces. At his entrance everyone stops talking.]

RICHARD [*with forced calm*]: What's happened? Is this a game?

[*Judith's face gives a slight twitch; then with a meaning look at Sorel and Simon, she answers him.*]

JUDITH [*with spirit*]: Yes, and a game that must be played to the finish!

SIMON [*grasping the situation*]: Zara! What does this mean?

JUDITH [*in bell-like tones*]: So many illusions shattered—so many dreams trodden in the dust——

DAVID [*collapsing on to the sofa in hysterics*]: Love's whirlwind! Dear old Love's whirlwind!

SOREL: I don't understand. You and Victor—My God!

JUDITH: Hush! Isn't that little Pam crying——?

SIMON [*savagely*]: She'll cry more, poor mite, when she realizes her mother is a—a——

JUDITH [*shrieking*]: Don't say it! Don't say it!

SOREL: Spare her that.

JUDITH: I've given you all that makes life worth living—my youth, my womanhood, and now my child. Would you tear the very heart out of me? I tell you, it's infamous that men like you should be allowed to pollute Society. You have ruined my life. I have nothing left—nothing. God in heaven, where am I to turn for help . . .

SOREL [*through clenched teeth*]: Is this true? Answer me—is this true?

JUDITH [*wailing*]: Yes, yes!

SOREL [*springing at Simon*]: You cur!!!

JUDITH [*rushing between them*]: Don't strike! He is your father! [*She totters and falls in a dead faint.*]

[*Myra, Jackie, Richard, and Sandy look on, dazed and aghast.*]

CURTAIN

~~~~~~

ACT THREE

IT IS SUNDAY MORNING, *about ten o'clock. There are various break-*
fast dishes on a side table, and a big table is laid down center.

Sandy appears at the top of the stairs. On seeing no one about,
he comes down quickly and furtively helps himself to eggs and
bacon and coffee, and seats himself at the table. He eats very hur-
riedly, casting occasional glances over his shoulder. A door bangs
somewhere upstairs, which terrifies him; he chokes violently. When
he has recovered, he tears a bit of toast from a rack, butters it and
marmalades it and crams it into his mouth. Then, hearing somebody
approaching, he darts into the library.

Jackie comes downstairs timorously; her expression is dismal, to
say the least of it. She looks miserably out of the window at the
pouring rain, then, assuming an air of spurious bravado, she helps
herself to some breakfast and sits down, and looks at it. After one
or two attempts to eat it, she bursts into tears.

Sandy opens the library door a crack and peeps out. Jackie, seeing
the door move, screams. Sandy re-enters.

JACKIE: Oh, it's only you—you frightened me!
SANDY: What's the matter?
JACKIE [*sniffing*]: Nothing.
SANDY: I say, don't cry.
JACKIE: I'm not crying.

561

SANDY: You were—I heard you.

JACKIE: It's this house. It gets on my nerves.

SANDY: I don't wonder—after last night.

JACKIE: What were you doing in the library just now?

SANDY: Hiding.

JACKIE: Hiding?

SANDY: Yes; I didn't want to run up against any of the family.

JACKIE: I wish I'd never come. I had horrible nightmares with all those fearful dragons crawling across the wall.

SANDY: Dragons?

JACKIE: Yes; I'm in a Japanese room—everything in it's Japanese, even the bed.

SANDY: How awful!

JACKIE: I believe they're all mad, you know.

SANDY: The Blisses?

JACKIE: Yes—they must be.

SANDY: I've been thinking that too.

JACKIE: Do you suppose they know they're mad?

SANDY: No; people never do.

JACKIE: It was Mr. Bliss asked me down, and he hasn't paid any attention to me at all. I went into his study soon after I arrived yesterday, and he said, "Who the hell are you?"

SANDY: Didn't he remember?

JACKIE: He did afterwards; then he brought me down to tea and left me.

SANDY: Are you really engaged to Simon?

JACKIE [*bursting into tears again*]: Oh no—I hope not!

SANDY: You were, last night.

JACKIE: So were you—to Sorel.

SANDY: Not properly. We talked it over.

JACKIE: I don't know what happened to me. I was in the garden with Simon, and he was being awfully sweet, and then he suddenly kissed me, and rushed into the house and said we were engaged—and that hateful Judith asked me to make him happy!

SANDY: That's exactly what happened to me and Sorel. Judith gave us to one another before we knew where we were.

JACKIE: How frightful!

SANDY: I like Sorel, though; she was jolly decent about it afterwards.

JACKIE: I think she's a cat.

SANDY: Why?

JACKIE: Look at the way she lost her temper over that beastly game.

SANDY: All the same, she's better than the others.

JACKIE: That wouldn't be very difficult.

SANDY: Hic!

JACKIE: I beg your pardon?

SANDY [*abashed*]: I say—I've got hiccoughs.

JACKIE: Hold your breath.

SANDY: It was because I bolted my breakfast. [*He holds his breath.*]

JACKIE: Hold it as long as you can. [*There is a pause.*]

SANDY [*letting his breath go with a gasp*]: I can't any more—hic!

JACKIE: Eat a lump of sugar.

SANDY [*taking one*]: I'm awfully sorry.

JACKIE: I don't mind—but it's a horrid feeling, isn't it?

SANDY: Horrid—hic!

JACKIE [*conversationally*]: People have died from hiccoughs, you know.

SANDY [*gloomily*]: Have they?

JACKIE: Yes. An aunt of mine once had them for three days without stopping.

SANDY: How beastly.

JACKIE [*with relish*]: She had to have the doctor, and everything.

SANDY: I expect mine will stop soon.

JACKIE: I hope they will.

SANDY: Hic!—There!

JACKIE: Drink some water the wrong way round.

SANDY: How do you mean—the wrong way round?

JACKIE [*rising*]: The wrong side of the glass. I'll show you. [*She goes to side table.*] There isn't any water.

SANDY: Perhaps coffee would do as well.

JACKIE: I've never tried coffee, but it might. [*She pours him out some.*] There you are.

SANDY [*anxiously*]: What do I do?

JACKIE: Tip it up and drink from the opposite side, sort of upside down.

SANDY [*trying*]: I can't reach any——

JACKIE [*suddenly*]: Look out—somebody's coming. Bring it into the library—quick. . . .

SANDY: Bring the sugar—I might need it again—hic! Oh God!

JACKIE: All right.

[*They go off into the library hurriedly. Richard comes downstairs. He glances round a trifle anxiously; then, pulling himself together, he goes boldly to the barometer and taps it. It falls off the wall and breaks; he picks it up quickly and places it on the piano. Then he helps himself to some breakfast, and sits down. Myra appears on the stairs, very smart and bright.*]

MYRA [*vivaciously*]: Good morning.

RICHARD: Good morning.

MYRA: Are we the first down?

RICHARD: No, I don't think so.

MYRA [*looking out of the window*]: Isn't this rain miserable?

RICHARD: Appalling!

MYRA: Where's the barometer?

RICHARD: On the piano.

MYRA: What a queer place for it to be.

RICHARD: I tapped it, and it fell down.

MYRA: Typical of this house. [*At side table.*] Are you having eggs and bacon, or haddock?

RICHARD: Haddock.

MYRA: I'll have haddock too. I simply couldn't strike out a line for myself this morning. [*She helps herself to haddock and coffee, and sits down opposite Richard.*] Have you seen anybody?

RICHARD: No.

MYRA: Good. We might have a little peace.

RICHARD: Have you ever stayed here before?

MYRA: No, and I never will again.

RICHARD: I feel far from well this morning.

MYRA: I'm so sorry, but not entirely surprised.

RICHARD: You see, I had the boiler room.

MYRA: How terrible!

RICHARD: The window stuck, and I couldn't open it—I was nearly suffocated. The pipes made peculiar noises all night, as well.

MYRA: There isn't any sugar.

RICHARD: Oh—we'd better ring.

MYRA: I doubt if it will be the slightest use, but we'll try.

RICHARD [*ringing and ringing bell*]: Do the whole family have breakfast in bed?

MYRA: I neither know—nor care.

RICHARD: They're strange people, aren't they?

MYRA: I think "strange" is putting it mildly.

[*Enter Clara.*]

CLARA: What's the matter?

MYRA: There isn't any sugar.

CLARA: There is—I put it 'ere myself.

MYRA: Perhaps you'd find it for us, then?

CLARA [*searching*]: That's very funny. I could 'ave sworn on me Bible oath I brought it in.

MYRA: Well, it obviously isn't here now.

CLARA: Someone's taken it—that's what it is.

RICHARD: It seems a queer thing to do.

MYRA: Do you think you could get us some more?

CLARA: Oh yes, I'll fetch you some; but mark my words, there's been some 'anky-panky somewhere. [*She goes out.*]

MYRA: Clara is really more at home in a dressing-room than a house.

RICHARD: Was she Judith's dresser?

MYRA: Of course. What other excuse could there possibly be for her?

RICHARD: She seems good-natured, but quaint.

MYRA: This haddock's disgusting.

RICHARD: It isn't very nice, is it?

[*Re-enter Clara with sugar. She plumps it down.*]

CLARA: There you are, dear.

MYRA: Thank you.

CLARA: It's a shame the weather's changed—you might 'ave 'ad such fun up the river. [*There comes the sound of a crash from the library, and a scream.*] What's that? [*She opens the door.*] Come out! What are you doing?

[*Jackie and Sandy enter, rather shamefaced.*]

JACKIE: Good morning. I'm afraid we've broken a coffee-cup.

CLARA: Was there any coffee in it?

SANDY: Yes, a good deal.

CLARA [*rushing into the library*]: Oh dear! all over the carpet!

SANDY: It was my fault. I'm most awfully sorry.

[*Clara reappears.*]

CLARA: How did you come to do it?

JACKIE: Well, you see, he had the hiccoughs, and I was showing him how to drink upside down.

MYRA: How ridiculous!

CLARA: Well, thank 'Eaven it wasn't one of the Crown Derbys. [*She goes out.*]

SANDY: They've gone now, anyhow.

JACKIE: It was the sudden shock, I expect.

SANDY [*observantly*]: I say—it's raining!

MYRA: It's been raining for hours.

RICHARD: Mrs. Arundel——

MYRA: Yes?

RICHARD: What are you going to do about—about to-day?

MYRA: Nothing, except go up to London by the first train possible.

RICHARD: Do you mind if I come too? I don't think I could face another day like yesterday.

JACKIE: Neither could I.

SANDY [*eagerly*]: Let's all go away—quietly!

RICHARD: Won't it seem a little rude if we *all* go?

MYRA: Yes, it will. [*To Sandy*]: You and Miss Coryton must stay.

JACKIE: I don't see why.

SANDY: I don't think they'd mind *very* much if we all went.

MYRA: Yes, they would. You must let Mr. Greatham and me get away first, anyhow. Ring for Clara. I want to find out about trains.

RICHARD: I hope they won't all come down now.

MYRA: You needn't worry about that; they're sure to roll about in bed for hours—they're such a slovenly family.

RICHARD: Have you got much packing to do?

MYRA: No; I did most of it before I came down.

[*Re-enter Clara.*]

CLARA: What is it now?

MYRA: Can you tell me what trains there are up to London?

CLARA: When?

MYRA: This morning.

CLARA: Why? You're not leaving, are you?

MYRA: Yes; Mr. Greatham and I have to be up by lunch time.

CLARA: Well, you have missed the ten-fifteen.

MYRA: Obviously.

CLARA: There isn't another till twelve-thirty.

RICHARD: Good heavens!

CLARA: And that's a slow one. [*She goes out.*]

SANDY [*to Jackie*]: Look here; I'll take you up in my car as soon as you like.

JACKIE: All right; lovely!

MYRA: You've got a car, haven't you?

SANDY: Yes.

MYRA: Will it hold all of us?

JACKIE: You said it would be rude for us all to go. Hadn't you and Mr. Greatham better wait for the train?

MYRA: Certainly not.

RICHARD [*to Sandy*]: If there is room, we should be very, very grateful.

SANDY: I think I can squeeze you in.

MYRA: Then that's settled, then.

JACKIE: When shall we start?

SANDY: As soon as you're ready.

JACKIE: Mrs. Arundel, what are you going to do about tipping Clara?

MYRA: I don't know. [*To Richard*]: What do you think?

RICHARD: I've hardly seen her since I've been here.

JACKIE: Isn't there a housemaid or anything?

RICHARD: I don't think so.

SANDY: Is ten bob enough?

JACKIE: Each?

MYRA: Too much.

RICHARD: We'd better give her one pound ten between us.

MYRA: Very well, then. Will you do it, and we'll settle up in the car?

RICHARD: Must I?

MYRA: Yes. Ring for her.

RICHARD: You'd do it much better.

[Sandy rings the bell.]

MYRA: Oh no, I shouldn't. [To Jackie]: Come on; we'll finish our packing.

JACKIE: All right.

[They begin to go upstairs.]

RICHARD: Here—don't leave me.

SANDY: I'll just go and look at the car. Will you all be ready in ten minutes?

MYRA: Yes, ten minutes. [She goes off with Jackie.]

SANDY: Righto. [He rushes out.]

[Clara re-enters.]

CLARA: 'Allo, where's everybody gone?

RICHARD: They've gone to get ready. We're leaving in Mr Tyrell's car.

CLARA: A bit sudden, isn't it?

RICHARD [pressing money into her hand]: This is from all of us, Clara. Thank you very much for all your trouble.

CLARA [surprised]: Aren't you a dear, now! There wasn't any trouble.

RICHARD: There must have been a lot of extra work.

CLARA: One gets used to that 'ere.

RICHARD: Good-bye, Clara.

[*He goes upstairs. Clara proceeds to clear away the dirty breakfast things, which she takes out. She returns with a fresh pot of coffee, and meets Judith coming downstairs.*]

JUDITH: Good morning, Clara. Have the papers come?

CLARA: Yes—I'll fetch them.

[*She goes out. Judith pours herself out some coffee, and sits down. Clara re-enters with papers.*]

JUDITH: Thank you. You've forgotten my orange juice.

CLARA: No, I 'aven't, dear; it's just outside.

[*She goes out again. Judith turns to the theatrical column of the Sunday* Times. *Sorel comes downstairs and kisses her.*]

SOREL: Good morning, darling.

JUDITH: Listen to this. [*She reads*]: "We saw Judith Bliss in a box at the Haymarket on Tuesday, looking as lovely as ever." There now! I thought I looked hideous on Tuesday.

SOREL: You looked sweet.

[*She goes to get herself some breakfast. Clara reappears, with a glass of orange juice.*]

CLARA [*placing it in front of Judith*]: Did you see that nice bit in the *Referee?*

JUDITH: No—the *Times.*

CLARA: The *Referee's* much better. [*She finds the place and hands it to Sorel.*]

SOREL [*reading*]: "I saw gay and colorful Judith Bliss at the Waifs and Strays matinée last week. She was talking vivaciously to Producer Basil Dean. 'I' sooth,' said I to myself, 'where ignorance is Bliss, 'tis folly to be wise.'"

JUDITH [*taking it from her*]: Dear *Referee!* It's so unself-conscious.

CLARA: If you want any more coffee, ring for it. [*She goes out.*]

SOREL [*sitting down*]: I wish I were sitting on a lovely South

Sea island, with masses of palm trees and cocoanuts and turtles——

JUDITH: It would be divine, wouldn't it?

SOREL: I wonder where everybody is?

JUDITH [*still reading*]: I wonder. . . . Mary Saunders has got another failure.

SOREL: She must be used to it by now.

[*Simon comes downstairs with a rush.*]

SIMON [*kissing Judith*]: Good morning, darling.—Look! [*He shows her a newly completed sketch.*]

JUDITH: Simon! How lovely! When did you do it?

SIMON: This morning—I woke early.

SOREL [*rising and craning over Judith's shoulder*]: Let's see.

SIMON [*over the other shoulder*]: I'm going to alter Helen's face; it's too pink.

SOREL [*laughing*]: It's exactly like her.

JUDITH: What a clever son I have!

SIMON: Now then, mother!

JUDITH: It's too wonderful—when I think of you both in your perambulators. . . . Oh dear, it makes me cry! [*She sniffs.*]

SOREL: I don't believe you ever saw us in our perambulators.

JUDITH: I don't believe I did.

[*David comes downstairs.*]

DAVID [*hilariously*]: It's finished!

JUDITH: What, dear?

DAVID: *The Sinful Woman.*

JUDITH: How splendid. Read it to us now.

DAVID: I've got the last chapter here.

JUDITH: Go on, then.

[*Sandy rushes in from the front door. On seeing everyone, he halts.*]

SANDY: Good morning. [*He bolts upstairs two at a time.*]

JUDITH: I seem to know that boy's face.

DAVID [*preparing to read*]: Listen. You remember when Violet was taken ill in Paris?

JUDITH: Yes, dear.—Marmalade, Simon.

DAVID: Well, I'll go on from there.

JUDITH: Do, dear.

DAVID [*reading*]: "Paris in spring, with the Champs Elysées alive and dancing in the sunlight; lightly dressed children like gay painted butterflies——"

SIMON [*whispering to Sorel*]: What's happened to the barometer?

SOREL [*sibilantly*]: I don't know.

DAVID: Damn the barometer!

JUDITH: Don't get cross, dear.

DAVID: Why can't you keep quiet, Simon, or go away!

SIMON: Sorry, father.

DAVID: Well, don't interrupt again. . . . [*Reading*]: ". . . gay painted butterflies; the streets were thronged with hurrying vehicles, the thin peek-peek of taxi-hooters——"

SOREL: I love "peek-peek."

DAVID [*ignoring her*]: "——seemed to merge in with the other vivid noises weaving a vast pattern of sound which was Paris. Jane Sefton, in her scarlet Hispano, swept out of the Rue St.-Honoré into the Place de la Concorde——"

JUDITH: She couldn't have.

DAVID: Why?

JUDITH: The Rue St.-Honoré doesn't lead into the Place de la Concorde.

DAVID: Yes, it does.

SOREL: You're thinking of the Rue Boissy d'Anglas, father.

DAVID: I'm not thinking of anything of the sort.

JUDITH: David darling, don't be obstinate.

DAVID [*hotly*]: Do you think I don't know Paris as well as you do?

SIMON: Never mind. Father's probably right.

SOREL: He isn't right—he's wrong!

DAVID: Go on with your food, Sorel.

JUDITH: Don't be testy, David: it's a sign of age.

DAVID [*firmly*]: "Jane Sefton, in her scarlet Hispano, swept out of the Rue St.-Honoré into the Place de la Concorde——"

JUDITH: That sounds absolutely ridiculous. Why don't you alter it?

DAVID: It isn't ridiculous; it's perfectly right.

JUDITH: Very well, then; get a map, and I'll show you.

SIMON: We haven't got a map.

DAVID [*putting his MS. down*]: Now, look here, Judith—here's the Rue Royale— [*He arranges the butter-dish and marmalade-pot.*] —here's the Crillon Hotel, and *here's* the Rue St.-Honoré——

JUDITH: It isn't—it's the Boissy d'Anglas.

DAVID: That runs parallel with the Rue de Rivoli.

JUDITH: You've got it all muddled.

DAVID [*loudly*]: I have *not* got it all muddled.

JUDITH: Don't shout. You have.

SIMON: Why not let father get on with it?

JUDITH: It's so silly to get cross at criticism—it indicates a small mind.

DAVID: Small mind my foot!

JUDITH: That was very rude. I shall go to my room in a minute.

DAVID: I wish you would.

JUDITH [*outraged*]: David!

SOREL: Look here, father, mother's right—here's the Place de la Concorde——

SIMON: Oh, shut up, Sorel.

SOREL: Shut up yourself, you pompous little beast.

SIMON: You think you know such a lot about everything, and you're as ignorant as a frog.

SOREL: Why a frog?

JUDITH: I give you my solemn promise, David, that you're wrong.

DAVID: I don't want your solemn promise, because I *know* I'm right.

SIMON: It's no use arguing with father, mother.

SOREL: Why isn't it any use arguing with father?

SIMON: Because you're both so pig-headed!

DAVID: Are you content to sit here, Judith, and let your son insult me?

JUDITH: He's your son as well as mine.

DAVID: I begin to doubt it.

JUDITH [*bursting into tears of rage*]: David!

SIMON [*consoling her*]: Father, how can you!

DAVID [*rising*]: I'll never attempt to read any of you anything again as long as I live. You're not a bit interested in my work, and you don't give a damn whether I'm a success or a failure.

JUDITH: You're dead certain to be a failure if you cram your books with inaccuracies.

DAVID [*hammering the table with his fist*]: *I am not inaccurate!*

JUDITH: Yes, you are; and you're foul-tempered and spoilt.

DAVID: Spoiled! I like that! Nobody here spoils me—you're the most insufferable family to live with——

JUDITH: Well, why in Heaven's name don't you go and live somewhere else?

DAVID: There's gratitude!

JUDITH: Gratitude for what, I'd like to know?

SOREL: Mother, keep calm.

JUDITH: Calm! I'm furious.

DAVID: What have you got to be furious about? Everyone rushing round adoring you and saying how wonderful you are——

JUDITH: I am wonderful, Heaven knows, to have stood you for all these years.

SOREL: Mother, do sit down and be quiet.

SIMON: How dare you speak to mother like that!

[*During this scene Myra, Jackie, Richard, and Sandy creep downstairs, with their bags, unperceived by the family. They make for the front door.*]

JUDITH [*wailing*]: Oh, oh! To think that my daughter should turn against me!

DAVID: Don't be theatrical.

JUDITH: I'm not theatrical—I'm wounded to the heart.

DAVID: Rubbish—rubbish—rubbish!

JUDITH: Don't you say Rubbish to me!

DAVID: I *will* say Rubbish!

SOREL: Ssshhh, father!

SIMON: That's right! Be the dutiful daughter and encourage your father——

DAVID: Listen to me, Judith——

JUDITH: Oh, this is dreadful—dreadful!

SOREL: The whole thing doesn't really matter in the least——

SIMON: —to insult your mother——

DAVID: The Place de la Concorde——

JUDITH: I never realized how small you were, David. You're tiny——

[*The universal pandemonium is suddenly broken by the front door slamming. There is dead silence for a moment, then the noise of a car is heard. Sorel runs and looks out of the window.*]

SIMON: There now!

SOREL: They've all gone!

JUDITH [*sitting down*]: How very rude!

DAVID [*also sitting down*]: People really do behave in the most extraordinary manner these days——

JUDITH: Come back and finish your breakfast, Sorel.

SOREL: All right.   [*She sits down.*]

SIMON: Toast, please, Sorel.

SOREL [*passing it to him*]: Here.

JUDITH: Go on, David; I'm dying to hear the end——

DAVID [*reading*]: "Jane Sefton, in her scarlet Hispano, swept out of the Rue Boissy d'Anglas into the Place Vendôme——"

JUDITH: I meant to tell you before, David—I've made a great decision.

DAVID [*amiably*]: What is it?

JUDITH: I really am going to return to the stage!

CURTAIN

The plays included in *Play Parade* were
originally dedicated to the following people:

DESIGN FOR LIVING: *To Alexander Woollcott*

CAVALCADE: *To G. B. Stern*

PRIVATE LIVES: *For Jeffery from Noël*

BITTER SWEET: *To My Very Dear Friends
Lynn Fontanne and Alfred Lunt*

POST-MORTEM: *To William Bolitho*

THE VORTEX: *To G. Calthrop with a good deal of gratitude*

HAY FEVER: *To Lorn Loraine*